D1509747

German Military and
the Weimar Republic

German Military and the Weimar Republic

General Hans von Seekt, General Erich Ludendorff and the Rise of Hitler

Karen Schaefer

Pen & Sword
MILITARY

First published in Great Britain in 2020 by
Pen & Sword Military
An imprint of
Pen & Sword Books Ltd
Yorkshire – Philadelphia

Copyright © Karen Schaefer 2020

ISBN HB: 978 1 52676 432 4
PB: 978 1 52676 627 4

The right of Karen Schaefer to be identified as Author of this work has
been asserted by her in accordance with the Copyright, Designs and
Patents Act 1988.

A CIP catalogue record for this book is
available from the British Library.

All rights reserved. No part of this book may be reproduced or
transmitted in any form or by any means, electronic or mechanical
including photocopying, recording or by any information storage and
retrieval system, without permission from the Publisher in writing.

Typeset by Mac Style
Printed and bound in the UK by TJ International Ltd,
Padstow, Cornwall.

Pen & Sword Books Limited incorporates the imprints of Atlas,
Archaeology, Aviation, Discovery, Family History, Fiction, History,
Maritime, Military, Military Classics, Politics, Select, Transport,
True Crime, Air World, Frontline Publishing, Leo Cooper, Remember
When, Seaforth Publishing, The Praetorian Press, Wharncliffe
Local History, Wharncliffe Transport, Wharncliffe True Crime
and White Owl.

For a complete list of Pen & Sword titles please contact

PEN & SWORD BOOKS LIMITED
47 Church Street, Barnsley, South Yorkshire, S70 2AS, England
E-mail: enquiries@pen-and-sword.co.uk
Website: www.pen-and-sword.co.uk

Or

PEN AND SWORD BOOKS
1950 Lawrence Rd, Havertown, PA 19083, USA
E-mail: Uspen-and-sword@casematepublishers.com
Website: www.penandswordbooks.com

Contents

Introduction

G eneral Hans von Seeckt (1866–1936) was the Chief of the Army Command of the Reichsheer at the Reichswehr Ministry of the Weimar Republic from 1920 until 1926.[1] As its supreme soldier, he had a military strategy and tried to implement it during his term of office. He failed, however. This study focuses on the issues of the military strategy he pursued, his inability to implement it and the factors that prevented him from achieving success.

The point of departure for this study is the end of the First World War and Seeckt's resulting task of re-forming, re-structuring and re-organizing the shattered forces of the German Empire for a republic under the conditions of the Treaty of Versailles. This introduction contains a brief account of the basic military and socio-political conditions that had prevailed in Germany since the winter of 1918 and a survey of the literature on the subject, including the interpretations, Seeckt's actions and influence in the Weimar Republic.

The End of the First World War

The last German government of the First World War, which had been formed under Reich Chancellor Graf von Hertling, was dissolved on 30 September 1918 and a new chancellor, the reformed monarchist Max von Baden, was named and appointed. On 3 October 1918, von Baden assembled a cabinet with the assistance of the majority parties in the Reichstag, the Social Democrats, the Centre Party and the Progressive People's Party. On 23 October 1918, the President of the United States, Woodrow Wilson, informed the German government that military chiefs were over-represented in the new governing body. He also said that the victorious powers were unwilling to accept a government that had been selected in such an autocratic manner for the Germans and demanded that it should be elected by the people instead. He pointed out that peace negotiations could only be conducted if the government were parliamentarized. On account of this demand, Ludendorff argued in favour of a continuation of the war, and the Supreme Army Command demanded the immediate termination of negotiations. The new cabinet, in which all the major parties of the empire were represented, refused to comply with this demand. It hoped that at least peace treaty negotiations would be held, and be conducted by a parliamentary government. The Emperor dismissed Ludendorff on 26 October 1918 and appointed General Groener as his successor. Yet Groener only consolidated the position of the Supreme Army Command.

The laws initiated on 26 October by the government for the introduction of a parliamentary monarchy did not meet with the approval of the victorious powers. They no longer offered negotiations and drew up no further offer for peace conditions, and simply issued the German government with their terms for an armistice. The political starting-point for the new government was the capitulation. Wilson called for more negotiating partners who were legitimized as representatives of the German people. In his view, this precluded the 'military parties and the men whose creed is imperial power'.[2]

The process of radical change was accelerated by mutinying soldiers in Kiel on 3 November 1918. They formed the first 'Soldiers' Council'. It was established to oppose the old military hierarchy, but it had no political aims, and its leadership was taken over by Gustav Noske, who was later to become the first Reichswehr minister.[3] The Emperor abdicated on 9 November 1918. Max von Baden conferred the chancellorship on Friedrich Ebert, a member of the Social Democratic Party, although he had no legal authority to do so and his only legitimation was the demand made by the victorious powers. The transfer of the legal power to Ebert has been interpreted in literature as the continuity in the revolution.[4] Friedrich Ebert became Reich Chancellor due to his being appointed as such by Max von Baden. One consequence of this appointment was that the future system of government did not take the form of the Bolshevist-style councils system, as had been demanded by the First German Congress of Workers' and Soldiers' Councils in Berlin in November 1918.

World War I ended with an armistice concluded between the Entente powers and the German Empire on 11 November 1918 in the Forest of Compiègne. The three victorious powers were represented by General Foch, General Weygand and General Wymis, the German Empire by Reichstag deputy Erzberger and Major General Winterfeldt.[5] The armistice treaty laid down the general political and politico-military conditions. One of the first conditions of the victorious powers that needed to be met without delay concerned the immediate withdrawal of German troops from occupied territories. This retreat was to be completed within 14 days.[6]

The armistice in November 1918 was followed by negotiations for a peace treaty, which was finally signed in Versailles and came into effect on 28 June 1919.[7]

The covenant for peace and security signed by the German Empire, the United States, Great Britain, France and the remaining Allies contained 231 articles.[8] It specified the future national borders of Germany and a new state order in Europe. As Germany was regarded as having influential military power during the days of the Empire owing to its troop strength of 817,762 men, its war materiel and its General Staff, the Allies demanded that its armed forces be downsized to 100,000 men and the General Staff be disbanded.[9]

Although Reichstag deputy Erzberger, as a member of the German delegation, was able to attain easier terms for Germany in a few instances at Versailles, the German people interpreted the peace treaty conceived by the Entente states as something that had been dictated wholly by the victorious powers.[10] The fundamental provisions of the Treaty of Versailles, which henceforth prompted undesirable developments in the domestic, economic and military policies of the Weimar Republic, remained at the centre of interest and were not amended.[11] Among the peace treaty conditions that were regarded as highly controversial by the military were a demand for the extradition of war criminals, among them the Emperor, and the issue of the war guilt (Articles 227, 231). The loss of large parts of the national territories in the east and west of Germany also met with vehement objections.[12] Although the new German Reich government, the majority of whose members were from the Social Democratic Party (SPD), resolutely opposed particularly to the articles mentioned concerning the issue of war guilt and the extradition of the Emperor and other war criminals, it was forced to sign the peace treaty at the Palace of Versailles on 28 June 1919. The location had been selected with an eye to a historical parallel. It was there that in 1871, the French had been forced to sign an analogous peace treaty dictated by Bismarck and containing terms that included reparations and the surrender of territories.

Part VIII of the Peace Treaty of Versailles contained obligations of far-reaching economic consequence for Germany. The Germans were required to provide reparation for all the economic damage inflicted on the victorious powers. The process for the payment of these reparations was designed to extend over the following fifty years.[13] In order to keep the economic burdens on the Germans at a bearable level, the Young Plan was to be introduced at a later date as a transitional solution.[14] For the young Weimar Republic, the high payments the Germans had to make to the victorious powers were an economic and financial burden and resulted in an impairment of its inner order and stability.

In addition, the Treaty of Versailles called for a clearly defined demilitarization of Germany.[15] The key foreign-policy conditions relevant to the Reichswehr in Part V were to be found in Articles 159–213. Articles 160 to 163 laid down the troop strength of the land forces, specifying the precise number of infantry and cavalry divisions the future German Reichsheer could have and their troop strength: The effective strength of the army was not to exceed the figure of 100,000 men, including 4,000 officers.[16] The organizational structure of the Reichswehr was established in accordance with these constraints. The land forces were to be divided into two group commands that, together, did not comprise more than seven infantry divisions and three cavalry divisions. The army was to have no more than two Army Corps headquarters, Reichswehr Group Headquarters 1 and 2. The 'Great German General Staff' (also called Prussian General Staff) was to be disbanded. The unauthorized manufacture of arms and ammunition remained prohibited for years and the introduction of compulsory military service was prohibited altogether.[17] A period of enlistment of twelve years was stipulated for non-commissioned officers and other ranks, while officers were to serve for 25 years. The Allies precluded the establishment of a reserve force by specifying that no more than five per cent of the effective personnel could be discharged in any year. In addition to the Reichsheer with its 100,000 men, the Weimar Republic was allowed to maintain a Reichsmarine (Navy) of 15,000 men.[18]

The Weimar Constitution regulated the supreme authority and power of command in the Reichswehr, vesting this not only in the Reich President, but also in a civilian Reichswehr Minister. In addition, Article 160 §1 of the Treaty of Versailles stated: 'The Army shall be devoted exclusively to the maintenance of order within the territory and to the control of the frontiers.' As a result of this constraint, the future tasks of the army were to be confined to protecting the frontiers of the Reich and to taking over policing measures in order to maintain public order in the interior of Germany.[19] Yet somewhat later, in agreement with the Allies, the duty of ensuring the internal order of the Republic was no longer assigned to the Reichsheer, but to the security police. Still later, after 1920, the Military Inter-Allied Commission of Control drew up further restrictions on arms and military equipment.[20]

Despite all these foreign-policy difficulties, the aim of Reich President Ebert remained that of establishing a parliamentary democracy. Led by him and Max von Baden, the members of the social democratic majority, the Independent Social Democratic Party (USPD), the Centre Party and the Progressive People's Party set up the 'Council of the People's Deputies'. They called for the election of a national assembly in order to provide the new state with its final political and social order. The first election took place on 1 January 1919, with the SPD emerging as the strongest party with 37.9 per cent (165 seats). It was unable to secure a majority, however. In order to take over the government, it had to enter into a coalition with the Centre Party (19.7 per cent, 9 seats) and the left-wing liberal DDP (18.5 per cent, 7.5 seats) – until the next election in June 1920.[21] The ability to compromise, to achieve a broad consensus, was something the parties were continuously called upon to demonstrate, but they hardly managed to do so. The numerous government reshuffles and changes of governments and coalition partners indicate that this was a prevalent problem in the Weimar Republic. No policy on how to establish a politico-social order for achieving a broad consensus had yet been developed. People held widely differing views on many issues and were none too ready to persevere with compromises for a whole legislative period.

One of the first orders of the national assembly was issued to Hugo Preuss, a professor of public law at the Berlin School of Commerce. He had already drafted a constitution in 1917. He took this as a basis and adapted the existing version to the political requirements of his day. His second draft of a constitution for the Weimar Republic was passed by parliament on its third reading on 31 July 1919 after some alterations had been made, these largely concerning codification details of fundamental rights.[22] In this draft, the Weimar Republic was set up as a parliamentary system of government with a republican form of government. This constitution represented the first German constitutional avowal of the sovereignty of the people. The German people were regarded as the subject of the constitution. The state unity was strengthened by the fundamental rights of the people, which mostly consisted of internal liberty and social equality. The position of the Reich President is of interest for the starting political situation. He was granted extensive powers in relation to parliament – in imitation of the Emperor and as a measure which the parties regarded as a safeguard against the danger of parliamentary absolutism. The constitution also included aspects of direct democracy. The Reich President was directly elected by the people for a seven-year term of office. He appointed and dismissed the government (Article 53), national officials and military officers of the Reich (Article 46). The legislative competence for the Wehrmacht was now vested in the Reich. The Reich President had supreme command over all the military forces (Article 47) and could declare a state of emergency in the event of domestic unrest, any disturbance of public order and safety (Article 48 of the Reich Constitution). In Article 48 in particular, which enabled him to dissolve parliament and proclaim a state of emergency, the President was provided with an instrument for enforcing power which the fathers of the Constitution believed to be an effective safeguard against parliamentary absolutism.[23] It did not occur to them that this very clause made it possible for the Reich President, on his part, to undermine parliamentary democracy. On the contrary, following examples from the past, the President was regarded both by the political parties and the constitutionalist Preuss as the guarantor of a continuous development of the democratic life of the state.[24]

A completely new but well-justified feature was the fact that workers' councils were included in Article 165 as representatives of worker interests in connection with co-determination. Trade unions were to be regarded as equal partners, a first step towards economic democracy.

The primacy of politics was established quite clearly in the Constitution of the Weimar Republic. The Reich President held supreme command. The first civilian Reichswehr Minister, Gustav Noske, held the power of command on behalf of the Reich President for the Reichswehr as a whole and initiated politico-military measures.[25] Within the hierarchy, he was followed by the last Prussian War Minister, General Walther Reinhardt. He resigned his post in connection with the Kapp-Lüttwitz coup, and General Hans von Seeckt became his successor in 1920. The influence of the Chief of the Army Command was no longer on a par with that of the Supreme Army Command in the days of the First World War. Even during Reinhardt's term of office, the politico-military constraints of the victorious powers and those of the new government had limited the post of the Chief of the Army Command to its purely military functions.

These domestic, foreign and alliance policy parameters resulting from the loss of the First World War in 1918 and the subsequent Peace Treaty of Versailles became the focus of attention for Weimar Republic politicians. For Hans von Seeckt, the Chief of the Army Command and hence the supreme soldier of the Reichswehr, new tasks ensued from the future socio-political and military preconditions. These had to serve as the basis for his conception of his military role and his mission, which he then had to implement in his orders to the troops and within the Reichswehr Ministry. In addition, he had to take account of the experiences that went with the loss of the world war and the attendant new challenges. During his term of office (1920–1926), Seeckt was responsible for assisting the state in accomplishing its new task with its army, for which he applied an appropriate military-strategic concept.

The picture of Seeckt that has been constructed in the history so far portay him as a stick-in-the-mud, old-fashioned, a closed-mind leader, perhaps even a revanchist. This book, however, will show that he has been widely misjudged due to indifferent engagement with the source material, which shows him to be of a quite different calibre.

Acknowledgements

For that understanding and support which can derive only from friendship, my gratitude is to Professor Beatrice Heuser at the University of Glasgow, to Kenton White at the University of Reading U.K. and Professor Claus von Rosen, fellow at the Führungsakademie der Bundeswehr, Germany.

Two complete drafts of the manuscript were critically read and edited by Lester Crook and Harriet Fielding of Pen & Sword Books Limited. Many of their valuable comments and their support are now part of this book.

For many years I have enjoyed the support of the Library of the Führungsakademie der Bundeswehr, Germany. Without the facilities of this library, without the professional and ready assistance of its staff, the completion of this book would have been impossible.

Remaining errors are my own.

Chapter 1

Seeckt According to Existing Literature

The existing literature on the Reichswehr and Seeckt has given his military strategy insufficient attention. Military historians have approached the subject in two waves. The first wave started after the Second World War with John W. Wheeler-Bennet, Harold J. Gordon, Francis L. Carsten, Samuel P. Huntington, and Jehuda Wallach.[1] Hans Meier-Welcker, Klaus Jürgen Müller, and Michael Geyer as the most well-known German military historians refer to the subject and initiated the second wave.[2] Finally, and just in recent years, the literature on the subject grew. Karl-Volker Neugebauer, James S. Corum, Gerhard P. Gross, Robert M. Citino and Gil-li Vardi, and also others like Peter Keller took up the old ideas and touched slightly on Seeckt's influence on the Reichswehr and his military ideas to strategy.[3] Of special importance to Seekt's military strategy is the only publication by Matthias Strohn .[4]

In specialist literature, Seeckt's ideas have been rather disparagingly regarded as merely fundamental questions of military training, equipment and tactical command and control.[5] While the specialists have assumed that Seeckt was concerned with national defence, his military strategy has not been recognized. Indeed, there is the suggestion that he had no coherent military strategy at all.[6] This is why his deliberations on military strategy have hitherto been almost entirely disregarded. The assumption that no military strategy had been developed by the military top brass prior to the First World War was later made to apply to the first Chief of the Army Command of the Weimar Republic as well.[7] In training, he was said to have merely emphasized a spirit of aggressiveness and 'manoeuvre warfare'.[8] It is suggested that Seeckt had little more than tactical and operational thoughts, merely a concept of mobile operations that was modelled on the service regulations of the old army prior to the First World War and based on the experiences of that war.[9] Moreover, he is considered to have exercised his office in an arbitrary manner, depending on the benefits and objectives of the Reichswehr, in order to keep it beyond political control.

Never fundamentally converted to belief or confidence in a republican Germany, von Seeckt was prepared, unlike many of his caste, to use the Republic for his own ends; and to cooperate with it as the existing constituted authority to restore the strength and power of those two institutions to which his devotion and loyalty were deep and answering, the German Reich and the German Army.[10]

Any statements Seeckt made to politicians were regarded as ambivalent, merely a cover for a military policy of his own: 'Using and abusing civilian authority according to its needs, accepting or avoiding involvement and responsibility at will, was a convenient cover for the Reichswehr'.[11] It has been argued that: 'Virtually all prominent German military thinkers in the 1920s saw war as the only way for Germany to re-establish its international status.'[12] These claims are supported by German military historians, who since the early 1970s onwards have reduced Seeckt's objectives to the 'renaissance of the nation state as a great power'.[13] As late as 2014, a treatise on the 'Wehrmacht der Deutschen Republik' ended with the well-known quotation from Gustav Noske at the end of its final chapter. Commenting on Seeckt's work, the former first Reichswehr minister of the young republic wrote in 1946 that he had only corrupted the Reichswehr.[14]

Seeckt had given no thought to the 'image of future war' during his term of office.[15] It has been claimed supposedly that he only paid attention to potential war scenarios after his discharge.[16] Seeckt was considered to have been 'no outstanding military theoretician during his tenure', because 'his publications … largely only appeared after his retirement from office'.[17]

It becomes evident that historians take hardly any account of the free time at the disposal of other well-known military theoreticians in their professional circumstances; this would tend to put their interpretations of Seeckt's activities into perspective. Alfred Thayer Mahan, a contemporary of Seeckt, had served at the Naval Academy and had elaborated a theory on naval strategy. In contrast to Seeckt, Mahan was able to use more than his private time. After all, his duties included research and teaching.[18] The same goes for Clausewitz (1780–1831); from 1807 onwards, he worked continuously on his ideas and entire *oeuvre*. Still, he only had a limited amount of time at his disposal to develop, write down and finalize his thoughts on what he had experienced in the Napoleonic Wars; this has unfortunately resulted in his incomplete work being regarded to this day as something that eludes any definite interpretation and leaves many questions unanswered.[19]

The public view of the Reichswehr has been rather negative from the days of Seeckt until quite recently. This young army seemed more like a band of 'troublemakers' rather than a disciplined force because since 1920, its leader was said to have been intimating to the Reich President that he headed a praetorian guard that claimed autonomy.[20]

The Politico-Military Situation in 1918

Seeckt comes across as an ideologically very problematic character in the existing literature. The politico-military situation Seeckt faced since his assumption of office in March 1920 was certainly conditioned by the defeat of 1918. Many members of the armed forces – in the view of the German historians – did not accept the defeat, and the lost world war also resulted in the 'disintegration of the army at home'.[21] While the new socio-political conditions had led to a change in the politico-military conditions as a starting point for the Reichswehr, the army in the Seeckt era still only chose to follow a 'separate path':

> It was unable to defend the German frontiers if its chances of doing so were calculated rationally. Thus the separate path the German army followed between 1918 and 1933 included its dependence on an ideological consensus that could only be directed against the Treaty of Versailles and the foreign policy of the Weimar Republic.[22]

This 'special path' is said to have contributed towards an 'increasing liberation of the executive authority from parliamentary control'.[23] Seeckt wanted to see the Reichswehr 'subject solely to professional military considerations'.[24] Michael Geyer's research on the Seeckt era is also used as a basis for recent specialist work.

> Geyer's findings were clear: Although many a Reichswehr officer might dream of an army that enjoyed 'complete freedom in its development and its independent existence' within the Republic, as

the notorious Seeckt once put it, seeking salvation in an inappropriate political isolationism could not be a viable medium and long-term option for the military decision makers.[25]

Michael Geyer and Rüdiger Bergien base their argument on Seeckt's rejection of the Treaty of Versailles on the year 1922. In that year, Seeckt had demanded that Germany have the right to defend itself and its borders. For Geyer, this was simply a roundabout way of demanding the revision of the Treaty of Versailles.[26] According to this interpretation, Seeckt not only wanted to achieve a revision of the Versailles Treaty, but was really aiming to have its provisions revoked as far as possible.

> Although Seeckt conceded that the Allies were entitled to make decisions on the disarmament of the Old Army and to verify their implementation, he objected to any control of the New Army that had been formally established on the basis of the Versailles Treaty ... He went much further in his positive demands: 'Yet the right by which all states justify their armaments, the right to defend our borders, we must also be able to claim for our small army and its training' ... The postulation of a country's right to defend its borders as the criterion for all the provisions of the Treaty of Versailles would hence have put the explosive charge of a revision into the Treaty itself.[27]

The military build-up measures initiated in the spring of 1923 are interpreted as mobilization preparations.[28] Thus some military historians argue that Seeckt took the first steps towards total mobilization that were to be used in planning a war of aggression.

Historians have thus suggested that Seeckt's military objective was not solely to establish a 'professional army'. His work on the military build-up and his continued attempts to circumvent the Treaty of Versailles were considered to be an immediate threat to German security:

> Seeckt's army accordingly took an active part in designing a separate strategic frame of action, as well as in setting its own foreign policy goals. The vast rearmament effort and military build-up that Seeckt promoted directly threatened Germany's security.[29]

Unfortunately, for his military goal of establishing a 'professional army' against the restrictive military constraints, Gil-li Vardi uses the term 'pygmy army' (*Zwergen-Armee*) in her translation. She claims to have borrowed the term *Zwergen-Armee* from Seeckt – 'The "pygmy army", in Seeckt's words'.[30] To my knowledge, Seeckt did not use this term, and I do not consider this translation correct for the 'small army' envisaged by Seeckt either.

The 'Problem of Professionalism' of the Military Elite and Total War

Klaus-Jürgen Müller considers Seeckt to have shown a 'wait-and-see attitude, a kind of inner reluctance, towards the connection between the army, political establishment and society in the era of the Weimar Republic'.[31] The younger generation of historians has followed him in this respect and interprets Seeckt's behaviour as that of someone 'reluctantly loyal to the constitution'.[32]

According to Müller, Seeckt's politico-military approach shows the will to achieve a

> ... correct, though provisional arrangement which was based on a genuine sense of responsibility for the 'state' as much as on the intention of maintaining the army as a basis and prerequisite for the national renaissance of the 'Reich' as a major power.[33]

In this context, Müller puts forward the hypothesis for the Weimar era that after 1918, the military elite was interested in the 'solely military professional task of ensuring the best possible mounting and conduct of a modern, a "total" war'.[34]

What his theory amounts to is that the new elite nucleus of the Reichswehr was aiming to regain 'political leadership of the nation' by planning a total war:

> The traditional claim of the political military elite to participation in responsible leadership in the state then found a new element of legitimation in the very phenomenon of the modern war that totally carries away society.[35]

Geyer suggests that the military planned to draw the entire nation, political establishment and society into the next war. Thus Geyer assumes that in the Seeckt era, the military developed into the 'organizer of force for society as a whole':[36]

> Accordingly, the military did not expand into society and the political establishment with the intention of conspiring and dabbling in politics in any Wilhelmine way to alter the balance of power in society in the interest of third parties ... but with that of going about their own particular task, that of organizing and using force.[37]

In this context, military historians contend that Seeckt planned and pursued the aim to wage a war of revenge against France.[38]

Furthermore, they draw attention to Germany's secret rearmament on account of the secret military training conducted with the Red Army. Besides the Weimar Republic, the USSR is regarded as 'another pariah in the international order' in this context.[39] This cooperation is interpreted as an attempt by the military heads to arm the Reichswehr for the next war.[40] Because of this cooperation, the next logical step, that of the 'removal of restrictions on force' and 'total mobilization', is inferred early on and this is then interpreted as Seeckt's principal concern.

Klaus-Jürgen Müller, Francis Carsten, Bennet-Wheeler and Rainer Wohlfeil have also emphasized that Seeckt regarded cooperation as the basis for 'returning to the status of an autonomous power'.[41] More specialist literature from Robert J. Neill follows their line of thinking and adds to it.[42] The purpose of this kind of military cooperation not only consisted of circumventing those provisions of the Treaty of Versailles, the 'disgraceful dictate', which concerned armament issues. With his 'exaggerated concept of a power state', Seeckt is supposed to have been intent on establishing a military power which could be built on to 'generate freedom of action in foreign affairs'.[43]

Seeckt is furthermore said to have given a speech to cabinet members on 9 February 1923 in which he supposedly advocated war.[44] Seeckt's long-term objective since the end of the First World War is considered to have been helping Germany to regain the position of a great power it had held before the war by means of the Reichswehr. Kurt von Schleicher and General Wilhelm Groener intended to join him in preparing for a forcible revision of the conditions in Europe. The views on this within the officer corps were said to have been 'different between the generations, but still complementary'. What mattered to Seeckt was 'the primacy of an operational leadership based on foreign-policy – and in this respect, primarily power-policy considerations'.[45]

One of the foundations for his plans is said to have been a three-stage programme for the 'restoration of our Wehrmacht'.[46] German historians like Bernhard Kroener interpret this as his first attempt to achieve a 'dilution of the army by a levy of masses', as his first thoughts 'on a war in the distant future'.[47] They are said to have been implemented and 'covert mobilization plans initiated' the very next day. The officers of the Reichswehr Ministry had conducted a survey 'of the personnel strength.'[48]

These scientific hypotheses are shared by British historians: 'In grand strategy, German military heads perceived war as the only way to solve political problems and to elevate the nation's – and the army's – prestige.'[49]

The view is that the events in the war had only been evaluated selectively and that had resulted in the 'inevitable confirmation of the principles concerning operational manoeuvre warfare and the significance of the attack, which were valid even before the war.'[50]

British military historians see German officers as stubborn and inflexible, despite their having lost a war. They also pose the question of how this kind of dogged persistence on the part of the military, the lack of perceptive awareness of new socio-political and economic conditions can be accounted for: 'What can thus explain such persistent military practice in face of a very different and indeed turbulent political, economic, and technological reality?'[51] Vardi explains the narrow-mindedness of German officers by assuming that the German officers believed that their military doctrine was not responsible for their defeat in the war: 'If army doctrine and practice had not failed Germany in 1914–18, there was no need to challenge them.'[52] Nor would Seeckt have made a paradigm shift over the period mentioned or learned anything from the lost war.

Military historians have attributed the image of the officer corps in the Reichswehr era and its military concept of itself to the Prussian tradition, 'old Prussian values' and the special position that the officer corps had held in society for centuries.[53] If this view is adopted, it can be said that the officer corps scarcely acknowledged the socio-politically new values of the Weimar Republic. In addition, Geyer and Müller develop the theory of the dualism of the military and politics, a two-pillar principle, for the Seeckt era. In the Weimar Republic, the 'military self-image of the commanders' was said to have been determined by a military policy that initiated a 'phase of autonomy secure from parliament'.[54]

Beyond that, the scientific specialist like Michael Geyer, presents the reduction of the Reichswehr officer to his military competence, to his purely military craftsmanship, as the objective of Seeckt, who wanted to keep his officers away from any political activity. 'Seeckt does come close to this tradition in that he created this separation, irrespective of the consequences to himself. This ... was accompanied by blindness to political developments'.[55] Admittedly the 'principle of non-partisanship ... [is] undoubtedly a well-tried principle for the conduct of an armed force in a well-established community that is supported unanimously by the will of the nation'[56]. Still, Seeckt's motives and his decision in favour of the principle of non-partisanship have been interpreted as being of 'paramount political significance' and regarded as misguided in the specialist literature of Ulrich Wehler.[57] At the same time, this attitude of his was associated with the 'adjustment of the army to the industrial and antagonistic Weimar society' of, for example, Geyer.[58]

German and British historians like Vardi, Frank Reichherzer and Robert M. Citino compare Seeckt's view of how the next conflict should be fought or would lead to victory to that of Schlieffen. Seeckt is thought to have the war aim of the annihilation of the enemy.[59] Although Jehuda Wallach pointed out contradictory statements made by Seeckt with regard to Schlieffen, the points at issue have not yet been settled.[60]

While Birk and Gross do not claim that Seeckt was a supporter of Schlieffen, they do regard his concept as a 'radicalization of the classic operational concept developed by Schlieffen to a point where the initial operations could not be speeded up any more'.[61]

The question that follows on from this is whether Seeckt, like Klaus-Jürgen Müller, Michael Geyer and Gil-li Vardi claim, actually favoured a war that carried everything away, that involved the whole of society, in order to circumvent the problem of military professionalism and the problem of integration into society and the state in the planning of it.

This in turn determines whether – as has been claimed – he regarded technology as a threat to the old elite position within the state or whether he intended to maintain his own social status quo in this manner. The hypothesis that Seeckt interfered with political decisions in the Weimar Republic is also scrutinized in the analysis of the military image he had of himself and his military strategy.[62]

The Organization of the Army and Advance in Arms Technology

Military historians regard Seeckt as someone who since the end of the First World War demonstrated that he had virtually no idea of strategy. He is considered to have learned little from the war. He is not believed to have had the professional competence needed to impart more than just a few improvements in training to the Reichswehr.[63] The hypothesis that he had no military-strategic planning to show for himself, that he had never moved beyond the operational command level, that he had even fallen behind the conduct of operations in the First World War, culminated in the assertion: 'Quite logically, if military failure had not determined the World War's outcome, then nothing more than minor improvements and better technology were needed for the next war.'[64]

The line of argumentation among military historians is based upon a draft concerning a way in which the army could be organized in the future, produced by Seeckt back in February 1919. The conclusion drawn from this is that he was out of his depth in his future position in the Reichsheer: 'The unbearable toll that Seeckt's reality-free optimism demanded … strengthened not merely the army's tendency to avoid present-day strategic and operational tasks, but ultimately shaped its evasion of future tasks as well.'[65]

Vardi believes that the fundamental flaw was to be found in the structure and organization of the army proposed by Seeckt. They were not adequately geared towards the prevailing political conditions either strategically or operationally: 'Seeckt unabashedly admitted that his solutions to Germany's strategic problems were not only operationally unfeasible and strategically insufficient for the present, but also possibly for the future.'[66] Vardi connects the army organization draft of February 1919 with the expectation that Seeckt had to specify a structure for the

Reichswehr which would be valid for all times. The fact that he had waited to see how the political situation developed and had not furbished any definitive answer was taken to mean that he had already failed as a military head early on.

> Yet Seeckt's fault did not lie primarily in his highly traditional approach to relations with the civilian leadership and to its authority. Rather, Seeckt failed in his duty as the commander of an army: to conceptualize his tasks, build his forces, and design a doctrine suitable to the military challenges of the present. Seeckt thus ultimately both saved and doomed the Reichswehr: he cut the last threads that connected German military planning to political, economic, and eventually operational requirements, limitations, and logic. Seeckt knowingly placed strategic and operational decisions beyond political restraints and outside the immediate context of Germany's security problems, and within an imaginary, one dimensional wish-fulfilment fantasy.[67]

As Seeckt was also unwilling to specify a definitive structure for the future army, Vardi comes to a conclusion which repeated the above mentioned idea:

> In doing so he impressed on future planning a pattern of studious indifference to real-world constraints; that was his most lethal bequest to the Reichswehr ... Seeckt's fault did not lie primarily in his highly traditional approach to relations with the civilian leadership and to its authority. Rather, Seeckt failed in his duty as the commander of an army: to conceptualize his tasks, build his forces, and design a doctrine suitable to the military challenges of the present.[68]

It is also inferred from this that Seeckt shrank back from making clear decisions on important issues and had no military doctrine.[69] This assumption is based on German military history research: 'Seeckt ... had neither the resources nor a convincing concept for the tactical implementation of his operational ideas.'[70]

Though he did devote attention to technological challenges, he is considered to have focused both on traditional things and the concept of the battle of annihilation, to have added only mobility to old technical ideas, to have based his ideas on Schlieffen and had no idea of strategy, and this is all regarded as evidence that he intended to achieve a victory in a decisive battle at the expense of the people:

> Above all else, Seeckt never doubted that the one decisive battle, whatever operational form it might take, would remain the key to successful campaigns and wars; he was incapable of envisaging, much less developing, a strategic outlook free of all-embracing tactical logic of the battle of annihilation (*Vernichtungsschlacht*). Seeckt's adherence to decisive battle of annihilation as the motivation, prime goal, and basic logic of strategic and operational planning can also explain the small to non-existent attention he devoted to strategic questions that extended to beyond the very narrowest operational framework.[71]

Gil-li Vardi concludes from this that his military leadership qualities were apt to enable him to handle the tasks he was assigned as the Chief of the Army Command. Seeckt is thus considered to have neither learned anything from the First World War nor added new aspects to the tactical and operational levels. Owing to his inadequate military skills, he is considered to have merely added a few new key technical points to training:

> Seeckt's clinging to old precepts and to the basic claim that deviations from orthodoxy had doomed Germany in the World War, coupled with his attempt to prepare the execution of traditional operations axioms with new technology that would promise victory in the next, was in effect the only policy he and his colleagues were capable of imagining and following ... And thereafter Seeckt's agenda legitimized the irrelevance of reality to military planning, and thus presented the army, along with the chance to prosper and excel for a time at the tactical level, its ultimate death-sentence.[72]

For instance, his regulations for training and exercises are said to have been limited to the tactical level – with few exceptions. It is claimed that there was no operational command and that his concept was neither new nor innovative. On the basis of this draft, she also assumes that 'thereafter Seeckt's agenda legitimized the irrelevance of reality to military planning', which in turn resulted in the 'exodus' of the army, 'its ultimate death-sentence'.[73] She claimed that his misinterpretation of the new conditions was already revealed in the 1919 draft and contributed towards the decline of the Weimar Republic.

Vardi asserts that if the draft of February 1919 proves his ignorance of real conditions, then he would scarcely be able to produce a plausible strategic and operational concept.[74] Accordingly, she rates his poor performance as 'the lesser evil'. In his planning, Seeckt was wide of the mark of 'real-world constraints'; she considers this 'his most lethal bequest to the Reichswehr'.[75]

In addition, he was accused of being ignorant of the problems of the present and of what the future had in store in terms of technical challenges. All this was said to have narrowed his slant. Vardi comes to the conclusion that Seeckt's mistake did not solely consist of picking up the thread of the old army and its tradition without giving it any thought. He also carried on with the old military doctrine in the Reichswehr without any breaks:

> Hans von Seeckt is the most clear-cut example of the argument at the core of the thesis, that between 1919 and 1938 no paradigmatic shift in military concepts occurred in the Germany army – and especially not during the 1920s, in which the most prominent of Germany's military brains closely followed and conformed to the army's organizational culture.[76]

Vardi can go on from where Jehuda Wallach left off. He had remarked that the army regulation H.Dv. 487 entitled *Führung und Gefecht der verbundenen Waffen* (abbreviated 'FuG'; approximately 'command and combined arms combat')[77] issued in 1921 and 1923 was largely modelled on outdated principles 'which had been valid during the Schlieffen era before the War'.[78] For this theory, Wallach quotes nine articles from army regulation H.Dv. 487 in Annex G of his work. The 1921 edition of the FuG contains 446 paragraphs. Altogether, slightly more than 1,000 more or less detailed paragraphs were contained in the two editions – not including The Hague Regulations Concerning the Laws and Customs of War on Land, which had also been printed in them.

Joachim von Stülpnagel, an officer at the Reichswehr Ministry, is cited as having provided proof that Seeckt was 'an old general, who held existing circumstances to be good, and desired no further innovations in the army once the Reichswehr had been conciliated'.[79]

Vardi updates this picture, stating that technology did change the Reichswehr after all. Still, she asserts that the officers only took account of the technical challenges of the twentieth century in order to make practical use of them in their war planning.[80] Although Seeckt put some effort into introducing several technical innovations, she believes that he showed no inclination to examine and alter his views on warfare and military doctrine: 'The only dramatic change was the technology it employed, but this technology served existing doctrinal maxims, rather than dictating new doctrine and conduct.'[81] Seeckt was said to have been more interested in formalities such as parades than weapons technology.[82]

In the more recent German specialist scientist like Marco Sigg, the view of Seeckt as someone who adhered to old service regulations follows the line of thought mentioned above. According to this, the army regulation H.Dv. 487, FuG, should be seen as an advance in quality when compared to pre-war regulations, but to some extent it represented continuity as well. It did not contain any guidelines for operational command; he deliberately rejected innovations or changes in order to maintain continuity in training.[83]

In 2014, other military historians took a close look, among other things, at the influence of Clausewitz on Seeckt's education and training concept. They emphasized that Clausewitz had no outstanding relevance for the Prussian-German General Staff.[84] The importance of Clausewitz for Seeckt is only touched upon in passing in more recent specialist literature by Sigg. There, it is assumed that the 'moral parameters' of Clausewitz were of some significance for Seeckt. For that reason, character traits such as will-power, mental agility and resolve became an integral part of military instruction and were trained in the Seeckt era. Their adoption by Seeckt was attributed to the influence of Clausewitz. The Seeckt quotation 'The essential thing is action' is presented by researchers as supporting evidence.[85] The question of whether Seeckt took account of more than merely the moral parameters of character will be dealt with in the main section on military strategy.

The assertions that Seeckt did not take sufficient account of modern challenges, that he failed from the very beginning as a military thinker because he did not have a profound operational concept, among other things, and that he therefore hastened the fall of the Weimar Republic, will be viewed and examined in the context of his military-strategic ideas.

An Army of 200,000

Some military historians take the view that from 1919 onwards, Seeckt pursued the military objective of establishing a 200,000-man army. His attempts to achieve this were thwarted by the political parties, above all the USPD:[86]

> ... the attempt had failed, according to Seeckt, because of the opposition of the Left: '[a]dmittedly a united front cannot be established, since the radical political parties on the Left under the leadership of the Independent Socialists have declared themselves against the claims of the armed forces', even before he had had the chance to face the French and their 'naked will to annihilation' at the Spa conference.[87]

In connection with the peace negotiations, Seeckt is accused of using political delaying tactics with the intention of circumventing the demands of the USPD:

> Seeckt's resentment of the Republic's governments [is] of course derived from far more serious causes; he held the Republic as responsible as the Entente powers for the harsh terms of Versailles. Reporting on the army's failure to secure changes to the Treaty's military clauses at Spa conference of July 1920, he bitterly commented that '... I spoke against the notion of handing over responsibility to

large numbers of individuals, the Reichstag, the Reichsrat [or] the cabinet members in Berlin, who would have permitted us to guide them in their decisions, or to be excluded and placed before a fait accompli.' That statement also expressed Seeckt's assumptions regarding the precise nature of the relations between the civilian and military echelons of the Weimar Republic.[88]

An address by Seeckt to the General Staff in 1920 is cited as evidence, and the content is compared to a poetic declaration of Germany and its army sharing a destiny: 'In poetically explaining their shared destiny, Seeckt went so far as to suggest a shared identity between the army and the state; that identity was, however, by definition a military one.'[89] In specialist literature, it is considered self-evident that in his aims, Seeckt did not go beyond military actions following purely traditional views.

Civil-Military Relations

After the Second World War, some historians have interpreted the personality and actions of Seeckt as making him 'want to have the Reichswehr regarded as the "support of the authority of the Reich and not of a particular government"'.[90] Not only Klaus-Jürgen Müller and Rainer Wohlfeil take this view. On the contrary, they concur with the hypothesis advocated by Francis L. Carsten. They agree with 'Carsten that Seeckt pursued anti-democratic objectives'.[91] Since 1920, he is said to have assumed a 'towards the new political order'.[92] Following the example of Geyer, Peter Keller in 2014 contends that Seeckt was deliberately attempting both to cut himself off from the Republican community and to strive for '*imperii in imperio*'. From 1920 onwards, Seeckt is said to have adopted an intentionally passive stance on democracy. He had avoided the Reichswehr adopting a clear political pro-Republic stance since the early years.[93] At the same time, a rapprochement between the military top brass and the Republic was also noticeable, but this was merely intended to promote remilitarization.[94]

There are references by Carsten and Wheeler-Bennet to the biography of Rabenau as a basis for its assumptions. As early as 1958, former Reichswehr Minister Gessler pointed out that Seeckt's anti-democratic traits in the literature were derived from the biased biography of Rabenau.[95] At any rate, Seeckt's superior, Reichswehr Minister Gessler, was somewhat more discriminating in his view of Seeckt. He wrote that Seeckt had been guided by the political and military realities. He averred that Seeckt had never been 'blinded by ideology' and that his strong point was a

> ... keen mind which kept to the nature of things and the realities. He was averse to all kinds of braggadocio, enthusiastic raptures, and playing at soldiers. These intellectually based traits were ... a reliable political guarantee for the state and the Reich government.[96]

Seeckt's personality and the reception of his actions have nevertheless been enlarged both in German- and English-speaking regions to an extent where more anti-democratic facets keep being added to his image. Not only is he said to have unwaveringly persisted in taking the traditional line of the old army in warfare against the political heads, but he did not care for civil-military cooperation either:

> He ... set in stone the army's faith in the infallibility of traditional operational notions...If battle was still the key to successful warfighting, why should anyone waste doctrinal effort and attention on minor matters such as economic mobilisation and cooperation with the civilian government.[97]

Younger German researchers round off this view and believe that Seeckt was only able to imagine a form of 'covert cooperation with civilian forces'.[98]

According to these interpretations, Seeckt was of the opinion that the Reichswehr command needed to be involved in important home affairs decisions and that he would occupy the dominant position in the state for the Reichswehr.

Vardi, too, assumes that this 'pygmy army' cooperated with the state, but that the civil-military cooperation was still dictated by the commanders of this pygmy army:

The 'pygmy army', in Seeckt's words, had no choice but to cooperate with the Republic; neither likes one another, but each was dependent on the other for survival ... Seeckt went so far as to suggest a shared identity between the army and the state; that identity was, however, by definition a military one.[99]

Other historians like Wheeler-Bennet, Carsten, Robert Neill and Gehrhard Gross believe that Seeckt showed little acknowledgement for the primacy of politics.[100] Even the officers educated by Seeckt were considered to have stayed away from politics, and for that reason remained ignorant of any modern concept of strategy and the significance of the primacy of politics underlying it.[101] They are only considered to have succeeded in 'operating free from politics'.[102] Vardi agrees with this assumption, but goes a step further by emphasizing that the military in the Seeckt era dominated political actions.

Seeckt naturally presented the two spheres – military and political – as distinct and separate from one another. The military sphere was wholly free, in its pursuit of victory – which Seeckt conceptualised in military terms alone – of the limitations attending the civilian sphere. Seeckt was as adamant as Germany's military heads before him that when it came to war, the army had the first and the last word.[103]

In 2011, she reiterated that 'the military leadership ... wished to subordinate all facts of civilian life to "military necessity"'.[104]

Although Seeckt had closed his mind to cooperating in any way with the government, he continued to work for military cooperation with the Red Army. This was intended to cut through the 'Gordian knot of the European post-war order' by means of power politics.

Soviet Russia was to be strengthened militarily and economically in order for Germany to have a powerful ally in the ubiquitous conflicts over the alteration of the entire European power structure that had evolved after the war from Germany's defeat. The main objective of the contacts with Soviet Russia was not to improve the diplomatic negotiating position, but to make long-term preparations for cutting the Gordian knot of the European post-war order by means of power politics.[105]

Seeckt's objective of entering into an alliance with another state and its armed forces is regarded by Geyer as the 'Seeckt concept of an alliance war'.[106]

Seeckt is considered to have pursued a military and alliance policy which did not pay much attention to the political constraints of the respective Weimar Republic governments. He saw himself as a critical adherent of the constitution and kept a 'curious system of bookkeeping with double entries which confused many of his subordinates'.[107] This also helped him to succeed in concealing his true military and political objectives. His concern was to achieve autonomy for the Reichswehr Command and to de-politicize the army in order to be able to put it out of the reach of [an] important political figure.[108] He himself is considered to have had a 'genuinely neutral attitude', but to have been unable to impose this on the Reichswehr.[109]

Owing to the fact that until the Second World War, no generally satisfactory solution to problems of civil-military relations had been found in America, experts like Carry J. Clifford, John. D. Huber, Charles R. Shipan and SamuelP. Huntington started to investigate this problem area in greater depth after the Second World War. They found that problems between the civilian and military leadership echelons in Germany had existed long before the establishment of the Reichswehr. As the comprehensive specialist literature published after the Second World War shows and Samuel P. Huntington has proved, the difficulties that arose in connection with civil-military work date back to the eighteenth century. In general, they have an adverse effect on the resolution of issues at the highest decision-making levels in ministries, departments and organizations; they can likewise be caused by key figures and superiors with specific interests. They normally arise between ministries. Yet even smallish departments may show signs of internal friction, precisely because of their limited sizes. In this way, any disagreement impedes inter-ministerial and joint work and thus the achievement of overriding objectives.[110]

In the literature of military studies after the Second World War, these difficulties are mostly examined under the aspects of advancing bureaucracy and 'group-think'.[111] It contains notes not only of egotistic attitudes and rivalries of individual ministries, but also a steady growth in the administrative machinery. The research results frequently concern deficiencies more than good cooperation and draw attention to the consequences arising from them. It is useful at this point to introduce some theoretical reflections on the problems of civil–military relations. In 1959, the leading US military sociologist, Samuel P. Huntington, explored this complex problem in *The Soldier and the State*, also touching upon Seeckt's concept of the state and politics:

> The one deficient element in Seeckt's formulation of the military ethic was certain haziness as to where the ultimate loyalty of the army lay. This reflected the ambiguity of the Weimar constitution and the political weakness of the republican government. Seeckt's description of the place of the army was contained in the formula: 'The Army serves the State; it is above parties'… This is fine as far as it went. But it left undefined the relationship of the military to the government. It was a state within a state, not a professional guild serving a government.[112]

Huntington pointed out the fundamental significance of civil–military relations to the military's understanding of its role:

> … modern, developed societies… are characterized by relatively highly institutionalized political structures and patterns of rule … and by relatively highly institutionalized and professionalized officer corps. The central problem of civil–military relations thus becomes the relationship between the military professionals and the political leadership. In theory, this problem is not dissimilar from the broader issue of the relations between the generalist and the specialist, the politician and the expert. In the case of military, however, it is often particularly intense and of central political importance to the society because of the nature of the functional imperatives that the military professional represents and because a highly professionalized and

bureaucratic military establishment is, by its very nature, a potential
source of political power and influence.[113]

Huntington was not the first military historian to tackle these questions,
but as one from the English-speaking world, he started dealing with them
after the end of the Second World War. He went into the issues in order to
define the 'military mind', the military self-image of officers in the post-
war era. He put it into the context of society as a whole and drew attention
to how soldiers saw military politics and their responsibility. He looked
into how officers saw their role, into their education, the professional
ethics, the military career and advanced training. He contrasted the
military self-image with the socio–political assignment of an officer,
which he could only accomplish on account of his professionalism and
responsibility as a military leader.[114]

Huntington sees social skills and ethical responsibility, the ability
to engage in civil-military cooperation and the will to keep extending
one's knowledge in a variety of other subject-fields as important factors
that contribute to the development of the 'military mind'. Still, the
professionalism of an officer cannot be judged solely by social and ethical
criteria. He should also have a 'deeper understanding of human attitudes,
motivations, and behaviour which a liberal education stimulates'.
Huntington also sees these traits as parts of his 'military mind'. Beyond
that, he believes that because an officer needs to deal with people all
the time, he must have more than his professional and social skills in
order to be regarded as suitable for his duties. Huntington has extended
the assumption that '[h]is behaviour within the military structures is
governed by a complex mass of regulations, customs, and traditions' so
that it includes the ability to engage in civil-military cooperation.[115]

Huntington has provided a complex definition for this. He has listed a
number of duties which an officer has to perform if he wants to remain
'on the top of his profession'. He has added numerous concepts to
professional skills and referred to the complex and grave responsibility
of the soldier:

Only if he is aware of the historical development of the techniques
of organization and directing military forces can the officer expect to

stay on top of his profession. The importance of the history of war and military affairs receives sustained emphasis throughout military writings and military education… requires a broad background of general culture of its mastery… The methods of organization and applying violence at any one stage in history are intimately related to the entire cultural pattern of society. Just as law at its borders merges into history, politics, economics, sociology, and psychology, so also does the military skill. To understand his trade properly, the officer must have some idea of its relation to these other fields and the ways in which these other areas of knowledge may contribute to his own purposes.[116]

Beyond the technical issues of his profession, Huntington demanded that an officer should keep working to extend his knowledge so that he can come up to the socio–political, international and social standards and expectations of the state he serves.

In 1977, Huntington listed other characteristics he believed a twentieth century-officer needed. He felt that the self-perception of the officer corps had continuously expanded in the modern age. Civic education and knowledge of the international situation and international relations were compulsory parts of this:

The modern officer corps is a highly professional body. It has its own expertise, corporateness, and responsibility. The existence of its profession tends to imply, and the practice of the profession tends to engender among members, a distinctive outlook on international politics, the role of the state, the place of force and violence in human affairs, the nature of man and society, and the relationship of the military profession to the state.[117]

He insisted that the 'military mind' needed civic education and added the demand for an officer to have the ability to engage in civil-military cooperation.[118] In his view, the military self-perception of the soldier in the late twentieth century was composed of this variety of characteristics. With more training, instruction and education, a soldier would develop more understanding for the military policy of his country and a more profound comprehension of his political task and role in the state. He hence believed that a soldier's understanding went far beyond the 'management of violence'. The national defence mission was no longer confined to providing military training to soldiers. Beyond his military training and instruction, civic education would enable the individual soldier to understand his mission towards state and society from a politico-military perspective as well. A soldier who is better informed, more able to enhance the performance of his military tasks with years of experience and political knowledge beyond his purely technical expertise, and proves himself in his service to the state by displaying a sense of responsibility and the ability to cooperate, is also more capable of 'getting involved' in political decisions. With more civic education and the ability to think along politico-military lines and to follow international politics, military chiefs could serve society better. There would also be another side to this political awareness: The influence of the supreme soldier on the political heads would grow as politico-military knowledge increasingly pervaded the ideas underlying the state. He would be able to influence how the political leadership made decisions. Matters would no longer be decided by civilians or politicians solely on the basis of political considerations, but also on that of military ones and be subject to politico-military influence.

As early as 1961, Huntington raised the question of political control over the military in connection with the issue of the 'military mind' and the understanding of its role, adding another critical question to his opinion. He asked whether the political method – of 'keeping the military out of politics' – was the best way of adequately settling civil-military issues.[119] Although he admitted that there was the danger of a politically-motivated soldier turning against the constitution, state system and society, he still postulated that the future challenges in politics did not include that of keeping the military away from politics and thus from civil-military relations.[120] On the contrary, after the experiences of the Second World War, he believed that thought should be given to determine whether this line was still the right approach when no solution could be reached by common consent owing to disputes between ministries. Military historian Hew Strachan posed this question again in 2006, adding that military subordination to the primacy of politics should be reconsidered whenever military resources were overtaxed by political objectives.[121] 'Policy is ill-conceived if it asks the armed forces to do things which are not consistent with their capabilities or with the true nature of war.'[122] For the twenty-first century in the western hemisphere, he concluded that 'a model of military subordination ... is now unhelpful, and even self-defeating. The fear of tanks in Whitehall or on the lawn of the White House is not founded in reality.'[123]

This demand formulated by English-speaking scholars is not only conditional on the acceptance of politics by the military, but is also characterized by reciprocity. Their expectations of the political and military heads are based on Clausewitz.[124] One of his demands was that the political leadership had to face facts about military capabilities and capacities in order to be able to achieve their political aims. Strachan followed this approach to its logical conclusion and emphasized that the primacy of politics was not questioned, but that politicians needed to assess which challenges could actually be met by the military: If the military was overtaxed by excessive demands from the government on military capabilities not actually available, there was the risk of military and political defeat. This conclusion also corresponds to Clausewitz's theory of war and will also be examined in its relation to Seeckt's military strategy.

This understanding of the 'military mind' and that of Seeckt's of civil-military relations will be gone into in some detail. In addition to the problems analysed by Huntington and his definition of the 'military mind', the question of whether there were no other central factors determining the military self-image of soldiers in general and Seeckt in particular – beyond the ability to reach responsible decisions from the politico-military angle and to ensure external safety by means of armed duties – will be discussed.

Those analyses dealing with Seeckt's defence concept have shown quite clearly that the prevailing image of Seeckt's professional skills and sense of responsibility among military historians is rather negative. According to them Seeckt disliked technology, was not a strategist and out of his depth as a military head from the very beginning. In the period from 1920 to 1926 he supposedly had military and political ambitions to establish a national dictatorship and effect the renaissance of Germany as a great power. One of his objectives was supposedly that of putting the Reichswehr at the head of the state. On the way, he was supposedly quite willing to prepare for a war of revenge against France. As the military elite, headed by Seeckt, faced a professionalism issue during the Weimar Republic, they were more willing than before to cooperate with the political and economic circles of the nation in planning a total war and the removal of restrictions on the use of force. Seeckt is portrayed as a revanchist with aims akin to those of the Reich prior to and during the First World War.

Outlook

A thorough engagement with original source material shows the above portrait of Seeckt does not conform to reality. To redress this picture, this book will proceed as follows. Better to contextualize, we shall first look at his opponent – Erich Ludendorff (1865–1937). A contemporary of Seeckt, Ludendorff was only a year older, but still the two soldiers could not have been more different on the political and military levels. This contrast will be discussed with the theory of total war at the beginning of Chapter 2. Seeckt's military strategy follows in Chapter 3. It is shown that Seeckt advocated neither the theory of total war nor the removal of restrictions on the exertion of force by means of the Reichswehr. The advantage of contrasting the two theories lies in the possibility it offers of concentrating on their focal points and the resulting incompatibility of their military-strategic principles. Whereas Ludendorff's theory of total war is briefly outlined in Chapter 2, Seeckt's military strategy is discussed in Chapter 3, with a clear line being drawn between the two men. The assumption expressed by specialists like Klaus Jürgen Müller and Michael Geyer that the civil-military cooperation during the Weimar Republic removed the boundary between the military and civilian society in order to allow a total war to be planned will be taken up once again and analysed. The inference made by scholars that the military, as an 'organizer of force for the whole of society', influenced domestic policy decisions and foreign policy objectives will be re-examined in the light of Seeckt's military strategy.[125] In contrast to the hypotheses concerning an autonomy vis-à-vis the government and parliament advocated in specialist literature, it will be argued that Seeckt did not aim at a militarization of society, that he did not intend to establish the Reichswehr at the head of the state, that his military-strategic concept for the Reichswehr did not require an 'autonomous position', but that, on the contrary, he showed a high degree of tolerance towards political interference in military issues.[126] There will be an analysis of Seeckt's military strategy in the context of whether he was truly anti-democratic and felt a '*reservatio mentalis*' towards parliament and the government, and whether he pursued a 'concept of an alliance war' in the military cooperation with the Red Army.[127]

The focus of Chapter 3 is on determining the fundamental principles of Seeckt's military strategy and finding out which factors he took into consideration and why he factored them in. The crucial question here is whether it may not have been true that Seeckt considered himself to be a member of the professional military and politico-social elite precisely because the fact of his membership of it made him recognize and accept his responsibility for the preservation of external security. It is emphasized that Seeckt must be reckoned to belong to the functional elite of the Weimar state because his politico-social and professional responsibility had its basis in fulfilling the true function of the military, namely the prevention of war. By means of a military-strategic concept, he hoped to be able to avert a war which would draw in society as a whole. Thus the antithesis to the interpretations of military historians cited in the introduction is that Seeckt must be considered a member of the elite of the state because he was aware of his special military responsibility towards its people. Another element of this argument is that he not only tried to prevent a war or civil war through his military strategy, but that his thoughts on a future war went beyond military-strategic considerations and included socio-political aspects. The question that will ultimately have to be answered is whether it was absolutely essential for him to belong to the 'new elite nucleus' of the Weimar Republic in order to be able to counter domestic and external threats.

Proceeding along those lines, it will be shown that any military policy can only be implemented effectively by the military chiefs if their actions are based on a military-strategic concept from the outset. This means that in addition to military and military-policy factors, Seeckt's decisions were not only influenced by military-strategic factors, but dominated by them. His military strategy was the basis upon which he tried to deal appropriately with the socio-political upheaval of his era and master the domestic and external politico-military challenges.

Seeckt was accused of having a trained professional army that was unable to safeguard the state externally against a war of aggression and of therefore having pushed for mass mobilisation. In this study, the opposite is assumed, namely that he rejected mass-mobilization and any operational planning for a total war in order to ensure the protection of the republic and prevent a people's war. His concept was to build up and train a small professional army and use it as a deterrent – for protecting and safeguarding the borders. These military-strategic deliberations more properly reflect his 'Prussian understanding' of military responsibility and fit his 'Prussian character'.

The assertion that Seeckt had a military-strategic concept from the very start raises the questions as to how he saw his chances of preventing a war by its implementation and as to what military-strategic solutions he offered. It will be shown that Seeckt accepted the primacy of politics and that he heeded this political premise both as the supreme soldier and as a holder of executive power. As the primacy of politics was part of his military strategy, the question must be asked as to how much priority it had in his deliberations on military and personnel policy. This not only shows that Seeckt was in opposition to Ludendorff, but also that he based his military strategy at least partially on Clausewitz.

In Chapter 3, the great extent to which Seeckt felt indebted to Clausewitz and the fact that he had already begun to think about the 'face of a future war' long before his period of duty as the Head of the Army Command will be examined. With reference to Huntington's definition of the 'military mind' and Strachan's understanding of civil-military relations, Seeckt's views on them will be closely analysed once again. The aim of this is to show that Seeckt did not hold one-sided views – as has been assumed by specialists mentioned above – and that he did not distinguish strictly between military and political responsibilities. On the contrary, he was extremely open to cooperation, just as Huntington and Strachan expect modern officers to be. The question of how great his openness was and whether it matched Huntington's military self-perception, his 'military mind', will be examined later.

The thesis put forward by military historians is that Seeckt embodied a '"middle course" of that group of officers who tried to find a way of preserving the army while being between an infeasible counterrevolution and an inner inability to approve of the political present'.[128] While it is true that he was a firm supporter of the Reichswehr being an instrument of power of the state for safeguarding its external borders, he did not aim for it to be used in a war of aggression, 'born' of the idea of military 'great power politics'.[129] Seeckt regarded the Peace Treaty of Versailles as a threat to development in home and foreign affairs and did not believe that it was a guarantor of peace. Still, he did not want to undermine it by means of the secret cooperation with the Red Army, and not even during the Ruhr crisis. He considered the unequal treatment of the negotiating parties to be the cause of the arising political instability. The terms of the Versailles Treaty, the economic crises, the social unrest and the socio-political development in the Weimar Republic prompted him to advocate a military-strategic concept which was intended to comply with the economic, financial and socio-political conditions.

The assumption that Seeckt's training was based on 'the Gospel of mobility' will be complemented by additional training criteria.[130] The assertion that Seeckt had also aimed at achieving a 'renaissance of major operational warfare with the ... operating army'[131] is countered by the thesis that he called for the professional army to be used as part of an international power and within an alliance. This is followed by questions concerning the aims of 'Seeckt's concept of an alliance war',[132] the kind of alliance policy he regarded as advantageous for a war and the way in which he intended to implement it. Actually, Seeckt put a great deal of emphasis on technology, referring back to his experiences in the First World War. In particular, his attitude towards defence technology, its brutal effects on the untrained masses, and the old military doctrines of the old army of the Empire will be reconsidered. The criticism voiced by military historians that Seeckt held onto the cavalry too much, that he showed an aversion towards anything new or technical and that his military training served to promote the renaissance of Germany as a great power both in the service regulations and in the secret cooperation with the Red Army will be scrutinized once again.[133] The contrasting theses are that Seeckt was technology-minded and aimed at integrating modern items of equipment into training to the greatest extent possible.[134] Seeckt no less reduced the military to the 'conventional combat unit' than he was critical of the old military doctrines. By means of the secret cooperation with the Red Army, he strove to use all the technical options not banned by the Versailles Treaty. He attached eminent importance to technology. For this, he even embarked on a course of action that violated the Versailles Treaty.

As Seeckt saw it, any military policy concerning soldiers was primarily an inward personnel policy or training and education directive. By means both of his decisions on enlistment, discharge, reassignment and promotion and of his training and education doctrine, he had an inward effect, on the troops themselves and on the morale among them. His inward military policy was the basis upon which he acted and advised in military-strategic matters. It was the foundation of the specialist military action he took to either respond to a foreign affairs crisis with war or to advice against doing so, intending it to have a deterrent effect.

A soldier will base his outward actions on how he has formed and organized a military force, trained it and familiarized it defensively or offensively with a peace concept. Accordingly, the military policy of a soldier is the foundation of his military strategy and the basis upon which he gives specialist military advice to the government.

Although Ludendorff was not a member of the Reichswehr, he still had a strong influence on the officers of the Army Command and thus initiated a military-strategic debate at the Reichswehr Ministry. This resulted in a military-strategic disagreement which developed into a factional dispute at the Reichswehr Ministry. This dispute and its progression will be discussed in Chapter 4 because this debate, which was dominated by Ludendorff's followers, set the tone in military-strategic and politico-military matters after 1926. The military-strategic dispute over the way in which the Reichswehr should develop ended when Seeckt was discharged.

Chapter 4 explores the differences between the diverse military strategies within the Army Command. Seeckt found himself at odds with another politico-military elite at the Reichswehr Ministry. His military-strategic concept can be regarded as the cause for the factional military-strategic dispute within the Army Command, which ultimately revealed that there were irreconcilable differences between General Staff officers. Seeckt's view of the primacy of politics and his military strategy based on it were the real reasons for his discharge. The irreconcilable differences between him and Ludendorff's followers caused the internal rift within the Army Command. While historians have noticed that the officer corps at the Reichswehr Ministry was caught up in factional conflicts, they offered only unsatisfactory explanations for it.[135] The questions arising from this are what military-strategic ideas divided the officer corps at the Reichswehr Ministry, who advocated them, and how and why. This military-strategic conflict still has an effect to this day. It is the precursor of the latest discussion between the reformers and the traditionalists within the Bundeswehr. This ongoing dispute is attributed to the divergent military strategies of Ludendorff and Seeckt.

In Chapter 5, Seeckt's political views as the holder of military power and his actions to preserve the Reich will be examined. The focus will be on analysing his political programmes in 1923–24. His political actions as the holder of executive power will be compared to his military strategy in order to show that his actions were inherently consistent with the guidelines he had already defined as a military strategist. Seeckt's further, above all political thoughts on how to preserve the republic will also be discussed in Chapter 5.

In Chapter 6, Huntington's definition of the military self-perception of soldiers will be cited once again and supplemented. The equally important criteria listed by Huntington, such as professionalism, expertise, experience, social and ethical responsibility and an ability to cooperate, are central aspects of the 'military mind'.[136] Yet, more criteria need to be added to them in order to get a full idea of a soldier at the interface with politics. Finally, the focal points of Seeckt's military strategy will be summarized and the incompatibility of his principles with those of Ludendorff will be highlighted. The next step will be to go into the criteria that form the basis upon which the military chiefs act and the factors that determine their actions at the interface with politics and within the forces. The aspects of a military strategy that military historians should also take into account in order to gain a better understanding of military chiefs will be examined.

Chapter 2

Military-Strategic Considerations in the Weimar Republic

Introduction

As has been shown, the existing historiography concerning Seeckt suggests, or at least implies, that he prepared the ground for Hitler's grand strategy of revisionism and military enforced expansionism. To illustrate the extent to which this picture is misleading, it is useful to contrast Seeckt's strategy for Germany with that of the man who competed with Hitler for the leadership of the National-Socialist Party (NSDAP) casually referred to in English as the 'Nazi-Party'. This man was Erich Ludendorff, a prominent general of the First World War, known for the victory of Tannenberg of 1916, and considered a great hero. Having turned his back on Hitler and the NSDAP because the 'Bohemi and Private' (Hitler) was preferred over him by their fellows Nazis, he published what nevertheless comes closest to a Nazi strategic concept in his 1935 book *The Total War*. It is useful to summarize his thinking, if just to contrast it with Seeckt's. To contextualise Seeckt's thinking in this chapter, the basic thinking of his main opponent Erich Ludendorff will be sketched. Ludendorff developed a theory, which differs markedly from the views of both Clausewitz and Seeckt. The differences between them can be seen most clearly in their attitudes towards the importance of the primacy of politics. This difference pervades military strategy to this day and reveals two irreconcilable positions, for their principles affect both the military and the political levels.

The most prominent German strategist of the inter-war era, Ludendorff and his theory occupies an important position because it had a strong influence on the officers at the Reichswehr Ministry. It led to a factional military-strategic dispute during Seeckt's term of office, the upshot of which was that it was not Seeckt who paved the way for the

Second World War, with his military strategy, but Ludendorff, with his theory of total war, and his followers at the Reichswehr Ministry, with their military policy. While speaking to him, Max Weber sketched his dangerous character very early. After the First World War he was the only scientist who had foreseen what impact this man could have had:

Prologue:
Max Weber (1864–1920) reproached Ludendorff for the political mistakes committed by the Army Command, whereas the latter held Weber responsible for the sins of the revolution and the new regime ...

W.: The honour of the nation can only be saved if you deliver yourself up of your own free will.
L.: I don't care a damn about the nation! This ingratitude!
W.: Nevertheless, you really must render us this last service.
L.: I hope to be able to render even more important services to the nation.
W.: Well, then your remarks obviously shouldn't be taken too seriously. Incidentally, this is not only about the German people, but also about restoring the honour of the officer corps and the army.
L.: Why don't you go to Hindenburg? After all, he was General Field Marshal, wasn't he?[1]
W.: Hindenburg is 70 years old – and anyway, every child knows that you were the number one in Germany at that time.
L.: Thank goodness!

The conversation soon turned to political issues such as the causes of the collapse and the interference of the Supreme Army Command in politics. With his back to the wall, Ludendorff tries to change the subject: Well, there's your highly praised democracy for you! It's your fault and that of the '*Frankfurter Zeitung*' newspaper! What is better now?

W.: You don't think that I take the mess we've now got for democracy?
L.: When you put it like that, we may come to some understanding.
W.: But the mess we had before was no monarchy either.
L.: Then what do you mean by democracy?

W.:   In a democracy, the people elect someone they trust as their leader. The person elected then says: 'Now shut up and do as you're told.' From that point on, neither the people nor the party have any say in what he does.

L.:   I could get to like this sort of 'democracy'!

W.:   Afterwards, the people can judge him – if the leader has made mistakes, it is to the gallows with him![2]

Ludendorff's Total War Theory

Erich Ludendorff was a General Staff officer in the Great General Staff of the Army during World War I and a contemporary of Seeckt. He developed the total war theory, as Leon Daudet (1867–1942) did for the French.[3] Ludendorff derived his theory from the French Revolution; its ideas provided him with the motives for a war, a people's war. What was special and new about the French Revolution was that the overthrow of the system was not initiated by a head of state, but that the people themselves intervened in politics and took the lead. Through the French Revolution, other forces came to power. The people devoted themselves to the service of the state and its underlying principles. As the new player in the state, they took over the reins of power in politics. The people now determined both domestic policy developments and the grounds for a future war. This had to result in a new kind of warfare. A few years later, Napoleon was able to draw on the masses when he waged war against other states. Once the politico–military balance in Europe was disrupted, the other states had to follow suit to avoid being overwhelmed by events.[4]

In Ludendorff's view, the new political demands of the French Revolution and the Napoleonic way of waging war had created a new relationship between politics and warfare, between the people and the government:

> Total war, which was not solely a matter for the armed forces, but also directly affected the life and soul of every individual member of the warring nations, was born, due not only to changes in policy … but to the introduction of compulsory military service, together with the rising population figures and weapons whose effects were becoming more and more destructive.[5]

The French Revolution had initiated a new form of government, but what evolved from it was a rising totalitarism. As far as warfare was concerned, it meant that the brutal effect of the massive use of weapons in war rebounded on the people themselves, that it could not help hitting the nations in the war.

In his theory, which was not supposed to be one, Ludendorff began with the words that he wanted 'to write no theory of war': 'That is far from my mind. I am, as I have so often said, opposed to all theories,' he added, concluding that general conscription had been introduced in Prussia by Scharnhorst because of Napoleon. Due to this, the relationship between the army and the masses, politics and warfare, was also said to have changed in Germany.[6] He stated that the new wars would now be governed by new forces, the people. He reasoned that this was bound to result in a new balance of power between politics, warfare, the army and the people.

Consequently, Ludendorff considered that the Napoleonic wars heralded the end of the European cabinet wars. The Franco-Prussian War of 1871 was to bring about the change for Germany. After the war against France, he believed that 'the days of the cabinet wars ... [were] over for Germany',[7] too.

Ludendorff denied that the previous cabinet wars had had any 'moral justification' whatsoever. He called them 'raids', because their sole purpose had been to enrich a small few. 'They were often "raids" more than fights with a profound moral justification, as total war is for the survival of a nation.'[8] He said that anything that cannot be 'sparked off for the survival of the people' served only 'greed'.[9] Ludendorff not only believed that the days of the cabinet wars were over, but also their 'raids'. In confirmation of his thesis on the end of the cabinet wars, Ludendorff quoted Bismarck: 'If we in Germany intend to wage a war with the full force of our national strength, then it must be a war with which everyone ... the whole nation agrees. It must be a people's war.'[10]

In the First World War, mass mobilisation was deliberately introduced. The steady rise in technical options increased the striking power at the cost of 'extreme suffering' being inflicted on an entire people.

The world war was completely different in nature to all the wars of the previous 150 years ... the nations themselves were put in the service of war, the war was also directed against them and inflicted extreme suffering on them.[11]

The planning and employment of the masses in the First World War seemed to bear out his theory on future total war and he developed it further.[12]

Ludendorff believed that in the future, a conflict would only have a 'moral justification' if it was a national, total one. In his opinion, a total war served the preservation of an entire people, and it needed to be prepared for war in its totality. He considered that the totality of a future war would result from the mobilization of the people. The people themselves were destined for the totality of war, were both the cause and the reason for total war. This was the only way they could maintain their existence. Ludendorff justified war with the argument that it ensured the 'preservation of the people'. Thus Ludendorff gave a rather archaic reason as the motive for war. He said that cause of war was the need to ensure the 'preservation' of an entire people, while the contents of politics were reduced to the fight for survival of a nation. The fight for survival and thus war itself needed no political goals. War became an end in itself for the people. Ludendorff had not even mentioned economic, geographical or other military-strategic considerations.

> The 'leaders in political dealings' should not only have an appreciation of war in order to manage foreign policy matters as warfare requires, but also more particularly of the nature that war has now assumed and how the tasks arise from it that the leaders of the entire people, that is the politicians, have to accomplish in all respects to ensure the survival of the people.[13]

'Nationalist policy' had to be put in the 'service of war'. Ludendorff became increasingly irrational in the phrasing and justification of his theory. To justify the fight for survival as such, to mobilize the unleashing of the force within one people against another, he did not feel the need to use universally comprehensible terms. At first, he referred to the forces the people drew from their 'racial heritage'.[14] Yet even as he tried to state the reasons for the 'fight for survival', he could only say that there were 'palpable causes'.[15] He believed that their fighting strength would maintain and enhance the 'emotional unity' of the people. He called the allies in this fight 'national siblings'. He said that the 'national spirit', 'Germany's recognition of God', the 'emotional forces of the people', their 'emotional unity' and the people's 'experience of God', would influence the fight and determine the result of a war.[16]

These terms are a far cry from a rationally worded, deductive line of argument for the justification of a war and served just as little to achieve the deduction of strategic interests. While he cited domestic reasons for the French Revolution, he primarily attributed emotional motives to Germany's policy of force, formulating them above all against minorities. In his eyes, they included the Catholic Church, which he saw as the 'black power' of Europe.[17] Among them, he also ranked the 'misguided intellectuals in society, some of whom [were] mind-numbed by occultism'.[18] He believed that the leaders of the people would have to realize that the people would be weakened by the 'discontented', the 'enemies of the German people'.[19] He failed, however, to give a definition of a person who was 'discontented' and to state why such individuals were discontented. Nevertheless, the theory of total war and of a people's war was to become one of the crucial theses of the twentieth century. He formulated his theory against the 'discontented' in society, against the intellectuals, Jews and Catholics in Germany, who in his view had caused the defeat in the First World War.[20]

His doctrine was not only racist and anti-Semitic, but also anti-Christian. It was directed as much against Jews and Christians of the Roman Catholic Church as it was against academics and freemasons. Ludendorff's demand for the mobilization of all the martial resources of a nation was not based on a rational justification of force, and his theory of the unleashing of the force within a nation was not rational.

Another thesis proved how anti-Christian his doctrine was and yet at the same time how much his thinking was based on the Old Testament despite his anti-Semitism; it also showed how much he lagged behind 2,000 years of civilization. 'Christian doctrine is a religious doctrine which is profoundly at odds with our racial heritage, destroys it, strips the people of their specific unity and renders them defenceless.'[21] In his opinion, it had ruined the people's 'conscious experience of race and God'.[22] For that reason, he regarded its effects on the individual and on the 'emotional unity' of the people as 'not salvific'.[23] Moreover, he endorsed the Old Testament principle of 'an eye for an eye'[24] as a guideline for the conduct of future wars. He went back on the religious and cultural progress of 2,000 years of Christianity, rejecting Christian doctrine and values and with them the way of treating people, which was based on moral and ethical understanding. Totality was put on an amoral and anti-Christian footing. Ludendorff rejected any compliance with ethical, Christian and moral principles. Everything was based on his idea of 'racial heritage'.[25]

Ludendorff's theory was formulated against his own people, for he accepted no Christian values in it which the people could have used to guide their actions in their fight for survival in the event of victory, failure or defeat. By turning against Christian values in his anti-Christian theory, he created very broad concepts of the internal and the external enemy. Abolishing all the previously applicable ethical principles, he demanded the total commitment of the emotional force of the people for the next conflict.[26] He believed that only the 'eye for an eye' principle fully unleashed the force of a nation, their 'emotional force'. He assumed that in a total war, the people fought as if they were in 'mortal danger'. He believed that this was what provided war its 'moral justification'.

> Today, in a total war, the word people and with it the people themselves have come to the fore, and at the same time the significance of the national spirit for the preservation of the people in their daily lives and even more so in mortal danger has been recognized … The emphasis is on the people in a total war.[27]

By then obviously a megalomaniac, Ludendorff put war above God. Having already rejected Christian doctrine, he next turned against God, because He 'determines everything in his [a man's] life …' For example, he considered 'Christian doctrine and the practice of living in accordance with it … the most profound cause of the collapse of the nation in the adversity of a total war'.[28] He believed that Christian doctrine was a kind of heteronomy over man and had rendered the people defenceless and weak in the First World War. He demanded that the next war be determined solely by the military chiefs and a government exercising total government. He argued that they alone would specify how the battle was fought and the people were employed:

> Total government that is intended to enable the people to exert themselves to their limits in a total war and to preserve it … can only accomplish its task if it … is given the position beside the man among the people and in the state that conforms to our racial heritage.[29]

In a racist total-war doctrine that has no connection whatsoever with Christian values, an individual could no longer count for anything in war. There were only the masses. Ludendorff granted few rights to the individual. For him, there were only the people, and its 'mental force' had to be mobilized for a war. The government had to pay attention to the 'unity of the people' and to oppose the influence of the Christian doctrine in peacetime.[30] As a consequence, totalitarian measures against individuals encompassing the repeal of rights and liberties were permissible in the event of war:

> It goes without saying that the state, i.e. the politicians advocating totality and the military chiefs conducting the total war, will have to take special measures such as tightening the censorship of the press, tightening laws against the disclosure of military secrets, closing off border traffic against neutral states, imposing bans on public meetings, arresting at least the chief figures among the 'discontented' …[31]

He demanded that all forces of the people, with the officers foremost, had to devote themselves to the preparations for a total war. They were not supposed to be concerned with ethical or Christian values, but to do as the 'code of honour of an officer' prescribed. 'His honour is to be a paragon, teacher and leader of his national siblings in the fight for the survival of the people.'[32] His aspiration must not only be 'to be a commander of soldiers, but to seize their souls and thus become their true leader'.[33] A soldier took on demagogic and therefore political tasks.

Ludendorff's theory was based on the assumption that the enemy would also take such total measures.[34] Such a concept of reciprocity put forward the idea of the fight for survival being fought to the death. All the forces of the nations would be devoted to the service of the war. A total war demanded the entire strength of a nation and its enemy. It would turn on the country's own people if it lost. As a logical consequence, defeat would mean doom. 'By its nature, a total war literally demands the entire strength of the people and turns against it as well.'[35] Unless the people were prepared in due time by 'total government', they would be annihilated in the next war. So government had to be 'like total war and assume a total character'.[36] This was why the people had to be given an idea of the necessary measures beforehand so that they would withstand a total fight. Total government constituted the foundation for preparations for a total war.

The task of 'total government' consisted of 'preparing [the people] in peacetime for this fight for survival and … consolidating the foundation for this fight for survival.'[37] Ludendorff left unanswered the question of what specific preparations were necessary with regard to equipment and training unanswered. Yet regardless of what factors were to be taken into account and what measures were to be taken, politics were devoted to total of war. Everything was directed towards the ultimate end, war itself.

In 1922, he defined the relationship between war and politics by reversing the approach taken by Clausewitz. Whereas Clausewitz endorsed the rule that war was the continuation of politics by other means and politics therefore determined the way in which war was fought, Ludendorff believed this: 'War is the conduct of foreign affairs by other means … Other than that, politics as a whole have to serve war.'[38] Ludendorff formulated his idea intentionally as an inversion of Clausewitz's argument.[39]

In order to substantiate his own theory, Ludendorff did not hold back in his criticism of Clausewitz.[40] He called studying the works of Clausewitz 'confusing'.[41] He was perhaps not alone in this, but he also strictly rejected the primacy of politics in war.[42] Right at the beginning of his book on total war, Ludendorff refuted Clausewitz's claim:

All the theories of Clausewitz must be thrown overboard. War and politics serve the preservation of the people, but war is the highest expression of a nation's will to live. Therefore, politics must serve war.[43]

Ludendorff's language was not only imprecise: his theory was not only irrational and denied the atrocities of war; it was not only contemptuous of humanity, anti-Christian and unethical; it also destroyed culture and civilization. 150 years earlier, Immanuel Kant had written about the absurdity of a war of this kind in his treatise on 'perpetual peace'. 'It follows that a war of extermination, in which the destruction of both parties and of all justice can result, would permit perpetual peace only in the vast burial ground of the human race.'[44] Accordingly, Ludendorff's idea of total war would result in military-strategic nihilism.

Hew Strachan believes that: 'Clausewitz the German nationalist was at times closer in his thinking to Erich Ludendorff, the German army´s first quartermaster general of 1916–1918, than we care to acknowledge or than Ludendorff himself did.'[45] But in fact, given Ludendorff's his fundamental attitude towards significance of politics, this is hardly the case.

It is sometimes suggested, as from the specialist historian of war theory Wilhelm Deist, that Ludendorff presented a theory, albeit an extreme one. It is considered to have answered questions concerning the budget, foreign policy, military policy and psychological warfare and to have addressed issues concerning the planning and implementation of equipment and training programmes.[46] However, it is hardly possible to deduce a rational comprehensive concept from Ludendorff's wordings and ideas or detect indications of a strategy. Strachan rightly emphasizes that '[t]he second point evident in Ludendorff's book was how little it said about strategy'.[47]

Ludendorff failed to provide extensive details on the formation, structure, organization, training and equipment the army needed to give the full 'strength of the people' any chance of survival at all in a total war. He devoted just five pages to the new weapons and their use on the battlefield.[48] It is true that in some parts of his exposition, Ludendorff did take account of heavy tanks, the Air Force and the Navy. But his remarks remained general in nature and provided few recommendations on how they were to be put into practice. Ludendorff took equally little account of important conditions such as the economy, the arms industry, geography or alliance policy. He gave even far less consideration to the country's geostrategic position.

Ludendorff conflicted sharply not only with Clausewitz with respect to his theory of total war, but also with Seeckt. In 1923, on the occasion of the coup he attempted with Hitler, he not only provided evidence of his anti-constitutional stance towards the state and society, but also of his having a different basic attitude towards the army and Seeckt with respect to military policy. He rejected Seeckt's objective of training soldiers to be inactive in party politics:

> Moreover, Ludendorff had also turned directly against Seeckt, who set so much store by keeping party politics out of the army, and claimed that the old Prussian army had been essentially involved in politics to a large extent, for every member of the Prussian army had been brought up to be a monarchist. The national idea was the force that was destined today to bind the future army together.[49]

In 1923, Seeckt merely commented sarcastically on Ludendorff's intervention in political events: 'He [Ludendorff] really is fighting … a war of missed opportunities and this time, too, will miss the chance to put a bullet through his head.'[50] Seeckt's analysis of the effects and results of the Napoleonic War was also incompatible with that of Ludendorff. He analysed the causes of Napoleon's downfall and came to the conclusion that his military-strategic dominance was the reason for his defeat. He believed that Napoleon had first lost the war and then his political leadership because his military objectives had predominated his political ones:

> The mistake that the military objectives completely eclipsed the actual idea of the state and that his [Napoleon's] policy was no longer in accord with his conduct of the war could not help but lead to setbacks which after a short while shattered the Napoleonic empire.[51]

In his continued analysis of the errors of Napoleonic warfare, Seeckt proved himself to be a disciple of Clausewitz, who had demanded that the military chiefs should not dominate politics.

Like Max Weber, Seeckt had considered Ludendorff's attitude towards the state and society to be dangerous, destabilizing, undemocratic and not based on the republican constitution. Less blunt than Max Weber, who wanted to send Ludendorff to the gallows, Seeckt had demanded that people of his ilk be kept away from government affairs.

> He [Seeckt] was a fierce opponent of Ludendorff, and he once told me [Minister of Justice Schiffer] that he would immediately resign if the latter should become Reichswehr Minister or obtain a significant influence on the government.[52]

Yet Ludendorff was not only Seeckt's adversary on account of his writing, he was far more. Compared with Ludendorff, whose views converged with those of the National-Socialism, Seeckt appears startlingly moderate. This will also become apparent in the following chapter. Ever since 1916, Seeckt like Max Weber 1918 had regarded Ludendorff's 'political attitude ... as misguided in many respects'.[53]

Epilogue

> The men [Max Weber and Erich Ludendorff] at first conversed in a very heated manner, then finally quite calmly and affably, although they were talking at cross purposes about their subject. Weber was profoundly disappointed, however. Not so much because the general had turned down his request ('he, of course, had no fear of death'), but in other respects. His conclusion was: 'Perhaps it will be better for Germany if he does not surrender himself. The personal impression he would make would be unfavourable. Once more, the enemies would think: the sacrifices made in a war that put paid to men of his kind were worth it! I now understand why the world defends itself against men like him trampling it underfoot. If he interferes in politics again, he must be fought uncompromisingly.[54]

Chapter 3

Seeckt's Military Strategy

Introduction

In this chapter, Seeckt's fundamental thoughts on military strategy, his acceptance of the primacy of politics and his connection to Clausewitz will be examined; it will also be shown that a line has to be drawn between him and Ludendorff's theory of total war.

The Concept of Strategy in Military History

The first theories concerning military craftsmanship and the waging of war evolved in the ancient world.[1] In more recent times, Sun Tzu, Thucydides and Clausewitz are among the thinkers who developed a theory of war by combining science, military craftsmanship and political leadership. Yet there was no definition of strategy or military strategy, particularly one in which a clear distinction was made between strategy and policy, military operations and tactics, until the days of Clausewitz. In the ancient world and the Middle Ages, the terms for strategic and military objectives were frequently synonymous and therefore not distinguishable enough in their usage for our modern age. Policy, however, a higher authority which provided the military with the strategic parameters for the objectives of their military operations, remained beyond the scope of theoretical reflections. It was only over the centuries that the terms 'operation' and 'tactics' became subsidiary to the terms 'military strategy' or 'strategy' and a clearer distinction was also made between them and strategy.[2] Clausewitz and Jomini (6 March 1779–24 March 1869) were the military theoreticians who decreed in their writings that the military principle should be secondary to that of political leadership.[3] This precept was subsequently taken up by other thinkers. They linked military-strategic considerations, military objectives and resources more closely with political ends. In the last two centuries, French, British and

Italian military theoreticians pursued this line of thought and maintained the close link between military resources and their use for political ends.[4] They established and structured a hierarchical system for tactics, operations, military strategy and strategy. Military-strategic reflections decreasingly tended to go off on a tangent as they were increasingly dominated by the political intentions of a government. This was regarded not only as a step forward in civilization. In the late twentieth century, this was confirmed as a positive development, because after the Second World War in Europe, decisions on the use of military resources were only made by a government and for political ends.[5]

As the close union between the political authorities and the military dissolved over the centuries in western Europe and the military came to carry out the orders issued by the political authorities, a hierarchy evolved between the political and military heads of a country and thus between the terms military strategy and strategy. The use of military resources depended on the political authorities. The political authorities pursued strategic interests by means of the armed forces. Military-strategic considerations depended on the strategy of the political leadership. Seeckt took account of this separation of tasks between the military and political heads.[6] This is why a clear distinction is made in this study between the political term 'strategy' and the term 'military strategy'. A 'strategy' is considered to be pursued by a political leader, whereas a 'military strategy' is pursued by a soldier. Military strategy refers to the military considerations of a soldier at the interface with politics. Its aim is to provide the political leadership with advice for his strategic decisions.[7]

Seeckt's concept of Strategy

Seeckt made no effort to provide a precise or detailed definition of strategy either in his orders, in the service publications, in the regulation ('Leadership and Combat with joint forces' *'Führung und Gefecht der verbundenen Waffen'*, henceforth FuG) or in his writings. To my knowledge, he only used the term 'strategy' a few times. On account of the experiences of the First World War, he asked in 1929 what strategy was to be pursued by the state and the army in order to avoid a repetition of the mistakes made in the First World War:

To what military success did this universal Levee-en-masse, this gigantic parade of armies lead? … Has the victor really rejoiced in his victory? Do the results of the war bear any just relation to the sacrifice of national strength? Is it necessary for whole nations to hurl themselves upon one another whenever recourse to arms is unavoidable. The soldier must ask himself whether these giant armies can even be manoeuvred in accordance with a strategy that seeks a decision, and whether it is possible for any future war between these masses to end otherwise than in indecisive rigidity?[8]

He applied the term strategy to the socio-political objective of waging a war and winning it quickly in order to minimize its consequences for the people affected. This option was passed up when, in the First World War, 'sight was lost of the great strategic objective of achieving an operational encirclement'. Schlieffen's 'Cannae concept' remained unsuccessful because 'a journeyman's bungling [referring to Moltke the Younger] attempt to improve the master's plan [referring to Schlieffen]' was unable to bring success.[9]

In another 1930 treatise on national defence, he again used the term strategy in association with politics, society and the army and answered his own rhetorical question above: 'The objective of a modern strategy must be to bring about a decision with mobile forces without or prior to masses being set in motion.'[10]

In his article on Clausewitz, written in 1930, Seeckt also applied the term strategy to military strategy.[11] Strategy was the result of the military skills of great generals. Their knowledge from previous wars determined their strategic theory and thus the way in which they waged war. Strategy was an expression of an advanced art of war; it was based on the experiences resulting from successes and defeats, errors and failures that could be summed up as general knowledge of war:

It is not the individual successes, the minor victories or defeats that are the basis of experience, but only the truly great qualities and the truly great errors that provide the opportunity to recognize eternal laws. This influence of the great geniuses, their deeds and their errors, puts strategy into the realm of the arts … Clausewitz does not teach any art of war … because he knows that personal genius cannot be taught ... Clausewitz deduces the eternal rules from the sphere of pure thought.[12]

According to Seeckt's understanding of Clausewitz's notion of strategy, there was not just one strategy, but there were many principles of strategy by which a war was waged and evolved. Seeckt ranked 'the doctrine of the state in its application to war ... and the doctrine of energy'[13] among the principles of strategy. He emphasized the progress which Clausewitz had achieved for the state in his strategy doctrine: A war should not be waged without political precepts and intervention:

> What is new in his [Clausewitz] train of thought [argued Seeckt] is that he sees war, the field of activity of the army, not as something outside the life of a nation, but regards it rather as one of the manifestations of political life.[14]

Seeckt followed Clausewitz, because the important questions for the army with regard to its task in the state were both asked and answered by the political authorities.[15]

Even the first basic military decisions concerning its formation and organization were made by the political heads. 'The larger questions of military organization are of a political nature, e.g. the choice between general compulsory service and a mercenary system.'[16] The question of whether a professional army or a people's army was formed, even when it was demobilized, was determined by political considerations:

> The government therefore has its say in the preparatory peacetime organization of the army, and there is no ruling out the possibility of the policy they pursue leading to a reduction of the army; as we are seeing at present, of the issue of arms limitation or arms compensation being a primarily political one in which the soldier is merely assigned the role of an expert adviser.[17]

He emphasized that government decided how a war was to be waged, aggressively or defensively: 'Politicians decide who is the attacker and who is the defender.'[18] They also specified who the allies would be in a coming war, another thing that can be traced back to Clausewitz.[19]

'The difficulties are doubled when a war has to be waged with allies.'[20] If the political leadership dominated questions concerning conscription or the length of military service in peacetime, then they also resolved questions concerning arms control policy: 'Competition in armament and limitation of armament are both political questions in spite of their military form.'[21]

Owing to these binding precepts for the military, any further military-strategic decisions concerning preparation, prevention and the use of the army also had to be agreed between the soldier and the political leadership. Seeckt regarded the role of the supreme soldier being to provide expert advice, which was covered by a military strategy.[22]

In his military-strategic principles, Seeckt started off from where there was no unity between the political leadership and the supreme soldier in the state, where the government and the army were required to cooperate.[23] Like Clausewitz, Seeckt also regarded all the departments as being subordinate to the political authorities in this initial situation.

> The essential point is that all the threads of political life are conducted to and from this centre, and that, to attain its ends, it controls all the departments of state, such as finance, foreign affairs – and defence.[24]

He did not base his military-strategic considerations on the politico-military restrictions specified in the Versailles Treaty anymore than he doubted that the Weimar Republic needed a larger army.[25] His view was that even a state whose government 'pursued peaceful objectives' would not be able to avoid favouring a strong army. Leaning on the political theory of Hobbes in this respect, he assumed a pragmatic attitude[26]:

> No matter how pacific the political aims of a state may be … It will depend partly on the strength of the army how far he may go in his demands and to what extent he must give way.[27]

In this, he assigned the army a power-politics role in the state:

> If we try nowadays to exclude the 'war of aggression' from the sphere of international relations, we therefore repudiate the dogma

of 'continuation of policy by military means', for policy will surely not be content to acquiesce in activity, in the renunciation of all aims which contemplate the acquisition of power.[28]

The army gave international weight to the state, was one of its political instruments which it was able to use as an '*ultima ratio*' to enforce its interests. The political leadership was able to assess the strength of the army and its abilities rationally. 'Starting out from the army, its strength decides the question of whether the politician can factor the "*ultima ratio*", war, into their calculations with any prospect of success'.[29] Seeckt regarded the employment of the military as the ultimate factor, the last resort of politics by which a government might attempt to safeguard its interests. At the same time, he took power-political scheming for granted, asserting 'that it cannot be anything but gratifying for its head when he can look, in the last resort, to a strong army for the execution of his plans'.[30]

Once war did break out, however, the declaration of war was not only the end of all diplomatic efforts, but also the declaration of bankruptcy of policy:

We shall not remove war from the world altogether, but it should only be waged to reconcile 'the great antitheses of life'. The statement that war is a continuation of policy by other means has become a catch-phrase and is therefore dangerous. We can say with equal truth: War is the bankruptcy of policy.[31]

War itself was the admission of the political heads of having failed to maintain external security and to achieve their own interests through diplomatic relations:

The first business of the Foreign Office is to prevent any menace from becoming a reality, to anticipate such by arbitration, and to gain allies in the event of an actual attack. Should war then really ensue, diplomacy must have done its utmost to provide that military operations may be conducted under the most favourable conditions possible.[32]

Seeckt's concept of strategy was at the interface to politics and was predominantly in compliance with the guidelines established by the political heads. As a military strategist, he saw his duty as that of achieving the military objectives determined by the political heads, acting within the framework of the political constraints throughout.

Seeckt did not take it upon himself to appraise the use and strength of the other two services. He confined himself to his experiences of World War I and to the provision of the requisite purely military capabilities and skills of a land force. He heeded the Versailles Treaty in his military-strategic deliberations just as little as he bothered to answer questions concerning naval forces:

> They are the product of my imagination and bear as little relation to the organization of the German Reichswehr as they do to the restrictions imposed on us by the Treaty of Versailles. Lastly, they refer to land forces only and leave naval matters to more expert examination.[33]

He remembered the First World War well enough to make use of his own experiences of war to complete his military-strategic concept. This meant that he had to take a good look at the errors of judgment made in the last war, those of the Supreme Army Command. They taught him a lesson on how not to plan, begin and continue an armed conflict ever again.

After the war, he voiced severe criticism of the operation of the First Army in the West initiated at the beginning of the war in the summer of 1914 and aimed at advancing across Belgium towards Northern France. He came to the conclusion that the western campaign had been organized quite badly.

> The entire front was equally strong, even the cavalry divisions were evenly distributed! That was what had become of the 'strong right wing'! And this form of deployment has become such in the 2nd Division under Ludendorff and deteriorated further under Tappen.[34]

One undesirable development in the war that Seeckt seems to have regarded as crucial was that of trench warfare.[35] He wanted the reasons for it to be found and the lessons from it to be learned:

A continuous front of trenches was built, which on the German west side extended to the sea with the right wing and to the Swiss border with the left wing, and it took a period of more than four years for this one front to be worn down and finally give way.[36]

Because the duration of a war was hard to estimate and even a single individual could hardly determine and limit it, Seeckt demanded: 'The goal of war is its end. All the factors involved are concerned to reach this end by the use of every means, military and political.'[37]

Seeckt's fundamental military-strategic considerations followed both the politico-military precepts of Clausewitz and the political ideas of Bismarck and leaned to some extent on the commission principle of Helmuth Moltke the Elder (1800–1891).[38] At the same time, he rejected the latter's claim to military leadership in war. Following the example of Clausewitz, the next logical question is whether the form of government of the republic and the foreign policy constraints of the victorious powers were the basis from which Seeckt systematically derived his politico-military and military-strategic objectives? It is a matter of debate as to whether further questions concerning personnel policy, training, equipment and military education in the army automatically derived from these restraints affected his policy as the supreme soldier.

For this purpose, it is useful to analyze the effects the orders, guidelines and service regulations issued by Seeckt had on military practice, everyday military life and the Reichswehr Ministry. An attempt will be made to answer questions concerning military personnel, military training, equipment and military education from the point of view of socio-political upheaval. It is necessary to understand whether and, if so, to what extent Seeckt was able to achieve his military – and particularly military-strategic – objective at the ministry and in the army.

Clausewitz – Bismarck – Moltke – Seeckt

Following the example of Clausewitz and Moltke, Seeckt developed a military strategy for the Weimar Republic which united the conduct of operations of a small army with tactics and combined arms combat. Seeckt proceeded on the assumption that only trained armies with appropriate equipment allowed political ends to be pursued on the battlefield. In conformity with Clausewitz, Seeckt quoted Bismarck, who only regarded the use of military force as promising if it was determined by the political authorities and they specified the professional army's objectives. 'No man did more for the development of the Prussian Army than the "statesman" Bismarck, because he used the army for his political aims.'[39]

Seeckt referred to the military theoretician Clausewitz, who had demanded 'the integration of war into statecraft and a foundation of general principles in the national political spirit of the time'.[40] He followed the latter's line of thought not only in his understanding of the relationship between the military and politics and in his acceptance of the primacy of politics. Beyond that, Seeckt followed Clausewitz in a definition which was to be found among Clausewitz' military principles: 'Destruction of the enemy's army, not destruction of the country, remains the supreme law of war, although at times it seems otherwise.'[41] In his theory, Seeckt took up issues from the First World War and criticized more recent wars in the post-war era. On several occasions he emphasized something that Clausewitz, too, took for granted: One of his first premises was not to destroy the population and, as shall be seen, not to mobilize it for war. In order to affirm this objective, he had the following guideline included in the Army regulation (*Heeresdienstvorschrift*) H.Dv. 487, '*Führung und Gefecht der verbundenen Waffen*' (FuG; 'Command and control and combined arms combat') of 1923: 'War is waged against an enemy state and its armed forces, not against its peaceful civilian population.'[42] In the last section of this H.Dv, he incorporated The Hague Convention with respect to the Laws and Customs of War on Land.

In a conscious attempt to dissociate from Moltke's views, he assigned the responsibility of being politicians' advisers to the chiefs of the armed forces. Seeckt demanded mutual acceptance. He argued that the soldier had to be able to give an appropriate military-strategic evaluation of the political objectives. The political leader, for his part, had to appreciate military parameters. 'Clausewitz … intends to teach the soldier political thinking, but also to teach the politician about the will of the soldier'.[43] Like Clausewitz, he was of the opinion that policy determined the use of the army.[44] No less logically, he concluded from this context: 'Precisely those who see in war only a continuation of policy by other means will have to admit that only a policy of aggression can lead to a war of aggression.'[45] The consequence of this is that if a policy is unfavourable for the country, its use of the army will be wrong; however, 'a good policy will make the right use'.[46]

Seeckt appreciated some other aspects of Moltke's views: who did not long for war, but 'was convinced of its inevitability just as much as of his duty to be so prepared for it that he had a good chance of waging it victoriously'.[47] Seeckt agreed with Moltke the Elder on the point that those wars that 'grew from decisions on the battlefield to decisions between nations' were detrimental to the population.[48] He assumed that Moltke had warned long before the First World War of the possible violent excesses, its long duration and the use of the masses, the excessive strain on them, also the economic consequences. While there had been political differences between Moltke and Bismarck, Seeckt believed their common denominator lay in the fact that both were concerned to end the war quickly.[49] Seeckt followed their joint objective in order to acknowledge the primacy of politics without being affected by the discrepancy between them.

Seeckt's position of mutual acceptance in combination with observance of the primacy of politics represents one of the fundamental differences to Moltke's opinion. With his understanding of civil-military cooperation and his acceptance of the primacy of politics, Seeckt broke with the tradition established by Moltke the Elder and upheld by Konstantin von Lossau and Field Marshal von Manteuffel in the wars in 1857, 1866 and 1871. Seeckt was aware of this and explored this contradiction:

> Moltke had to ask himself whether he could still bear the responsibility for the military operation under these circumstances ... but most of all, his personal honour was not at stake. It certainly could not be damaged by such a king and such an opponent [Bismarck]. This calls to mind words of Frederick the Great, who wrote to his brother: 'You talk about your honour; it lay in leading the army well.'[50]

Seeckt followed the statesman Bismarck.[51] He regarded his policy as representing the right 'statecraft' for Germany. Bismarck had succeeded in 'preserving Germany's freedom of action and decision-making'.[52] As early as 1920, the demand for the state to have freedom of action was at the fore of his military-strategic considerations. It remained so until the end of his term of office: 'A nation is free if it is able to protect its freedom; we cannot do so.'[53] His military-strategic concern was to regain that freedom while preserving the primacy of politics and without embarking on lone military solutions.

With Moltke, Seeckt put the commission principle to the fore in military training and education. Even before the First World War was over, Seeckt realized that an adequate way of dealing with soldiers in a war scenario had become less important due to the masses and effects of the weapons involved. Since the Napoleonic Wars, the political and military heads had increasingly lost track of the overall situation in a battle and of the operational consequences of the weapons used on the masses. No single soldier was any longer to dominate or determine the course of a battle. Because individual human eyes had lost track of events on the battlefield, soldiers needed to be trained to assume more military responsibility. The result was that the commission principle gained in importance.

Moltke the Elder was an example for Seeckt when it came to placing high demands on the education of officers and General Staff officers and commission tactics.[54] Seeckt took over the crucial command and control asset from him: commission tactics. For Seeckt, it remained one of the most important supreme principles in military training that the soldier used to plan and execute his operations:

> In the execution of this task [the waging of war] the soldier is absolutely independent. The nature of the task is best indicated by reference to the principle which it was once the fashion to term 'commission tactics'. In the early stages of the Great War this principle was perhaps too widely interpreted, later on, unfortunately, it was too much forgotten, yet its soundness remains. We understood by the term the indication of the end to be attained together with the assignment of the means, without any direction as to the execution of the task – in contradistinction to the principle of issuing binding instructions as to the details of execution.[55]

To conclude, Seeckt therefore pursued a military strategy, which revealed a critical attitude towards Moltke, leaned heavily on Clausewitz, and was deliberately directed against Ludendorff and his followers at the Reichswehr Ministry.[56]

In the following section, certain aspects will be further developed and put first in consideration of their significance for Seeckt's military strategy. These are civil-military cooperation, a people's army and an operating army, a professional army and technology, training and mass. This will be followed by several no less important factors such as population, arms control negotiations, geostrategic position and alliance policy.

Civil-Military Cooperation

Seeckt acknowledged the importance of civil-military cooperation for because 'we [had] lacked this cooperation before the war'.[57] To begin with, Seeckt did not put the blame for the final stage of the war and the defeat of 1918 on the political leadership, but said that the loss of the war was caused by the lack of ability of both sides, the military and the political, to exercise leadership:

> My only concern now is to fix the responsibility for the fateful war plan of 1914 – not as criticism after the event, but in exemplification of the principles which must underlie the cooperation of the political and military heads.[58]

Henceforth, cooperation of a kind which was already established in peacetime was called for in the future.

> Let us turn first of all to the conditions that obtain in time of peace. The statesman must ask himself what he wants and what he can do. The answer to the first question lies wholly in the political sphere and is his business alone. To answer the second he will have to pay attention to military as well as to political considerations.[59]

One of the 'political considerations' mentioned by Seeckt was that the civil and military departments worked towards a common end. This concerned the army just as much as it did the Foreign Office. Only thus could the achievement of a political goal by military means be planned and implemented efficiently and effectively:

> Differences of opinion between Foreign Office and Army have frequently occurred, and have not been confined to Germany. It is the task of the statesman to reconcile them. The nature of their respective duties demands of both departments a close, constant, and frank cooperation. As long as there is no guarantee of permanent peace, foreign policy must take account in its calculations of the strength of home military forces and of those of other countries ... The question of a country's security is first and foremost a political question ... It is for the statesman to decide whether the possibly superior prospects of a military offensive are not outweighed by political disadvantages, ...[60]

Hew Strachan took this idea to its logical conclusion: 'The principal purpose of effective civil-military relations is national security, its output is strategy.'[61] According to Strachan and implied by Seeckt, strategy is a result which is achieved through 'common sense' in the departments concerned.[62] Seeckt did not consider it right for military specialists to be left to their own devices when it came to resolving conflicts. Besides the Foreign Office with its diplomatic connections, they also had to involve other departments in their planning.

> The soldier's prime task is to secure his country against attack, and to effect this he must seek assistance from the most diverse civil departments. Finance, transport, industry, commerce, agriculture are involved in the task, not forgetting the Foreign Office.[63]

The soldier with his military advice was only one of many. Still, Seeckt drew attention to the special position held by the soldier in political cooperation before and during a war:

> The necessity for the cooperation of statesman and soldier, and especially of the Foreign Office and the War Department, in the preparations for a possible war is thus established. The closer and franker this exchange of views the better it will be for all ...[64]

Cooperation based on trust was essential and the starting point for the success of the strategy pursued by the government. If a lack of cooperation had manifested itself in a lost war, then the political leadership had a special responsibility. In the event of differences of opinion, the politician was supposed to mediate between the departments and make a decision. Friction between the departments and the army representatives was to be smoothed over by the political leadership, while 'it is the duty of the head of the state to secure this cooperation'.[65] If no agreement is reached between the civilian and military department heads, the government had the decisive vote: '... the statesman's fiat will have to decide.'[66] On the subject of the problem of cooperation and the ensuing friction, Strachan wrote in 2006: 'The true evil in war is the inability to hammer out how the two are to be reconciled.'[67] Seeckt offered a solution in his acceptance of the primacy of politics and the claim to power of the politician.

Civil-military cooperation was to be initiated in peacetime in preparation for a potential conflict. A joint course of action had to be planned at the political and military levels. The soldier informed the political leadership about the levels of military training and equipment, whilst the political leadership disclosed his objectives in return. 'The statesman asks the soldier: What can you do? What can they do? And the soldier asks in turn: What do you want? What do they want?'[68] During this dialogue, the soldier learns whether and, if so, how he must re-arm.[69] The politician had to alert the soldier leader to the possibility of a war in peacetime. The political leadership called for the military data and facts in order to estimate the strength and striking power, the potential duration of a conflict, and the military will. The soldier provided information on strength and quality of materiel while receiving information on the interest pursued by the government.

Seeckt described the cooperation between the political leadership and the supreme military head as a dialogue. He not only pointed out that no lone decisions were to be made, but also that these two departments were crucial interfaces that influenced the course of a war. They had to cooperate on a permanent basis. The soldier informed the political decision-maker of the levels of training and equipment. The latter based his decisions on this information:

It will depend partly on the strength of the army how far he may go in his demands and to what extent he must give way ... As a result of this exchange of views the statesman discovers what value he may attach to the military pawn in his game, and the soldier receives a hint as to the direction in which his preparations require completion.[70]

The most obvious precondition for adequate military advice was the provision of sufficient and permanent support for the soldier by the political leadership on the political aims and ends. Civil-military cooperation was a means of preserving external security:

Every state will desire to see its frontiers as well secured as possible, and it is only by the joint deliberation of statesman and soldier that it can be successfully determined what concession can be made on military grounds ...[71]

The provision of military advice for political interests took place in a dialogue between equals. It was necessary to ensure mission accomplishment. If the government put too much load on the military capacities, this would put the political aims at risk, as Napoleon had already provided and Clausewitz had noted in his tenets.[72] For Seeckt, the provision of military advice was based on parity in responsibility, not on equal political status. The responsibility lay in the provision of military-strategic advice. The military strategist was the responsible adviser of the statesman in all military issues. Prior to and during a war, the soldier and the government determined the advantages and disadvantages of military operations together.

Wrong assessments, however, led not only to military means being employed inappropriately and planned to be used beyond their capabilities. The politicians would assign them missions which would not correspond to the nature of military skills. On the basis of the lessons learned from the 2003 Iraq War, Strachan had this to say on the subject: 'Policy is ill-conceived if it asks the armed forces to do things which are not consistent with their capabilities or with the true nature of war.'[73] It is shown quite clearly what Clausewitz and Seeckt expected from the political leadership in order to counter an overload of the military instrument, namely expertise in estimating the military situation.[74]

The politician first listened to the general military view, then he made his decisions in war. His political decision-making was complemented by a hearing of the various departments:

> He will constantly receive the opinion of the soldier on the military situation, its prospects and possibilities, and his diplomatic adviser will likewise report to him concerning the effect of the course of the war on other states, while the internal departments will keep him posted as to the country's capacity.[75]

It was only by taking account of the departments concerned that the government was able to determine and gauge whether the political aims were attainable. The more intense the exchange of views is, particularly between the soldier, the politician and the Foreign Office, 'the better it will be for all'.[76] Resolving a conflict required a great amount of different expertise, and this could only be reliably provided by consulting the various ministries. A maximum of efficiency would be achieved by the departments making the right decisions, and this could prevent undesirable developments.

On the other hand, dissension among the departments and offices resulted in negative consequences. In 1928, Seeckt wrote that 'the dissension between the military and political departments or even a mere lack of coordination in their activity must produce the most disastrous consequences'.[77] In 2006, it was said that '[t]he true evil in war is the inability to hammer out how the two are to be reconciled'.[78] While these frictions continued, both Clausewitz and Seeckt regarded it as an indication that the political interests were no longer pursued in the best possible way.[79] The view that deliberation on how a war was to be waged and what course it was to take should not be limited to those who made political decisions was also expressed by Strachan.[80]

If differences of opinion developed between the departments, Seeckt recommended more understanding and obligingness in interpersonal communication for the benefit of the higher objective:

> ... nothing can avail save tact on all sides and a recognition of identity of aim – or the arbitrary decision of the statesman. The goal

of war is its end. All the factors involved are concerned to reach this end by the use of every means, military and political.[81]

Consultations led to compromises, but also to mutual understanding. In view of the difficulty of civil-military cooperation in war, Strachan in 2006 recommended: 'The application of the principle in practice cannot proceed without personal goodwill. Obviously, strong personal relations between civilians and soldiers…help.'[82] A country's strength was preserved for the course of the war because '[c]ompromise among departments can be a strength rather than a weakness'.[83] By implication, this meant that constant bickering between the various departments had a negative influence on the course of the war. It is also possible to judge the way a conflict had been resolved and its success by the quality of civil-military cooperation.

The orchestration of the departments and their means had to be ensured in case of a declaration of war. This was an important task, which Seeckt assigned to the statesman and expected him to discharge. Accordingly, the soldier and the political leadership had to pursue an aim together, but the soldier had to bow to the will of the political leadership. The soldier's agreement with the political ends was the first basis for this joint and yet subordinate position of the soldier during the cooperation. A key requisite for the cooperation between the soldier and the politician was that the former had to be in agreement with the political heads of the country and their objectives: 'The ultimate aims of a war are always political ones … It follows from this that the measures of the soldier have to correspond with the objectives of the politician.'[84] With reference to Clausewitz, Seeckt pointed out what was expected from waging a war: 'What Clausewitz demands is that war be pervaded by the idea of a state which makes use of many forces and many assets for its development and to which all is subordinate.'[85]

As it was essential for every further decision on the drawing up of war plans, 'whose drafting requires a good knowledge of the political situation and political judgment in equal measure',[86] that the political leadership and the soldier kept each other informed, Seeckt demanded political thinking and understanding of his senior commanders.[87] And like Clausewitz, he expected just as much from the political heads.[88]

Clausewitz had demanded that the soldier needed to have political knowledge, and Seeckt reaffirmed this view on the day of his discharge. For him, this was the basis on which the troops had to be strengthened in their relationship to the state and the military heads.

> The army was to be built on three pillars: on the idea of the state, on discipline and obedience, on comradeship. We have been reproached and praised for making the army unpolitical. This is correct insofar as we wanted to keep ourselves free from party and parliamentary politics: it is one of the many misunderstandings that occur when this kind of politics is mistaken for the propagation of an understanding of the state. On the contrary, it was necessary to teach understanding of the nature of the state and our duty.[89]

Lieutenant Colonel Joachim von Stülpnagel from the Reichswehr Ministry reported from the Seeckt era that the so-called 'Thursday Society' [Donnerstags-Gesellschaft] had been established in the Reichswehr Ministry for a specific purpose. The aim was to maintain links between active and former officers in order to

> inform the non-active on developments in the Reichswehr and our political views and convey economic knowledge to the active General Staff officers. For example, a lecture followed by a discussion was given at every meeting … Frequently we also invited speakers who did not belong to our circle, for example, well-known professors, economists and politicians.[90]

To enable him to measure up to his military-strategic task, Seeckt set standards for the soldier at the interface to politics. The military strategist had to have an interest in and a knowledge of politics. Only then was he able to provide the government with accurate information on the military firepower of a potential enemy. The military strategist at the interface to politics had to keep himself continuously up to date on politics. At the same time, this allowed the military capabilities and interests to be adequately presented. The soldier required civic education for presenting the military situation, which served as the basis for providing advice to the political heads of the country:

The demand that the army be kept out of politics is undoubtedly correct if it is taken to mean that the troops themselves should exert no influence on government measures and be kept away from any parliamentary or party machinations. This principle of an apolitical army must not be interpreted as an excuse for keeping the leaders of the army, i.e. the Reichswehr Ministry, away from developments in general state policy. If it wants to exert a justifiable influence on it, the Ministry must have knowledge on which to base its own judgment. It must therefore enlist and train the necessary personnel for these studies and hence add a further task area to its other tasks.[91]

This resulted in what is to this day a key demand on the soldier, namely that he undergoes advanced politico-military training:

It is one of the great errors in political and politico-military as well as strategic doctrine that war takes place in a vacuum or – more precisely – a political vacuum and that it on the other hand could one day be locked away behind bars, leaving the field open for pure politics.[92]

Even before 1930, Seeckt had added a principle to his concept of political leadership which Clausewitz had already formulated:

What Clausewitz demands is that war be pervaded by the idea of a state which makes use of many forces and many assets for its development and to which all is subordinate. It will have to be admitted that these requirements appear obvious and simple and yet we seldom enough see them met. The most simple and at the same time most seldom way of solving this conundrum is to have policy and war, statesman and soldier united in one person. If this is not the case, then the idea of the state must ensure the unity of action.[93]

Seeckt expected the military to accept the primacy of politics. He was, however, no less convinced that the government might be assumed to feel respect for the military heads. This is another assumption in which he followed Clausewitz:

Some may have in mind that there is a danger of the politician spiking the soldier's guns all too easily and inopportunely and of pen-pushers ruining what has been gained by the sword. However, Clausewitz aims his doctrine on war at both the statesman and the soldier; he wants to teach the soldier political thinking, but also to imbue the politician with the will of a soldier.[94]

The high hopes placed in civil–military cooperation have been borne out in more recent military history literature: 'If strategy today is defined as operating on the boundary between war and policy, then it is being expected to be prudent and far-seeing while also being contingent and adaptive.'[95] Prompted by several errors of judgment during the Iraq War in 2003, military historian Strachan analysed civil–military cooperation and the way in which the political leadership had been advised by the military. He concluded that the political objectives would not be achieved by overtaxing military assets, by government overruling military advisers or even by military subordination: 'The issue now is not that of overall political direction, but of coherence among policy, military capabilities and the events on the ground.'[96] This is a demand which Clausewitz had partly made and which Seeckt endorsed.[97] The appropriate strategy can only emerge from the interaction of the various elements of the military and civic as political capabilities. This strategy in war promises success if attention is paid to employing suitable assets (including military assets) and keeping up a continuous dialogue between the sectors concerned. It was the result of a sharing of responsibility in war which was strengthened by a dialogue between the departments. 'Strategy is therefore the product of the dialogue between politicians and soldiers, and its essence is the harmonisation of the two elements, not the subordination of one to the other.'[98] However, the government would expect too much of the military instrument of power if they failed to appreciate the capabilities of the army sufficiently or indeed at all. Huntington pointed this out in 1977.

The politician must be aware of overcommitting the nation beyond the strength of its military capabilities. Grand political designs and sweeping political goals are to be avoided, not because they are undesirable but because they are impractical.[99]

With regard to the potential difficulties in the cooperation with the military administration and friction with individual figures, Seeckt had had few illusions from the outset. Not knowing what the future would have in store for him as Director of the Truppenamt (Troop Office), he wrote in 1920:

> I do not underestimate the difficulties of my new position. I have taken it up and will try to fill it ... I will have to wait and see whether I have enough strength to prevail against personal opposition and bureaucracy; and if I do not succeed in getting my views accepted in fundamental issues, I will have to hand over the task to others.[100]

After his tenure of office, he once again touched upon the difficulties that had resulted from the cooperation with an administration. With typical irony he commented:

> There are three things against which the human spirit struggles in vain: stupidity, bureaucracy, and catchwords. All three are perhaps alike inasmuch as they are necessary. I prefer to leave the hopeless fight against stupidity to my more sagacious contemporaries; admit unqualified defeat in my struggle with military bureaucracy; and propose in these pages to join battle with a few catchwords in the military sphere at home.[101]

Seeckt also regarded the 'conservative character' of a military organization as a problem for civil–military cooperation. He believed that this prevented it from moving with the times. Proposals for changes were rejected out of hand. Only when negative consequences appeared would even the military realize that it was to initiate reforms:

> Proposals for changes often have something revolutionary about them. The decision to exchange something old and proven against something new is a difficult one to take. The variation of conservative thinking, the rejection of what is coming into being for reasons of inner laziness, also plays a part in this. Thus military organizations tend to outlive themselves until an often painful experience proves their infirmity.[102]

Seeckt put the primacy of politics and its political precepts first in his military-strategic deliberations. The supreme soldier had to deal with political intervention in fundamental military issues and civil-military cooperation. An attempt was made to put the assertion that 'the battle was still the key to successful war fighting, why should anyone waste doctrinal effort and attention on minor matters such as economic mobilisation and cooperation with the civilian government' back into its military-strategic context.[103]

Moreover, contrary to what has been claimed about him[104], Seeckt had not ignored the political intentions of the USPD (*Unabhängige Sozialdemokratische Partei Deutschlandsat*) in the peace negotiations in Versailles. The USPD had opposed the conservative parties demand of an army of 200,000, and was happy to settle for 100,000. But Seeckt had bowed to the terms of the peace treaty. Seeckt's address to the officers and civil servants at the Reichswehr Ministry was an explanation and justification of the political and military decisions. This is to say, it was anything but a 'poetically explaining of their shared destiny ... a shared identity between the army and the state'.[105] It is necessary to quote the complete speech here in order to put Vardi's theory concerning it into perspective:

> You know that our own matter proceeded in the way that we resolutely took up the 'battle for a 200,000-man army' and submitted our demands with extensive reasoning and that we have tried to gain as much public support for this issue as possible. And I believe that I may add that everything that could be done in this respect was done, and I can gratefully acknowledge that the overwhelming share of the public was on our side. However, it was not possible to achieve a united front, as the radical leftist political parties under the leadership of the USPD declared themselves against the military demands.
>
> In view of the fact that the majority of our people supported our matter, not emotionally but by soberly recognizing the logic of our demand, in view which the attitude of the entente powers may come as a surprise to some. The only explanation for this is that the enemy only knows his own circumstances, has his own subjective view of the German ones and accordingly gets a wrong idea ...

The *notes* which we received shortly before the meeting in Spa on the matter of a 200,000-man army contained a brusque rejection of our demands: the reduction of the army on this day in the form which is prescribed by the Treaty of Versailles! Further negotiations and counter statements were regarded as pointless. It was, of course, impossible to implement it by 10 July. Not even the entente could ignore that.

The *disarmament issue* was put at the top of the agenda in Spa, but this did not mean that we were required to give reasons why we are unable to reduce the 200,000-man army, why we must retain it, but instead we were told: You have received our notes, you have signed the peace of Versailles, therefore any discussion of the 200,000-man army is superfluous. You only have to state how you intend to fulfil the peace treaty as soon as possible … It was impossible to achieve a 200,000-man army, or any major deviations from the terms of the Versailles Treaty at all! There was no doubt that the entente powers were seriously prepared to break off the negotiations and force through their demands with instruments of power. The whole situation in Spa indicated this: The whole British headquarters was assembled, all the leading generals of the entente nations were present, and new troop movements were in progress. The situation for us was similar to that in Versailles – accept or refuse. And in the latter case, the entente would have regarded this as proof that we had broken the peace and that they now had the 'right' to obtain the necessary securities themselves.

We were unable to say 'no', instead for our part made certain formulated proposals on how we intended to implement the reduction of the army. The members of the delegation and I are the *sole people responsible* for this decision. Only someone who had an impression of the situation there was able to vote on the decision and so *I spoke against the notion of handing over responsibility to large number of individuals, the Reichstag, the Reichsrat, [or] the cabinet members in Berlin, who would have to permit us to guide them in their decisions, or be excluded and placed before a fair accompli* [Italics used to mark the text quoted by Vardi].[106, 107]

Quoted in context, we see that Seeckt made the decision in agreement with those present, that he was *not* thwarted by the USPD, that he took on the responsibility for the acceptance of the terms in front of the officers, and that he had seen no other option due to the prevailing foreign affairs situation and a realistic evaluation of the domestic situation.[108]

Seeckt did not act unreasonably at the negotiations. He rejected a mobilisation and reported back to the Ministry:

> I [Graf Westarp] have already declared that we are not in a position to offer military resistance. Quite apart from all the figures, a present-day war simply requires technical equipment, heavy guns, aircraft, tanks, particularly ammunition. And how are things with us? We have nothing. And the people? If I am not sincerely convinced that the German people as a whole will support me to the utmost if I placed myself at the head of a major movement, I refuse to act in this manner, because it is a game and not the action of a man. I am not prepared to do this.[109]

The hypothesis that there was a lack of understanding of civil-military cooperation and committee solutions within the Reichswehr and that this could be attributed to Seeckt's 'high-handed and arbitrary' behaviour may have been put into perspective a little with regard to the understanding of civil-military cooperation prior to and during a war in his military strategy.[110]

If Seeckt strove to obtain the position of the supreme soldier which would be established as an 'independent executive only advised by Parliament', he still did not claim a position above that of the top political echelon for it.[111] In the period of upheaval between the end of the war and the first years of the young republic, Eugen Schiffer was the deputy of the Reich Chancellor in 1920. In 1921, he became Minister of Justice. He depended on cooperation with Seeckt. He wrote of his experiences with him:

> He continued to cooperate very closely with me and followed my political guidelines ... At that time, he had a great influence on the cabinet, although he did not formally belong to it, but only

attended the meetings from time to time. He regarded himself as the representative of the armed force in which state authority is vested.[112]

Carsten conceded that even in the Ruhr crisis in 1923, 'Seeckt [who] continuously participated in the cabinet meetings, agreed with the policy of the government and was opposed to any active resistance'.[113]

A contemporary document testifies to how much he was guided by the time with Reich President Ebert in his military-strategic understanding of civil–military cooperation:

> I [Kuno Westarp 1864–1945] remember a conversation with Herr von Seeckt from the time after the Field Marshal [Hindenburg] had become Reich President in which he explained to me – in his calm matter-of-fact manner, yet perhaps with a certain bitterness – that his political influence had decreased considerably. Ebert and his governments also discussed general decisions, particularly ones on foreign affairs, with him, from one power to another as it were, whereas the Field Marshal usually merely listened to him on military issues.[114]

Seeckt considered his position to be that of an expert adviser who respected the primacy of politics. His responsibility for cooperation was part of his military professionalism.

Further evidence can be found in Seeckt's thinking about the relationship between the state and the chiefs of staff which will be analysed from the point of view of realpolitik and crisis-prevention. This will be considered in the following section.

Realpolitik and Crisis Prevention

Owing to Seeckt's thinking, policy was directed by a 'statesman' who either ruled as a monarch in a monarchy, as a dictator in a dictatorship, or by a government, a cabinet and its politicians.[115] This political leadership not only determined the socio-political lives of their citizens but also made decisions concerning peace or the entry into a war. They ended wars, formed alliances and secured peace. An offensive or preventive war was an option for them or a defensive war might be imposed on them. The army was merely one power factor among many that the government included in the practical political plans for their own aims. Given that, the army could be employed in the conduct of offensive, defensive or preventive wars:

> The overall thrust of the policy of a state determines the extent and manner of its armament; in case of markedly expansionary objectives, it may require the greatest possible expansion of the armed forces in all areas … This policy is affected by the attitudes of the neighbours … If the politicians regard a sudden enemy attack as conceivable, if they intend to bring about a favourable situation through a fast blow, they will demand combat-ready forces; on the other hand, if they consider the outbreak of a war to be something solely contingent on their own free decisions, they may resign themselves to lengthy preparations for a war.[116]

The state's political leadership decided whether their country should wage an offensive or preventive war and began a conflict.[117] If the political leadership had decided in favour of an offensive war, this could still be indicative of a 'defensive policy, because they thought that the foreseeable future would be still more dangerous'. Still, a policy, which began a war, was a 'policy of aggression' even in Seeckt's eyes.[118] Like a war of aggression, the government ordered a preventive war. Seeckt's deliberations took on an almost fatalistic note, because the leading politician bore the full responsibility for each of the three kinds of war. This representative of a country was also 'the statesman, who is exalted above theories and notions of law and owes no duty save to the welfare of his own people'.[119] The statesman would not shrink back from a decision to go to war, if he thought it would enable him to secure his political interests. The political leadership would 'surely not be content to acquiesce in inactivity, in the renunciation of all aims which contemplate the acquisition of power'.[120] If a policy of pursuing political interests met with resistance, followed by a threat and – as the next phase – the endangering of the state's existence, then the aggressive policy would change from a political to a military one.

The political leadership can thus formulate their political interests quite extensively and declare war at the first sign of resistance. In Seeckt's view, the First World War had also been a defensive war for Germany: 'Attack became a means of defence.' When asked about the issue of war guilt, he was of the opinion: 'Whoever insists that we ought to have awaited the enemy's attack in order to prove our own peaceable policy, admits that he would rather have seen the war fought out in his home than in France.'[121] We have no way of knowing to which extent Seeckt was informed about the political machinations of the last German Emperor, Wilhelm II. There are no records of Seeckt's library.

This attitude does by no means alter Seeckt's basic opinion of a preventive war, however, which like an offensive war is solely demanded and initiated by the political side. Politics dominated the life of the state, its development both in peace and war. 'National policy determines the use that is made of the army: if it is poor, the wrong use will be made of the army; if it is a good policy, the right use will be made of the army.'[122] In the final analysis, Seeckt followed the doctrines of Clausewitz who had formed an opinion on the power politics of Napoleon and drawn his conclusions from this:

> He [Clausewitz] comes to the conclusion that the more energetic and deliberate the policy of a state is, the more energetic will be its conduct of war, and this conclusion is explicable in a man who witnessed the triumph of Napoleon's methods of warfare over those of his opponents.[123]

By contrast, the commander-in-chief was expected to take an indifferent view of the decision of whether an offensive or defensive war was to be conducted. His task consisted solely of defeating the enemy:

> First of all, the soldier does not care whether the statesman who bears the responsibility for the outbreak of war, even though war has been forced upon him, is fighting simply in defence of his own interests or to attain a definite end. The soldier has one task only and that is to destroy the enemy's forces as quickly and as completely as possible, and thereby force him to renounce his political aims and make peace.[124]

Both in his planning and in the preparation of the war, the soldier was subject to the government's guidance. 'The preparation of plans for the eventuality of war is the soldier's business, but he requires the basic political guidance of the statesman.'[125]

Whereas the political leadership controlled the operation and whether a defensive, preventive or offensive war would be conducted, the strategist tailored his preparations to this. It was his duty to function as an 'expert adviser' who was able to correctly assess their own capacities for the required operation. He gave advice concerning the intended form of war and the most favourable position from a military point of view without influencing the political decision:

> It is vital to the efficacy of his measures that he should know whether it is permissible or desirable, from the political point of view, to anticipate a threatened attack or whether the general situation requires a purely defensive attitude. The soldier will expound the advantages and disadvantages of both methods of action, and the statesman will decide whether political and military interests are identical or, should they diverge, which is regarded to be vital.[126]

Once the decision for an offensive war had been made, the political leadership bore the responsibility:

> It is for the statesman, not for the soldier, to decide whether the possibly superior prospects of a military offensive are not outweighed by political disadvantages, whether it is expedient and permissible to anticipate the enemy's declaration of war instead of waiting for it.[127]

In the course of the war, the commander-in-chief was supposed to keep informing the politician on the state of affairs, while the political leadership listened to the soldier. 'He will constantly receive the opinion of the soldier on the military situation, its prospects and possibilities....'[128] Still, the soldier's estimate of the situation was only one among many. The reports from all departments had to be taken into account; it was on this basis that the government made its decisions on a continuation of the war or initiating peace:

> Weighing all these items of information the statesman will ask himself day by day whether the end of the war is drawing near, whether he has already attained his object or whether its attainment is within reach, whether this object is worth further sacrifices, or whether the enemy is at last ready to make peace.[129]

If the government wanted to end the war and initiate peace negotiations, the soldier had to fall in with this, even when he believed that he could very probably continue to conduct the war successfully.

> Should the statesman decide on such grounds to enter into negotiations for peace, military considerations must recede into the background. It may be hard for the soldier, in view of the previous favourable development of his operations, to relinquish the promising prospect of exploiting his success to the full, but he must acquiesce in the political decision of the statesman.[130]

This consideration most clearly demonstrates the difference between Moltke and Seeckt.

Seeckt fully understood that military advisers were able to tip the balance in the pursuit of political aims towards a peace or towards a continuation of war through military successes or failures. Even the most basic information concerning military capacities could make politicians initiate a war. 'As a result of this exchange of views the statesman discovers what value he may attach to the military pawn in his game. …'[131]

The government determined everything not of purely military nature. There were innumerable individual orders and regulations to which the soldier was subjected. Thus political leadership were authorized to intervene continuously in the theatre of operations.

> The prime responsibility for deciding against which enemy his forces must be launched to secure a decisive issue falls to the soldier, but even this decision involves possible consideration of the possible and probable consequences of a victory over one adversary or the other.[132]

The politician was even able to exert influence at the operational level of the theatre of war. For that reason, and in conformity with the doctrine of Clausewitz on the principles of strategy, in which interference by politics in the conduct of war was included, Seeckt wrote:

> With the beginning of the war, the effect of politics on its leaders does not end … Admittedly, the choice of the road to the attainment of the objective must be left to the strategist, although even this choice and that of the means will be affected by political considerations. Even the war plan may be subject to political interference, as for instance in the selection of the direction of attack and of the main enemy, or in the attention afforded the influence which an operation may exert on neutral powers or those to be kept neutral. Both the continuation and ending of the war are subject to political considerations.[133]

As a military adviser, prior to a declaration of war (no matter whether of an offensive or defensive war), he was merely able to point out the military advantages and disadvantages of the forms of war and alliance policies concerned. During its course, he was supposed to notify the political side concerning negative military developments. If the military forces had become too weak, the strategist had to report this to the government within a short period of time: 'Finally, he may foresee a gradual weakening of the enemy's forces, but also of his own, a contingency of which he must be in duty bound inform the statesman without delay.'[134]

In Seeckt's view the commander in chief could initiate peace either after a victory or a defeat. Because military 'failures require the cessation of a belligerent policy and necessitate looking for other ways', his responsibility consisted in acknowledging his own defeat in time.[135] The responsibility of the commander-in-chief lay not only in providing information and advice concerning the form of war chosen by the political leadership, but the course of the war and the victories won. Even more, it was to be found in a timely notification of any failures. '[Likewise] he may regard his own defeat as so decisive that further resistance seems to offer no prospect of success'.[136] The strategist had to anticipate his own defeat quickly and early on. He 'must not hesitate to make an admission of the approaching weakness of their own forces, however distressful, if this enables the statesman to pave the way for the conclusion of peace while this is still possible'. With regard to the outcome of the First World War, Seeckt added: 'before a catastrophe perhaps necessitates much more unfavourable terms'.[137] What is important is that the government determines whether the war is continued. 'When defeat has to be admitted the statesman must face the question whether he ought to try to make peace – a peace obtainable, of course, only on unfavourable terms...'[138]

The government evaluated and decided whether his political demands which had given rise to the war were met, and whether the war could be ended. If the military forces were no longer sufficient, making peace seemed like a good idea, then the statesman had to ask himself 'whether he was to attempt to make peace as quickly as possible?' At all events, 'he [the statesman] takes upon himself the responsibility for the prolongation of the war'.[139] If required to do so by the political leadership, the strategist could only try to continue the conflict by employing his best forces, without any hope of a military victory. The politician bore the responsibility for the prolongation of the war, while the soldier had no other duty than to 'continue it to the best of his ability, without hope of military success'.[140]

In Seeckt's military-strategic conception, the government not only determined when, with whom and against whom and in which form a war would be waged; he also influenced events on the battlefield and was responsible for the decision about its continuation. In the final analysis, political leadership was solely responsible for determining the future of the country.

The military were allowed to provide the means, while even their direction of attack was politically determined, allies were named and the conduct of operations was influenced by political vision. Both had the objective of quickly bringing about the end of the war. Military victories or defeats, military advice during the course of the war and status reports during its various phases were the basis for further plans of the government, for peace negotiations to be initiated or for his decision to prolong the war. The military did not dominate the course and result of the war but the political leadership determined its beginning, course and end.

Politicians have a special influence on the beginning of the war, just as the decision in favour of war is a purely political one, although it does take military elements into account ... Political aims can seem to be achieved and secured by military successes, which makes a continuation of the war unnecessary ... for the conclusion of the peace, the military results will form the basis for the negotiations leading to the new policies.[141]

Despite all military-strategic evaluation, the strategist refrained from a political analysis and any interference with the politically founded decision once made before, during and after the war:

The soldier has only one task and that is to destroy the enemy's forces as quickly and as completely as possible, and thereby force him to renounce his political plans and make peace ... As a rule, the campaign is complicated by the emergence of problems in which political interests interfere with purely military interests ... The statesman may have had his own definite aims and objectives at the outbreak of war, and these aims may change, contract or expand during the war and after its conclusion. He will constantly receive the opinion of the soldier on the military situation, its prospects and possibilities, and his diplomatic adviser likewise will report to him concerning the effect of the course of the war on other states, while the internal departments will keep him posted as to the country's capacity. Weighing all these items of information the statesman will ask himself day by day whether the end of the war is drawing near, whether he has already attained his object...[142]

If the political leadership demanded that the war should be continued, although the soldier had warned him that their own military forces were insufficient for this, the politician was able to overstress the military resources and overrule the commander-in-chief in the final analysis. Although Seeckt assumed a dialogue and a close and trusting cooperation, the decision of the government remained binding on the military and was the determining factor for the actions of the latter.

The necessity of a consultation in dialogue form did not only apply to the preparation of the war, its course and its victories, but also to providing timely information about defeats or weaknesses. At crucial points during the course of the war, mutual understanding for the political and military situations turned out to be essential. In the end, this is what Seeckt took for granted and used as justification of the subordination of the military. With another approach, with the military decisions dominating over the political ones, the government would risk failure. For the fact that this development resulted in defeat, Seeckt cited the doctrine of Clausewitz and substantiated it with the course of the French wars under Napoleon. The reversal of the priorities, of the hierarchical relationship between military means and political objectives, the predominance of warfare over politics, had initiated the downfall of Napoleon. Because the military objectives had prevailed over the political ones, his armies – victorious until then – were defeated. Napoleon had committed this error because his 'military objectives completely eclipsed the actual idea of the state and his policy was no longer in accord with his conduct of the war; this inevitably resulted in setbacks which within a short period shattered the Napoleonic empire'. Like Clausewitz, Seeckt deduced the overarching principle in his eyes from this: 'As a consequence, in all cases where politics separate from the conduct of war, we see either a political or a military defeat, and frequently both occurring at the same time'.[143]

Whereas Ludendorff considered the Napoleonic Wars to be an example for a promising employment of the masses and for what warfare would be like in future, Seeckt pointed out a fundamental error of Napoleon. Moreover, he was of the opinion that some mistakes had been repeated towards the end of the First World War, namely when Ludendorff took over the political leadership within the Supreme Army Command. From 1916 onwards, Seeckt regarded Ludendorff's 'political attitude ... as misguided in many instances; it would have had a less disastrous effect if his diplomatic counterparts had not been dead losses or worse'.[144] In Seeckt's eyes, this was a serious blunder.[145] Concerning this, he criticized the political heads of the last war for having allowed power to be taken from them and for having failed at their task by taking second place to the military leadership.[146]

While it is true that Seeckt continued a 'traditional conception of the military' with his assessment of practical politics on the part of the political leadership, he had drawn this from the doctrine of Clausewitz. Seeckt's military-strategic attitude is at variance with the assumption of military historians 'that the strategist has to go to the top of the pyramid in a war'.[147]

Together, the political leadership and the soldier strove 'for supremacy via the destruction of the enemy'. Both pursued 'a fight for supremacy. And a fight implies aiming for the destruction of an opponent, whereas peace means the brief enjoyment of power.'[148] If unavoidable, a war was a means to an end. For all power politics, it was necessary to bear the objective in mind during all political and military planning: 'The goal of war is its end'.[149]

With the Swiss military theoretician Jomini, Seeckt justified an offensive conduct of war, if a country had been attacked.[150] As has been shown, however, this decision was still subject to political deliberation. Seeckt shared the view of his French and British contemporaries that an attack was to the advantage of the operating army.[151] A military attack could be a better defence if it was supported by an aggressive policy.

He cited the manoeuvring regulations of the French infantry to substantiate his interpretation of how a potential opponent would react: 'Solely an attack enables us to deal crushing blows to an enemy. The side which attacks first exerts an influence on its opponent by demonstrating its superior will – an echo of Marshal Foch's "victoire = volonté".'[152] Parallel to the German and French interpretation of defence, Seeckt wrote: 'In the British Field Service Regulations published in 1920, it says in volume II on page 14 under "The Principles of War": "A victory can only be won as a result of aggressive action".'[153] This part of his military doctrine was not only mandatory for him, but also for two other European states.

The quotation concerning a 'notorious Seeckt' who was said to have demanded 'full freedom in its development and its own life' for the Reichsheer, was taken out of its context by military historians.[154] When quoted fully, it should be put into perspective by the context of Seeckt's understanding of civil-military relations.

In any healthy political organism the government, whatever its form, disposes, within the limits laid down by law and constitution, of all the resources of the state, and therefore of the army, too. The army, in accordance with its nature, becomes the first servant of the state, of which it is a part. The army may therefore legitimately demand that its share in the life and being of the state shall be fully recognised. It is subordinate to the state as a whole, that is, to the state as represented by the political head, but it is not inferior or subordinate to single parts of the political organism. This brings us to the duties of the state towards the army. The army must have perfect full freedom in its development and in its own special sphere, in so far as they are reconcilable with the general structure of the state. In internal and foreign policy, the military interests represented by the army have the same claim to existence as the other needs of the state. It is the business of the political head to weigh them one against the other.[155]

Mass and Technology

The weapons technology used in the First World War had increased an army's striking power considerably. At the same time, the masses deployed in the war were no match for the modern weapons technology and, contrary to the expectation of the Supreme Army Command, the idea of employing masses of soldiers had not been successful. 'The mistake lies in opposing an immobile and almost defenceless human mass to the brutal action of materiel.'[156] The consequences of the mistake were that the cursorily trained soldiers became mere 'cannon fodder'. Materiel had prevailed over mass: 'The more we increase the mass of combatants, the more certain is the triumph of materiel.'[157] These experiences with technology, mass armies and their inadequate weapons training were some of the fundamental lessons learned from war that Seeckt incorporated into his military-strategic concept.

> Anyone who has the smallest idea what technical knowledge, what numerous instruments, operated only by carefully trained experts [...] are necessary [...] must admit that these essential qualities cannot be taken for granted with men whose training has been brief and superficial, and that such men, pitted against a small number of practised technicians on the other side, are 'cannon fodder' in the worst sense of the term.[158]

Moltke the Elder already drew attention to future developments that had begun with the war of 1870–71. He believed that 'an armed mass of people [was] far from being an army and … [it was] "pure barbarism to lead them into battle"'.[159]

Seeckt did not shy from addressing the new technical challenges when he assumed that future wars would be fought with high-tech weapons. Only the professionally trained and armed professional army would have the advantage:

> The army that has been victorious in the first act of war will, while drawing on its own reserves of men and materiel for the necessary maintenance of its striking power, try to prevent the newly-formed masses on the other side, superior in numbers but inferior in quality, from developing their strength and above all from forming compact and well-equipped fronts.[160]

A further disadvantage of deploying masses was their inefficiency. This made them a hindrance to operations. The mass got in the way of conducting decisive operations:

> What until then had been understood as operating, had to be ruled out for another reason; there were, to put it simply, too many people there; the theatre of war available was too small for an operation with such masses after the first attempt at it failed on all fronts.[161]

The soldier was unable to bring about the military decision by means of decisive operations. The growing number of the mass and their low military quality prevented him.[162] Seeckt's premise, 'to decide the war quickly', could not be met with the mass.[163] His saw his opinion confirmed by the developments in the First World War. Military war-winning operations were abandoned by the mass in the war of position. For the states involved, the war had led to a 'series of exhausting struggles for position until […] the springs which fed the resistance of one of the combatants, the sources of its personnel, materiel, and finally of its morale, dried up'.[164] His demand for the establishment of a small army with a high degree of mobility is also based on these experiences.

Seeckt also drew attention to the fact that for the Weimar Republic, a large standing mass army would have the disadvantage of being a burden on the financial budget on account of its personnel, training and cost-intensive weapons-training and equipment.

> The accumulation of great reserve stocks is the most uneconomical process imaginable. It is also of doubtful military value owing to the natural obsolescence of materiel [...] There is only one way to equip masses with weapons, and that is by fixing the type and at the same time arranging for mass production in case of need.[165]

He rejected mass mobilisation for the Weimar Republic from the financial and economic points of view. On account of reparations, a weak economy and the recession, it was natural for the governments of the Weimar Republic to shy away from such spending. In the post-war era, it became apparent that the economic power of all the states involved in the war had suffered. The economic situation was affected, particularly of those countries that had fought in the last war:

> The general economic situation compels all states to pay attention to the limitation of expenditure on armament and consequently to reduce its most expensive form viz., high peace strength with a long period of service and lavish equipment, and incidentally to limit as far as possible the unproductive retention of male labour in military service.[166]

He believed that other states in Europe would also avoid such high ensuing expenses with the result that the strength of the army would be reduced due to cost-pressure: 'The equipment of a large army with a new type of weapon is so enormously costly that no state undertakes the task unless compelled [...] The cost of this requirement is in itself sufficient to limit the strength of the professional army.'[167]

Since financial burdens had arisen after the war as a result of its long duration, which ultimately proved an economic disadvantage for everyone, military-strategic considerations also had to adapt to these socio-political conditions.

It was in the interests of the states suffering from the consequences of the war to avoid both a war of the masses and also an unnecessary extension of war and with it the bleeding dry of whole nations in the next conflict. In Seeckt's opinion, this must have become obvious to every soldier. Rationally, based on experience, every soldier had to ask himself 'whether these giant armies can even be manoeuvred in accordance with a strategy that seeks a decision, and whether it is possible for any future war between these masses to end other than in indecisive rigidity'.[168] The war of position had been caused by the immobility of the mass. Taking a critical view of this scenario, the military strategist had to ask: 'What has become of the spirit of warcraft?'[169]

These were the lessons that were to be learned from the lost war. Seeckt's military-strategic considerations took account of financial, economic, socio-political and technical criteria. Based on the military knowledge of mass armies and the effect of weapons on the events of war, a mass army had proven to be inappropriate with regard to the use of technology and the conduct of operations. These war experiences were key to the development of his military strategy and its adoption for the benefit of mobile warfare and a qualified operating army.[170]

Due to the assumption that at least the enemy had learned from the lessons of the past war that all weapons would be used in the next war too, measures had to be taken to protect one's own people.

> The arming of masses must be placed on a totally new basis. It becomes impossible to stock modern equipment for armies of millions when it is urged, and with justification, that these masses, in view of their inferior military training, are most particularly in need of the support of materiel.[171]

Other weapons training measures had to be taken for the people. Seeckt wanted to only allow them to be used for defensive purposes, namely border defence. With this first military premise, he pointed out the socio-political advantages. These were of an economic and financial nature:

> [T]he military demands can be reduced if the task of a people's army is a purely defensive one. This will avoid the concerns that arise from

the movement and command and control of large masses, there will also be no difficulty involved in training the mass to become fully adequate aggressive combatants, and finally the enormous costs will be reduced that equipping an army of millions with modern assault weapons requires.[172]

Seeckt distinguished between the people's army and the mass army. In a proposal in 1930, that did not take the Treaty of Versailles as a basis, he recommended a separation of the two army organisations, as they performed two different tasks:

> The term people's army, as I understand it, that is an army that harnesses the full strength of the people and utilizes it for military purposes, is also given due attention in the proposed organisation. In addition to the standing army, a militia army is to be established and prepared.[173]

The militia was provided by the people. The people's army differed from the professional army in that it had to be trained for defensive tasks. The levee-en-masse was to be prepared for the 'battle of despair' and established for an unprepared attack and for border defence.[174] It was limited to a few tasks since it could not be given the same level of military training in the use of weapons as a professional army. It was to be called up in the event of an attack and assumed the second line of defence, that is to say, home defence, which took place within the country's own borders.[175] The people's army as a levy in mass thus acquired a defensive task.[176] In comparison, Seeckt understood the mass army as it was deployed in World War I as being merely a cursorily trained force.

Recruitable members of the public were to be trained separately from the professional army. A staff division of the professional army would assume responsibility for their training.[177] It would provide the recruitable youth military training at regular intervals.

> Side by side with this professional army and in the closest union with it there is a permanent cadre of officers, non-commissioned officers and men, through whose training units and schools pass all the fit young men in the country.[178]

On account of the different military demands, young men capable of bearing arms were assigned to schools for recruits where they were trained by active duty officers of the professional army. 'Through the assignment of active duty officers in regular rotation during the training formations they learn the different kind of training, treatment and command in establishing the people's army.'[179] The intention was that state schools should already support this project by conveying young people a sense of the duty of self-defence. This would make it easier for them to understand and devote themselves to the 'ideal cause'.[180]

The better the people were educated in military principles by state schools and later at schools for recruits, the stronger their moral will to defend their country would be. With this kind of support, Seeckt saw this as home defence, as training for the 'second line of defence'.[181] The duration and success of a war could also be influenced in this respect. Passive resistance and a defensive posture against the enemy were psychological aspects that he took into account in his military strategy. If the outcome of the war is to be decided by the operational readiness and high military standards of

> a professional army and if its fighting spirit and ability to attack are decisive factors, the levy in mass should use passive resistance to defend the country against an attacker. In addition to this military purpose, the ideal – or let us say political – task of the system lies in drawing to the attention of all the people their duty to defend themselves and to enable them to do so ... Whether the state then calls this trained mass to arms wholly or partly if required is a matter for the state and depends on various circumstances.[182]

With regard to his military-strategic ideas, he complained that the 'demand for general military training ... did not yet [mean] the general military assignment of those trained'.[183] He also believed that military equipment and preliminary military training did not immediately mean mobilization, but primarily served border defence.

Seeckt assumed that the regular training of the levy in mass was subject to the political will that introduced the necessity of the battle of despair in response to an enemy attack.[184] The state legally regulated the establishment of this levy in mass trained to support the mobile army and thus military training for the recruitable youth.[185]

> In this way a military mass is constituted which, though unsuited to take part in a war of movement and seek a decision in formal battle, is well able, after a hurried completion of training and the supply of suitable equipment, to discharge the duty of home defence and at the same time to provide from its best elements a continuous reinforcement of the regular, combatant army in the field.[186]

Seeckt based his wording of this form of general compulsory military service on the motivation that the Swiss had for general compulsory military service.[187] He believed that the purpose of defending national borders was adequately preserved in Swiss general compulsory military service.

The professional army trained the 'second line of defence' in the event of war, with the people being trained to deal with an enemy attack on home territory.[188] Its recruitable youth prepared themselves for the defensive tasks at regular intervals. They were only to be armed temporarily, during the three-month training courses. Permanently maintaining ammunition and equipment for the levy in mass was superfluous and uneconomical.[189] With his demand for the establishment of a 'second line of defence', Seeckt drew attention to the stated political framework conditions in order to emphasize their importance for a professional army.[190] The recruitable youth provided the silent reserve for a mobilization in the battle of despair.[191] The possibility arose for the operating army to draw its new recruits from the best of the levy in mass.[192] What preparation for a war emergency, a state of defence and a hasty attack, meant for Seeckt was neither initiating total mobilisation nor planning war. Enabling the people to mount a strategic defence meant preparing it for the 'self-sacrificing defence of the homeland'.[193] In a future state of defence, it had to bolster up the army.

> If the outcome of the war is decided by the operational readiness and high military standards of a professional army … the levy in mass should use passive resistance to defend the country against an

attacker … This inherently moral patriotic duty must be transformed into a legal one … The arming of the people's army must be put on a different basis. Weapons, ammunition and equipment will already have to be available for certain border protection formations that can be formed immediately from it, for manning permanent fortifications, barriers, bridges and the like.[194]

The people as the 'second line of defence' played only a subordinate role in military terms. The levy in mass was supported by the highly qualified, mobile army, which had to assume responsibility for the defence proper.[195] The people's army was neither able nor allowed to decide a battle or conduct an operation.[196] The 'second line of defence' was in its own country and served to defend it against the invading enemy. The aim was to prevent mass mobilisation. 'The objective of a modern strategy will be to bring about a decision with the mobile, high-quality operating forces without or prior to masses being mobilized.'[197]

The levy in mass received military training, which prepared it and enabled it to provide support services. The main burden of military action lay with the high-quality 'small peace army'. Military historians thus concluded that 'in comparison, the mobilising masses of the people's army [were] of only secondary importance.'[198] Seeckt deliberately avoided equating the tasks of the levy in mass with those of the professional army or a mobilized mass. The recruitable youth, members of the public with military training, were earmarked for purely defensive tasks. Their military training included 'the establishment of military foundations, a sense of order, the spirit of comradeship, discipline, the use of weapons'.[199] Even these military-strategic considerations served to protect the people. They were to be prevented from becoming mere cannon fodder.[200]

In 1919, Seeckt saw a link between the threat in his own country, the unstable situation immediately after the First World War, and the experiences of that war. 'With full awareness I advocate the replacement of the present people's army with a professional army, a kind of mercenary army, if you will.'[201] Seeckt was confirmed in his rejection of mass mobilization by the domestic unrest in 1920 and 1923. In those years, officers were politically active and sought to bring down the republic. In 1923, the Hitler-Ludendorff coup had confirmed the anti-constitutional attitude of other officers. Seeckt's attitude towards a soldier being politically active was justified not only over the earlier years. In the year when the National Socialists seized power, Seeckt concluded that arming the people would pose a greater threat than the small army. Legitimized by the introduction of general compulsory military service under Hitler, this made him

> think that even today, a people's army is a reflection of the moral and philosophical state and that arming the people, as general compulsory military service entails, involves major internal concerns and dangers.[202]

Seeckt considered the hasty, unqualified arming and mobilisation of the people under the mantle of general compulsory military service to be dangerous.

From the mercenary army he was able to demand 'the fighting spirit' that he believed was 'the prerequisite for success', but to permanently maintain this in a people's army appeared problematic to him in his day.[203] The people's army was a 'reflection of the people's will', irrespective of whether the military mission was affirmed or negated, of whether an attack or a war of defence was concerned. As a result, Seeckt believed there was 'the danger that if this will is misguided, the military setback will lead to a national disaster'.[204]

From 1919 onwards, Seeckt had rejected the introduction of general compulsory military service for the Weimar Republic. It was known at the highest political levels that he rejected general compulsory military service and the arming of the people. Following the publication of the second part of Rabenau's biography of Seeckt, Hitler criticized Seeckt's position on military policy. Through his adjutant, Schmundt (1896–1944), Hitler made it known not only to the head of the Wehrmacht press division V (Army) that he 'disapproves of Generaloberst von Seeckt being assigned the role of a Scharnhorst'. Schmundt also reported that particularly Seeckt's description as 'the staunch representative of the idea of a professional army, but not of a conscript army' had displeased Hitler.[205]

It seemed that the young republic would protect its own system of government and constitution better if it did not train the general public to use weapons. A nation in arms could develop into a threat, one of the most dangerous weapons that could be used in the state against itself if it rejected its system of government. In 1920 and from 1923 to 1932, it became clear that more and more citizens had voted for anti-constitutional parties. In 1932, more than 50 per cent of Germans obviously had their doubts about the republic because they had turned to the Communist Party of Germany or the National Socialist German Workers' Party.

Seeckt derived a further argument against a nation in arms and against general compulsory military service from the French armed forces legislation and military history. Since the French Revolution, though not between 1815 and 1830, France in particular had maintained a people's army and increasingly waged wars in Europe.[206]

Apart from the fact that, according to what has just been said, the participation of the entire people in war, albeit in a different form, is envisaged and the professional army no less a part of the people than the levy in mass, the last war has shown that this form of armed forces legislation has no influence on a nation's willingness to participate in war. If one wishes to see the difference, this willingness was greater in France, with its people's army, than in England with its professional army.[207]

He therefore did not regard the *levée en masse* as the remedy for preventing a future war. He derived a further argument against a nation in arms and against general compulsory military service from recent war history.

Among the French revolutionary notions which persisted was that of general compulsory military service. This notion found acceptance in different forms and in different measure throughout the whole of Europe, excluding England. It governed our endeavours throughout the Great War, and was powerful enough to claim first England, then America.[208]

Basing his judgment on military history and the experiences of the First World War, he summed up: 'The objection of our time, that a strong standing army leads to a policy of conquest, is invalid.'[209]

The First World War served as a warning not only on account of the technical challenges. Generally accepted conclusions had to be drawn from the inadequate weapon training for the mass army and from the military spirit of the last two centuries. Seeckt drew attention to the fact that the inadequacy of the general compulsory military service implemented before the First World War had exposed masses untrained in the use of weapons to an embittered, bloody and exhausting people's war in the early twentieth century.

In order to also gain support for his ideas among political leadership, Seeckt reminded them of the political consequences of a long war. He said that the government's primary interest was not to wage a war for too long and certainly not to permit the initial factors and framework conditions to develop that would additionally prolong and worsen it. The government should be interested in ending a war swiftly. 'Today, a statesman should ask his military leaders whether a future war cannot be brought to a successful end more rapidly, if not with less use of energy and power'.[210] He also drew their attention, and not for the last time, to the consequences of mass mobilisation in the last war: 'The problem now finally arises. Is this vast number necessary for national defence? ... The goal of deciding the war swiftly has not been achieved.'[211]

Due to domestic concerns, the state should legally regulate the temporary issue of weapons to the people and the conversion from peacetime to wartime production that must be introduced. Seeckt called for 'the identification of the necessary models, including all necessary drawings and lessons, the provision of the necessary raw materiel under state supervision'. In addition, 'legally specified preparations of the required factories to switch from peacetime operations to military production' were to be made.[212] The government made decisions not only on economic interests and military ambitions, but also on arms production and on sending recruitable youth on training courses.

Mass mobilization was no solution in a future war for either the political or the military authorities. Rather, the last war had led to the complete exhaustion of entire nations, which in turn had had economic, financial and social disadvantages for each one in equal measure. Seeckt was justified in asking: 'Do the results of the war bear any just relation to the sacrifices in national strength?'[213] He not only adopted a military position when he asked his military strategy question. He took account of the economic and financial consequences of a military confrontation. Taking account of the consequences of a mass army for the national economy, he drew attention to the positive factors associated with only a small, but highly equipped and well-trained army. In addition to the smaller financial burden, the 'relatively low strength of the professional army and thus the lower amount of equipment that has to be maintained [would facilitate the making of the]... changes in weaponry that are in line with the developments in technology and the economy'.[214]

As for the question of why it was necessary for 'whole nations to hurl themselves upon one another whenever recourse to arms is unavoidable', Seeckt provided a subtle answer with his approach, based on experiences in the past wars.[215] The idea that a small professional army was the economic alternative that also promised to considerably reduce the duration of a future war and protect the people, cursorily trained and deployed, from being used as mere cannon fodder, led to the development of an appropriate theory for the times. The economic postulate was: 'The smaller the army, the easier it will be to equip it with modern weapons, whereas the provision of a constant supply for armies of millions is an impossibility.'[216]

Contemporaries said that Seeckt was right. General JFC Fuller and Liddell Hart considered a professional army appropriate. Liddell Hart, a British military historian, concluded that the focus should in future not be on the battle of men against materiel, but rather against the military authorities and the cohesion of the enemy's armed forces.[217]

Great Britain and America had reverted 'in general to their pre-war systems, i.e. to the principle of maintaining small armies ready for immediate employment'.[218] France would basically follow their example in the organisation and build-up of such armies, but had reintroduced general compulsory military service.[219]

Seeckt listed far more advantages than disadvantages for a numerically small army in order to provide the state an adequate means of power. The small professional army that was capable of quickly mounting a decisive and also offensive operation was an integral part of his military-strategic concept. This could be put into practice by means of lengthy training being provided in the use of the new weapons, among which he included not only heavy artillery, but also light combat vehicles, heavy battle tanks and the air force.[220] His concept was an attempt to find an alternative to the experiences of World War I; neither the cursorily trained mass, nor the entire population should be affected by the next conflict.

Due to Seeckt's placement of the emphasis on a professional army, the establishment of militias became a matter of secondary importance and concerned with passive defence issues. Seeckt's military policy concept was based on the experiences of the First World War and so he was not one of the people who, as a specialist like Bernhard Kroener assumed, had forgotten its horrors.[221] He believed that instead of a large standing army, a small professional army was required for reasons of social policy and included this in his military-strategic considerations. The result was that instead of the mass, a professional army that in peacetime assumed the task of a cadre army was established. It was responsible for training recruitable youth in three month-long courses and preparing the public to mount passive resistance and provide logistic support for home defence in the country. The policy of protecting the country against a war of aggression with a highly qualified professional army could not succeed if this army was only supported by a cursorily trained mass. 'The gospel of mobility'[222] of the small army was only one of the essential factors of his military strategy.

The Professional Army

Neither the Weimar Republic nor Great Britain or France were thinking of creating a large army.[223] The global economy was suffering from the reparation payments and the recession. The small army specified for Germany in the Treaty of Versailles was ultimately in the interest of the republic. During the peace negotiations in Versailles, Seeckt had aimed for a 200,000-man army. He regarded this size as the best prerequisite for defence. He believed that a strength of 200,000 did not mean the automatic activation of the war machine, but offered sufficient protection against attacks.[224] In 1919, he wrote to General Groener: 'Within these limits [specifications of the victorious powers], the wish of everyone who still believes that we have international standing must be for a standing army to be as large as possible. This has nothing to do with foreign policy goals and principles.'[225] In the early days of the Weimar Republic, he believed that an army of 200,000 adequately trained men could be established in a future international confederation. It would grant this confederation an adequate negotiating position in international negotiations.[226]

The 100,000-man army, by contrast, could be no more than a qualified cadre army, the nucleus of the small operating army favoured by Seeckt.[227] All he saw in forming and equipping such an army was a provisional solution for the Weimar Republic. He remained aware of its inadequacies until the end of his period of service and beyond. In 1933, he recalled 'that the Reichswehr [...] is still a long way from this future image'.[228]

Seeckt had developed a draft for a possible new army structure in 1919 and at the time was already working to establish a professional army. He preferred to leave the question of whether the people's army should be allowed to mix with the professional army open for the time being. He wrote:

Whether use of the whole military power in the field involves a combination of the standing army with the militia units and whether the former should be an assault force is something over which the future Chief of the General Staff will have to rack his brains.[229]

Seeckt was subsequently able to provide the answer when he became Chief of the Army Command. His advice was this: 'The levy in mass should not ... be dispensed with as a means of national defence. It should just not be ranked among the cadres of the peace army.'[230] He recommended separate training for the people and equipment that was adapted to the training. A people's army that was only envisaged as a support for defence of the country could not provide the qualifications and skills that a professional army could.

In 1919, he deliberately avoided precisely specifying the strength and formation of the army. He drew attention to the fact that 'even this organisation [is] not created for eternity [...]; the future of the republic and of the global situation is so uncertain that it is impossible to predict whether the further development will sway towards a professional or a purely people's army'.[231] When the draft was being elaborated, not all the negotiations with the victorious powers had been concluded and he was still able to advocate a 200,000-man army in Versailles. In February 1919, he was convinced that the political factors were crucial and that the formation and strength would be determined by them. Since 1919, Seeckt had expressed not only his own military wishes: he had been convinced that future military decisions on formation and structure would depend on domestic and foreign policy factors. He already took account of the limiting conditions in his draft: the establishment of a people's army would depend on the 'financial and economic situation, probably also on the will of our enemies and later neighbours'.[232]

By 1930, he had added further ideas to the earlier ones in order to align military negotiations and agreements with future international ones.[233]

'The peacetime army or covering or operating army', that was trained to bring about a decision quickly, was in the overall interest of a rationally led state.[234] It afforded 'at least [...] security against hostile attack'.[235] The army also served as a deterrent because 'adequate armament is not in itself a threat of war but, on the contrary, can be a guarantee for maintaining and securing peace in a country'.[236]

The professional army was well equipped and it 'is best when [this "operating army"] requires no reinforcement at all for its first move, i.e. when no special mobilisation is necessary. In any case, it should require very little.'[237] It had a deterrent effect on a potential enemy because it was always fully armed.

To justify a small professional army, Seeckt put forward an argument often used in military history against professional armies:

> These strike-ready professional armies will be seen as containing enticements to war, since it is assumed that a nation not directly involved will more easily decide to place the lives of its 'mercenaries' on the line ... [By contrast,] the last war has shown that the form of armed forces legislation has no influence on the willingness of a nation to go to war ... No risk to peace will be seen in the mood and influence of a professional army.[238]

Seeckt had taken a close look at the technical implications for the people that had been recognized since the First World War, the deployment of a mass army and its inadequately trained soldiers. The mass army on the one hand and technology on the other had prolonged First World War. 'After the number and quality of the first formations had failed to bring about a decision, it had to be continuously postponed despite the increasing number and declining value.'[239]

After comparing a mass army and a professionally-led small army, he came to the conclusion that in the case of a future conflict only the latter would rapidly achieve success or a decisive outcome. 'In a few words then, the whole future of warfare appears to me to lie in the employment of mobile armies, relatively small but of high quality and rendered distinctly more effective by the addition of aircraft ...'[240] Trained for high mobility against the war of position, he believed that the 'war of movement, i.e. the clash of two adversarial armies in free movement, released from and unhindered by a system of positions [...] will again predominate in future'.[241] The first Chief of Staff of the Bundeswehr, Adolf Heusinger, who during the Second World War II served in the operations centre of the Army General Staff, had been in the Reichswehr since 1920. He confirmed Seeckt's assumption about the start of the next war, which had become more dynamic as a result of force mobility: 'A war of movement developed immediately in World War II in a form that no-one expected, and a purely aerial war did not develop.'[242] Heusinger attributed the increase of mobility to the training provided under Seeckt.

A high level of force mobility was meant to enable a future war to be brought to an end more rapidly. There is no discussion at this point of whether the thought was based 'on an illusion that had been cherished since before World War I that the war would short'.[243] The focus here is on the conclusiveness of his overall concept. A small army that was efficient and technically well-equipped guaranteed that operations could be conducted. It provided an alternative to the mass army and thus to the exhausting four-year war of position:

> The more efficient this army, the greater its mobility, the more resolute and competent its command, the greater will be its chance of beating the opposing forces rapidly out of the field, of hindering the enemy in the creation and training of further forces and perhaps of making him immediately ready for peace.[244]

Seeckt recalled the Thirty Years War, which spared the people as little as the First World War did. Just as the consequences of defence technology of the modern age were unacceptable to the people, he regarded the use of the sword or the 21 cc. high explosive shell as one that destroyed cultures:

> There is nothing humane about the sword or the 21 cc. high explosive shell. We need only remember the Thirty Years War and the many spots on the map, now marked 'Waste', which were once the sites of flourishing villages, to realize that in the past, too, war spared neither wife nor child, house nor home. After all, it is doubtful whether the blessings of our much-boasted culture are more valuable than those which were destroyed long ago by the Germanic torch and sword.[245]

Since attacks on the hinterland, on the civilian, were nothing new, it was important to prevent them.[246] The well-trained professional army would not wage a war against the civilians. 'War is waged against the enemy state and its armed force, not against the peaceful people.'[247] He regarded land warfare against the civilians as a violation of international law, the Hague Convention of 1907. He had the provisions contained in the Annex to The Hague Convention respecting the laws of war on land included in the FuG of 1923 with the words:

> The agreement reached at the Second Hague Conference on 18 October 1907 concerning the laws and customs of war on land with the Annex to the Convention (Regulations Respecting the Laws and Customs of War on Land) aims to 'diminish the evils of war, as far as military requirements permit' (introduction). The agreement is the only international one to this effect and is binding on German nationals.[248]

Seeckt did not limit the Hague Convention to being observed only by soldiers, but meant it to be every German citizen. The introduction to the Annex to the Convention was followed by nine pages in which its most important provisions were listed. These included the ban of toxic gases, poisoned weapons, murder, robbery, extortion, theft, arson, property damage, rape, treacherous killing or wounding of members of the enemy's army or people, malice, contemptible action and 'what is not expected of a decent enemy'.[249] Seeckt took care to ensure that international law was observed, attempting to protect his own and the enemy's civilian populations.[250] The annual 'Observations of the Chief of the Army Command' also contained statements regarding warfare and the 'relations behind the front line'. He told the superiors: 'Early commands issued by the commanders and independent action by drivers of motor vehicles and pack animals must rule out behaviour that does not comply with the rules of war.'[251]

He was particularly critical of the use of gas and air raids on the civilians in future warfare. 'It would be frivolous to deny or extenuate the dangers and horrors of an attack by air on the "hinterland", especially when coupled with the use of gas.'[252] In addition to the Thirty Years War, the 'Turkish invasions, and Heidelberg', he regarded air raids as 'wars which have destroyed civilizations'. But unlike his contemporaries – General Douhet from Italy and Air Marshall Trenchard from the Royal Air Force – it was not the chief towns that would form the first and most important objects of attack. In the first instance, the attack would be aimed at the 'opposing air forces, and only after the defeat of the latter will the attack be directed against other objects'. He believed that building up an air force was a matter of urgency as the next conflict would 'begin with an air attack on both sides, because the air forces are the most immediately available for action against the enemy'. Whereas fighting had hitherto been limited to land and water, a decision would then be able to be obtained 'in the air as well'.[253]

Training for the air force had to be initiated in good time and as 'the provision of passive security for the country's vital centres.'[254] In view of the anticipated role of the air force in the next war, which would be directed by the enemy power against the adversary's people, a country had to make preparations for its own defence.

Mobility could be enhanced by technical innovations such as tanks. In the 'Annual Observations', he remarked:

As technology advances, motorisation in the army becomes more important. We must study these questions theoretically and, as far as possible, practically, because the momentum of mobility and rapidity is of key significance particularly in a small army ... Any amassing of convoys must be avoided.[255]

Besides mobility and rapidity, the high levels of armament of the infantry and cavalry were important. Motorized transport and the air force complemented the 'gospel of mobility'. Seeckt's concept of defence was more than just a 'renaissance of classical warfare'.[256] Mobility supported a well-trained army and reduced the possibility of a people's war developing. The combination functioned as a deterrent. Tactical and operational training formed the basis with which surprise, delaying tactics and attack were practised for the benefit of a war of movement. The focus of training was on the joint deployment of all the branches of service with their different weapons.[257]

Tactical and Operational Training

Seeckt uses these two concepts to refer to different levels in military training. The tactical level corresponds with the lower level, i.e. that in the companies, battalions and the brigade. The operational level refers to corps and divisions. While the commission principle is exercised in tactical training, the directive style of command is used at the operational level.

Army Regulation 487, also known as the FuG, was issued in two parts. The first part was issued in 1921, the second in 1923.[258] The service regulations provide an overview of command principles, the higher duties of command and control and the various types of combat operations. Aware of the disadvantage of their epic breadth, due to the more than 1,000 items they comprised, the Chief of the Army Command in 1924 had all the key command principles consolidated and an index of keywords produced. Laconic by nature, and not entirely out of character for him, he wrote: 'Not everyone has time today to study in detail a regulation as extensive as the FuG.'[259] In addition to the FuG, Seeckt had complemented military training with the 'Observations of the Chief of the Army Command' since 1922. In them, he consolidated his instructions, advice and guidance that he had given to the regiments during his troop visits and manoeuvres.[260] The difference between the FuG and the annual 'Observations of the Chief of the Army Command' is due to the fact that the annual observations referred to the tactical, the lower level of command. They contained the problems and deficiencies addressed during the troop visits and the solutions proposed by the Chief of the Army Command. At the end of the year, the regimental commanders received the proposals for improvements, which they were to implement so as to complete military practice. In the annual 'Observations', he made generalisations in order to express the overarching goal for the tactical level. Seeckt used these observations to continuously expand and enhance the training of the small army.

The FuG went beyond the tactical level. Right at the start of the regulation's preface, Seeckt emphasized in 1921 that a national defence could not be mounted with the German army. Advanced goals had to be set in training: 'The regulation is based on the strength, weaponry and equipment of a modern major military power, not only the 100,000-man German army formed in accordance with the peace treaty.'[261] Whether Seeckt's visions of the future, for which he was already attempting to lay the foundations in the regulations and exercises, actually lost their shine as a result of the Ruhr crisis in 1923 is not discussed here.[262] He himself certainly did not have any illusions about the capabilities of the small army of 100,000 men. Since 1921, he had planned for preparations to be made in training for the Reichswehr to become a cadre army with a strength of 200,000.

In the FuG, he referred to the command of several army corps, the new types of weapons fielded, all the branches of service, even the non-existent air combat units, the heavy artillery, tanks and the intelligence services.[263]

In Army Regulation 487, not only attack operations were analysed, but also defence, the capability to withdraw rapidly and delaying tactics. Mobility was often the focus of attention and had to be practised with all weapons. The theory of combined arms combat was taught. Even the air force was discussed in combination with the armoured units, the heavy artillery and the other branches.[264] The modern technologies of the telegraph and telephone were included, as far as possible, in addition to the traditional long-range reconnaissance method of using carrier pigeons.[265] In the manoeuvres and exercises, practical training was conducted in those aspects that were suggested in theory in the FuG, but not stipulated in their 1,000 items.

The FuG focused on the attack, war of position and delaying tactics. These had to be practised by the service branches at the higher command level. At division level, the FuG dealt with the operations with the various service branches and the supreme command authorities. Assuming that the matter of mobility in battle was understood at the tactical level, the next step was to provide training at the operational level of command. The theoretical training on mobility in the divisions given at the tactical level was consolidated and preparations were made for it to be used in a war of movement.

Although activities had to be based on a fictitious battlefield scenario and the troops had neither heavy artillery equipment nor tanks, the higher command authorities responsible for intelligence, transportation and logistic support in the area of operations had to be more integrated than in the preceding war. Cooperation at the higher command level and between the command authorities and the various service branches had to be practised.[266] Their interaction was necessary to ensure that all the forces were employed in pursuit of a specific objective.[267]

Each command post had to maintain contact with the neighbouring one both during periods of rest and in battle. There were several violations of this rule, and Seeckt reacted to them with particular sensitivity. He felt it was just as wrong to wait for orders as it was to break off contacts. 'The contact between the infantry and artillery is of critical importance. Its failure can endanger the entire combat action.'[268] The intelligence service officers had to maintain close contact both with the units and commanders. They could only be kept continuously informed of the situation if the necessary contacts were maintained.[269]

> The basis for successful command is a liaison staff that is well set up and works quickly and reliably. It enables all the elements to take unified action to accomplish a specific mission and, particularly in battle, all the weapons to interact.[270]

In the FuG, he referred to the higher command level, pointing out that it required important information from the engineers, long-range reconnaissance forces, the army cavalry and the airmen to make the right battle decisions.[271] With respect to troop training, Seeckt focused his attention on the military information that directly concerned the enemy on the battlefield. He took account of the principle that 'even apparently unimportant details [could] acquire significance in connection with the other existing information'.[272]

The higher command authorities were required to assist and complement each another, since only precise knowledge of the situation allowed conclusions to be drawn about the enemy's position, intent and direction of attack.

The way the service branches and command authorities had to coordinate had to be expressed clearly in the orders. A distinction was drawn between an order, a combat order, a warning order and an operation order. The operation order comprised important details for the troops and the higher command authorities. It contained the particular orders 'for liaison between the command authorities and the troops'.[273] It differed fundamentally from the order, in which 'not all units [were] included in the overall picture'.[274] But it was to 'contain the information most necessary about the activities and missions of the other service branches, particularly of the infantry and artillery, as otherwise there is no guarantee of the weapons interacting'.[275]

The type of combat operation concerned had to be expressed clearly in the order:

> The term delaying tactics is expressed in the mission and the commander's decision. In defence operations, he must know whether to take on or evade the enemy's decisive attack, and in the case of an attack, whether he should seek a decision, or simply want to delay the enemy, withdraw or force a development.[276]

By contrast, the aim of neither the order nor the operation order should become lost in the details of the mission.[277] The mission had to be expressed in the concept of operations in such a way that the subordinate commander got the freedom of action that allowed him to execute the mission in accordance with the possibilities on the ground and with the means made available to him. This freedom had been granted to him on the basis of mutual trust and conveyed in tactical training by means of regular instruction based on unified military principles. This capability was the basis of the commission principle:

> The nature of the task is best indicated by reference to the principle which it was once the fashion to term 'commission tactics' [...] The 'commission' principle embodied the sound idea that the man who is responsible for success must choose the way to attain it.[278]

The ability to conduct the various types of combat operations, for the mobile deployment of the other combined service branches and for adaptation to different situations was taught by means of the commission principle.

The commission principle was a principle that ensured that the commander could accomplish a broad range of tasks. The decision on the situation was based on the ability to repeatedly align a decision once taken to the current situation. This was necessary to avoid having to wait for orders from above.[279] Seeckt believed that waiting for orders was a mistake that had been made all too often in the First World War and that should not be repeated.[280] A central principle of the Reichswehr evolved logically from this guideline: 'The independent execution of orders by subordinate commanders must not be pre-empted.'[281]

Every decision made by a commander on a battlefield had to take account of the current military capabilities on the ground and the location of the troops and be included in information about the overall situation. The soldier had the ability to make decisions in order to adapt the course of the operation, and therefore the order, to changes on the battlefield. 'When the mission is no longer sufficient as the basis for action and no longer reflects events, the decision must take account of these conditions.'[282] It could be necessary to make a change to the order that would abort a battle in order to initiate the withdrawal. The commander was even responsible for the mission if he had not had it executed or altered. This was something Seeckt called for as a result of his own experience of war.[283] In the regulations, the soldier was urged to act responsibly and independently.[284]

The regulations therefore did not contain any binding requirements concerning how a soldier had to act on the battlefield. Rather, uncertainty in war was the rule and dealing with it was something that had to be learned in exercises. No regulation could be issued to specify what action had to be taken in each individual case. 'In terms of tactical action, it is not possible to issue regulations that are suitable for every case. They would lead to one-sidedness, and that is opposed to the diversity of war.'[285] No regulation could be binding in specific cases. But each regulation could be adapted to such cases.

These skills were taught during officer candidate training. Officers were trained according to standardized rules and prepared for their assignments at the next higher level. The introduction and intensification of the commission principle and the subsequent directive-style command, which was put into practice in everyday military life and which enabled soldiers to take on the next task up, involved the actual mobilisation of the troops.

> This effort to continuously raise the level of training was further justified by the idea of the cadre army that was based on the Reichswehr's own will, not on the Treaty of Versailles. If instructors and commanders of a future people's army were to be groomed, requirements must be established for which a period of service of twelve years was not too long. In the course of service, one soldier will be promoted from a recruit to a serviceable section leader, while another acquires the capability to command a militia company, and as few as possible remain at the level of a simple front line soldier.[286]

Specialists objected that some regulations contradicted the concept of independence and responsibility in the commission principle. In item 13 of the FuG, it says that in delaying operations, the troops should not be informed that this is the combat operation they are conducting.[287] The specialist Gross believed that the instruction was issued 'probably out of fear that the troops would not be able to fight or defend resolutely enough'.[288] Item 332 of the FuG also contradicts the commission principle. The 'intent to attack and timing must be kept secret from the troops for as long as possible.'[289] The fact that Seeckt had had this approach altered in his "Observations of the Chief of the Army Command' had not been taken into account:

The concept of delay is expressed in the mission or decision of the commander. In the defence, he must know whether he wants to take on or evade the enemy's decisive attack, and in the attack, whether he seeks a decision, or simply wants to delay the enemy, withdraw or force a development ... In delaying operations ... it must therefore first be clear where it is to be developed.[290]

The mobility practised in training with the commission principle was intended to qualify the small professional army for fighting a decisive battle. Mobility was a means for the small operating army to compensate for the inferior strength of its forces. 'Concentrating all available forces to bring about a decision is the unique art of command and control. Inferiority in numbers often has to be compensated for by greater mobility.'[291] Being important for operations, mobility had to be combined with the commission principle. Both capabilities were essential criteria of military leadership. But contrary to what military historians assumed, Seeckt did not regard them as a substitute for the lack of forces. The assumption that 'the lack of modern means of combat should be compensated with the aid of the commission principle and mobile warfare' reduced training to only two aspects, which was generally inadequate.[292]

Seeckt adhered to the principle of economy. He valued the saving of forces even when strong opposing forces had to be contained. 'It will always be important to save forces oneself and hold down as many opposing forces as possible.'[293] It was not important for him to 'go the whole hog'. Wherever it was not possible to contain the enemy's strong forces, he recommended withdrawing.[294] The commission principle complemented the training concept. It was a sound command and control principle in both economic and military terms. The commission principle and mobility offered ways and means to be successful in battle.

Seeckt did not assume there would be a people's army in the war, and maintaining inferior forces had to be considered in the event of a hasty attack. Such an attack had to be contained by an appropriate defence strategy. Defence did not mean leaving the decisive steps to the enemy. Even when he has 'less strength, the defender will endeavour to end the battle with an attack and thus inflict a decisive defeat on the enemy'.[295] Since defence was to be offensive, military historians concluded that 'destructive all-arms fire' was used. Defence through attack was declared the 'main battle line'. In contrast, Seeckt used the term to describe repelling the enemy attack. His first concern was to ensure the establishment of effective coverage, though he advised against batteries being deployed too close to the enemy's 'main battle line' for this purpose. He concluded his advice with the sentence: 'Otherwise, binding rules for the deployment of the artillery cannot be issued, as it will primarily depend on the terrain.' Another possibility was that 'annihilating fire can be delivered' by the artillery at the request of the infantry or surveillance aircraft.' His final general remark was: 'Only in rare cases will the delivery of annihilating fire along the entire front be effective and necessary. It leads to the unnecessary piecemeal employment of the troops.'[296] Similar guidelines applied to the use of tactical means of the artillery. It had to be 'manoeuvred by concentrating the strongest annihilating fire against the identified main points of resistance of the enemy'.[297] The artillery batteries had to be 'kept mobile and deployed in alternate positions.'[298] Seeckt urged more restraint and advised commanders to use delaying tactics if enemy fire prevented their troops from advancing and attacking. He recommended waiting. If the enemy was strong and their own troops were exposed to gun battles during the advance, 'this must not be forced, and commanders must wait and see what effect the fire has.'[299] The troops must not be used as cannon fodder.

The FuG referred to the conduct of operations by several divisions that fought a decisive battle with combat vehicles. But in theory, he did not assume that large, and therefore what he regarded as inevitably immobile armies, would determine events on the battlefield. This is why he continued to see the use of tanks as a subordinate, albeit modern resource assigned to the infantry.

In the FuG, a distinction was drawn between heavy and light fighting vehicles, wheeled armoured fighting vehicles, armoured fighting vehicles, tank platoons and their operational capabilities. The fighting vehicle, fitted with light or heavy equipment, light or heavy machine guns, was to be used in such a way that it was able to 'confuse the enemy, break his resistance and destroy his obstacles'.[300] Its penetrating power depended on 'how well it succeeds in appearing on the scene unexpectedly'.[301] Tanks were a means of combat that provided support in deciding a battle and helped the infantry with their advance, being deployed in large numbers, but deeply echeloned and on a broad front:

The higher commander deploys the fighting vehicles where he . seeks the decision. They must be deployed unexpectedly, in large numbers, on a broad front, simultaneously and deeply echeloned, and ample reserves must be kept separate.[302]

They were to be positioned behind the foremost front of the division 'in order to have at hand on an early stage'.[303] Even though they did not yet constitute a branch of service of their own and remained under the control of the infantry, tanks were regarded as a decisive resource in the attack, defence and breakthrough battle. Seeckt had a similar view of the capabilities of tank platoons. Their task was also to exploit surprise, speed and mobility. Tank platoons were under the control of the highest command authority. They were flexible in the way they could be deployed.

Tank platoons are a highly mobile means of combat. They have great combat power and a powerful moral effect, particularly on inferior opponents ... Exploitation of the element of surprise promises the greatest success. Consideration must always be given to whether or not the more mobile wheeled armoured fighting vehicles can accomplish the mission more reliably.[304]

The use of tanks was dependent on the infrastructure, the standard of roads and the terrain conditions. On account of their size, they themselves could become a target, the ability to conduct observation from a tank was limited, and this 'severely hampered command and control and communication'.[305] If, on the other hand, the field had 'few roads' and the countryside was spacious, 'tank platoons under enterprising commanders have a wide field of activity.'[306] Initiative was also called for and was necessary. If a soldier was able to control a situation, the infantry would operate in mixed service branches 'under the protection of the tank platoons'.[307] The use of tanks was not limited to the war of position. 'Training for the war of movement is the main thing and must not be neglected.'[308]

It was possible to bring about a decision if forces were deployed at the right position, with the infantry deployed appropriately deep and adequate ammunition provided. This was also true for the deployment of tanks, whose strong forces were assembled in a limited area and concentrated specifically for making deep thrusts:

> In attacks deep into enemy positions, it is recommended to deploy the fighting vehicles in several leapfrogging echelons … In the defence, it would be wrong to use fighting vehicles solely for the purpose of deterrence. On the other hand, they will have frequent opportunities to intervene in counterstrokes and counterattacks.[309]

Since tanks were of paramount importance, in 1923 an order was issued to the individual military districts to design wooden models of tanks. In 1924 the first cardboard models were delivered to the troops.[310] These replica fighting vehicles were used as a 'useful means' to prepare the commanders and troops for battle using fighting vehicles.[311] Although the improvisations provoked a 'furious reaction one moment and mockery the next, but rarely understanding' among the public because they were 'just ridiculous dummies', Seeckt was 'deadly serious' about them.[312] During manoeuvres, the cardboard dummies were used for the purpose of improvising in order to practise their capabilities and use for the war of movement.[313]

Wallach, who had recognized what was new in Seeckt's theory, believed that he had to qualify this by maintaining that Seeckt had not 'recognized the important role of mobile armoured units'.[314] The second part of the FuG, however, was dedicated to the technical innovations and their potential in the manoeuvre in 311 items.[315] And Citino corrected this view and referred in his work to the importance of armoured units in training in the Reichswehr.[316]

Since 'adequate account was often not taken' of surprise during manoeuvres and military exercises, a mistake that had already been made in the war, Seeckt focused more on one of 'the most important means for success in battle'.[317] The surprise that was achieved by change, manoeuvrability and movement in battle was a psychological advantage. When applied with the tactics of deception and diversion, this could hastily contain enemy forces.[318]

Attack, defence and delaying were practised by the troops on manoeuvres. The combat operations of envelopment, extension of the lines/dispersion of forces, breakthrough and head-on attack were types of combat operations that were able to reintroduce movement into battle.[319] The combat methods of surprise and mobility had to be practised for attack and defence operations. They were used both for defence in a war of movement and for breaking out of a war of position.[320] They were important for regaining an advantage over the enemy. Also on the subject of attack in the war of position, the instruction was issued: 'It is even more important to surprise the enemy [in attacks in a war of position] than in a war of movement.'[321] With the aid of surprise, it was possible to break out of a position: 'An attack in a war of position presupposes surprise. Where and when the attack is to take place must be concealed from the enemy long enough to prevent him from taking defensive action and bringing in reserves in due time.'[322] Surprise confused the enemy and could make it easier for a commander to mount an attack in the breakthrough battle.[323]

The troops would break out of immobility or attempt to gain an advantage from their surprising or deceiving the enemy by mounting an attack. Above all, in order to break out of a war of position, it was

> important to surprise the enemy ... Special measures are therefore needed to conceal one's own intent and deceive the enemy ... A change in the method of attack must therefore always pose the defender new tasks.[324]

A sudden attack, however, using the concealed realignment of forces, decoys or changes in one's own positions at night, a well-known method since ancient times, could also be used by the enemy.[325] In the 'Annual Observations', Seeckt warned:

> On the other hand, the troops must protect themselves from surprises in all situations ... must secure and organize themselves in such a way that they cannot be attacked unexpectedly in what is an unfavourable position or grouping for them and can themselves be ready for battle quickly.[326]

The most favourable position for a breakthrough was the enemy's most sensitive position. In the breakthrough battle, the commander had to 'identify the weaknesses of the enemy front and shift the point of main effort of the attack there. It is seldom right to evenly distribute forces along the entire front.'[327] And, drawing on his own experience of war, Seeckt wrote:

> After a lengthy war of position, the attack usually encounters a defence system that has been set up with ample thought and all the means of field fortification and that cannot be enveloped ... The mass of attacking soldiers surging forward should hit the enemy's sensitive point.[328]

Since the Battle of Cannae, envelopment, including double envelopment, had played a special part at the operational level.[329] This was only permissible, however, and Seeckt again drew on his First World War experiences for this, with adequate manpower.

> An envelopment will succeed if the attacker ultimately has more forces opposite the point that is to be enveloped than the enemy so that the enemy cannot extend the battle any longer. If it is apparent that this ratio of forces cannot be established, it is often right to threaten envelopment, but then to break through.[330]

His World War I experiences were the basis for his idea that envelopment should not follow the same pattern practised repeatedly in manoeuvres.[331] What had to be taken into account was rather the military and civilian infrastructure for one's own troops, the geographical factors, so that combined arms combat became more dynamic due to mobility. In addition, operations in the East had to be planned differently from an envelopment in the West:

> The constant striving for tactical envelopment on the right wing had the result that the great strategic aim of envelopment on a large scale was forgotten. When we finally succeeded in making the great 'break through' battle in the East, the higher command had the greatest difficulty in accustoming the troops and subordinate leaders to the unfamiliar conditions of this operation ...[332]

Seeckt had strongly advised against the envelopment being repeatedly attempted in every exercise. There were other types of combat operations than just envelopment. The FuG and his 'Annual Observations' took account of this instruction. In the 'Annual Observations', he wrote that field training exercises should not proceed according to the book.[333]

The objective of operations was to plan the fighting in such a way that the required forces were able to go into battle at the right time, at the right place, and with the appropriate method of fighting. If the envelopment could not be ventured, the point of main effort had to be shifted so that the operation weakened the enemy at another decisive point. The mobility of this branch of service had to be practised both for the breakthrough and for delaying operations.

In actual fact, Seeckt rejected the doctrine of the Schlieffen school. He regarded envelopment as only one of many possibilities and did not favour it if it could not be successfully secured with appropriate military strength. The principles of both the envelopment and the breakthrough battle were set forth in the FuG. The war of position was mentioned so that it was possible to learn from the mistakes of the past war.[334] As a battalion commander, Seeckt had had the breakthrough battle practised since 1909.[335] He had not achieved success at Gorlice in 1915 with the aid of Schlieffen's dogma, but with a breakthrough battle.[336] On Schlieffen's Day, 28 February 1928, he recalled that the general staff should not concentrate on a 'one-sided dogma', i.e. that of envelopment. 'The destruction of the enemy is the goal of war, but there are many roads to this goal. Every operation must be dominated by one simple clear idea … Decisive force must be thrown in at the decisive point.'[337] Seeckt was of the opinion that Schlieffen had only one lesson to offer, but that there were others that needed to be considered:

> Should no possibility of any kind of envelopment arise – and we have known cases of the kind – then the general cannot simply declare that he is at his wits' end; he will be acting quite in the spirit of Count Schlieffen, if with a clear object in view, he launches his masses at the most effective point – even though it be in a frontal attack, for the success of which Schlieffen, we must admit, coined the sarcastic term 'ordinary victory'.[338]

The breakthrough battle and frontal attack had to be practised particularly as means against the war of position.[339] Seeckt had adopted the war of position in order to develop new solutions. The breakthrough battle in a war of position had to be conducted if one's forces were inadequate in terms of number and equipment for an envelopment. The breakthrough could succeed together with tanks and lead to a turnaround by means of surprise. The psychological element also gained importance here:

> The higher command level deploys the fighting vehicles where it seeks the decision ... At the end of a day of battle, the appearance of fresh fighting vehicle units can hugely increase the chances of success.[340]

The purpose of battle had to be adapted to the terrain, and the materiel quality had to be ensured in addition to the necessary forces, equipment, arms and ammunition.[341] The mission and means had to match. This was also a requirement derived from Seeckt's own experience. He had experienced the negative consequences, namely that troops were overtaxed, at an early stage:

> [W]hile advancing to the Marne, a lot was demanded of the troops, but it was within their powers. When the operation failed, however, their powers were also exhausted. The troops needed rest. Restoration of order, which had been deeply shaken in part, the replenishment of the severely thinly manned lines, the replacement of the lower-level leaders, ample ammunition – and trust in the supreme command. They did not receive any of this ... Instead, the troops received 'new missions in the old direction' that 'far exceeded their powers and that, discernible to them – not the higher command – bore the signs of hopelessness'.[342]

In the 'Observations of the Chief of the Army Command', he also repeatedly asserted that the lessons of war should be borne in mind and taken into account in exercises.[343]

He wrote that delaying operation tactics should be used if the forces were distinctly inferior. What mattered was to buy time. 'Delaying

operations are intended to deceive and contain the enemy and buy time
... The commander's task is initially to defer a serious battle.'[344]

All the branches of service with their effects were brought together
by the operational level and their operations geared to the objective.
Conducting the various types of combat operations, the different
branches were able to exert a decisive influence on the events by including
the respective higher command authorities. At the tactical level and in
the conduct of operations, movement, change, surprise and camouflage
remained important methods of fighting for the troops.

The operational level had to prepare for the major operations and was
not allowed to waste combat power on minor battles. The operational
objective was to concentrate forces at the main point:

> The general cannot be equally strong at all points; he must, however,
> be as strong as possible at the point he has identified as being decisive.
> In order to achieve this, he must accept the risk of becoming too
> weak at another point, of suffering setbacks and losses that will be
> offset if he succeeds in the main decisive strike.[345]

On account of the terms of the Treaty of Versailles, Seeckt had to put the
infantry and army cavalry first. His statements on heavy artillery, fighting
vehicles, aircraft, air support and defence therefore had to remain
theoretical. Nevertheless, he repeatedly referred in the regulations to
the direct interaction of all the branches of service, and in particular to
the importance that tanks, air forces and heavy artillery would have in
the future.[346] He acknowledged the fact that the 'development of motor
transport [was] one of the most urgent questions of military organization';
even if as a result of technical developments it was not yet the case that
'the armies of the world [had been] transformed into armoured engines
and the horsemen entirely superseded by the motor soldier':

> Things have not gone so far yet, and we shall do well to reckon
> with present conditions if we would satisfy the demands of the
> present and of the near future. We certainly ought not to close our
> eyes to the development of the motor vehicle and its employment
> for military purposes. We shall not ignore it, but rather try to lay

the theoretical foundations and, as far as possible, the practical foundations for its use, but we must take care not to neglect existing, tested, serviceable appliances in favour of something that may be possible in the future.[347]

Seeckt always assumed that the army would be a small operating army, so in his regulations, he did not place the focus at the operational level on the training of the army corps of one branch of service or on that of the divisions of the same branch. He was concerned about movement and surprise, which had to be practised by the various branches in coordination with each other and for each other. The various weapons used in battle promised victory in battle. The emphasis was above all on ensuring smooth interaction between all the branches with their different weapons at all levels of command. Liaison had to be maintained between the armies while they fought separately. Manoeuvres were to be used to study above all the different effects and combat strengths of all the weapons employed. Under the generally restrictive terms of the Treaty of Versailles, the functions and technical conditions of the unknown weapons had to be known at least theoretically and improvised versions of them created for use in exercises. The interaction not just of all the branches of service and their weapons, but also cooperation between the different levels of command were prerequisites for the success of an operation. Although an inadequate means, improvisation helped to make war games reflect real war conditions. Due to the broad, general description of the different war scenarios and the improvised manoeuvres contained in the FuG, General Guderian and General von Senger und Etterling were able, after years of theoretical training, to prove their military capabilities and mental agility with the employment of tanks in the Second World War.[348] They put what they had practised with wooden models into effect on the battlefields of World War II.[349] General Frido von Senger und Etterling attributed his ability to his training in the Reichsheer. He attributed both the first successes in the campaign in France and the Battle of Monte Cassino to the doctrine of Seeckt, who had taught the Reichsheer mobility with the modern means of 'dive bombers, armoured forces, paratroopers' and anti-air weapons for a modern conflict.[350]

During their training in the Reichswehr, the officers learned what Seeckt initially had taught commanders in the FuG: 'In terms of tactical action, it is not possible to issue regulations that are suitable for every case. They would lead to one-sidedness, and that is opposed to the diversity of war'.[351] Mental agility to deal with the expected uncertainty was something that the commanders had learned. The merely theoretical imagination of the officers, trained with the aid of cardboard and wooden models, had enhanced their creativity and improvisation skills during manoeuvres and matured their operational capabilities for the Second World War.

Under the restrictive terms mentioned, the Reichsheer was far from being an elite army.[352] This was particularly so as Seeckt had rejected the establishment of such an army.

In the early years of the Reichsheer, the proposal was once made to form special units, companies or battalions, entirely from people with a higher education, secondary school graduates and academics … The wish to create elite forces, as it were, from such elements on account of their homogeneity and the higher standards which their education entitled them to meet was understandable. From the point of view of creating a school for commanders of a future people's army, this proposal was not unjustified. It was not, however, to the army's advantage and was not compatible with the main idea of raising the entire Reichswehr to the highest possible level and making the whole German army an army of leaders. One would have … followed paths similar to those that led to the formation of 'youth corps' at the start of the war. They had consumed materiel that could have been of use to the whole army.[353]

Seeckt endeavoured to make the soldiers comprehend the horrors of battle, but he had never regarded them as 'highly motivated fighters of the elite army'.[354] The aim of his military training was to 'educate the soldier to become a thinking fighter'.[355] This enabled him to apply mobility, the commission principle and directive-style command with the various branches of service jointly and independently.

It is of fundamental importance that our subordinate leaders are educated to become men who think and act for themselves. They will only become so if they are taught to understand the wider context, if they free themselves from exaggerated dependence and from waiting for orders. There was always a penalty to be paid – even in the World War – when orders from above were too detailed.[356]

The 'Observations of the Chief of the Army Command' were of fundamental importance for training the troops from 1922 to 1926. The topics addressed at the tactical level were the employment of tanks, the experiences of the troops and not just theoretical, but real-life deployment. The 'Observations' reflected the challenges the troops faced.[357] They included the permanent improvement of training and education goals for the troops, enabling Seeckt to increase the value of the troops.

If the Reichswehr is granted both tasks, those of being an instrument of outward and inward state power … and also of forming the core of future development, one is forced to admit that the demands on its intrinsic value cannot be high enough.[358]

The FuG was more than just continuation or supplement of the old service regulations. It offered a lot of new things compared with Field Service Manual DVE No. 267 from 1908 and introduced the full range of new weapons. With his idea of mobility, Seeckt consciously followed those guidelines in the Drill Regulations of 1906 that corresponded with his theory.[359] The above-mentioned service regulations, however, are not comparable either in terms of their structure or the military regulations they contain, nor do they permit any parallels to be drawn between Seeckt and Schlieffen with respect to the establishment of priorities.

In the 'Annual Observations', Seeckt had turned his attention to tactical training and tried to optimize military training in everyday military life. In the FuG on the other hand, he went far beyond the capacities and equipment conditions of the Reichsheer. He did this to challenge the army and to stimulate achievement. This consisted of practising speed and mobility, surprise and deception, between the various units, encouraging the use of improvisation when required facilities were not available. The commission principle and directive-style command at a higher level were styles of leadership that optimized operations. Reducing Seeckt to only a few training criteria does not do him justice.

In the military regulations, Seeckt did not devote himself to those aspects that influenced the conflict between the political antagonists, i.e. diplomatic relations or the interactions between political actors. The overarching significance of information that would have introduced stability and cooperation at the political level was not taken into account in the FuG. It remained a matter for the political leadership.

The Passive Electoral Rights and Political Activities of Soldiers

Seeckt agreed with the British and French of his generation that constitutional reservations were an argument against granting soldiers active electoral rights. What he felt was appropriate for his day in the Weimar Republic was already true before his day in Britain with its aversion to a large standing army and in France for the period after the French Revolution. Justified for the first time by the Kapp Putsch, Seeckt was like the French military philosopher Hippolythe Comte de Guibert before him in regarding a politically active soldier as a danger to the state and its constitution.[360] Owing to the change in the political system from a monarchy to a republic, which had caused the domestic instability in the Weimar Republic, Seeckt also believed that introducing the active electoral rights was problematic.[361]

Seeckt's demand for the Reichswehr to be politically neutral has to be attributed to both communist and extreme right-wing agitation. Since the early days of the republic, this agitation had aimed for the Reichswehr to engage in politics. In February and May 1920, decrees in which they were instructed to refrain from expressing any judgment on political matters were issued to the troops. No political comments were to be made, above all in writing such as in the bulletins of command authorities.[362] Even before the Military Law was passed in 1921, Seeckt banned troops from participating in elections.[363] He went a step further, however. He also called on the troops to 'remain informed of the course of political events even though the Reichswehr is to keep out of politics. This internal information service must not, however, lead to political activity on the part of military agencies.'[364] Commanders were not to exert any political influence. The matter was to be decided by accepting the constitution and relying on political education. Only the politically-educated soldier could deal appropriately with indoctrination and ideology, and the force of arms would not help. For this reason, Seeckt ordered the commanders to issue the instruction through the student companies that

> [i]n addition to extensive welfare for the troops, which will always constitute the best propaganda, what is needed in my view is constant education as stipulated in Art. 35 of the Military Law, in which the topics of both the significance of the soldier in the state and the knowledge and assessment of political directions and parties and on the political situation in Germany and abroad are dealt with.[365]

The troops had to be informed about important domestic developments. For example, on 24 February 1921, when Seeckt first informed the commanders and division chiefs and, on 26 February, when he had the order issued to the troops. He emphasized the danger of an existing right-wing *coup d'état* in which Ludendorff was involved. He warned that '[a]nyone who should attempt to force his will on the government and leave the path of legality would only ruin Germany completely.'[366] And he personally called on the officers and public officials who had been assigned to the ministry to follow the Reich government.[367]

Seeckt had met and spoken to Hitler in Berlin on 12 March 1923. Although some of his contemporaries seemed to hope that he was more than just impressed, he informed the troops on 22 March 'that any involvement of army personnel in matters related to National Socialism would be regarded as disobedience.'[368] In spite of this, some officers joined the National Socialist Party in 1923. But Seeckt left no doubt about his position on this either:

There have been incidents of officers expressing their political views in public … In these cases, I was forced to intervene with disciplinary action, even with dismissal. Furthermore, the National

Socialist movement under the leadership of Lieutenant Rossbach (retired) has gained access and sought to gain access to several agencies ... All those involved are facing court proceedings; the instigators must be dismissed immediately; the commander of the Reichswehr Bloc is in custody at the Supreme Court of the Reich. Two of those involved, who have been proved to have connections with Rossbach, have been dismissed, all those involved have been subject to disciplinary action.[369]

Deprivation of the civil right to vote and the ban on attending political assemblies were important aspects of his military strategy.[370] Seeckt was unrelenting on this point, even against President of the Reich Friedrich Ebert. There is documentation of a conversation Seeckt had with Ebert regarding his attitude towards party politics in 1923:

President of the Reich Ebert was aware of the efforts of the right-wing groups to make the Reichswehr its party force, while being pressured by his own people to exert a social democratic influence on them. He asked me where I stood on the issue. I abruptly rejected both influences, upon which he asked me with a degree of agitation: Who is the Reichswehr actually behind? My reply was: 'The Reichswehr is behind me.' The discussion ended there and was never again resumed.[371]

Seeckt reverted to the position that a politically neutral military means of power, an operating army whose members did not have active electoral rights, who were banned from attending political assemblies, was useful to the government. He believed that it was in his power to educate 100,000 men to be politically neutral, that unconditional obedience could be demanded of officers and men, particularly since the military hierarchy was in his view based on obedience:

A Reichswehr that remains united and obedient is invincible and the strongest factor in the state. A Reichswehr in which there is political discord will break apart in the hour of danger.[372]

Colonel-General Hans von Seeckt, Chief of Army Command, who re-built the Reichswehr under the restrictive terms of the Treaty of Versailles, and followed Clausewitz in advocating supremacy of the civil power.

Group picture of the German delegation to the Versailles negotiations in 1919 (left to right): Walther Schuecking, Johannes Giesberts, Otto Landsberg, Ulrich von Brockdorff-Rantzau, Robert Leinert, Carl Melchior.

Colonel-General Hans von Seeckt as creator of the Reichswehr with infantry students on manoeuvres in 1925.

Friedrich Ebert with Hans von Seeckt in the background celebrating the progress of the Weimar Constitution in August 1922.

Friedrich Ebert, *circa* 1918,
Reich Chancellor (1919–1925).

Friedrich Ebert at his desk, who with von Seeckt safegarded the primacy of civil over
military power.

Major General Erich Ludendorff, promoted Lieutenant General and Chief of General Staff, and reputed hero of the battle of Tannenberg in defeating the Russian army in 1914.

Erich Ludendorff, Quarter Master General of Imperial German Army in 1916, promoter of theory of 'total war' of the nation in arms, supporting the military over civil power, in opposition to von Seeckt.

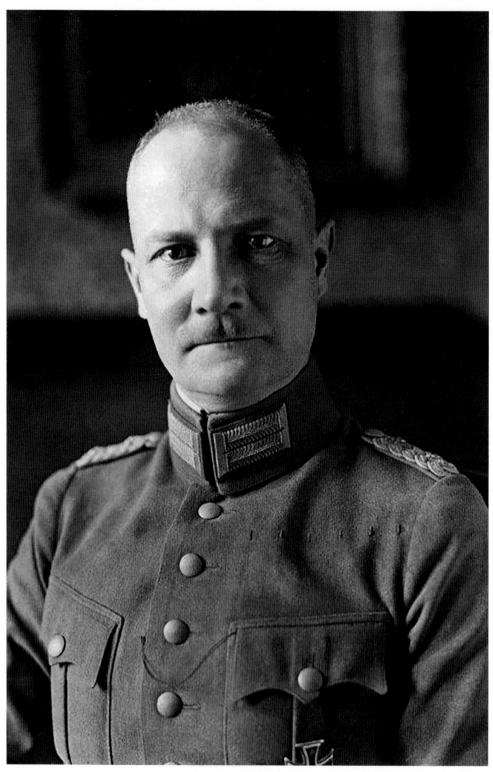

Lieutenant Colonel Joachim von Stülpnagel, follower of Erich Ludendorff in promoting theory of 'total war' and forerunner of Nazi militarism.

Adolf Hitler and Erich Ludendorff at Munich for their trial in March 1924.

Hitler and Hindenburg at the Garrison Church in Potsdam, 21 March 1933 – the 'Day of Potsdam'.

Hitler with Werner von Blomberg, Minister of War and Werner von Fritsch in 1935, a successor of Hans von Seeckt as Supreme Commander of the Army.

Consistently pursued, a 'politically neutral instrument' of the state that remained subordinate to the government's political interests would not be a threat to the state and the constitution. Since 1920, he had called for the state to have a politically neutral instrument of power and, as the holder of executive authority, defined his idea of how it should be used.

> The interests of the officer and of the nation are not connected to those of a class: They lie in the German state, which we have to safeguard against all class and party struggles, which must demand the same sacrifices from every class and to which it is our moral duty to devote ourselves and to serve, with disregard for our own person.[373]

He did not want neutrality to be seen as an attitude that implied non-participation in the face of anti-constitutional efforts.

> The emphasis on the 'neutral' political viewpoint must not be able to be interpreted wrongly. 'Neutrality' naturally refers only to the political 'parties'. In contrast, doubt must not arise in any party that the Reichswehr is the unconditionally reliable pillar of the constitutional government.[374]

He also thought it was wrong that civic education would 'transform into a party political influence.'[375]

As Chief of the Army Command, he held the view, in opposition to the National Socialist Party, that an intervention by soldiers in domestic matters for the benefit of that party would not only be anti-constitutional, but also provoke civil war. On 4 November 1923, he emphasized:

> that well-being does not come from one or the other extreme, not from external help or internal revolution – whether from the left or right – but that only hard, sober work allows us to carry on living. We can do this solely on the basis of the law and the constitution. If it is abandoned, there will be civil war ... It is in our vital interest to refute this doubt [in the unity of the Reich and security, peace and order], to exclude the party struggle that is destroying all of

Germany's other forces from the army, to serve only the non-party needs of the state and not to let ourselves be thrown off this course either by the hatred or the temptations of the political directions.[376]

In a further bulletin issued in 1924, he again clearly highlighted how the individual soldier had to behave:

Two things are fundamentally important for the relationship with the public. Unconditional neutrality with respect to all political movements as long as they are not working towards a violent overthrow of the government, and a readiness to help anyone ... Complete impartiality is the foundation stone of trust. For this reason, I cannot impress often enough, or strongly enough, upon each member of the Reichsheer this impartial attitude that has always been a characteristic of the best servants of the state. It must never be the case that sections of the population feel they are being discriminated against by the Reichswehr on account of their political views. Every German, regardless of his political persuasion, and as long as he understands the word national only in the positive sense, has the right to equal treatment by the Reichswehr.[377]

As far as Seeckt was concerned, ideological blinkers, political infiltration by left- and right-wing extremists, were just as much a threat to the troops as to the still fledgling form of government. The demand he had voiced since 1920 for soldiers to be deprived of active electoral rights was confirmed by the various political events, though particularly by the Hitler-Ludendorff coup in 1923. He favoured a professionally led professional army for the Weimar Republic whose members did not have civil electoral rights.

The historian Ulrich Wehler rejected Seeckt's actions as Chief of the Army Command. Wehler believed that it was primarily Seeckt's denial of active electoral rights that prevented the republicanisation of the army.[378] It should also be noted that with his call for party-political neutrality, Seeckt also prevented the Reichswehr from falling into line behind the National Socialists.

Further Focal Points of the Military Strategy

After the political will, Seeckt ranked the population, the economy, industry, the territory of a country, its geography, natural resources, geostrategic position, financial system and diplomatic ties among those factors which determine the domestic and foreign policies of a country.[379] These aspects were 'sources of the inner power of a nation'.[380] The religious faiths, the education system and the administrative apparatus of a country also had an effect on its civilization and culture. Seeckt did not incorporate the three latter aspects in his thoughts on military strategy.[381] Yet formation and structure, organization, personnel, the arms industry and the materiel quality of the armed forces were determined by these factors. 'The creation and maintenance of a military force is not a question for the consideration and decision of soldiers alone.'[382]

The People

In Seeckt's view, no concept of security could be measured. There could be 'no more than a sense of security' and it would be more or less believed or perceived in relation to an alleged threat. This sense depended on the strength of the potential opponent and on the continental situation. While the 'sense of intimidation' could certainly fluctuate, the geopolitical position of a country was its fixed point. The people's very perception, their sense of 'intimidation', was a political reason for promoting military build-up or could prompt the government to initiate negotiations aimed at achieving a balance of armament.[383]

This shows that Seeckt included psychological factors in his military strategy. It was the people's sense of being intimidated by their neighbour, their political limits and political relations with a neighbouring state that were the primary driving force behind the policy of assuming negotiations with this neighbour:

> The decisive sense of security is the one that can be described better than the possible or probable threat and that is made up of quite different components, among which, for example, the relationship with the neighbours and their political aims number as something changeable and the geographic position as something permanent.[384]

The imposition of excessive armaments limitations on the state and thus its people that leave it no possibility of self-defence 'increases the sense of insecurity in that state and thereby increases the risk of war'.[385] They would also have to endure the negative economic and social effects in the aftermath of a war. If the people were no longer prepared to endure them, their political will could gain a momentum of its own.

Though Seeckt did not believe that natural protective factors such as mountain ranges and rivers could be translated into battalions, they were nevertheless of incomparable psychological value for the people.[386] They could strengthen their 'sense of security'.[387]

Seeckt's reflections contain only one reference to a military operation being legitimate when it is supported by the people. He cited the Wars of Liberation, deducing from the interdependency of the army and the people that there was close interaction between the two in a hopeless situation. He recalled the zenith of the beaten army after its defeats at Jena and Auerstedt: 'The victor whose army was not so long ago defeated at Jena and Auerstedt became the people in arms because their political will was in concert with the policy and warfare.'[388] The attitude of the people of a country towards the political system and the opponent could influence not only the duration, but also the success and end of a war.

One responsibility of the people was to be prepared for enemy attacks. They had to protect their country's borders. This served the country's defence. State schools were to instil the idealistic duty to defend the country in young people, to teach them how to mount a defence and develop their 'will to defend themselves' as that of the 'survival instinct' of the country.[389]

In peace and war, the state could impose restrictions to ensure that the administrative and business sectors in the country were not deprived of all young manpower at the same time:

> The state can confine its call-up for national defence to certain age groups or regions in response to the situation. It goes without saying that material considerations, the strength and will of a nation, will have a say in how the state exploits its military power. A nation's will to defend itself and survival instinct are backbones of the system, which can also require sacrifices to be made and have nothing to do with 'imperialism' and 'militarism'.[390]

The people were an integral part of political life. Their sense of intimidation had a determining impact on political antagonism; they were able to demand bilateral negotiations and, when they supported the state's military action, to contribute to the success of a conflict.

Competition in Armament – Disarmament – Balance of Armament

Seeckt studied competition in armament, deterrence and disarmament. His focus was on the question of how peace could be preserved and secured. Taking the people's feeling as the yardstick, an offensive arms build–up or a heavily armed neighbour would raise the sense both of insecurity and of intimidation in a country. To maintain greater security, the states concerned should take up negotiations. International agreements were one way to 'diminish the character of an immediate threat to the other or to others as this is what a country's armament is associated with'.[391] He was in no doubt that disarmament was a central political objective, but that a few obstacles had to be overcome on the way to it:

> The question therefore was: 'Is it worthwhile to strive, in the political sphere, to limit the risk of decision by force of arms?' To answer the question in the affirmative is sufficient to imply an adequate political idealism and recognition of the fact that progress is slow and only imaginable in stages.[392]

Not only 'mistrust of the power and effectiveness of peace efforts and peace treaties' had to be overcome, but also scepticism if a basis was to be established for negotiations.[393] Moreover, there was a need for 'a lot of optimism and trust in the good will of all the parties to assume that the nations of Europe would be able to achieve a real and fairly just balance of armament'.[394] While a common basis for conclusive negotiations might have been found, the major ideological differences still had to be overcome.[395] As for the question of the worth and continuance of an alliance, Seeckt attached importance both to the neighbours' political interests and proceeded on the assumption that the people's desire for peace was genuine and that there was trust, optimism and idealism in politics. He rated them as the political driving forces and basis for international agreements.[396]

He assumed that the people's desire for peace was genuine and knew that, besides good will and political idealism, sincerity, trust and optimism were part and parcel of any negotiations.[397]

> The good will, that is the willingness, to not only defend one's own interests, but to give room to those of the others is a prerequisite without which no objective agreement would be possible. The naval agreement between England and America proves that there is no reason to despair of a possibility of mutual consideration such as this one.[398]

By contrast, it would not be possible to detect hidden intentions and in 1930 he was not very optimistic about the global political situation. His strong sense of pragmatism and political realism was enough to stop him from drawing attention to the downside of general armament efforts. For example, hardly any government would cite another reason for its military build-up in addition to the 'natural drive for survival', the necessity of self-defence and deterrence. 'A state would [not] admit that the purpose of its military build-up was to pursue intentions to achieve conquests.'[399] No distinction could be made between a defensive and an offensive military build-up.[400] The breach of an agreement, the start of a war, would, in contrast, only result in the opponent being morally discredited. All that the other states could do was 'to threaten to morally ostracise the state which breached the peace'.[401] Seeckt, however, believed that these tendencies to disturb peace emanated from the political leadership, 'the threat to peace lies in the specific nature of the politician who creates them.'[402]

For that reason alone, mistrust and scepticism were difficult to overcome and political idealism was difficult to maintain.[403] Seeckt regarded the imbalance of military power as a driving force behind political action and negotiations. The objective of armament negotiations was not to achieve unilateral or complete disarmament, but rather a balance of armament. It was a 'balance of power' that was to be achieved:

The risk of war lies essentially in the inequality of military forces, which leads the stronger power to secure its political interest by the threat or the exercise of violence against the weaker. ... Such an adjustment would enhance the general sense of security, just as the increase of security by treaty favours in turn the reduction of armament.[404]

The objective of negotiations on disarmament was not to achieve a zero in armaments. 'Lasting peace' would remain unattained: 'Accordingly, the current aim, for the time being more theoretically than practically, is not to abolish armaments, but to reduce them.'[405] Seeckt believed that disarmament negotiations were more in line with the wish to limit spending than in fact meant to lessen the danger of war.[406] Economic reasons favoured a balance and opposed unlimited competition in armament. He thought that adequate armament was 'a guarantee for preserving and securing peace in a country' and unilateral disarmament implied 'an immediate danger of war because a less equipped neighbour was an inducement to war'.[407] As all negotiating partners would 'recognise a minimum level of armament' 'as necessary', this could be assumed to be a given fact.[408] This was especially so because a country's armament policy primarily served the purpose of deterrence.[409]

Equality had to be guaranteed at the disarmament negotiations:

If specific armament regulations are to be drawn up and adopted at all, they will be acceptable, or be of any worth, to Germany if the condition of full equality in all issues concerning security is met.[410]

There had to be general acceptance that negotiations on reciprocal armament limitations would be conducted on an equal footing. Cemented inequalities made it difficult for rapprochement to be achieved in international negotiations and political idealism and trust in the observance of the treaties were put at risk.[411] Only full equality between the allies that concluded treaties and entered negotiations could strengthen the 'feeling of security' and assure its continuance.[412] Equality at international level did not just allay the psychologically determined sense of intimidation among the nations.[413] State-induced self defence did not result in a military build-up either that would otherwise lead to a policy of aggression.[414]

The above factors made it more difficult to initiate disarmament negotiations. The primary concern with respect to the negotiations was to 'redress inequalities or to weigh them up against each other fairly'. This again proved to be a problem 'because one cannot alter the fact that a big and rich country will, in the military sphere, if we use the term in its broadest sense, always remain stronger than a small and poor one'.[415]

On account of these parameters, Seeckt assumed that the political leadership were only able to see their primary objective in armament negotiations in those that concerned a reduction in army strengths. 'The only tangible figures available for calculation on either side are those of the armies in being.'[416] For the military chiefs, this 'issue of armament limitation or a balance of armament was primarily a political one … in which the soldier only played the role of an expert adviser.'[417] The soldier had to accept the results of international armament negotiations:

> Competition in armament and limitation of armament are both political questions in spite of their military form. The soldier cannot be blamed if he makes large demands on behalf of the interests he has to represent. It is the business of the statesman to adapt these demands to general policy. […] but he will come to terms and adapt himself if policy requires him to do so and if the statesman compels him.[418]

Where negotiations had been entered, it was possible in the next step to compare the armies of different strengths and their level of armament and to reduce their armament. Seeckt commented on this with the words that 'it would be useless to weigh up the value of the various factors that, combined, make up the military strength of a country, against one another, indeed to translate them into figures.'[419] Structure, organisation, training and equipment were variables that could only be calculated to a degree. And then there were factors which were difficult to assess. The only option that remained was to offset the strengths of the armies against one another:

> When determining what was an adequate strength for a country's peacetime army, very different circumstances such as size, the

geographic and economic positions, concern about overseas interests, the people's military spirit and willingness to make sacrifices naturally come into consideration; nonetheless it seems conceivable to achieve an acceptable balance of armament at international level and guard against the return of competition in armament by limiting the strengths of peacetime armies.[420]

The more difficult factors in the calculation were the size of the population, natural resources, other resources and the geographic position of a country. A full comparison was hardly possible. Especially rivers and mountain ranges were natural strong points in terms of national defence and Seeckt concluded that it would be 'somewhat difficult ... to translate these into battalions or batteries'.[421] Yet, besides the non-calculable factors, there were also negotiable factors, which permitted the achievement of a balance of armament, and one was the strength of the army itself, which could be reduced:

> If we accept that the general desire for peace evinced in the disarmament negotiations as sincere, then there is in the existing military organisations no irreconcilable antithesis ... This sense of intimidation cannot be represented in disarmament calculations in terms of figures. The only tangible figures available for calculation on either side are those of the armies in being.[422]

Military manpower and equipment were quantifiable. By contrast, the organization, the efficiency an army achieves through training and education, was regarded as a non-quantifiable variable. Above all, he considered that the level of training and hence the professional capabilities of soldiers were almost impossible to quantify. Seeckt's permanent effort to gear soldiers to the next-higher task and to continually improve their skills through training and education, which, for him, was inseparable from the enhancement of inner values, also entailed the danger of unequal forces for him.[423]

He did not, however, rule out a ban on the currently proscribed weapons:

There will be competition in armament in the fields of organisation, training and armament, where each state will be allowed complete freedom, unless thought is given to an international ban on specific weapons such as gas and submarines.[424]

The national arms industry had the task of meeting military requirements and being prepared for an emergency:

> A prerequisite for meeting this demand is the existence of a national arms industry which is capable of meeting current requirements, but at the same time can increase its capacity to meet higher requirements.[425]

In times of economic prosperity, the state needed to do less for the arms industry, while in times of recession and inflation it was required to bolster the industry with state subsidies.[426] 'We did see that the legitimate desire for a reduction in armament was limited by the state's obligation to ensure the capability of self-defence.'[427] The arms industry should not dominate state spending either, because the preservation of peace was still the better deal.[428] Seeckt's comparison between a large army and a small army was also of importance in this context: when the armament for a small army is state-subsidised, 'these subsidies will cost the state less than the accumulation and maintenance of large stocks and obsolescent equipment.'[429]

In the event of mobilisation, the necessary raw materials and materials for the production of machinery had to be made available and industrial operations had to be switched from peacetime to war production. Close cooperation between the military and the arms industry was necessary at all times.

> The army is able, in cooperation with technical science, to establish the best type of weapon for the time being by means of constant study in testing shops and on practice grounds. An agreement must be made with industry to ensure that this fixed type can be produced at once and in the necessary quantities. They must be made with the closest collaboration between the soldier and manufacturer ...[430]

Co-operation between the civilian and military sectors, which industry and the Army High Command had already begun in peacetime and been ordered to continue, was based on the requirements for military equipment.

Military build-up was an answer to a threat that existed along the borders and was caused by neighbours who were better equipped and served the purpose of defence. Seeckt agreed with Moltke the Elder that being militarily prepared for war was the best guarantee for peace, and 1930 was not the year in which he emphasised this basic military strategy idea for the first time:

> It is essential to remember that armament in itself is no threat of war; on the contrary, it can be a guarantee for maintaining and securing a country's peace, while the refusal of sufficient armament for the purpose of security, and thus for the capability of adequate self-defence, implies an immediate danger of war, albeit the respective country is not actively involved in war, but will forcibly become a mere passive theatre of war for the others.[431]

A sovereign foreign policy was dependent on armament capacities, the strength of the army, its resource and the geographic position. A sovereign foreign policy was the activity of a state whose freedom was in its political decisions:

> The larger a country, the greater the threat to its geographic position, the closer its connection with world events, the more urgent the demand for armament to ensure its freedom of decision-making and conduct.[432]

Despite the danger of military build-up, he rejected the assumption that military build-up was equivalent to a policy of aggression. The purpose of armament was firstly to maintain peace, a defence and deterrence. Thus, he considered it appropriate that the respective states kept a 'minimal level of armament'. The purpose of the disarmament negotiations in favour of a balance of forces was to limit spending, to reduce the sense of insecurity and intimidation, which would create the possibility to 'eliminate the risk of war'.[433] As mentioned previously, full equality was taken for granted at the negotiations, as this was the only way to ensure compliance with the negotiated measures.

Accordingly, Seeckt was convinced that the sense of intimidation could only be countered by a balance in armament, by a 'balance of power'. An attempt by two states to reciprocally adjust in the assessment of their armaments was the first step towards securing peace. 'Such an adjustment would enhance the general sense of security, just as the increase of security by treaty favours in turn the reduction of armaments.'[434] It would be utopian to seek to abolish armaments. A balance of power offered the better guarantee for peace.[435] A balance of armament secured peace through international or binational negotiations, and this peace would last if all the parties had equal rights.

A Balance of Armament through International Negotiations and Alliance Policy

Seeckt occupied himself in quite some detail with how competition in armament could be avoided and a balance of armament achieved for the security of all. International negotiations and agreements were one option.[436] Alliance policy was another. It offered a better possibility to contain the probability of war in the military field. International negotiations not only enabled negotiations on balance to be conducted, but also offered the negotiating partners the chance to coalesce and form an alliance.

Seeckt believed that the improbability of an end to the competition in armament had been evident long before the First World War. Before the First World War, the nations' views on the obligation of self-defence had

> led to competition in armament, in essence, to a continual build-up of active forces. Their availability and possible huge reinforcement in a minimum of time constituted a permanent threat to peace, more so in psychological than in material terms perhaps.[437]

Current armament efforts could also end in competition in armament. Competition in armament had not been halted in Europe after the First World War, but had been continued:

The general feeling of the nations is that all the treaties and peace regulations are not adequate today or perhaps yet to provide the sense of security necessary for each state and so that everyone must fend for themselves.[438]

This development in particular was a problem because it made it harder to recognize the true intents of a country:

An attempt was made to distinguish between offensive and defensive armament and to describe the former as a threat to peace and the latter as permissible. It is difficult to define such a distinction.[439]

He did not, however, see the ideological antagonism between the East and West as a hindrance to starting negotiations on armament balance. Rather, he advocated negotiations between the nations which would demonstrate an honest will, trust, political idealism and optimism.

Where the road was open to alliance negotiations, Seeckt suggested that the weaker neighbour should enter negotiations with a potentially stronger opponent in order to achieve a balance in armament through agreements. States of unequal strength could join up to enter an alliance for the purpose of protecting themselves and of jointly forcing an even stronger neighbour into accepting a balance in armament.

Military alliances are rarely formed on the grounds of a general security need alone; such alliances are certainly desired by a weak state because it rightly lives in permanent fear of a stronger neighbour.[440]

A militarily weaker state should deliberately strive to enter an alliance, to balance out its inferiority through an alliance in order to achieve an aspired balance in armament. Alliance policy could mean a gain in power for the weaker state and have a deterrent effect. Moreover, an alliance had the advantage that its members would watch out that none of its members became much stronger than two of them:

It is, however, feasible to bring the available peace strength of one army into such a relation with the peace strength of another that no state has a force at its disposal which is superior to the combined forces of several other states.[441]

Alliance policy was not only ruled by politics in peacetime, but also in war. 'The enemies which confront him, the allies which are at his side, are the politician's work'.[442] Circumstances could arise in war, which suggested that a military alliance should be abandoned. But even then, it would be up to the government to decide on the acceptance or abandonment of an alliance. A commander could only give advice:

> Just as the prosecution of a pre-war policy of alliance is the statesman's business and includes therefore the making of alliances and military agreements, similarly the cooperation of the allies in war is constantly dependent on political support. ...The sacrifice of an ally may appear desirable from the military point of view, but inadmissible from the political point of view. It is precisely in a war that is waged jointly with allies that the dissension between the military and political departments or even a mere lack of coordination in their activity must produce the most disastrous consequences.[443]

Alliance negotiations were sought when there was an imbalance of power between individual neighbouring states, when the imbalance of power was perceived as a risk to peace. Agreements were concluded to create a balance of power. Foreign policy was able to forestall a threat through arbitration agreements, to initiate a more extensive alliance policy and to find further allies. International agreements, international disarmament agreements primarily served the purpose of answering the people's security need, to lessen the sense of intimidation and to prevent competition in armament.[444]

The aim of becoming an ally, of entering an alliance was not achieved because of Germany's military weakness:

> A state that is defenceless and kept in a disarmed state is not capable of forming alliances because it has nothing to offer in terms of power; nor is it master of its own decisions because it does not have the power to secure peace. The grand peace manifesto of the Kellogg Pact must recognise the right of self-defence, a state's right

to defend itself; the Reich has been deprived of the possibility to exercise this right and has thus been deprived of the right itself.[445]

Since 1918, Seeckt had had a precise idea of the means with which Germany could defend its interests and could rise to become a 'desirable ally'. A sufficiently strong army was a prerequisite for being recognised as an equal partner in political negotiations and for being accepted as an ally:

> A state that has international respect and wishes to pursue a foreign policy, needs a reliable, that is to say, a trained and equipped army … The plan for a League of Nations – devised to secure peace – requires its participants to have a standing army, as part of an international police power. No major state can escape this obligation unless it wishes to sink so low as to become a mere object of world politics.[446]

The point is that other foreign policy conditions had been approved and initiated as a result of the Treaty of Versailles, and the result was that Germany was not given equal status in Europe. There was no basis for negotiations that could have yielded lasting results.[447]

In his deliberations on the arms negotiations, Seeckt had considered many a factor and idea which have been described in the literature on the subject as 'soft skills', but they are of no lesser importance as they can impair the course of negotiations. He had urged this to be taken into consideration at the negotiations. This is described as an expression of cultural understanding in the literature on the subject:

> In such studies, balance-of-power calculations and considerations of nations' interest are the key to understanding interactions among nations, and there is little room in such a 'realist' (or 'rational actor') analysis for 'soft' or 'irrational' factors like ideals, visions, or prejudices… All realities in a way are imagined realities, products of forces and movements that are mediated through human consciousness.[448]

The Geographic and Geopolitical Positions

Seeckt believed that the geographic position was also affected by specific geopolitical conditions. These conditions had to be linked to Germany's foreign policy and taken into consideration by that policy to enable protection against a sudden attack to be successfully provided:

> Germany's overarching political objective is more alienated from the concept of attack today than ever before, yet it has the keenest interest in preserving its military security vis-à-vis attacks from the west and east, for its geographic position has on the whole remained the same, but worsened in specific respects).[449]

The geostrategic worth of a country was determined by its geographic, its continental position and by geopolitical factors such as who its neighbours were. An infrastructure that was both poor and unsuited for the employment of heavy tanks and a region rich in mountains or rivers would influence the choice of an ally and at the same time mitigate the people's sense of intimidation.[450] The geographic conditions could increase a country's worth as a potential ally for a neighbouring country. Besides its geographic position, natural resources such as minerals could influence alliance policy and thus the choice of allies.[451]

> The worth of a state as an ally is expressed most easily in its number of battalions and cannons, then in its geographic position in relation to a hypothetical enemy and in the concurrence of economic or political objectives.[452]

Depending on the territorial and geographic features of a country, mountains and rivers constituted natural obstacles that further increased its worth as a potential ally. The improvement of civilian and military infrastructure also had to be taken into consideration in cases where motorised means of transport would be used in a war.[453] From the geographic point of view, a country's regional and territorial features made it unique, for they not only determined the people's sense of security, but also had to be taken into account if a country had to defend itself.

Seeckt considered Germany's central geographic position to be a vital reason for the country to pursue an alliance policy. Alliance policy was valuable for a country that was in a central geographic position; even it did not want to pursue a policy of war.

Commerce

In 1932, Seeckt gave a lecture entitled: '*Deutschland und Europa* (Germany and Europe)'.[454] In it, he primarily broached the political situation in specific European states and in North America, making particular reference to their economic and foreign policies. Seeckt made a distinction between the continents of Europe and Asia and the USA. His next step was to separate the European region from the American. He believed that there had been a rapprochement between the countries of modern Europe of the past century through diplomatic and commercial channels until World War I broke out. He noted that progress had been made in the nineteenth century in a commercial and political rapprochement between all the European states. This positive development had produced a balance of power with a

> tendency towards a rise in understanding and cooperation in the commercial and colonial sectors, but without precluding healthy and natural competition between the various nations.[455]

All this had been conducive to Europe's development in the past century. However, the geographic position of a country in Europe, its history, culture and economic system had also influenced the internal and external development of Europe. Germany's central position had gained in political and commercial influence in the past century. At the same time, its economic growth and political influence had been eyed with suspicion by its neighbours. Germany's rise was first viewed with anxiety over its 'expansionist intentions or intentions to achieve hegemony' and then halted by the outbreak of the First World War. One consequence of this war was that it marked the end of what Seeckt saw as an overall positive development in Europe.[456]

Developments in Germany had taken an unfavourable turn over the past decade.[457] In the years following the First World War, Seeckt saw the political ambitions of certain countries as elements of uncertainty for Germany's borders, in particular as far as France and Poland, the immediate neighbours in the west and east, were concerned. He believed that these uncertain relations would force Germany to recognize the relevance of an alliance policy or the necessity of finding an ally. However, the intention was to prevent this and ensure that Germany became 'the erstwhile strong ally no more.'[458]

The post First World War generation experienced 'fresh political antagonisms' in Europe. There were 'fresh economic struggles which were conducted with all the more trenchancy for they affected the sheer existence of each single state'.[459] Commerce and newly prospering societies determined the socio–political relations and development of their countries and thus of Europe. The military defeat and the Treaty of Versailles were not only meant to bring about a detrimental development in politics, but also an unfavourable development in commerce. In contrast to the views Seeckt held in 1918, when he had still been open-minded about alliance policy, he rejected it in 1932. He considered Germany's accession to the League of Nations a politically disadvantageous decision. He thought that the idea of international reconciliation was like 'an insurance institution for securing the victor's successes and suppressing the defeated and weak'.[460] Seeckt posed the question of how Germany could find a way out of what was a messy situation for the country. He saw economic recovery as the solution. He believed that it could be achieved through political cooperation in Europe and through the reduction of 'France's absolute political and economic preponderance.'[461] The political calming of Germany, the securing of order in the country, was only achievable if there was an economic upswing.

> The existing economic interdependence and the necessity of all to work together for the common weal will only be recognised when the principle of mutual cheating and the preponderance of one power are renounced.[462]

Seeckt judged the foreign policies of France and Poland to be directed against Germany's sovereignty. He believed that both countries were trying to prevent other European states from cooperating with Germany on an equal footing. With their political cooperation, they caused both short- and long-term damage to Germany in the commercial sector and at the level of foreign and domestic policy. Seeckt's view had little to do with Germany having a policy of war objective and a plan for the conquest of Central Europe. It was the analysis of Germany's weak economic development and, as a consequence, precarious political development that highlighted his rejection of the idea of placing priority solely on foreign policy. Furthermore, he pleaded for a trustful co-operation in commerce as the basis of prosperity.

Post-War Economic Systems and Ideology

Despite the world economic crisis, which had been ongoing since 1929, he held the opinion that capitalism would prevail as an economic system. He believed that while economic fluctuations would recur and hamper the development of capitalism and its economic principles, the communist system would not spread. He did not let himself be infected by the general fear of communism on the domestic front:

> Capitalism will remain the economic foundation of civilization, albeit in a modified form, and the ideas of Bolshevism will not be the ones that rule the world … Yet there is no denying that the Eastern economic tendencies may spread further, and it is easily possible that Europe as a whole or in part will have to go through heavy fighting against the new economic system.[463]

Seeckt saw the two ideologies, capitalism and communism, as the new economic antagonisms of Europe. Even so, it appears that he considered neither the political unrest in Germany a sufficient hindrance, nor the ideological antagonisms towards the East a sufficient danger for Western civilisation, its culture and values.

He showed even less tendency to associate himself with the 'hysterical panic' in some circles and regarded the duration and effect of the communist ideology in Europe as short and meagre.[464] But Seeckt thought in terms of periods and developments which went beyond those of his generation: 'We should guard against even rating the importance of phenomena such as Bolshevism higher than the perpetual laws of geopolitical conditions.'[465] For him, the communist ideology, which would be overtaken by the economic and geopolitical developments in Europe, was a momentary occurrence. Like President de Gaulle of France later, he was one of those figures who put the ideological dimension and its influence on politics into perspective. While the 'concept of Bolshevism' constituted an internal danger, which had hitherto been the cause of many uprisings, it could not be fended off by military measures. It could only be countered by civic education in the army.[466]

In his lecture on 'Germany and Europe (*Deutschland und Europa*)', Seeckt expressed his conviction that Germany suffered most under the economic and political conditions of the day. Since the conclusion of the Treaty of Versailles, the reparations payments and the 'loss of its colonies', it had been unable to achieve economic growth. Internal instability was only one consequence of the Treaty of Versailles. The country was in the grip of economic downturn. By contrast, Seeckt reckoned that a prosperous state was a guarantor for peace in Europe. Not only did he think that a 'totally unfounded anxiety *vis-à-vis* Germany's alleged intentions to seek to expand or to achieve hegemony' existed, but he also believed that this anxiety was merely a means to an end for others. He believed that their objective was to bring about Germany's military and economic decline. With respect to the consequences of these economic and disarmament policies in Germany, he hoped that a political awareness process would set in at the international level and that

> perhaps the only benefit of this economic catastrophe [would be] that the rest of the world begins to appreciate the situation and to pose themselves the question of whether Germany's ruin is in the interest of the rest of Europe and the whole world.[467]

Seeckt went on to reiterate his assessment and said that France was responsible for Germany's economic weakening.

But he not only said that economic policy in Europe had the consequences stated. He believed that France was pursuing a further objective: he expressed the view that it was not just aiming to weaken Germany economically, politically and militarily, but that the economic policy, which was primarily implemented by France, yet pursued in concert with other nations, was being used as a means to secure politico-economic hegemony in Europe. He said that this hegemony had not only led to the highly unstable political situation in Germany, but also to the new economic struggles in Europe. The consequences were already being felt throughout Europe. For a

> reshaping of Europe on the basis of sound political, economic and geographic aspects ... it would be necessary to not hamper the evolution of the freshly created circumstances artificially, and to render recovery impossible. Whilst superiority is recklessly exploited and the natural rebellion against such an abuse constitutes the essence of European policy, an economic upswing, the prerequisite of which is political pacification, is unthinkable.[468]

In December 1918, he had said that economic recovery could not be achieved in a politically powerless country.[469] His view had not changed much by 1930. Even in 1930, he maintained that not only a militarily strong, but also an economically strong country defined European policy and secured peace.

The Right of Self-Defence

The general advice given by Seeckt was that in the event of the threat of a war of aggression, the order for military mobilization should be issued to protect Germany's territorial borders, but added that the 100,000-man army permitted under the restrictive conditions of the peace treaty would not be sufficient for this.[470] He quickly became aware of this fact due to Polish incursions and began making secret preparations for the protection of the border as early as January 1921.[471] He had no illusions about the military weaknesses. Seeckt warned against the pursuit of an overt, offensive-orientated military policy as the Reichswehr was cut off from all the latest technical assets such as heavy artillery, tanks and aircraft.[472]

The idea of a war of aggression being started by Germany was and remained inconceivable because of the restrictive requirements. In

1922, Seeckt had addressed France's foreign policy, which he believed constituted a threat to Germany, in a presentation to the members of the cabinet. All he could advance was that in the event of an attack, Germany had the right to defend itself. In view of the armament situation in Europe, he drew the following conclusion from the necessity of the 'right to defend our borders':

> The states allied with France and surrounding Germany maintain armies in peacetime that, together, are twelve times stronger than the German Army. It has been reduced to an eighth of its pre-war strength. None of the powers that faced Germany in the war has reduced its armament on anything like a comparable scale.[473]

He invoked the right of self-defence guaranteed by international law in the event of a hostile attack, the crossing of the German border: 'A ban on the aversion of hostile acts with arms would not find justified support in any historic event, nor in any provision of international law'.[474]

Whilst, in 1922, he dwelt on the event of an attack from the angle of the right of self-defence, he at the same time rejected the idea of the Reichswehr taking rash or independent military action.[475] He considered the military attack an act that had no prospect of success from the outset, especially since Germany's central geographic position appeared to be threatened by many strong neighbours.[476]

The issue of clarifying how the right of self-defence should be interpreted and applied in practice became topical when French troops occupied the Ruhr region in January 1923.

Germany's Foreign Policy during the 1923 Ruhr Crisis

Military conflicts, whether local or trans-regional, can be triggered by different cultural, territorial, ethnic, religious or ideological interests. They can clash when only one of any two states believes that its political interests are not sufficiently respected by another state or party. When it comes to resolving a conflict, a state is bound by its system of government and by its constitution. It will seek to manage the conflict in the way these institutions permit it to. Its foreign policy and diplomatic relations can be of key help. Other factors such as party-political orientation, ideology, religion, history and culture are directly or indirectly part of the process of resolving a conflict. The way a nation reaches a decision is also a manifestation of its culture.[477] These factors not only write the story of a country, but also determine its culture and history. Other factors that influence a country are its climate, geography, territorial borders and neighbouring states. All these factors play an important part in understanding what kind of conflict has arisen and in resolving it. It is always recommendable to take account of these aspects when a military strategy concept is being prepared. It is equally important that the military can act on the authority of the political heads and their political objectives and interests when faced with military problems. This requires clearly formulated guidance from the political heads.

Seeckt integrated some of the factors listed here into his military strategy. He above all considered the continental focus and the historical development of a country influencing factors.[478] He also held the view that, besides clashes of geographic and economic interests, a sense of intimidation could trigger a conflict.[479]

Seeckt was notably faced with the political challenge of not only presenting a military strategy concept, but of acting in accordance with it in January 1923, when French troops marched into the Ruhr region. The German government was confronted with the occupation of the Ruhr region because of its failure to fulfil its annual payment and reparation obligations. Instead of delivering 13.86 million tons of coal in 1922, Germany supplied France only 11.7 million tons. The German government also failed to make further payments of arrears to the French government.[480] By ordering the occupation of the Ruhr region, French political leadership wanted to collect the debt themselves. The German ambassador in Paris at the time held the view that France was dependent on the deliveries. The French government had run up a high budget deficit of over 340 billion French francs, and it rose by a further 40 billion francs a year due to the absence of fresh revenue. The German coal deliveries were one way of avoiding having to impose new taxes in France.[481] The reparations had failed to come in since 1922 and added to the rise in tax losses. The occupation of the Ruhr region apparently offered the French government the possibility of easing the financial situation.[482]

The German Chancellor interpreted France's policy as a policy of aggression. He accused the French government of covering their policy of power with a veneer of justification, of attempting to stir up the neighbours in the east against Germany and of trying to create an unstable situation in Germany.[483] Chancellor Cuno saw France's attempt to become the dominant power in Central Europe as its overarching political interest.[484] The German Foreign Minister even spoke of France pursuing a 'policy of force'.[485] Despite the ensuing tensions, the German Foreign Office explained to the German ambassadors in London, Washington, Rome, The Hague and Copenhagen that Germany would be 'purely passive and absolutely non-aggressive'.[486] That was it. At no point in time did the German government consider using military power. For Seeckt this meant acting 'in concert with the Reich government'.[487]

In January 1923, Germany's foreign policy was primarily geared to preserving the country's territorial borders. The Reich government expected France to leave the area it had occupied. The German government protested against the French government's policy of occupation in several official notes. It went on to attempt to win over other nations as mediators. Yet the German government's letters of protest met with little support in diplomatic circles due to the lost war and the weak economy. It broke off diplomatic relations with France, calling back its ambassador from Paris.[488] It otherwise confined itself to issuing appeals to the German people.

The Reich government discussed its actions against the French government under two criteria: it sought to enforce its view that the occupation was an act committed in violation of international law and endeavoured to promote passive resistance among the people and to provide it moral and financial support.[489] At the same time, the Reich Chancellor had to guard against the danger of unemployment rising in the occupied region. He secured financial support from industry. With its help, the government-initiated defensive resistance among the people lasted eight months, from January to September 1923.[490] The socio-political cost of this appeal (which was increased by unemployment, loss of production and the separatist NSDAP [Nationalsozialistische Deutsche Arbeiterpartei] movement) caused a huge financial loss. The consequences were profound and lasting. The 'swastika movement', the national socialist wave, had rallied against the government and been able to canvass for their political aims in a sustained manner.[491]

In the further course of events, the government had to clarify whether the peacetime occupation was permissible under a treaty. France would have had to invoke the Treaty of Versailles to settle the issue. If the answer was no and the Treaty did not contain such a clause, the occupation could have only been an enforced one.[492] Accordingly, the Reich Chancellor, on 12 January 1923, accused the French government of acting unlawfully, substantiating his charges with the assertion that the Treaty of Versailles did not contain any such paragraph which permitted a military occupation. He said that the French government's action had required to be examined with the other signatories to the Treaty in advance and approved unanimously. While it was right that Germany had to make repayments, the French government was only allowed to repeatedly request that the payments be made, and then in cash only.[493] The Reich government considered the invasion by French troops, which were deployed on 11 January and accompanied by an engineer commission, a violation of its political, economic and financial interests.

The French government did not consider the occupation of German Reich territory a military invasion. It justified the occupation with the claim that it wanted to collect the outstanding payments directly and locally.

Seeckt had concerned himself with matters of defence in response to hostile border crossings since 1920. In 1922, he wrote his position paper 'on issues of national defence'. In April 1923, Seeckt delivered a presentation to members of the cabinet he had prepared in March of that year. He presented his interpretation of the right of self-defence. Prompted by the invasion by the French troops, he outlined the military capabilities, options and his personal view of the matter.[494] In his deliberations, he made neither direct mention of the current political problems nor indirect mention of the French government's motives for the occupation of German territory. He defined the military interests which he believed Germany had to safeguard in general terms and with reference to the military clauses of the Treaty of Versailles. He subsumed them in three categories and deduced the current threat to German interests from them. He said that the German government had met all the demands since the Treaty of Versailles had been signed and complied with all the requirements for demobilisation. The requirement to reduce the armed forces to 100,000 men had been met in full and further demands over and above the terms agreed, such as ammunition limitations and the razing of fortifications, were met. Seeckt took this as a basis for deriving political objectives for the German government. He advised it to safeguard its rights and reject any military claims that exceeded the terms of the Treaty. He justified this by pointing to the military build-up being undertaken by the neighbouring states. He said that the current situation in those countries constituted a permanent threat for Germany.[495] In his comments, he stated that Germany also had the right of self-defence, declaring it a vested right under international law.

He differentiated between the terms self-defence and mobilization. He first addressed the ban on mobilisation laid down in the Treaty of Versailles and then moved on to the right of self-defence:

> The question that it should be made impossible for Germany to wage a war of aggression was fully supported, while the question of whether Germany had the right to defend its borders and its rights remained open or, rather, it had to be answered in the affirmative as a guarantee to respect Germany's borders was neither given nor intended to be. After all, the French chamber negotiations in the autumn of 1919 provide quite a clear picture. The right of military self-defence had to be accepted on principle.[496]

Seeckt demanded that Germany should initiate political and military border defence measures to counter the occupation of its territory by enemy troops. Militarily and politically, 'the right of defence – self-defence – had to be conferred as a matter of principle ..., this implies the right to prepare for this self-defence'.[497] In rejection of the occupation in the spring of 1923, he held the view that it was possible to observe the Treaty of Versailles while making preparations to protect the borders.

> Applied to the present case, it follows that Germany has the right to make all the preparations for this self-defence which are not

explicitly prohibited by the Treaty of Versailles ... as otherwise Germany would acknowledge the one-sided interpretation of the terms by the opposite side, which, as demonstrated above, intends to expand the term disarmament, that is to say, the destruction of the offensive power, into that of defencelessness. This endeavour must be rejected and a state's right of self-defence and of making preparations for it must be acknowledged. Above all, any expansion of the term 'mobilisation' must be rejected.[498]

These were hair-splitting statements, since all military measures were regulated in the Treaty of Versailles. A defence could only have been prepared in secret. Activities for a secret border defence to guard against Polish border violations had been ongoing since January 1921 in the form of passive resistance and had been reinforced *vis-à-vis* the West in agreement with the government.[499]

In his speech to members of the cabinet in April 1923, Seeckt advised the government 'to anxiously mind its right to reject demands that go beyond the Treaty'.[500] All the terms of the Treaty of Versailles had been fulfilled, while compensations had not been provided. The 'justification given for the disarmament demand in the Treaty [of Versailles] itself [was] not respected ...: The general limitation on the armament of all the nations.'[501] Non-compliance of a unilateral treaty resulted in a breach by both parties to the treaty.

Seeckt said that the disparity in Europe with regard to arms, the unilaterally enforced disarmament of Germany, inevitably strengthened its right of self-defence. In his very military strategy, he had emphasised that 'the strongest inducement to war ... [was] a defenceless neighbour'.[502] The occupation of the Ruhr region confirmed his words. Yet, even in this case, it was the political heads who decided whether and, if so, what military measures were to be imposed in 1923. Their implementation lay in the 'dutiful discretion of the German government'.[503] Seeckt believed that the secret self-defence preparations were legitimate, while he neither demanded nor wished for a forthright policy of aggression.[504]

In his military strategy, he expressed the view: 'Starting out from the Army, it can be said that its strength will decide the question of whether the political heads can factor the ultima ratio, war, into their calculations with any prospect of success.'[505] However, the German government was not in a position to mount either a political or a military attack, let alone hold its country's borders. Germany could not even work for an alliance policy aimed at protecting the country against incursions at that time. The demand for 'participation in treaties and agreements and in deliberations on them' was justified. [506] It was not possible for Germany to defend its interests either militarily or by means of power politics.

Given the foreign and military policy situation, Seeckt considered it reckless to initiate a war of aggression or a war of defence. He was in no way prepared to take military action without the consent of the government.[507] After the end of his active service, he once again addressed Germany's situation and its right of self-defence. He admitted that Germany would at no time have been able to exercise the right of self-defence.[508]

It was particularly due to the foreign and military policy situation that Seeckt did not call for Germany to pursue a policy of expansion and war. He wanted to see the establishment of a German border defence, but it could not apparently be guaranteed in 1923 on account of the current strength.

Seeckt's Orientation towards the East and his Policy of Alliance with the USSR

In 1918, Seeckt believed that two basic requirements should be 'a matter of course' for Germany, though neither was to be met in the Weimar Republic: Germany's integration into European alliance policy, and its attainment of equal rights in negotiations.[509] Despite the lost war, Seeckt did not yet assume in 1918 that there could be antagonism from within between Europe and Germany. The purpose of membership in a community of nations was to ensure the security of a country's borders. Military power was a means to sponsor admittance to an alliance. It remained the task of the political heads to establish the foundations from which the country would become 'capable of being an ally' and thus become an 'attractive ally'.[510] In April 1919, Seeckt still believed that it was possible to establish these foundations:

What I mean by help is not soldiers, but bread and butter, raw materials and jobs, an army of one's own and, not least, a national identity. There is still the chance that the pursuit of a reasonable policy by the enemy could give us all that, and his terms could well be hard without taking our lives.[511]

He expected Germany to back its capability to be an ally by building up a military instrument.[512] The plan for a League of Nations offered it the possibility to play an active role in an international alliance. In February 1919, he presented his idea in more specific terms. An internationally recognised government would only be able to establish security through its army.

> The government needs a standing army to govern. The strength of this standing army will be dictated to us by the peace treaty. It will further depend on our materiel power. Within these limits, everyone who still grants us international recognition should wish the standing army to be as large as possible. This has nothing to do with foreign policy objectives and principles ... our political business is conducted by men who insist, not just endure, not one of them will consider a strong army to be detrimental to the policy he pursues.[513]

As early as in 1919, he made the use of the army dependent on a policy and the government that pursued it: 'National policy determines the use that is made of the army: if it is bad, the wrong use will be made of the army; if it is a good policy, the right use will be made of the Army).'[514] In his February 1919 blueprint for the future organisational structure of the army, at the peace negotiations in Spa and also later, Seeckt considered a strength of 200,000 troops appropriate.[515] He reckoned that six years of service were sufficient for the rank and file, while senior officers should serve for longer.[516] He thought that this was adequate to satisfy the requirements of national defence and allow sovereign foreign and alliance policies to be supported. When the Treaty of Versailles was signed, it became clear that Seeckt's hopes for equal rights, the build-up of an armed force and thus becoming an equal partner in Europe were shattered. The German Reich was isolated and left without a political ally. The Reichswehr was cut off from the developments in advanced heavy equipment (tanks, heavy artillery, aircraft). In view of the disarmament, the ban on tanks, heavy artillery and a state-of-the-art air force, this meant 'no air forces for Germany' at the time and certainly not only for Seeckt.[517] On the subject of the military requirements concerning the length of service of non-commissioned officers defined in the Treaty of Versailles, he remarked in a laconic undertone: 'A non-terminable twelve-year contract is a novelty in the labour market.'[518]

Because of Germany's difficult geopolitical position, which resulted from its central geostrategic position in Europe and the recent socio-political challenges, Seeckt had, from 1920 until his retirement, advised a balanced policy to be pursued *vis-à-vis* the East and the West. He deemed it crucial for Germany's foreign policy to be geared to the whole of Europe. His assessment was based on the assumption that Germany would have to take care not to be crushed by the national interests of other states owing to its central geostrategic position between the East and West. It would have to develop a policy *vis-à-vis* its neighbours in the East and West that was not geared to just one side and so was a unilateral commitment. On account of Germany's position in central Europe, the political heads would be well-advised to cultivate their contacts with both sides.[519] A balanced alliance policy would take account of Germany's geopolitical and geostrategic positions:

> Germany belongs to the West and East because of its geographic position. This can be to our disadvantage as well as to our advantage, and has worked to our advantage previously. In the end, the geopolitical factors are the crucial ones ... Germany cannot deny that it has a long border with Eastern Europe. This border, greater in length and importance, was once a German-Russian one – that harmed Germany because it was caught between two fires, when it antagonised Russia unnecessarily over its policies, without being able to form an alliance with the West. All the same, this closeness of the two nations, which another constellation could have easily united, remained a threat to the Western powers, which, as a precaution, edged in the new states, of whose anti-Germanism they could certainly be convinced ... This is how the problem of Russia and us is caused, and it can never disappear from our policy. As a consequence of the conditions in Russia, the problem has gained

momentum, and this makes it much more difficult to deal with at present, and yet we should take care not to put the importance of even contemporary phenomena such as Bolshevism before the permanent laws of geopolitical conditions ... The task to be solved is to safeguard the German nationhood, placed as it is between the West and East, neither by siding against Russia to sink as low as to become, along with Poland, a western colony dependent on the Anglo-Saxons or on France, nor by becoming dependent on Russia in a situation where we might be threatened with an attack by the Western powers first and on our own, and, finally, to avoid the third danger, namely of becoming the battlefield between the East and West.[520]

Anything other than a balanced policy that was open to both sides would jeopardise Germany's position in Europe. Moreover, having a strong military instrument would underpin sovereign foreign and interest policies, since it would protect Germany, in its central geopolitical and geostrategic positions in Europe, against incursions. However, political relations that in Seeckt's view were maintained as a result of a one-sided political orientation and neglected national interests *vis-à-vis* the other side would in time weaken Germany's position in Europe. Germany would degenerate into a 'Western colony' because the power of the West European nations would force it to assume a one-sided attitude towards the East. At the same time, Germany should avoid becoming dependent on the USSR. That would simply offer the West possibilities for launching political attacks. Finally, at worst, Germany might become the 'battlefield between the East and West'.[521]

The military isolation and enfeeblement, which in the opinion of Seeckt were what France was aiming to attain, remained in place for him during his period of service. From an early point, Seeckt believed that the isolation could be overcome by means of military cooperation with the Red Army.[522] On account of the peace treaty, he sought a secret form of cooperation. The first contacts were established in 1920 and maintained until 1933.[523] The conclusion of the Treaty of Rapallo in April 1922 provided Germany further options. The agreement with the USSR offered the German business world and arms industry the opportunity to invest in the Soviet Union. This cleared the way for cooperation in the field of armament. The military were able to intensify their existing connections. The ally's ideology remained a negligible factor for Seeckt not only in theory, but also while the cooperation continued.[524] Nonetheless, he warned the military of the implications of his own military policy: 'No foreign policy advantage can make up for the damage caused by internal Bolshevisation.'[525] In order to cope with the foreign policy obligations of establishing a military defence and to win and retain the USSR as an ally, Seeckt demanded that the military should distinguish between 'conditions in Germany and any attempt to allow Bolshevist objectives to find their way in.'[526]

In the years that followed, Seeckt undertook the balancing act of engaging in military cooperation with the USSR while rejecting its ideology. 'The only way for Germany to be steered through the present dangers is for it to assert itself against the Entente and Bolshevism, and to do so in strict neutrality vis-à-vis the two.'[527] However, this by no means meant he himself was neutral vis-à-vis the nations of the Entente. As he took security into his reckoning, he distinguished between the expansionism of communist ideology and Germany's interests.[528] Since 1921, he had on the one hand pushed for military cooperation and on the other successfully used daily routine orders to avoid communist ideas finding their way into the Reichsheer. He had to assume that communism aimed at abolishing the republican constitution of the Republic of Weimar. And he considered France and Poland the countries which aimed at weakening Germany economically and militarily. His rejection of communism was a result of the security situation in Europe. The rejection of communism did not in his view justify an alliance with Poland and/or France either, as he believed that such a move would not result in military cooperation between Germany and the other European armies. Germany's establishment of a power base of its own was more important to him, and the question of whether it was because he pursued a 'policy of war' or enabling Germany to defend its own borders remains to be examined.

He hoped that the USSR would be an ally against France and Poland.[529] The view that it was not the USSR, but France and Poland that constituted the external threat to Germany may have reinforced his intention to enter into some form of military cooperation with the USSR. He also believed that the USSR would be an ally against Poland and that the Poles would see Germany as their primary enemy rather than the USSR. As far as he was concerned, France and Poland pursued the aim of weakening Germany economically and politically. This may have strengthened his resolve to take the path of secretly cooperating with the Red Army.[530] He was convinced that Russia would focus more in its foreign policy on the East, Persia and far-away Afghanistan. 'In the far East, Russia will soon ... take on its role as a bulwark against the yellow people.' If this reckoning was right, however, it would mean that the USSR would not be moving in a 'detrimental direction' for Germany. He concluded that 'all the causes of friction and antagonisms between us and Russia [would be] gone.'[531] He analysed Stalin's five-year plan, recognised the danger of a future military build-up, and considered that the government was 'peaceful in order to buy time'. Nonetheless, his advice was to maintain contact with the USSR: 'It is better to assist Russian industry politically and industrially than to leave this to others, than to make an enemy of the Russians.'[532] Besides military and strategic aspects, politico–economic assessments were at the centre of his political view on the geostrategic position of Germany.

In his attitude towards Germany's foreign policy, Seeckt had drawn attention to the necessity of openness towards both the East and the West. As he had called for Germany to pursue a balanced policy towards either side, these demands were added as factors in his thoughts on military strategy, amid considerations of the country's geographic and geopolitical positions. He needed the secret cooperation for two reasons. He intended to train the army in the use of the prohibited weapons in order to enhance Germany's future defence of its borders. And he attempted to turn the Reichswehr into a cadre army for a 200,000-man force that would strengthen Germany's position in Europe. In Seeckt's view, Germany as a possible future power had too many fronts, too many strong neighbours and should preferably aspire to form an alliance.

Military Cooperation with the Red Army

The decline of Tsarist Russia had begun in 1917 before the November Revolution in Germany in 1918. The old Tsarist army was destroyed by the revolutionary leaders. The Council of the People's Deputies issued a decree laying down the establishment of the Red Army and the introduction of conscription. The army was to be made up mainly of peasants, workers and partisans from the previous war.

In Germany, the soldiers' councils held a share in military power for a short while in 1919. With respect to developments in the two countries, Lenin commented 'that it will not be long before we are marching side by side with a German councils' government'.[533] Both German and Soviet intermediaries campaigned for the establishment and maintenance of contacts between the new Soviet Russia and the Reichswehr. One of their better-known representatives was Karl Radek, a close associate of Trotsky and people's commissar in the USSR.[534] Karl Radek maintained contact with the German soldiers' councils and mixed with military and political circles in Germany. He was considered a driving force on the Soviet side. He believed that the connections were useful for both sides and continually tried to expand them.[535]

On the German military side, Oskar Ritter von Niedermayer, Major Herbert Fischer (Seeckt's adjutant), Major Fritz Tschunke, Major von Schubert and Colonel Hasse made their mark.[536]

In spite or because of the rapprochement, Seeckt warned against ideological indoctrination and both rash and arbitrary action:

The Russian victory over Poland has stirred up the mood and hope, which now threaten to blur the clear guidelines of the Reichswehr. It has particularly revived the idea that Germany could evade the Treaty of Versailles only by rushing into the arms of communism and, powered by this idea and the Russian Army's advance through Poland, could start a fresh war against the Entente. I cannot warn explicitly enough against such trains of thought. The Red Army owes its great successes against Poland, as even Radek admits, to a national spark borne by an old popular hatred for which the Polish resistance was no match.[537]

In the following years, Seeckt ventured to walk the line between cooperation with the class enemy at the military training level and rejection of the communist ideology of the USSR at the military policy level.[538] He informed the German military of this ambitious objective and advised them of what they had to bear in mind:

> If we wish to enter a friendly economic exchange with Russia ... we will have to approach her as a united nation and very strongly reject international Bolshevism. This requires absolute order at home and a ruthless fight against revolution.[539]

The Special Group R (*SondergruppeR* (R= Russia)) was established in 1920.[540] Assigned to the Truppenamt ('Troop Office'), Special Group R was integrated into Division T3. Schubert had been one of the first members of staff of Special Group R at the Reichswehr Ministry under Colonel Hasse since 1921.[541] The division 'dealt with basic issues concerning the cooperation of the two armies'.[542] Besides Herbert Fischer, his former adjutant, and von Schubert, Seeckt assigned other officers to work in this field and to cooperate with the Junkers company.[543] On 11 November 1921, a German-Russian airline (*Deruluft*) was established, one half of its capital shares being provided by the German armed forces and the other by the Red Army. Another contract was concluded between Junkers and the Soviet Union in the spring of 1923. The construction of aircraft was agreed. One German-Russian corporation, by the name of *Bersol*, was founded for the purpose of manufacturing poison gas, and another for that of producing artillery ammunition.[544] In 1925, former fighter pilots attended the first refresher courses after the First World War. By 1926, the first young Reichswehr officers had completed the new fighter pilot training.[545] In February 1926, a farming equipment company was founded to develop and produce materiel for a chemical air war.[546]

Military equipment was developed and tested with the help of the officers detached by the Army High Command to Fili a Moscow suburb. The personnel contributed their knowledge. In turn, they were trained in the Soviet Union in the use of some equipment prohibited under the Treaty of Versailles. In 1925, Red Army officers for the first time took part in Reichswehr army manoeuvres. In the autumn of 1926, Red Army general staff officers underwent principal staff assistant training.[547]

When it became increasingly clear that the Western powers were disassociating themselves from Germany, in a move intended to render Germany defenceless, Seeckt obtained the consent of the leading government parties and the Reich Chancellor in spite of the Treaty of Versailles. Seeckt justified his maverick moves concerning the cooperation with the arms industry in Russia by stating that this would allow the Reichswehr to enhance its operational capability. Although he initially acted in concert with the government, he bypassed the President of the Republic, Friedrich Ebert. It was only some time later, on 6 December 1922, that Seeckt informed the Reich President of the ongoing negotiations.[548] Ebert mistrusted the Kremlin leaders. His deep-seated anti-Bolshevism would have allowed him to approve neither the unauthorized actions of his Reich Chancellors, Cuno and Wirth, and of the Chief of the Army Command nor the conclusion of the Treaty of Rapallo. 'There was inner resistance, not least on the part of Ebert and the Social Democratic Party of Germany (SPD), and the attempted communist coup of March 1921 reinforced his concerns further.'[549]

Seeckt emphasized the advantages of the cooperation. He said that it would yield economic and foreign policy advantages for Germany.[550] He did not see any domestic danger in the cooperation. 'Germany will not be bolshevised, not even by way of accommodation on external issues'.[551] He hoped that the strengthening of the military would increase Germany's political power.

In the initial stages of the cooperation, Seeckt could still hope to find an ally. In December 1922, Trotsky let the German ambassador to Moscow, Brockdorff-Rantzau, know this: 'Should Poland, at the behest of France, attack Silesia at the same time, we will under no circumstances stand idly by; we cannot tolerate that and will intervene.'[552] The French invasion of the Ruhr region in January 1923 in Seeckt's view confirmed the assumption that the French had not only intended to weaken Germany militarily.[553] The French invasion had removed the government's remaining doubts which had accompanied the German-Russian cooperation. The business contacts became even closer, and the Reichswehr was granted a higher budget.[554] The Association for the Promotion of Business Enterprises established in the summer of 1923, intensified its connections with the Reichswehr Ministry.[555] Army Command staff were assigned to the association for the purpose of issuing instructions and orders for military projects.[556]

Events took a favourable turn for the Reichswehr, for the executive power was transferred to Reichswehr Minister Gessler by Reichs-President Ebert in view of the eruption of civil unrest in September 1923. Seeckt worked to intensify the cooperation, saying that while 'Communists in Germany [should] be strangled, Germany [had to] associate with the Soviet Union'.[557]

The military interests, which were initially defended mainly by the private company Junckers and limited to the construction and operation of aircraft, were expanded. Yet, there was only little technical progress. Until September 1926, the Junkers work in Fili was more like an assembly facility than a production facility.[558] By 1927, 170 aircraft had been built with the involvement of Junkers' support. Nonetheless, the 73 aircraft delivered to the Soviet Union in December 1924 did not comply with what had been agreed in the contracts in respect of maximum altitudes, speeds, load capacities and weights.[559] Despite the limited capabilities, the Reichswehr Ministry in 1924 ordered 100 Fokker fighter aircraft, the initial 50 of which were delivered to Germany in 1925. They were tested during military exercises, and a total of 120 fighter pilots and 100 aircraft spotters were trained on them.[560] In 1927, Gessler assumed that the number had been higher and publicly announced after Seeckt's retirement that the annual number of aircraft built during Seeckt's term in office was 300, of which 200 were intended for Germany and 100 for Russia.[561]

In the following years of cooperation, from 1922 to 1926, the Soviet Union under Stalin showed no willingness to come to their partner's defence in the event of an attack by the Entente. The Soviet Union estimated that Germany, 'due to its hopeless armament situation, [was] currently far too weak and its military situation too desperate' to be capable of forming an alliance with the Soviet Union. Moscow's counterproposition was:

We must first become strong jointly before there can be any talk of military agreements. This requires more intensive arms cooperation, with the German representatives, as a first prerequisite, having to name a definite sum of money with which they are prepared to embark on restoring the fallow Russian arms industry.[562]

So Seeckt had not won an ally.

In the summer of 1926, when Seeckt was still in office, the German Army Ordnance Office (*Heereswaffenamt*) planned, under the direction of Major General Max Ludwig, to buy artillery guns produced in the Soviet Union. These guns were marked as having been manufactured in 1896 to 1916. Krupp had once produced and delivered them for the Tsar. The German military were quite unconcerned about purchasing fully obsolete arms. They were prepared to pay the inflated price for the weapons. The real problem was the production of ammunition for these old weapons. Disclosures in the German press were made just at the right time and forced the Reich Defence Ministry to issue a denial.[563] The deal was called off. Some time later, the Reich Defence Ministry arranged a successful transaction for ammunition that had been manufactured at the Russian works in Tula and Zlatoust. In 1926/27, 4,500 tons of artillery ammunition were purchased and stored in clandestine arms depots in East Prussia and Stettin.[564]

Germany's orientation towards the East slowly came to an end as three political developments appeared to render it superfluous. The negotiations in Locarno, which were taken up in October 1925 by Great Britain, France, Italy, Belgium and Germany and concluded in December 1925 with a satisfactory outcome for Germany, resulted in a reduction of the occupation forces, the withdrawal from the remaining areas along the Ruhr river, a solution for the Saar issue and the final closure of the Military Inter-Allied Commission of Control. Much of this was owed to German Foreign Minister Gustav Stresemann, a deputy of the German People's Party.[565] It was now in the interest of the government of the German Reich to devote more attention to the Western powers. In 1926, this reorientation was rewarded with membership of the League of Nations. Germany's foreign policy towards the USSR in the military domain became more reserved and pragmatic. The Soviets saw Germany's admittance to the League of Nations as a violation of their interests. 'Scheidemann's Reichstag speech, in which he disclosed the existence of the GEFU organisation and its discreet activity', did its bit to end the military cooperation for good.[566] Another reason for the end of politico-military orientation towards the East was Seeckt's resignation in October 1926.[567]

After Seeckt's term in office, some of the land and naval force cooperation projects continued in various fields (poison gas production, aviation and tank development). Press publications continued to hamper any intensification of the business activity, exchange of personnel and production of defence goods.

After five years of cooperation, the later General of the Luftwaffe, Fiebig, who in March 1926 was still a major and military adviser to the Red Air Fleet, ascertained that the result was rather unsatisfactory for the Germans: 'All in all, I cannot see a worthwhile benefit resulting in the near future from our activity under the present circumstances either for the Russian side or for the German.'[568] In the original, this comment was highlighted with a double mark in the left margin of the text. The German view was that the USSR had been maintaining the contact primarily to serve its own interests, and this had not made cooperation with the USSR easy:

Experience shows that intergovernmental agreements leave room for interpretation even though their details are carefully worded. One soon learned that Soviet Russia avoids breaking them de jure, but is de facto inclined to circumvent the obligations laid down on them where this is expedient, while it at the same time stubbornly insists on these obligations being fulfilled by the other party.[569]

The German-Russian cooperation appears to have been negatively affected by continual mistrust and mutual reservations.

Like some German officers, the Soviets also estimated that the cooperation was fruitless for the Germans. In December 1926, Y.K. Berzin, chief of the fourth administration of the Red Army general staff (intelligence service), wrote to Stalin, addressing the subject of effort and cost:

Assessing the cooperation to date, we reckon that expectations have not been met on either side. We have received only partially usable equipment from the known works, equipment that could only be used if we put in a great deal of work to alter it. They used all the means available to them, disgraced themselves and used these works for their political ends.[570]

Berzin believed that 'Germany's non-compliance with the agreements …. cost the USSR valuable time in its own war production. Political damage was in particular caused by the disclosure of the grenade deliveries.'[571]

He made the attempt to calculate the costs the Germans had incurred over the years and found out how much more worth it had been to Germany than to the Soviet Union to invest in specific facilities in Russia. Berzin listed the expenditure for Tomka, where chemical tests were made, for the upkeep of the tank school at Kazan, for the aviation school at Lipetsk, for Junker's investments and for the state subsidies and other financial losses which were known, and came to the conclusion that the costs for the Reichswehr were enormously high in financial and material terms but did not match the results achieved. Nonetheless, he emphasized in his report the positive aspect that Soviet officers had taken part in manoeuvres and attended various courses (poison gas tests, tank school, pilot training). The true motive for Seeckt to continue the cooperation was in Berzin's estimate the wish to extend the training and enhance knowledge:

The Germans spend large sums of money on the planning, establishment and upkeep of the above-named enterprises; we do not know the exact amount (apart from the direct costs that incur on our territory for building work and for the sustenance of personnel, and the expenditure for equipment that has to be delivered completely from Germany must also be factored in), yet the expenditure for 'Tomka' (chemical tests) already amounts to a million Marks, the costs for the planning, establishment and maintenance of the tank school amount to over 500,000 Mark, and the costs for the school at Lipetsk – with the equipment included – amount to more than a million Marks. When we factor in the previous Reichswehr expenditure for subsidies paid to 'Junkers' for the cooperation with us and the amount of 20,000,000 Marks which the Reichswehr lost in the deal with Stolzenberg (mustard gas factories), then it must be said that the Reichswehr expenditure for the 'enterprises' in the USSR is extremely high and cannot be justified by any concrete results produced by those factories.[572]

Seeckt's main concern was the training on equipment that was not available. The success of those investments was, and this was Seeckt's intention, of qualitative worth. The fact that this worth had been far-reaching became apparent at the beginning of the Second World War, yet had begun to be 'watered down' due to the army's speedy expansion before the war.[573] Quality suffered due to the rapid recruitment of personnel who since 1935 had no longer been properly trained. The quality had been deteriorating since the establishment of the Wehrmacht and was to decline further until well into the last years of the war.[574]

For Seeckt, the purpose of cooperation was to create the foundations for Germany to be able to defend itself against France and Poland. He had ruled out Germany waging a war of aggression since 1920. He did not stop issuing warnings against any kind of 'resistance policy'. Even in 1930, he still considered any policy of military of aggression negligent:

What is needed to be able to accomplish this task is a prerequisite which we do not have at present, that of military importance and, as a consequence, significance to engage in power politics. As long as we do not have that, any decision in favour of either East or West is extremely dangerous, if not indeed impossible.[575]

If anything, he expected enemy incursions. The aim of the training was to prepare for defence: 'Germany is certainly in no position at present to put up resistance to France. Our policy is aimed at making preparations to render this a possibility in the future.'[576] He left no doubt about the objective of his military strategy, which was politically motivated and included Germany's ability to defend itself, 'it is Germany's resurrection as a power state.'[577] But his concern was to build a politically powerful state which would not distinguish itself by promoting a policy of military aggression, but whose political heads would decide the ways in which Germany's interests were to be defended. He knew that he could not cut the Gordian knot of the post-war order in Europe with the Reichswehr and did not want to.

Where the quality of the Reichswehr was concerned, he was more realistic and less imaginative of a national renaissance as a great power. Due to the assessment of the situation by German and USSR officers, Seeckt was neither inclined to believe in an 'allied war concept [*Bündniskriegskonzeption*]'[578], nor did he consider the contacts a surrogate for future great-power politics. Instead, he used a deterrent military tool to pursue a crisis prevention strategy against Poland and France.

Chapter 4

Factional Dispute over Military Strategy at the Reichswehr Ministry

Introduction

Military historians have pointed out that the Reichswehr Ministry had developed 'ideas of a war of liberation with features like those of a partisan war'.[1] Research was based on presentations given at the Reichswehr Ministry. Inconsistencies in Seeckt's personnel decisions had been noticed. It was assumed that Seeckt had posted 'minor opponents' away from the Ministry for no reason in 1925 and 1926.[2] Since 1923, however, Seeckt had met with opposition from officers who felt he had acted too passively against the state and the people since the Ruhr crisis in 1923 and especially since he had given up executive powers on 1 March 1924.[3] The aim of this chapter is therefore to clarify the question as to whether Seeckt's military strategy was in conflict with that of officers at the ministry and whether some did not agree with his politico-military approach and consequently pursued different plans. Their ideas about the 'war of the future', about a people's war and total war, will be presented in the chapter.[4] The differences between this group of general staff officers and the military strategy represented by Seeckt, the most prominent advocate of which was Lieutenant Colonel Joachim von Stülpnagel, are illustrated by means of presentations, indoor exercises and presentations given by and to officers of the Army Command of the Reichswehr Ministry.

Joachim von Stülpnagel and the Ruhr Crisis in 1923

There were fractions among the Army Command general staff officers who discussed their different ideas about a possible future war and developed them further in a way, which made them quite different from Seeckt's ideas. There was a group of general staff officers at the

Reichswehr Ministry who developed the ideas on future warfare, who were driven by the idea of a war of revenge against France and who had wilfully turned against the political leadership, against the Republic and its Constitution. Their concept was based on Ludendorff's ideas and conflicted with Seeckt's in the politico–military respect.

Joachim von Stülpnagel was one of those who had largely thought through their ideas and presented almost a ready concept for a war of liberation. During the First World War, he had served as an officer under Ludendorff. Since that time, he had described himself as 'his [Ludendorff's] follower'. He and a few other officers 'admired him [Ludendorff] and his willpower and work very much then'.[5] Stülpnagel started working for Seeckt on 1 May 1920 and was assigned the responsibility for the personnel management of the general staff officers and for the build-up of the officer corps. In this function, he accompanied Seeckt on his field visits. On 1 April 1922, this follower of Ludendorff's became chief of Army Division T I at the Truppenamt in Berlin at the Reichswehr Ministry.[6] In 1925, he was promoted to the rank of colonel and was assigned to Braunschweig. After Seeckt had been discharged, his successor, General Heye, had him posted back to the Reichswehr Ministry in Berlin in January 1927 as the director of the Army Personnel Office.[7]

As Francis Carsten has pointed out, Stülpnagel wanted to 'start a small war', a war of revenge against France aimed at achieving the cancellation of the Treaty of Versailles by force.[8] This expectation became acute when the French occupied the Ruhr region in 1923. The government's and Seeckt's reactions were too passive for his taste.[9] He wanted 'revenge' for the Treaty of Versailles. Both the political and the military authorities were to 'turn … the people's passive resistance into an active one'.[10] 'Hatred toward the enemy without' was to be fomented among the people. According to his interpretation, France was acting 'out of a sense of superiority and motivated by robbery and lucre'.[11] 'Seen from the national and military standpoint of that time,' the soldier was not allowed to fail in his mission. He was to be deployed on the very front line in the war of liberation.[12] Preparations were to be made for mobilization; the war of liberation against France was a national matter. Of course, 'all these measures …' were to be 'approved and financed by the Reich government.'[13]

Since the occupation of the Ruhr, Stülpnagel had begun to present his expectations of a future war to a wider audience of officers.[14] The arming of the people promised the possibility of taking the first step in the 'right direction', of shaking off the Treaty of Versailles. The war of the future was a people's war:

> The objective must be to prepare for a war of defence to safeguard Germany's needs and to fend off enemy attacks. As long as we are shackled by the Treaty of Versailles, the preparations can be made only secretly … Since a war of the future will be a people's war from the beginning, even more so than the world war, the following requirements will have to be met to build up the military strength: a) the people must undergo physical training and b) our people's will to defend themselves must be revived by the schools and propaganda.[15]

In his presentations and speeches, he explained how the Treaty of Versailles was to be overcome and developed ideas on a border war and small war, on a war of revenge that was to be waged with the help of the people.[16] He did not shy away from accepting the 'crucial importance of aerial combat and gas warfare – even against the people'.[17] Over the years, the people's war was to be turned into a military war of aggression.

He knew that the people were still far from backing him. Thus, he initially placed his hopes in his closest colleagues. As Stülpnagel stood fairly alone with his ideas at the beginning, he first had to form a circle of officers around him. Stülpnagel believed that 'we must continue breeding the concept of attack both in little things and in big ones in the Army, too, in particular for moral reasons'. His presentations were above all intended for the general staff officers because they already had the task of 'pondering the problem posed by the future war in detail under the likely conditions and of leading with force in a spirit of unity'.[18] The people's war would lie in their hands:

> The tighter the people's war is controlled and the more surprising and fierce the way in which it is waged, the better it will be. It cannot be that the people's war is left to itself, flaring up here and there, irrespective of the overall situation. It must be controlled by

a central authority in close coordination with the Army Command and be taken up as the situation requires, either everywhere or in a limited area.[19]

These plans were to take on a life of their own[20] in the course of the years under the responsibility of Joachim von Stülpnagel. He won over an increasing number of officers at the ministry for his idea of a people's war, especially when the Ruhr crisis broke out in January 1923. Among them were the lieutenant colonels von Falkenhausen, Erich Freiherr von dem Bussche-Ippenburg, Friedrich von Rabenau, Pawelz and Bogislaw von Bonin.[21] Stülpnagel, however, presented his proposals not only to his peers, but also to his superior, Colonel Hasse, the Director of the Truppenamt. The political events in the Ruhr region made his hopes rise. In March 1924, he explained his priorities for a future war to his superior in writing:

> I am convinced: firstly, that Germany must wage a war in the foreseeable future in order to free itself from the diktat of the Treaty of Versailles and to free the Rhineland from the French rabble and, secondly, that until that time, we can rearm neither in terms of manpower nor in terms of materiel in a way that is remotely equal to the enemy's armament.[22]

Stülpnagel's Concept of a People's War

Even though the ideas presented by Stülpnagel only heralded the start of a new politico-military era after Seeckt, he nevertheless began to develop the basic concept of a war of liberation in the shape of a people's war during Seeckt's term of service together with officers of the Reichswehr Ministry.[23] Stülpnagel can be regarded as their most prominent advocate, as he exerted considerable influence through his presentations, papers, drafts of war games and letters to the various authorities at the Reichswehr Ministry.

Stülpnagel had been in Seeckt's service since 1920, and he tried to base the exercises conducted during the field visits and the generals' tours upon his ideas of how a future war should be waged. While he was only tolerated by Seeckt in his early years, Stülpnagel achieved a certain breakthrough during the occupation of the Ruhr region. In April 1924, Seeckt was more inclined to approve of Stülpnagel's proposals than before so that the latter was able to present his ideas during a commander's tour.[24]

> After two days in Berlin, the commander's tour under Seeckt started in Wildungen. I was in charge of the staff again and I was glad that Seeckt based the war game more than in the past on my ideas of how to wage a future war and that he approved of the critique I had prepared.[25]

Stülpnagel had called upon the officers to think through the concept of a people's war months before: 'We must share our ideas in order to gradually achieve unanimity in our views and implement the results both in theory and in practice in all our doings.'[26] This was because the way in which a future war would be waged had not yet been worked out clearly enough for his taste. The still imprecise use of the terms people's war (*Volkskrieg*), mass military force (*Massenheer*), quality army (*Qualitätsheer*), war of the future (*Zukunftskrieg*), small and large war (*kleiner Krieg/grosser Krieg*) showed that the terms had yet to be defined and used in a more precise way. The officer corps was to first discuss the definitions and then use them.[27] Thus, the officers of the T1 Subdivision (Army Division) of the Truppenamt began to plan the 'desperate struggle'. Stülpnagel also believed that his concept of the conduct of a people's war (*Verlauf der Volkskriegshandlung*) could be adapted to the special situation in the Ruhr region. He thought that the dense population would favour an uprising and that there would be 'a lot of people who have nothing to lose and who are … capable of anything'.[28] While he had started out with a border war, he developed it further during the Ruhr crisis of 1923.[29] What evolved was a system of acts of sabotage, which included raids on, and disruptions of the enemy intelligence system.[30] During one of the war games, he explained how the acts of sabotage would have to be conducted during the occupation of the Ruhr region:

> When sabotage is carried out, not only are the usual punishment measures to be implemented, but also all towns and villages within

a radius of 7 km of the act of sabotage are to be burnt down, the people are to be driven out, private property is to be seized, the people fit for military service are to be taken away and hostages to be taken away for deportation to Cayenne.[31]

In 1924, he gave a speech on the 'war of the future' at the Truppenamt.[32] It was based on the assumption that the next war would be a 'war of liberation' of the German people, that it would be a people's war.[33] When he began his planning, Stülpnagel could not immediately think of 'the destruction of the enemy' because he did not have enough forces for this. Thus, he first demanded 'the uprising of the whole people for liberation in a primitive defence battle'.[34] He answered the question as to whether 'mass military forces' could 'not be quality armies at the same time' in the affirmative.[35] He assumed that Germany's inferiority could be compensated and made up for 'by superior command and control and the best training of our 100,000-man army'.

Stülpnagel not only called to arms, but he assigned the task of preparing for war to the political authorities. He argued that the government had to 'lead the way towards and prepare for the war of liberation'.[36] Stülpnagel's hopes were vested in extensive measures that were to be taken by the government in order to 'prepare the war of liberation, the only means to regain the Ruhr and Rhine provinces'. In 1924, he hoped that a government would be found 'to create the economic and moral preconditions in a dictatorial way'.[37] A 'new government' would have to be formed to pass the necessary 'dictatorial laws' for building up the 'people's strength'.[38]

Stülpnagel stated that political leadership and diplomats had to orientate themselves towards military views. The parliamentary institutions in the Weimar Republic were to be abolished and the wrong conditions to be put right. Pacifism and the Internationale were considered '*Underman*'. 'Reinforcing the pacifist-democratic ideology would be Germany's end.'[39] Stülpnagel demanded that 'all the government institutions be adapted to support the preparations for the war of liberation', and, thus, politics be made subordinate to the military.[40] Political leadership had to convene a 'war cabinet', which would then call for 'a ruthless people's war'.[41] Stülpnagel deemed it necessary not to declare war officially so as not to give the enemy the opportunity to prepare defensive measures in time.

In other drafts, speeches and presentations, he planned the bombardment of the enemy people, because he assumed that the German people would be attacked by enemy air forces.[42] While he had shown little reservation about the use of the people, he was to lose it entirely by 1925. 'We must bear in mind that the war of the future will be directed against the entire people. Not only the field army, but also the sources of power and the nerve centres of a country will be the objects of warfare.'[43] His military ideas were based on a people's war, which, as in Ludendorff's theory, would 'most profoundly affect' the country from the outset:

> There will be no consideration for the people when winning the war is at stake ... The tighter a people's war is controlled, the more surprising and fierce the way in which it is waged, the better it will be ... We must ... focus our attention on this fact and do everything possible without exaggerated expectations in order to trigger the people's war and make it become as intense as possible.[44]

He rounded off his ideas with Freiherr Erich von dem Bussche-Ippenburg, Lieutenant-Colonel Bogislaw von Bonin and Falkenhausen into a 'war of liberation' concept at the Reichswehr Ministry. Their expectations seemed to match his. They too regarded the arming of the people as a means of waging a war of liberation. Their common goal was the mobilisation of the masses.[45]

In August 1925, the T2 Division of the Army Organization at the Reichswehr Ministry drafted another memorandum. It pointed out that the 'war of the future, even more than the world war' would be 'a people's war from the beginning'.[46] The director of the T2 Division of the Army Organization at that time was Bussche-Ippenburg. He advocated a modern form of mass warfare that was based on the technical innovations.[47] Not only Stülpnagel and Bussche-Ippenburg, but also Bonin dedicated the entire nation to war.[48] They demanded that the mobilisation of the entire 'strength of the people' be prepared in a foresighted way and planned in detail for the government so that the country was prepared for a war of aggression,[49] although Stülpnagel himself pointed out that 'large proportions of the people are still today suspicious of the possibility of war against a France that is bristling with arms.' For example, he believed that he could lend a certain amount of truth to his demand by using the 'sense of history' as an argument. Referring to German military history, he was of the opinion that the majority of 'the German people' would be open to the necessity of liberation. He believed that 'law is based on power and that it would be against nature and experience if Versailles and the League of Nations rang in the era of eternal peace.'[50] His arguments were based on the concept of the nation state and on emotion. A bit like Ludendorff, albeit not quite as irrational as he was in his theory, Stülpnagel referred to the 'traditional German concept of being able and willing to fight' in order to oppose disarmament, reconciliation and the League of Nations, diplomatic measures and measures initiated by the government.[51] Like Ludendorff, he called the unjustified cabinet wars raids because they served the greed for profit.[52] He shared Ludendorff's view that politics served war.

Stülpnagel's urging to win Seeckt over for his ideas probably started during the occupation of the Ruhr. In February 1923, Stülpnagel had prompted Seeckt to meet Ludendorff. He hoped that this would bring about a politico-military agreement and provide the impetus for a war of liberation.

> After I had encouraged Seeckt to meet Ludendorff secretly for private talks at a neutral location, a talk took place between the two at Wannsee. Seeckt seemed to be satisfied by this talk and told me that he had explained to Ludendorff that he would leave his position to him at any time, but only on the one condition that Ludendorff respected the Constitution.[53]

Seeckt met Hitler in Berlin on 12 March 1923. The consequence was that Seeckt warned the forces on 22 March in an order 'that any pro-national socialist activities by members of the Army would be considered as disobedience'.[54]

Stülpnagel urged Seeckt once more, in October 1923, to install a dictatorship. By the end of 1923, Stülpnagel had not only tried several times to urge Seeckt that he as a soldier and not Gessler, a civilian, had to take over the executive power.[55]

I [Stülpnagel] tried to present my estimate of the situation to Seeckt in private as I had once done to Ludendorff. I called by in the evening, when he had already gone to bed, and appealed emphatically to the responsibility he had for the nation as a leading soldier. He dismissed me ungraciously, but on the following day, he nevertheless went to Ebert and Stresemann as I had suggested. What those men suggested, I do not know, but we heard that a board of directors headed by Seeckt or Wiedfeldt would come.[56]

However, no politico-military agreements were concluded between Seeckt and Ludendorff, and no board of directors replacing the government was formed either.

Contrary to Stülpnagel's expectations, no agreement was reached with Ludendorff and Seeckt did not decide in favour of a board of directors. However, differences arose between him and Seeckt. The events that followed were not very encouraging for Stülpnagel.

The personal consequences of my actions at that time meant that my predominantly warm relationship with Seeckt became strained because my constant urging had got on his nerves and he usually treated me only 'correctly' from then on.[57]

It was not the first and the last time he came to the conclusion that 'Seeckt didn't like my vehement urging'.[58] Stülpnagel condemned the defensive attitude which Seeckt adopted during the Ruhr crisis as inappropriate for the times. He insisted on an approach being adopted towards the French invasion of the Ruhr that was offensive both politically and militarily.[59] And he was to be more successful with his demands with the political leadership rather than with the military leadership:

I [Stülpnagel] was then of the view, and I still am, that soldiers must not refuse and I presented my view to General Seeckt in many presentations. He hesitated for political reasons, probably rightly so, and he always remained very cautious in his attitude. Reich Chancellor Cuno, Minister Gessler, State Secretary Hamm and in particular Employment Minister Braun argued strongly for action so that I got, with Seeckt's approval, the authority and a considerable budget for acts of sabotage in the Ruhr region.[60]

As the Ruhr crisis unfolded politically, Stülpnagel began to understand that Seeckt would not follow his ideas. From 1923 onwards, he had hoped that Seeckt would act in a more nationalistic way, but was increasingly disappointed by Seeckt's behaviour.[61]

At the end of November, Stresemann resigned from the post of Chancellor and became the Foreign Minister in Marx' 'Grand Coalition' cabinet. He held this position in different cabinets until his death. We soldiers were disappointed by this development. In our opinion, they muddled on. The President of the Reich, the governments of the Reich and of the Länder, the Parliaments, everybody was talking, and only Seeckt, the all-powerful master of the state of emergency, was silent.[62]

Stülpnagel had to recognize that Seeckt would not give in to his 'vehement urging'.[63] Stülpnagel was more successful with his views with his superior, Colonel Hasse, and the other officers mentioned than with Seeckt. However, as Stülpnagel noted, Seeckt might have been more than just hesitant. Blomberg, too, stated to his peers that Seeckt did not support the military demands of the younger officers: 'In fact, his and our basic views of the Reichswehr were contrary.'[64]

Stülpnagel considered the situation at the ministry critical and he treated the army leadership with contempt. He wrote to his peer Geyer at the General Staff of the 5th Division about the state of affairs at the ministry

that they will even now prefer to muddle on in small steps … Today, there is a risk of us enjoying what we have achieved in our military work, of us adapting to the calm situation, of us working multa instead of multum, of us being intolerant of prophets of doom and preferring figures who are easy to manage.[65]

After Stülpnagel's such modest success, he did not attribute the lack of success to his basic political and military attitudes being wrong, but blamed the country's political leadership:

Unwaveringly staying on this path will yield greater successes than groping around like the Reichswehr has done in all questions of mobilisation with its domestic and foreign policy risks! It will not be enough in the long run for the bellicose spirit to remain the intellectual property of the Army, which, despite the Versailles diktat, will have to prepare for war in the future ... If the government creates a body in the Reich Defence Council and then procures the funds, the path can be taken. Still, a decision must be taken as to whether we remain wilfully defenceless or not.[66]

Initially tolerated by Seeckt, Stülpnagel had time and again presented his politico-military thoughts at the Army Command. However, the more the political developments in the Ruhr crisis progressed, and the more Stülpnagel showed what path he was ready to take, Seeckt recognized the incompatibility of their approaches. Stülpnagel was in fact slowly becoming 'bothersome' to Seeckt.[67] Completely failing to recognize the differences between Stülpnagel and Seeckt, General Werner von Blomberg wrote the following lines to Stülpnagel:

We had finally summed up our thoughts on the necessary development of the Reichswehr in a fairly long report, in which we had proposed in particular the creation of a Führerheer as a framework for a large-scale *military build-up* ... This document ... was not well received by General v. S. at that time. His marginal notes were rather unfriendly and his final judgment was that we younger officers were trying to disabuse him.[68]

Disappointment about Seeckt's hesitance since the events of 1923 could be caused only in those who had expected Seeckt to be prepared to push forward 'more actively' in favour of a 'national dictatorship'.[69]

Stülpnagel also attributed Seeckt's rejection to his age. 'As I have mentioned before, he had lost much of his former elasticity, was satisfied with what the Reichswehr had achieved and was inclined to resignation regarding all political and military issues.'[70] Even in 1955, Stülpnagel would blame the Reichstag for the fact that the Weimar Republic had rejected what he claimed were the right policies. He recalled the 'undignified attitude of the Reichstag', arguing that it had conducted a 'policy of appeasement'. He still rejected the policy of rapprochement with France, the government's efforts to achieve reconciliation and Germany's accession to the League of Nations.[71] Until his death, Stülpnagel would not understand what had motivated and moved Seeckt.

However, not only Stülpnagel, but also the coming generation, and with it Reichswehr Minister Gessler, blamed the Chief of the Army Command Seeckt for the fact that the Reichswehr had over-aged during his term of service, that the Reichswehr had 'not moved on militarily', that he had not wanted to listen to the truth, had hindered progress, had allowed 'the old to triumph,' preferred 'formalities, festivities and parades', and had not contributed anything to the 'liberation of the people'.[72]

Seeckt had not supported Stülpnagel's proposals ever since the questions arose in 1923 as to whether a 'fight for liberation' was to be initiated and how sovereignty in the Ruhr and Rhine regions could be regained militarily.[73] Rather, Seeckt had tried to have Stülpnagel reposted, but he failed because of objections from the Reichswehr Minister and three officers: Freiherr von Fritsch, Kurt von Schleicher and the Truppenamt Director, Colonel Hasse. 'However, when the Personnel Office tried to hastily post me to Stuttgart (maybe Seeckt was behind this!), the Minister and Hasse objected.'[74] In the following years, 1925 and 1926, Seeckt had to order the postings of two lieutenant colonels, those of Bussche-Ippenburg and Stülpnagel. Stülpnagel was promoted to the rank of colonel and 'banished' from the Reichswehr Ministry to the 'back country', Brunswick, on 1 February 1926. His posting was less due to Seeckt's airs and graces, a 'Sphinx-like nature',[75] even to personal sensitivities, personal animosities, than to profound military-strategic discrepancies, which had caused Seeckt to take these personnel measures. He was forced to intervene because he had declined 'to create the framework for the war of the future'.[76]

Some of the mentioned specialists have not been able to clarify the cause of and reason for Stülpnagel's posting, and the consequences of his reintegration into the Reichswehr Ministry have not been examined.[77] In the winter of 1926, immediately after Seeckt's retirement, Reichswehr Minister Gessler, General Heye and Lieutenant Colonel Kurt von Schleicher planned to call Joachim von Stülpnagel back to the

Reichswehr Ministry.[78] In January 1927, the successor of Seeckt General Heye appointed him director of the Army Personnel Office.[79] He was now back at one of the steering wheels of the Reichswehr Ministry. Thus, Stülpnagel was again, and better than before, in a position to let those officers move up who, like himself, endorsed his preferred principle of the people's war, the war of liberation and the mobilisation of the people.

In a presentation which he gave to the Reichswehr Ministry officers on 28 January 1927, he wanted to establish an overarching council at the ministry: 'The establishment of a Wartime Defence Council as a supreme authority would be welcomed.'[80] Like Ludendorff, he rejected the Constitution and demanded a dictatorship:

> The future war will necessitate from the outset the use of the entire strength of the people – that is to say, universal conscription – whether it be in armed combat, in the war industry … Dictatorial laws, the strictest discipline, very exacting demands on the commanders of every level will be a matter of course.[81]

In his presentation, Stülpnagel compared a numerically limited quality army with a mass military force. He demanded that the quality army be supplemented by a mass military force. He concluded that 'the great masters in the art of war …' 'simply liked large battalions'.

> At least, they sought to be numerically superior at the decisive place. They actually sought to use the superior quality of their forces only with respect to the greater mobility it gave them so as to have not only more quality, but also numerical superiority on the battlefield.[82]

Stülpnagel developed a concept according to which a war of liberation would be brought about by a people's war.[83] He could to some extent count on a mass military force being established by the Reichsheer. The presentation in January 1927 contained the proof he had of the benefits of a mass military force that was to be built up, trained and armed militarily on the basis of an existing highly qualified cadre-strength army. He built upon plans according to which war was initially to be fought with 21 divisions and later with 63.[84]

The 'disciplinary posting to the back country' did not have a lasting effect. The posting was of little effect because the ministry did not and could not stop staff from thinking about the central questions concerning the future priority military strategy objectives in an armed people's war – a war of liberation.

Seeckt's retirement in October 1926 not only led to Stülpnagel being posted back to the ministry. The politicians and officers Hindenburg, Schleicher, Heye and Gessler helped him, as the director of the Army Personnel Office, to find the young officers who suited him, to set a new, different politico-military and military-strategic course at the ministry that provided for soldiers to be more actively involved in matters of the state.[85] They built on the old objectives of war from before the First World War and developed new ideas of how Germany could assert itself militarily against the supremacy of certain states in Europe.

Stülpnagel was now able to develop and pursue his ideas further without being disturbed. Nobody opposed his demands for making the people fit 'to wage an independent war' any more.[86]

Now, he was able to voice his view that victory would not be brought about by quality, but by superior armament and technology without being challenged.[87] He built upon the small 100,000-man army which had been established by Seeckt under entirely different premises. 'The commanders at all levels for the new, larger people's army that was to be established' were to be able to 'rise' from its cadre.[88]

Little remained of Seeckt's military-strategic approach after his term of service. All that was pushed ahead by the officers at the Reichswehr Ministry was confined to force mobility. Not only were mobility and quality to be decisive on the battlefield henceforth; quantity, mass and technology gained crucial importance, too. Stülpnagel not only diluted Seeckt's concept, but also recreated the First World War conditions that Seeckt wanted to avoid. The general staff officers around Stülpnagel had not learned anything from the war; they had only formulated and propagated their politico-military doctrines against the state and society in a more radical way.

Contrary to the supposition among military historians that Stülpnagel was one of those officers who 'were the least averse to recognizing the existing order of the Weimar Republic as a basis of the military preparations', it becomes clear that his views in particular clashed with the parliamentary authorities and the political system.[89] He was not prepared to respect the existing order either – even in the year 1955. As claimed by specialist historian Heinz Hürten, Stülpnagel did not show any 'positive acceptance' of the existing form of government. In 1919, he had written that he vested 'all his hope ... in the Crown Prince'.[90] In 1924, he preferred dictatorship. 'It is our ill fate that we should not have a man of outstanding qualities in Germany who is able and willing to rule in a dictatorial style in Germany.'[91] He rejected the parliamentary system of the Weimar Republic. He demanded 'the creation of a strong Reich government and the elimination of the pathological parliamentarianism.'[92] He did not believe in political attempts at arbitration that 'only sought to find solutions by means of negotiations and economic struggle.'[93] He voiced his demands in his presentations: 'The task of foreign policy is for the time being that of buying time for rearmament ... Its firm objective must be to prepare for the war of liberation.'[94] Just like under Ludendorff, politics was made subordinate to the military objectives. It was his military-strategic concepts and not Seeckt's that paved the way for 'total and terrorist war'.[95]

Synopsis

The basis upon which Seeckt planned the use of the military was the primacy of politics. Accordingly, he did not want to conduct a coup d'état, the reason for this not being, as some specialists like Walter Mühlhausen, Michael Geyer, Johannis Hürten and Francis Carsten believe, that he placed his hopes in change without revolution and in the long-term development in foreign affairs. The reason was that, as a follower of Clausewitz, he adhered to the primacy of politics. The military foundation upon which he based his military strategy was wartime experience. Seeckt's answer to the past war years was the establishment of a qualified professional army, heavily armed and well trained, serving as an instrument of deterrence in the hands of the political authorities. His politico-military basis and military-strategic foundations were opposed to the political motivations of Ludendorff and Stülpnagel, who urged the government to work for mass mobilisation, the rearmament of the army and a war of revenge.

The difference between Seeckt and Ludendorff in politico-military terms lay in the contrast between the totality of war and the primacy of politics, between the mass military force that Ludendorff sent off to war with insufficient training and Seeckt's opinion that only heavily armed and well trained soldiers using technology would be able to stand up to war. The idea of deterrence by means of a qualified and high-quality army on the one hand, and the untrained mass military force on the other, marks the militarily irreconcilable contrast between these two opponents in the Weimar Republic. On the political level, the incompatibility of the two concepts lay in their relationship to policy. Ludendorff proceeded from the assumption that there was a policy of war, which gave it its totality, while Seeckt respected the primacy of politics, which relativised the military actions. The seriousness of the effects of this war theory can be seen in the total war that Ludendorff demanded be fought to the end, and the demise of the enemy or his own people. In contrast, Clausewitz and Seeckt assigned the full responsibility for the aims, ends, means and ways of war to the political authorities. Seeckt assigned soldiers the responsibility for giving expert advice to the political authorities.

After Seeckt's era, the questions concerning war were raised and discussed again. The question as to how the next war was to be waged, if it was demanded by the political authorities and considered 'inevitable' was no longer answered by the officers on a constitutional basis and was no longer to be accounted for by the preservation of the republic. Stülpnagel gave the 'traditional German concept of being able and willing to fight' as a reason to mobilize against the Treaty of Versailles. The more he devised his military-strategic thoughts on a war of revenge that was to be waged by means of acts of sabotage, the clearer the passivity of the government and Seeckt during the months of the Ruhr crisis became to him, the more vehemently he demanded policies to be made subordinate to military policy as a means of shaking off the Treaty of Versailles and the more frequently he pointed out the benefits of a mass military force. The further military-strategic discussions were conducted among the Army Command officers, both from the politico-military and a purely military standpoint. They did not adhere to public law guidelines in their assessments and the development of their plans, but indeed demanded their revocation. The consequence of the dispute was that Seeckt's postings of personnel were not only revoked by his successors, but that Stülpnagel was able to begin the advance planning for a people's war and direct it into military-strategic channels as a war of liberation or a war of revenge. His plans were also to have other consequences for society and the state. The idea of a people's war, ultimately of a total war, as Ludendorff had imagined it since the end of the First World War was to catch on with help from Stülpnagel, who was a supporter of the ideas of total war.

While specialists like Vardi and Geyer believed they had understood Seeckt's actions, i.e. the planning and implementation of a systematic armament programme, the ideas only acquired their penetrating power under Seeckt's successor, Major General Heye. The assumption expressed by specialists Geyer and Müller that the boundaries between the military and civilian society broke down in the inter-war period and a 'concept of an alliance war' gained acceptance is true for the post-Seeckt era. The observation made by military historians that, until Seeckt's retirement in 1926, nothing had come of the idea of a large-scale insurrection, the organization of the entire people, because Seeckt had allegedly been a ditherer, and the claim made by academics that, in Seeckt's day, the Army Command's military plans had existed only on paper because Seeckt had only wanted to unleash the full force in steps have merely drawn attention to inconsistencies in Seeckt's actions. They have not, however, been able to recognize and to explain how this was connected with military strategy. Seeckt's military strategy and politico-military attitude had prevented the very implementation of such plans to militarize society and the rapprochement of the army and the industrial and antagonistic Weimar society claimed by specialists Klaus Jürgen Müller and Michael Geyer.

The reason why Seeckt cannot be seen to have adopted a clear position in the period from 1920 to 1926 is that the above mentioned specialists did not distinguish between the different military-strategic deliberations, some of which were incompatible with one another. Thus, the factional dispute over military strategy that was going on between the factions in the Army High Command did not surface either. The factional dispute at the Reichswehr Ministry had broken out by January 1923 at the latest, i.e. at the beginning of the Ruhr crisis. The military strategy dispute was decided and terminated in October 1926 upon Seeckt's retirement. After his retirement, the organization of force started, for the 'ditherer', who did not want to be a 'malicious civil war general', the 'Cunctator Seeckt', had been given the send-off by his own officers. The military strategy dispute in the years 1923 to 1926 over the question as to what path the military should take in future was the reason why the Army Command Directorates at the ministry were divided into several interest groups. It was the reason for nepotism and a number of personnel changes. At least two Army Command Directorates drafted ideas of their own about a future war, but pursued different military objectives to Seeckt. Accordingly, the military strategy dispute went right through the Reichswehr Ministry, as specialist Harold J. Gordon correctly pointed out. However, contrary to what the specialists believed, the factional conflicts did not follow political class divides or socio-political contrasts, but focused on the general staff officers' real subject, i.e. the question of the military-strategic objective, of a military strategy at the interface with politics. This was linked to the significance of military counselling for politics.

The questions regarding the military-strategic concepts of the Weimar Republic were not addressed by the specialists for several reasons and there was no debate on them. Military historians had initially assumed that Seeckt had not a military-strategic concept. The analyses referred to the operational plans, still more to the tactical level and to command and control, whereby the basic differences about military-strategic ideas with respect to war theories and the different military-strategic ideas held by the officer corps were left out from the beginning. In addition to that and to reinforce their own arguments, the academics stated that Seeckt was a 'traditionalist' and had been opposed to the fielding of modern ordnance. He was accused of having held on to traditions and of not being receptive to new challenges. The basic military-strategic contrast between Seeckt and Ludendorff was, thus, not even touched upon, not even when Seeckt's biographer Meier-Welcker remarked on the subject of Seeckt's behaviour and said that Seeckt had felt put off by the loud public ovations for Ludendorff, attributing this to Seeckt's 'vanities'. Military historians believed that the deliberations made at the Reichswehr Ministry had developed in a consistent way and that the officer corps had agreed on its objectives. They also assumed that the officer corps had held the same political views. Even though specialists have had some objections, they have conceded that the officer corps could not only be seen as a monolithic block. But they put forward sociological reasons, believing that the discrepancies had been caused by personal backgrounds, experiences or interests or that they had been generation-specific. The much discussed controversy about the necessary rejuvenation of the officer corps or its overaging, about a lack of technical progress and about the importance which Seeckt allegedly attributed to formalities at Reichswehr parades was only superficial. The dispute over technology and equipment, modern weapons and training standards after all only revealed a difference between the 'traditionalists' and the 'reformers', between the followers of Clausewitz and Ludendorff. The entire debate on Seeckt among military historians has taken place at the exclusion of the parties' military-strategic concepts. This is a mistake if they want to understand the supreme soldier at the interface with politics.

It was therefore not the publications by officers such as Max Schwarte or Kurt Hesse that had left the intellectual basis upon which the officers reflected on future warfare. Rather, it was Ludendorff's follower Joachim von Stülpnagel who continued to systematically proceed along the latter's path. It was not Max Schwarte and Kurt Hesse who were successful with their works on the psychology of war and of the supreme soldier at that time. But it was Stülpnagel in the background and with his speeches and presentations at the ministry, his ideas on war games and manoeuvres for a people's war and mass mobilisation, who influenced the military and political heads. By 1927, 'Ludendorff's disciple' Stülpnagel, who not only claimed that he had remained imperial at heart, but that he had felt very close to Ludendorff since the First World War, was firmly established at the Reichswehr Ministry. He was successful in gaining support among his listeners and supporters for his theory of mass warfare, thus contributing to and preparing the horror of the Second World War.

Judging by the questions they raised, with the exception of Matthias Strohn, all above-mentioned specialists did not understand what concerned Seeckt and what position he had adopted. Researchers concentrated on the German military's policy of war objectives, which had existed long before the First World War, and derived Seeckt's military policy from it. However, the discussions at the Army Command were not coherent and pursued no common goal, but rather showed differences of opinion on the interests that the Weimar Republic could and should pursue. The different attitudes and answers led to upheaval and division in the officer corps. The questions raised by the officers around Stülpnagel and the answers they gave were a counterdraft to Seeckt's military-strategic concept. Their answers went beyond the legal limits of the Weimar Republic because they demanded the revocation of the Treaty of Versailles. Their thoughts on military strategy concerned central, vital interests of the Weimar Republic because they wanted to abolish the parliamentary republic.

The answers given by the Reichswehr Ministry officers, whose position differed from Seeckt's, to the question of how the military-strategic objectives of the Weimar Republic should be pursued, clearly revealed Seeckt's disinclination to support the younger generation. This generation was open-minded about military technology for entirely different reasons, and the military strategist Seeckt knew what political consequences mass mobilization, mass armament and a war of revenge would have for Germany. As a military strategist, he understood the officers' demands and his far-sightedness showed that he had not forgotten the horrors of the previous war. The 'ditherer Seeckt' quite consciously hesitated and reined in the upcoming generation. He reined it in to prevent rash nation-state action being taken that was not within the framework of peaceful objectives. He rejected the mobilization and armament of a mass military force on account of his wartime experience and for military-strategic reasons. Seeckt was therefore one of the people who were bound to reject the technical challenges for the masses, yet not for the 100,000-man army. He worked against the spirit of the upcoming officers, who demanded the mobilisation of the people. There are two sides to the argument raised in the Anglo-Saxon countries that he had hesitated to make changes, in contrast to Groener and Stülpnagel. Seeckt respected the limits of military force set by politics and Germany's military capabilities. He may have been an 'aging general' in that respect. However, as an elder general who accepted the existing politico-military conditions as the point of departure and who did not want to see progress being made in the way that Stülpnagel did, he held on to the Weimar state and its Constitution. The assumption that Seeckt and Stülpnagel pursued the same objectives and were willing to irresponsibly plunge the people into war should have been disproved by the presentation of their fundamentally different military-strategic concepts.

Clausewitz' military-strategic approach remained binding for Seeckt and ruled out compromises. Stülpnagel and Ludendorff were equally uncompromising in their aim to end the 'pathological parliamentarianism' of the Weimar Republic. Seeckt had tried to bring about a paradigm shift in the military doctrine in place after the Schlieffen era. However, when it came to enforcing his military strategy line, he was defeated not only by Ludendorff's follower, but also by the personal differences between himself and Hindenburg, who was later to become the President of the Reich. The reasons for the steady weakening of his position at the ministry and his retirement did not lie in the Crown Prince affair; the younger generation had a different opinion on military strategy and military policy, one which could not be reconciled with the political system of the Weimar Republic, and it found open ears among both the political and military heads in the Reich.

Accordingly, Seeckt's behaviour was based on politico-military and military-strategic principles. In the politico-military respect, he exerted an influence on the forces. He tried to build the Reichsheer around his military-strategic concept by means of training and education, equipment and personnel policy. At the interface with politics, he represented a military strategy which ensured that the politicians' aim, the defence of strategic interests, would be achieved. He took into account important military-strategic factors for this. They included the people and its sense of being intimidated, the strong and the weak neighbours, the armaments policy and the resulting possibilities of armaments negotiations and alliance policy, a small operating army, civil-military cooperation, geostrategy, the economic policy, finance policy and public and constitutional law of his country.

In the politico-military way of acting as expounded discriminately above, the Reichsheer trained by Seeckt was able to become the best possible basis for the later Wehrmacht and the Second World War. The differences found in the officer corps of the Reichswehr and Seeckt's military strategy should prompt thought to be given to re-evaluating the Seeckt era. Also against the backdrop of the contradictory views on a mass military-force and a professional army, military technology and the Hague Conventions, the primacy of politics and total war, this dispute not only divided the officer corps of the Reichsheer. Rather, it was to resurface under new circumstances and a new subject heading, namely as one between traditionalists and reformers in the Bundeswehr. Both the follower of Clausewitz and the man who had rejected Clausewitz from the outset were to dominate not only the military-strategic debate of their time but, far beyond that, also the Second World War and the more recent era.

Chapter 5

Seeckt's Political Programme in 1923/24

Introduction

In the autumn of 1923, the Weimar government evoked Article 48 of the Reich Constitution and declared a civilian state of emergency. By using the full executive powers, it tried to counter the separatistic aspirations of radical parties, especially in Prussia, Saxony, Thuringia and Bavaria. Another reason was the attempted coup by right-wing radical paramilitary units under Hitler and Ludendorff in Bavaria. Officers of the 7th Division in Munich, including its commander, were involved in this attempt.[1] In the night of 8 November 1923, executive power was conferred on the Chief of the Army Command, Seeckt, and the military state of emergency started. It lasted until the end of February. This action was the government's attempt to restore order and security and to impose its central authority. The following passage does not contain an analysis of the causes and events that led to the state of emergency. A lot has been written about them and the socio-political consequences have been analysed.[2] An attempt will be made to analyse Seeckt's concept of politics during the time when he held executive power and to answer the question of whether his politico-military actions were in contradiction his military strategy. This introduction to this chapter, too, will include references to the historical studies and interpretations of Seeckt's actions.

The Holder of the Executive Power in Specialist Literature

Seeckt was allegedly trying 'to establish the "most severe executive power through the Reichswehr and police" at the time of the military state of emergency'.[3] As the holder of the executive power, he is said to have pursued 'far-reaching goals', such as strengthening the Reich's executive power.[4] It was argued that his true ambitions, namely 'to rise to become the decisive power factor' had become visible during the state of emergency.[5]

He is said to have aspired to gain control of 'the Ministry of the Interior in Prussia through a change of government there'. As early as December 1923, he allegedly sent a letter to Severing, a Social Democrat, with 'an appeal to his patriotism' in order to gain his support for strengthening the Reichswehr. To corroborate this assumption, a passage from a letter from Seeckt to Severing is offered:

> To be able to accomplish the economic turnaround that has been begun and that demands the greatest of sacrifices from everybody, and to be able to conduct at least a small measure of foreign policy, the Reich will in the time ahead need a strong executive power, which, in the given situation, can only be ensured by the military state of emergency. What is ultimately at issue is the big German problem: If we want to play power politics, we will have to eliminate slack on all levels – it is especially huge due to the federal structure of the Reich (some 90 ministers and 2,100 deputies) – pool all the productive forces and strengthen the Reich's executive power [government], or if we want to buy economic advantages from our neighbours at the price of national prestige, then it is understandable that we should want to strengthen the states and provinces.[6]

Seeckt, it was argued, was unsuccessful because of the reservations of the Prussian government.[7] Only Ebert and the Stresemann cabinet allegedly ensured that the 'primacy of political leadership' was safeguarded.[8] The public in the Weimar Republic and posterity must have gained the impression 'that the forms of domestic administration [by the Reichswehr] ... can be better compared with the police regime of the Ancien Régime, which acted at its own free moral discretion'.[9]

More recent socio-political interpretations coincided with this assessment and considered President of the Reich Ebert to be the key figure who, distrustful of Seeckt, had thwarted a coup d'état and thus a dictatorship, in a 'masterly move'.[10] Besides Ebert, it was allegedly Reich Chancellor Stresemann's 'well considered action' that enabled the realization of 'the military' ambitions to be prevented.[11]

If Seeckt had only hesitantly abandoned his political aspirations at the end of February due to 'resignation over too much resistance', he was often quoted with a curse on his lips against the parliamentary republic and his aversion to parliamentarianism. It was argued that he must have recognized his 'strategic defeat' only in 1924 when he 'abandoned his risky game' and had gone back to 'government normality'. And, once more, emotional or mental characteristics were cited to explain his return to 'government normality' and the abandonment of his far-reaching ambitions. His 'tactical skills' and his behaviour were said to be the 'expression of greater sceptical prudence'.[12] The fact that Seeckt had not taken over the political leadership is said to have been due to his Prussian origin. It was allegedly 'his nature, which was bent on service, not on power' and his 'Prussian character' that made him averse to the misuse of power.[13] The latter assumption, however, is in contradiction to the test of strength in domestic affairs which he pursued for reasons of power and by means of which he sought to rise to become the decisive power factor.

Civil-Military Cooperation during the State of Emergency

The legal status permitted the strengthening of the Reichswehr in the state of emergency. The central and local government authorities remained in power during the state of emergency and were 'only made subordinate to the Reichswehr Minister … Executive power could therefore often be limited to general directives given to civilian government authorities and the drafting of guidelines.'[14] It may not be surprising that there were still differences. Civil-military cooperation was still one of the challenges.

At the beginning of the state of emergency, states such as Wurttemberg and Baden voiced reservations because the borders of the military districts did not match those of the states.[15] They pointed out that departmental issues would inevitably lead to overlaps in the different fiscal and economic areas. Double subordination would make government of the states more difficult in general. Differences between civilian and military forces therefore arose not only in the states of Wurttemberg and Baden.

One fairly frequent consequence of this overlap in responsibilities for the cooperation was that both sides felt that they were treated unfairly. The civilian side believed that it was just as much passed over as the military side. The commander of Military District IV, Lieutenant General Müller, wrote to the Saxon government:

> It has been reported to the Military District Command that the address given by Minister-President Dr. Zeigner in the Parliament of the State of Saxony on 12. October [1923] has been put up in public in the Free State of Saxony. I consider this public posting a distribution of pamphlets which ... required my authorization. Since it was not obtained from me, I have the honour to hereby issue the authorization of the Saxon government for this posting belatedly.[16]

At the beginning of the state of emergency, Reichswehr Minister Gessler held civilian power. Thus, Seeckt knew from the beginning of the state of emergency onwards that he was in agreement with the President of the Reich Ebert. Together with him, both Carl Severing, a Prussian minister, and Wilhelm Sollmann, a minister of the Reich, (both SPD) had demanded the declaration of the state of emergency in September 1923. The reasons they gave for this were that the NSDAP [Nationalsozialistische Deutsche Arbeiterpartei] in Bavaria and radical left-wing parties in Prussia, Saxony and Thuringia were threatening government business and order in the Reich.

Prussia's Minister of the Interior, Carl Severing, reckoned that the domestic situation in Prussia should be stabilized by 29 December 1923. He demanded that the state of emergency be lifted.[17] Seeckt was of a different opinion and explained his assessment of the political situation. His assessment is taken from the same letter that is reproduced in the introduction above as an excerpt from specialist literature of Johannes Hürten:

> The Reich had to concentrate its entire power in the hands of one person if it wanted to enforce its rule. I know that you, Minister, defended the standpoint yourself in the night of 26 September and that you also expressed the view to the former Minister of the Interior of the Reich that the government had to rule with the state of emergency for a long time to come in order to finally achieve calm in Germany and the possibility of rebuilding it.[18]

Seeckt went on to address the difficulties of civil-military cooperation during the state of emergency. He was, however, equally convinced that cooperation was possible and that it was still too early to revoke the state of emergency. First of all, he drew up a list of the frictions that had arisen around the state of emergency:

> From your oral and written statements I believe that I may assume that you too attach great importance to trustful cooperation between the military and civilian authorities. The best of intentions must remain unsuccessful if events as referred to in the attachments (1–6) make the Reichswehr agencies suspect that they are under surveillance or, to use a stronger term, being spied upon. It is always the same old story: instead of contacting the responsible command authorities in confidence, inquiries are made behind their backs and then full-blown official reports are sent to the Ministry of the Interior ... Let me say a few more basic words in this context about the military state of emergency in general. I appreciate that it demands a certain amount of self-denial from the states and all the civilian authorities. Nevertheless, I am of the opinion that these inconsistencies must be accepted when the existence of the Reich is at stake; for I am firmly convinced that without the military state of emergency, neither the Reich nor Prussia would have been able to withstand the united attack by radical right and left-wing forces.[19]

If, as Seeckt estimated, the state of emergency was lifted as early as December 1923, the risk of the Reich falling apart would still exist. Even if 'exceptional things have been done to consolidate the authority of the Reich in the past few weeks', Seeckt believed that the military state of emergency had to be maintained because of the NSDAP. Because of it, there were still 'unsatisfactory conditions in Bavaria'. He thought that the NSDAP was the driving force and 'believed that nothing can help more than strong Reich power in resolving the Bavarian conflict in particular. I therefore think that it is very dangerous if the lifting of the military state of emergency is talked about time and again.'[20] The power politics Seeckt aspired to conduct was intended to serve the Reich's existence, and it seemed to be directed not only against a Prussia with a social-democratic government, but above all against the NSDAP.

Seeckt's estimate that Bavaria's separatist aspirations would not diminish was confirmed by a second motion on 4 January 1924. The Bavarian envoy Preger transmitted to the Reich government a demand for a revision of the Weimar Constitution. The State of Bavaria demanded a revision of the relationship between the Reich and the states – for example, the restoration of their own fiscal sovereignty and the return of the tax authorities.[21] Seeckt reckoned that another aim of this demand was to circumvent Article 48 of the Weimar Constitution so as to prevent the military state of emergency being declared and the Reichswehr being used in Bavaria.[22]

The Reichswehr was a political instrument during the state of emergency, for use not only against Saxony's and Thuringia's communists. It also seemed to be the government's ultimate tool against the troops of the 7th Division, who were revolting in Bavaria. The conflict between Bavaria, which demanded a national government excluding the SPD, and the Reich became more acute.[23] On 3 November 1923, the President of the Reich demanded that troops be used against those in Bavaria. Seeckt refused to allow Ebert to use the Reichswehr against the 7th Division in Bavaria. To Seeckt, this was a repetition of what he had declined back in 1920 during the attempted coup by Kapp and Lüttwitz, i.e. the use of troops against other troops. He rejected it for a second time. And, as specialist Andreas Dietz has stated, Seeckt again disregarded the primacy of politics, and 'the German government had to look on powerless'.[24] Ebert was considerably shocked by this insubordination, and the first tensions between him and Seeckt arose.[25] The order to deploy troops against the 7th Division in Bavaria was of a purely military nature and did not take account of its possible long-term political consequence, the civil war that would be caused by the forces. Seeckt's answer was a political response, and not a military one.[26]

Accordingly, Ebert changed his position the following day, 4 November, showing understanding for Seeckt's rejection of his call for the use of the Reichswehr against the Reichswehr:

4.11 … On the other hand, Ebert today endorsed Seeckt's position on this matter and also Seeckt's statements on the political leadership of the Reich. He too no longer considers a Stresemann cabinet possible. While Ebert considers Seeckt a possible chancellor, he considers him undesirable for reasons of foreign policy. He does not want to go without Seeckt as the Army chief either because there is no suitable successor.[27]

While Seeckt had tried to build up a force that would be neutral from the party political angle and usable against the right as well as the left, he had to accept after three years of service in the republic that he had not succeeded. Despite his explicit orders against both the right and left, the right-wing radical movement in Bavaria had caught and carried away the 7th Division and the cadets of the Munich school. Even after months of dispute with General Lossow in Munich, Seeckt did not manage to enforce the government's political will via the military chain of command in Bavaria.[28] General Lossow did deploy the 7th Division against Ludendorff and Hitler in the night of 8 November 1923 and then had the two imprisoned.[29] But it had taken months for this to happen. Ebert had demanded the use of troops on several occasions and seen his demand turned down by Seeckt. Seeckt himself had demanded the dismissal of General Lossow in Bavaria on several occasions in writing, but was unable to assert himself against the general and the Bavarian government. All that Seeckt could do was to insist on the military chain of command being respected. This was the politico-military way which he trusted.[30] The military hierarchy was the only instrument he had to demand obedience and the discipline based on it from the troops under his command.

Seeckt's Political Programme in the Years 1923/24

Politics is the art of the possible,
not that of the desirable.[31]

Until well into 1923, officers such as Colonel Hasse, Lieutenant Colonel Joachim Stülpnagel, political and business figures and even Friedrich Ebert asked Seeckt whether he would be prepared to be a member of a board of directors, and not only while he held executive power.[32] This board of directors was to be a transitional body with extraordinary powers staffed by business, political and army figures. Seeckt drafted two hand-written documents on the subject. The first one was written in September 1923, the second one in November 1923. Only the latter was entitled a 'statement of government policy'.[33] In the September edition, he wrote just one item in the first person. 'Where I described the maintenance of state authority as a necessity at the beginning, this meant the suppression of all aspirations for a coup d'état.'[34] The 'statement of government policy' of November 1923 equally clearly expressed the view that 'a military policy openly set on attack' was not an option.[35] He judged, on the basis of his military-strategic estimate, that the Reichswehr would not be strong enough and that the primacy of politics would still also be valid for a military member of the board of directors. The September programme was based on the assumption that the 'cabinet' would be only a 'state of emergency and transitional government'.[36] This remark is not included in the November statement.

In both editions, the following step was to itemize those measures which ruled out mobilization and a policy of military aggression. His concern in both editions was the right of self-defence, the right of a country to defend its borders. He concluded that Germany fundamentally acknowledged the duty to pay reparations, but that it was limited by [Germany's right of] self-preservation.[37] While Hans Seeckt had begun to counter this emergency with volunteers and a secret armament programme as early as January 1921, his belief that it was necessary to defend Germany's borders was only confirmed by the occupation of the Ruhr.[38]

The government programmes did not cast doubt on Germany's compliance with the Treaty of Versailles, and they included the duty to pay off the war debts. Furthermore, the entente nations were offered the chance to acquire shares in German companies so that the debts could be paid off faster.[39]

In both editions, the government programme was based on an intensification of the relations with the USSR and emphasized that contacts would have to be maintained both with the West and the East. The contrast between the two forms of government would 'not be an obstacle ... as the Reich has equally little intent to interfere in Russia's domestic affairs'.[40] As in his speeches and other papers, he did not aspire to put the political and economic relations on a one-sided footing either.[41]

Since the idea of such a board of directors would bring about domestic unrest, both programmes contained the advice that no changes should be made to the Constitution at the present time. Federalism ought to be strengthened in such a way as to give Prussia more weight in all political issues 'in the way the great founders of the Reich had had in mind'. Here too, the domestic policy goals of Bismarck the politician were to be found in the programmes of September–November 1923.[42]

Contrary to the expectation that a national dictatorship would be sought, both statements advocated the independence of the judiciary, especially of the judges, and opposed the establishment of extraordinary courts for political offences.[43]

In another two memoranda of 1924, Seeckt discussed the political dangers and lessons learned from the time of the military state of emergency. The first one was his memorandum entitled *Preussen und das Reich* of 4 February 1924. It was the answer to the Bavarian demand of January 1924 in which more fiscal, financial and administrative independence was claimed. In his counter-proposal, Seeckt assigned Prussia the central position with respect to future ministerial responsibility and decision-making power. The second memorandum followed in August 1924. It was drafted in the directorate headed by Major Schleicher, Truppenamt T 1[44]. Both are identical as regards contents, because Prussia, the strengthening of federalism and the issue of the use of the Reichswehr pursuant to Article 48 of the Constitution of the Weimar Republic are just as much the central issues as they were in the memorandum of 4 February 1924.[45] As there are no contradictions in terms of contents, it shall be assumed that Seeckt initiated and fully approved of this second paper.

In his paper of August 1924, Seeckt emphasized that the lessons learned in Thuringia, Saxony and Bavaria showed that the governments of the individual states rejected the policies of the Reich and that they could blackmail and influence the Reich government. Only by using the Reichswehr had the government been able to exert its authority and prevent separatism. However, he 'unexpectedly' emphasized the Reichswehr was not the adequate means for him to use repeatedly for preserving the state and its Constitution.

Only when the Reich becomes a real state will it be able to stop implementing its domestic policy time and again solely by means of the military state of emergency. The creation of a large and cohesive state, of a strong power base inside the Reich, inside northern and central Germany, is imperative, especially to ensure the supremacy of government power over the military and to keep the armed forces out of politics. I refer to the first part of my statement on the Bavarian memorandum.[46]

Rather, he believed that the integration of smaller states into a strengthened Prussia would help fight separatism. Creating a central power base meant to him 'amalgamating Prussia with the Reich'. In his opinion, the small particular states were the cause of separatism, while the integration of the small states into the large and stable ones would create new majorities at the state parliament elections and thwart the small separatist movements of minorities. However, besides the lessons learned during the state of emergency, there were also financial, economic and fiscal reasons for an amalgamation.[47] Centralization through amalgamation would have the advantage of reducing the number of government authorities and hence of bureaucracy, and this would improve and speed up the cooperation between the authorities. The amalgamation of the state government authorities in question would yield tax relief, and he believed that the overlapping of departmental responsibilities could be prevented:

This paper cannot and is not meant to be an examination of how many ministers, government agencies and state parliament deputies can be saved if the proposed reorganization is implemented, whether one Prussian President [*Oberpräsident*] or one head of the administration of a countryside [*Landrat*] could not replace several ministers and whether it is not enough in certain cases to reinforce the next responsible *Oberpräsidium* by assigning it a few civil servants. Beside these savings in manpower, it is not possible to estimate the savings in unnecessary work and time which the reduction of parallel and so often opposing structures of the states' and the Reich's authorities will bring with it.[48]

Seeckt insisted on citing a few examples from administrative practice of how more efficient administration would result from it and what the problems were:

> The major share of the food of the Reich is produced by Prussian farmers, so the matter of feeding the people is primarily one of the Prussian Ministry of Agriculture ... However, we have a particular Ministry of Food in the Reich that has no executive power and direct influence. So here, either opposition arises or two-thirds of one ministry are superfluous.[49]

He believed that it was possible to overcome an 'unrestrained financial policy' and a 'policy made solely by civil servants with a party affiliation'. He thought that the state governments would no longer be able to designate members who negated the constitutional foundations of the Reich.[50] However, he also indicated what other internal difficulties his proposal would face. Besides the already existing interdepartmental, civil-military frictions, there would be others in administration:

> The resistance lies in general less in a particularism which is afraid that not all of its particular interests will be taken into account and more in the large number of those who are afraid of losing their undeserved status in public and see themselves threatened as the safe posts they hold become superfluous.[51]

He was in no doubt that 'in all the other hitherto particular states, including the Hanseatic cities, the amalgamation with Prussia [would yield] only advantages for Germany as a whole as well as for themselves.'[52]

None of his programmes or memoranda included a mention of the strengthening of the Reichswehr at the expense of other ministerial or parliamentary bodies. Rather, Seeckt hoped that the whole matter would strengthen Germany's international position, which had, up to then, suffered due to departmental egoism and particular interests:

> The political will must strive for the Reich to gain as much strength as possible internationally, and this can be achieved by reducing

sources of friction inside the country and by developing all elements which preserve and consolidate the state. The two cannot be achieved by centralization, but by the amalgamation of viable, independent confederations to form a Reich.[53]

He demanded the dismantling of federalist structures for the purpose 'of firmly distinguishing responsibilities between governance and self-management'.[54]

Neither in his proposals of 1924 nor in the political programmes of 1923 did he think of immediately or violently changing the Weimar Constitution. He advised that the Constitution be revised slowly because

a nation does not evolve in bounds, and as small and very small German states and cities amalgamate to form fewer and bigger states we can even now only take those steps which take account of the present-day situation.[55]

Stresemann, who was the Reich Chancellor until November 1923, was also of the opinion that a revision of the Constitution by which the federal structure and the states would not be abolished would be a political objective that could be used to prevent internal unrest. In

the much contested area of the interpretation of Article 48 where the distinguishing of the rights of the states and of the President of the Reich are concerned, a federal law should be initiated, and a way will be found here to safeguard the responsibilities of the states also on the issue of internal unrest.[56]

Seeckt felt neither drawn to dictatorial adventures nor did he enjoy the life of a politician that promised power and influence. His aide-de-camp, Selchow, passed on a few of his remarks. These were often quoted by specialists whenever they were at a loss when giving explanations and were unable to interpret his actions and character in a technically coherent way.[57] These remarks are not untypical of him and allow a glimpse to be obtained of his character. Regarding the search for qualified figures to be members of the board of directors, Selchow wrote into his official diary:

In those days, he once said to me something like: 'Governing takes men who know the trade: soldiers for military affairs, bankers for finance, farmers for questions of food production etc. The first precondition which they must fulfil, however, is having a clean record.' These are the people I am looking for and I find only few.' Thus, he rejected Warburg as finance minister because he was Jewish[58] after all, and he rejected managers of the Landbund because he had the impression that they applied more out of personal ambition than out of the will to help Germany; he dismissed general manager von Stinnes after a conversation of two hours 'because he has presented only sparkling wine and not mixed it with a single drop of water'.[59]

Regarding the question asked by many as to whether Seeckt wanted to defy the President of the Reich, specialists like Heinz Hürten, Otto-Ernst Schüddekopf or Michael Geyer quoted a cutting and also condescending remark. 'If it's going to be a comedy, I'm not going to play at all, if it's a drama, then I will enter in Act 3.'[60]

During the internal unrest, which had, at that time, not yet developed into a drama, and during the commotion around him, he wrote home: 'Were I Reich Chancellor, I would not make any general's trips. Well, I am the Chief of the Army Command, so I do not need to engage in politics ...' or to his sister, Marie von Rothkirch: 'trying out a new horse ... is better than politics.'[61]

After having laid the power back into the hands from which he had received it, unexpectedly for some of his contemporaries and much too hesitantly for posterity, the sentence which he allegedly said in 1922 may sound less Sphinx-like, that is 'that he alone could stage a coup d'état, but he would not do it'.[62]

Such remarks were unfortunately often put into an ambivalent context by some specialists, with the aim of reflecting his rejection. In the context of his military-strategic and politico-military concepts, they refer rather to an aloofness to power, influence, dictatorship and a unilateral strengthening of his own institution, the Reichswehr.

Chapter 6

Conclusion

The images of Seeckt that we have constructed differs considerably from that which has been painted by previous historians. This is particularly true of Seeckt's strategy concept for the Weimarer Republic.

The primacy of politics was probably the most important idea behind Seeckt's strategic concept. It was the politico-military basis upon which he judged the new military setting after the lost war. It was the foundation upon which he decided what measures the Army had to take and what political terms it had to observe. Civil-military cooperation was of prime importance to him in conflicts and in his view already had to be taken up in peacetime. The First World War had proven the extent to which the civil-military element influenced events and the course of a war and how the lack of good cooperation impeded success. Seeckt believed that cooperation between the political leadership and the military top brass in particular was indispensable and had to be consensual. He also wanted to include those government departments that would be affected by a conflict and have to provide resources. They, too, had to prove that they were always willing to cooperate in the interest of ensuring that success was achieved in war through tact, concessions and goodwill. Mutual acceptance was as natural to Seeckt as the equality of the partners in international negotiations. The political leadership set the guidelines for all government departments and decided on the course a conflict should take, the priorities and the objectives. The fact that soldiers came under the control of the government due to the primacy of politics did not relieve them of their socio-political responsibility of continuously providing information about the capacities and potentials of armies before or during a war. Because of Germany's military weakness, the political leadership had to be informed about the state of the army in due time. A soldier was eminent on account of his capability to make correct assessments of the military situation and his knowledge of how a war could be started and ended. His responsibility was not founded on the equality of politicians and the military, but on the equality of the responsibility they held both for war and peace. Seeckt took account of the criteria that Huntington considers a 'military mind' meets. According to Strachan, all the government departments concerned not only had to be functional and professional, but also good-willed and united in the pursuit of the political objectives. Like both military theorists, Seeckt considered technical responsibility and the technical capability for civil-military cooperation keys to success.

The fundamental change in the system of society caused by the change in the system of government from a monarchy to a republic by way of a revolution formed the political foundations of his thoughts on military strategy. The change in society and the ensuing change in the system of government in 1918–1919 had created new socio-political challenges for the people. From the political standpoint, cooperation was called for between the different parties; the defeat could be dealt with from the economic angle; and personal unemployment could be handled from the financial one. What made the socio-political setting even worse was the Treaty of Versailles, which posed more immense difficulties for all the sections of the population. The sense of rejection felt by the people of the Weimar Republic for the Treaty of Versailles also caught hold of the state's new army. Given the domestic unrest in 1919 and the Kapp-Lüttwitz coup in 1920, the Reichswehr seemed to be a potential threat to the state. Since there was a threat of more domestic unrest, Seeckt rejected any form of party politics within the Reichswehr and refused to allow any political influence to be exerted on it either from within or without. Conscription was controversial for political reasons because an increasing number of people in the Weimar Republic voted for extremist parties. By 1932, almost half of the people had voted for anti-constitutional parties, proving that Seeckt was right after all in his rejection. Such conditions were not only the reason why he did not grant soldiers active electoral rights and the right to participate in political rallies, but also accounted for his decision. In contrast, Seeckt attributed great importance to civic education for themselves and for which soldiers were responsible. They had to educate themselves politically and form their own opinions. They were to develop their own ideas about current political events without being influenced by party politics and by the people around them. Above all, the higher a soldier rose in the military hierarchy and the sooner he assumed responsibility for troops and their public image, the more civic education he was required to have. Seeckt's concept of military strategy is shown to be modern by the fact that soldiers at the interface with policy were themselves responsible for always staying abreast of political developments and international relations and familiar with the factors that influenced them.

The after-effects of the lost war were at the basis of his assumptions, either in economic or socio-political terms: the First World War had not only demonstrated to all the warring parties involved how much the people of Germany had suffered through mass mobilization, but also how the national economy had shrunk and prosperity had been lost for generations to come. The purchasing power of the global economy was paralyzed, a development that weakened the state's finances owing to lower tax revenue, and debts rose everywhere. The country could not afford to maintain and arm a mass-military force. Seeckt counted these economic conditions among those factors which, besides Allied guidelines and his war experience, prompted him to decide in favour of a small operating army.

In his regulations, in FuG and in his publications, Seeckt worked on the assumption that Germany would have a 200,000-man army, orientating the training of the Reichsheer towards the new weapon-related challenges in order to form a professionally equipped army that would be ready for the future. To him, a well-trained and heavily equipped army was a deterrent for the enemy and, thus, served the purpose of securing peace. To him, deterrence was both a psychological and a military means for avoiding war. This made him a proponent of the modern theory of deterrence.

His sense of responsibility in the politico-military and socio-political fields had its roots in his war experience and in the understanding that a professional army would prevent the total violence of a people's war. Seeckt looked at his task and official function from the angle of military professionalism linked to a political and social élite status from which he derived the duty to prevent an escalation of violence, civil war and a people's war. He neither regarded this attitude as a threat to his military professionalism nor did he have a problem with integrating it into the Weimar Republic. Rather, it was his sense of professional responsibility that made him part of the political and social élite and made him think about a potential future conflict. It was precisely because the First World War had clearly shown him, the professional soldier, what the consequences of a possible future conflict might be that he claimed to be part of what was the ruling class of the country in 'traditional political and social terms'. His military experience gave him the technical competence to take on a responsible task to safeguard peace both at home and abroad in times of international crises. This was his professional responsibility vis-à-vis the state and society.

Owing to Germany's changed geopolitical situation after the war, the military strategist, too, had to revise his situation assessment. It was dependent on the country's position on the continent, its neighbours, its armament policies and its readiness to shape a policy of alliances. Disarmament negotiations were a way of banning the danger of war, and international negotiations were deemed to be qualified for leading to an alliance policy that would secure peace among neighbours. It was the military strategist's task to make geo-strategic situation assessments, but those depended on foreign policy guidelines and on the political objectives and priorities. Seeckt believed that Germany's borders were threatened. His opinion had been confirmed by illegal Polish border crossings since 1919 as well as by the occupation of the Ruhr by French troops in 1923. His demands for a right of self-defence were addressed at the government, but contained calls neither for mass mobilization nor for a war of revenge. Seeckt's preparations to fend off enemy incursions meant secret rearmament to reinforce Germany's borders. He continued to be well aware of the insufficient training the Reichsheer had, warning against hasty plans and preparations being made until long after his retirement. Seeckt would have rejected a four-front war not only on account of his war experience, but he also warned against the danger of Germany being crushed between the powers of the East and West. Seeckt had not rejected a League of Nations from the beginning, but believed that the equality of Germany in international negotiations and agreements was an essential foundation of such an alliance policy. His military-strategic considerations were based on the concept of political interests being equal in international negotiations. His position clearly ruled out a war of aggression, even though he wanted Germany to become a great power again. His military-strategic considerations were founded on his assessment that international negotiations and alliances would secure peace.

Seeckt's geostrategic analysis favoured a balanced foreign policy, not a biased one. His political views corresponded with Bismarck's in that respect. His geostrategic assessments were not guided by ideological opposites, especially where a border was shared with a strong neighbour. He recommended negotiations and rapprochement. He believed that the end of Germany's foreign policy was to enable the country to pursue its strategic objectives with respect to both Western and Eastern countries, irrespective of political ideologies. Since it was not possible for Germany to realise this objective during the first years of the Republic, the result had to be a one-sided orientation towards the East. In military terms, he was primarily interested in technical training with the prohibited weapons. It was not his objective to pursue a concept of an alliance war in favour of Germany's renaissance as a great power. Rather, it must be assumed that Seeckt took precautions to protect Germany from incursions by powerful states.

At the tactical level, Seeckt was a supporter of the commission principle as advocated by Moltke the Elder. Like Clausewitz, Huntington and Strachan, Seeckt was also opposed to putting too much strain on military means. This principle was based on the commission principle, which required the means needed have to be made available in order to accomplish a mission.

Seeckt believed that he would be able to control the military in operations and at the interface with policy by means of directive-style command. What he expected from soldiers, from their military concept of themselves within the state, was not less than what Huntington and Strachan expected. Seeckt lived up to Huntington's expectation of a 'military min' and he was generally far ahead of his time. To him, other factors such as civic education, and the expert and professional advice given to the political leadership by the military were essential. While Huntington warned against soldiers being influenced by politics, Seeckt had pointed out long before Huntington the importance of military advice and placed the latter under the primacy of politics and under the responsibility vis-à-vis the state and society. Soldiers at the interface with policy had to be able to make political assessments in order to give the political leadership military advice and serve political interests. Part of their military advice came in the form of assessments of how to prevent crises through deterrence and assessments of the geostrategic situation that safeguarded political interests.

Seeckt had therefore met Huntington's expectations regarding a 'military mind' long before his day and had added essential factors. Changes which Seeckt made were his demand for politically independent education for soldiers as well as military strategies devised by soldiers so as to ensure that expert military advice could be given to the government. These factors were part of Seeckt's identity as a soldier because he believed that this was the only way the soldier at the interface with policy was able to inform politicians on all aspects of the state's legal recourse to force.

A military strategy was required that took account of geopolitics and geostrategy, foreign and domestic policy, financial and economic policy, public and constitutional law. Seeckt was in no doubt that soldiers had to respect armament and disarmament agreements, but believed that it was the political leadership who specified the policies regarding alliances, including military alliances, and that the conduct of war was also constantly subject to political considerations, so that all that soldiers had to do was to be able to make military assessments and to give military advice.

The criteria stated show not only a contrast between Seeckt and the military doctrines of previous decades, but also a contrast between him and Ludendorff. The acceptance of the primacy of politics, the rejection of a mass military force for moral, socio-political and military reasons, the focus on good civil-military cooperation, the expectation that soldiers acquire civic education on their own, and the emphasis on a technically very well armed small operating army, are central elements of his military strategy.

He had accepted these terms so as to be able to give adequate military advice in the sense of Clausewitz. Compared with Stülpnagel, it has become clear that a biased interpretation or the omission of one or more military-strategic criteria resulted in unbalanced advice being given and thus in military advice which compromised or changed the political objectives themselves. Such advice was only given in a responsible way with regard to the state and the people if the factors specified by the government, i.e. the observation of public and constitutional law, were taken into account. Another prerequisite for successful military-strategic advice being given is the need to ensure that the political leadership get full information about the military strategy so that they are aware of the consequences and effects on their political objectives and of the main elements and weaknesses of the strategy. This is the only way to ensure that they are able to assess whether they will be able to realise their political interests by means of the legal recourse to force. The political leadership must be aware of this concept and understand it so as to be able to assess its effects on their own objectives in socio-political and foreign policy terms. If, as happened after the Seeckt period, the military and the politicians are not aware of the military foundations and its consequences, they will neither succeed in drafting a joint political strategy nor be victorious in military conflicts.

Here too, Seeckt followed Clausewitz, who had demanded that the military aims should converge with the political ones, that political leadership should 'think in a military way' in order to understand the political consequences of the military-strategic advice given. The supreme soldier knew the aims and ends of policy and was able to not only organise, train and educate the forces accordingly, but to also adequately advise politicians. What this means is that political leadership must know the military strategy in order to be able to assess what the effects and consequences it has on domestic and foreign affairs on the strategic objectives. Differences and disagreements in Seeckt's day, too, caused failure or compromised the success of political objectives, just as Huntington and Strachan had warned. Mutual understanding for others' views, ends and aims not only facilitates cooperation, but also ensures that objectives are achieved.

The policies of Seeckt, the chief executive, have been presented and analysed in Chapter 5. The chapter covered the question as to how his policies and political views complied with the principles of his military strategy and as to whether they were conclusive and in conformity with his military strategy: his political programmes were based on the military guidelines made by the Allies and by the Weimar Republic, and he stipulated that the primacy of politics was binding, just as he discarded the idea of a war of aggression being waged for military or political reasons. Thus, he not only based his military strategy on Clausewitz, not only upheld the primacy of politics at the interface with policy, but was also faithful to these principles in his role as chief executive. What he considered necessary, if anything at all, was a transitory board of directors, and even then, he did not advocate an amendment of the constitution that would have put the Reichswehr at the helm of the state. Quite the opposite is true: he considered that the constant use of the Reichswehr as a last resort for maintaining the unity of the Reich was wrong and discarded it on political grounds. As chief executive, Seeckt made political proposals on how the Reich could be held together. He even remained a military strategist when he gave political advice, for the precise reason that he did not want to implement it by taking the legal recourse to force.

The last open issue regarding Seeckt's military conduct is his refusal to obey orders from Reichswehr Minister Noske in 1920 and from the President of the Reich Ebert in 1923. This refusal to obey orders seems to be the only inconsistency in Seeckt's attitude towards the primacy of politics and in his military-strategic attitude towards the government. He declined to use the Reichswehr against his own forces on several occasions. One was in 1920, two years after the end of the war, in which the forces, bound in comradeship, had held out against the enemy without for four years in a trench war, and a second was after the change of system in 1923. In that year, President of the Reich Ebert had even issued several demands for him to use the Reichsheer against the Bavarian troops in Munich who were sympathizing with Ludendorff, Hitler and the NSDAP. The motives for his decisions were, however, more political than military.

He believed that a force that was required to fire at fellow soldiers at the very beginning of a break of a system and then in the ensuing change of the system, would not trust their fellow soldiers anymore and would be like a gang of thieves, the sole difference being that their own fellow soldiers had become political opponents. Not only would it be a force void of comradeship, but it would be unable to secure the existence of the Reich either. It would no longer trust either the state or its politicians who had issued them the order to fire at soldiers alongside whom they had once fought in the trenches. Such a force would be able to protect neither the state nor its citizens, especially at the beginning of a change of system. It would be worn out politically and ultimately turn on itself. These are the reasons why Seeckt not only rejected outright any party influence being exerted on the Reichswehr, but also the unmilitary demand for soldiers to fire at fellow soldiers. This may have prompted President of the Reich Ebert to give way in November 1923. Seeckt's only remaining instrument of power within the Reichsheer was his insistence on the military hierarchy, i.e. the discipline, of which obedience was an element, being maintained. He argued that anyone who did not obey had not understood the principle of military hierarchy and should be discharged. Consequently, Seeckt believed that the value of a military force did not depend solely on such factors as training and equipment, technology and military exercise, but also on trust in the political and military heads. He believed that the command of the state's legal instrument of force did not rely solely on the principle of order and obedience, as General von Lossow demonstrated to Seeckt, but also on political opinions and, as Stülpnagel showed, on politico-military convictions regarding war and peace. Both soldiers, Lossow and Stülpnagel, lacked political appreciation of the consequences of their socio-political and politico-military demands. They lacked trust both in the state's political and military heads. The use of force against his own troops and commanders was out of the question for Seeckt, and this accounted for his refusal to obey Noske's and Ebert's orders. Seeckt failed because he was unable to instil trust in the state and the constitution among the forces; this would have required civic education that was supported by the state and the Army. In the Weimar Republic, he could merely rely on obedience. The directive style of command, which was Seeckt's style of command towards the commanders within his own institution, can only be successful if the political heads and the system are appreciated militarily and politically.

In contrast to Clausewitz, Jomini, Leon Daudet, Ludendorff and other war theorists, Seeckt was the military strategist who not only advocated a modern military strategy, but who was also able to apply it at the interface with policy. He was not one of those theorists whose military strategy is only implemented by others. Due to his eminent position in the Weimar

Republic, he was one of the few soldiers who had the possibility to train, educate, advise and thus operate according to their military-strategic principles.

Combining all military-strategic aspects, Seeckt proved to be a representative of the primacy of politics, of the theory of deterrence and of civic education and a follower of Clausewitz. Seeckt's actions took firm shape when his conduct was seen in the light of military-strategic ideas, considerations and thoughts. Especially his personnel policy, his conduct vis-à-vis the up-and-coming generation, his attitude towards defence technology and his political actions can be seen in this context. Moreover, his rejection of a mass military force, of electoral rights, of defence technology and of certain people gained a rational basis. It was not based on politically emotional feelings, a hitherto undefined character or double-entry bookkeeping. His political actions, too, were influenced by the military-strategic factors stated. His attitude towards public and constitutional law, the primacy of politics, civil-military operation, his assessment of the geostrategic situation, armament and alliance policies, the people's political opinions, the formation and organization of armed forces, directive style command, the commission principle, personnel policies, civic education as well as defence technology provides an overview of his attitude towards politics and the armed forces.

The military-strategic position was central to his actions, especially since it not only provided a different dimension to his policy on the East.

The analysis shows that the supreme soldier's military professionalism and politico-military responsibility can be gauged by his military strategy. His sense of responsibility and his capability must be measured by whether he informed government fully and on all aspects. At the same time, military strategy is the key to understanding his actions and his sense of responsibility vis-à-vis the state and society. There are few cases in military history in which such a clear contrast between two very different military strategies is demonstrated. There are few cases in which two contemporaries define their theories in such different ways and can also substantiate them. In contrast, there are frequent cases of mixed types of military strategies whose essence and focal points military historians find difficult to work out.

What this means for military historians is that mysteries surrounding the person, his 'Sphinx-like' conduct, indeed contradictions in his conduct can only be clarified and open questions can only be answered if the military-strategic factors are taken into account. The military-strategic concept of the supreme soldier must be analysed for military history research to be done. It is the source from which his actions at the interface with policy as well as his effect on the troops must be derived. His military-strategic ideas leave their mark not only on the advice he gives, but also on his bearing and actions within the force. Military strategy is at the centre of the supreme soldier's actions. It characterises his instructions, orders, guidelines, advice. It is at the heart of his actions. This is why academics cannot confine themselves to just a few facts or disregard some facts from the start when they analyse it. The argument that Seeckt's publications were not published until after his retirement, and therefore do not need to be taken into account, is invalid. Especially since, if it were so, many a biography would never have been written, because, to be thorough and paint a full picture of the figure concerned, a biography must take account of files and documents which were produced after their productive period and which are still unpublished. Military historians, too, may assume that a soldier at the interface with policy has a concept according to which he consistently pursues his objectives and that he is not a split personality who has one personality while at work and another after hours.

Military history analysis must also take account of politico-military and military-strategic principles because it has become clear that contradictions in politico-military or military-strategic principles must be resolved as they cannot be combined logically into one theory. Military-strategic principles which cannot be combined must be taken away and presented separately, and the different approaches they propose must be traced back to their origins. However, this research has shown that the interpretations tend to lead to confusion and even greater misunderstanding if this approach is not adopted. Nowhere has this become as clear as in the dispute between Seeckt and Ludendorff and Stülpnagel respectively. The discussion on the future military-strategic and the politico-military orientation of the Reichsheer not only considerably hampered the force's development in its day. It also created the possibility to build up a mass-military force and thus helped bring about the Second World War and Germany's initial successes.

Even after the Second World War, both the followers and opponents of Seeckt and Ludendorff influenced the establishment of the Bundeswehr. To this day, the factional dispute between Seeckt and Ludendorff underlies the disputes between traditionalists and reformers. The military strategy conflict has not yet been resolved. Seeckt's followers, among them Wolf Graf von Baudissin, and Ludendorff's followers, who comprised the first Bundeswehr Chief of Staff, Adolf Heusinger, not only marked the period before and during the Second World War, but also helped build the Bundeswehr. Their military-strategic lines have not yet been analysed. Their importance for the forces with respect to military policy and their effects on them have so far not been attributed to Seeckt or to Clausewitz or Ludendorff, a step that would result in their actions alone yielding a clear indication of their positions on military and social policy. Researchers and politicians will not be able to appreciate the effects these figures and their military strategies had until the factors and influencing criteria stated have been presented.

The time has therefore come to analyse the military strategies of the theorists and practitioners who influenced the post-Seeckt period. It is no less urgent to use the approach taken here, i.e. to present the differences between both Ludendorff and Clausewitz and Ludendorff and Seeckt as a starting point for highlighting those general staff officers who made the preparations for the Second World War much more than Seeckt did. This would allow the dispute between the followers of Ludendorff and Clausewitz to be pursued, i.e. the discussion between traditionalists and reformers, into the Bundeswehr era.

What is important for the political leadership is that the supreme soldier clearly explains to them his military strategy and the effects it will have both on domestic and foreign affairs. For soldiers can only achieve the objectives set by politicians when they know them. The government can only be certain of having been adequately informed on whether the strategic objectives they have formulated can be achieved by military means after they have thoroughly analysed the military strategy. It is just as important for military policy to be conclusive and for all of its factors to be coordinated among the relevant authorities as it is for military strategy at the interface with policy to be consistent with this policy.

Abbreviations

FuG: *Führungs und Gefecht der verbundenen Waffen*

H.Dv.: Heeresdienstvorschrift

NSDAP: Nationalsozialistische Deutsche Arbeiterpartei, National – Socialist Party

SPD: Sozialdemokratische Partei, Social Democratic Party

DDP: Deutsche Demokratische Partei, German Democratic Party

USPD: Unabhängige Sozialdemoratische Partei Deutschlands, Independent Social Democratic Party

Bibliography

List of References

1. Unprinted Sources Federal Archive Military Archive, Freiburg im Breisgau, Germany (BArch): Stock description: Military history collections

MSg 1/266 Aufzeichnungen des damaligen Majors Fleck über seine Tätigkeit im Kriegsministerium, insbes. als Adjutant Kriegsminister Reinhardts während der November-Revolution 1918 (Handschrift, Kopien), 1917–1919. [Notes of Major Fleck at the time about his activities in the Ministry of War, in particular as adjutant of the Minister of War Rheinhardt, during the November Revolution 1918 (handwritten copies), 1917–1919]

MSg 1/269 Handakte des damaligen Majors Fleck als Adjutant des Kriegsministers Reinhardt, 1919. [Reference file of Major Fleck at the time as adjutant of the Minister of War Rheinhardt, 1919]

Msg 2/2168 Donald Shearer: Truppenbewegungen, II. Notes on Early Mobilization Planning: 1921–1926, o. A. des Ortes: 1978. [Donald Shearer: movement of troops, II. Notes on Early Mobilization Planning: 1921–1926]

Stock description: literary remains

N 5 Nachlass Joachim von Stülpnagel [literary remains of Joachim von Stülpnagel]

N 42 Nachlass General Kurt von Schleicher [literary remains of General Kurt von Schleicher]

N 62 Nachlass Friedrich Rabenau [literary remains of Friedrich Rabenau]

N 86 Nachlass Walther Reinhardt [literary remains of Lieutenant General Walther Reinhardt]

N 247 Nachlass Generaloberst Johannes von Seeckt [literary remains of Colonel General Johannes von Seeckt]

N 386 Nachlass General der Artillerie Erich Freiherr von dem Bussche-Ippenburg [literary remains of Artillery General Erich Freiherr von dem Bussche-Ippenburg]

Bestandsbeschreibung: Reichsheer (RH)

[Stock description: German Imperial Army]

RH 2 Reichswehrminister / Aktenbestände des Heeres [Minister of Defense/ files of the Army]

RH 8 OKH / Heereswaffenamt [German Army Ordnance Office]

RH 12–1 Inspektion der Waffenschule des Heeres (In 1) [Inspection of the Army Weapons School (In 1)

RH 12–2 Inspektion der Infanterie des Heeres (In 2) [Inspection of the Army Infantry (In2)]

RH 37 Verbände und Einheiten der Infanterie des Heeres [Military units of the Army Infantry]

RH 53–3 Wehrkreiskommando III (Berlin) [Military District Command III (Berlin)]

RH 53–4 Wehrkreiskommando IV (Stettin) [Military District Command IV (Stettin)]

RH 61 Kriegsgeschichtliches Forschungsanstalt des Heeres [History Research Institution of the Army]

RH 61/2279 Kurzer Überblick über den Wiederaufbau des Heeres-Nachrichten- und Abwehrdienstes 1919–1929. Ehemaliger Bestand der Kriegsgeschichtlichen Forschungsanstalt des Heeres (Konkordanz W 10 / 52127). [Brief overview about the reconstruction of the Army's intelligence and counterintelligence agency, 1919–1929. Former stock of the History Research Institution of the Army (concordance W 10 / 52127)]

Stock description: Reichswehr (Rw)

Rw 6/Allgemeines Wehrmachtsamt

RwD 6 Reichswehrministerium / Reichskriegsministerium [Reichswehr Ministry/ Reich War Ministry]

RwD 6/5 OKW Allgemeines Wehrmachtsamt, Drucksachen Richtlinien zur Beurteilung der Tauglichkeit für das Reichsheer und die Reichsmarine (Musterung), 23. Februar 1921 [printed documentation and guidelines for assessing the suitability of the Reichsheer and the Reichsmarine (military physical examination), 23 February 1921]

2. Printed References
Files and Collections of Documents:

Files of the Chancellery of the Reich (Akten der Reichskanzlei), Weimar Republic, ed. for the Historical Commission at the Bavarian Academy of Science by Karl Dietrich Erdmann, for the Federal Archive (Bundesarchiv) of Hans Booms, Boppard/Rhine: 1968, Cuno cabinet (Das Kabinett Cuno) 22 November 1922 till 12 August 1923.

Files of the Chancellery of the Reich, Weimar Republic, ed. for the Historical Commission at the Bavarian Academy of Science by Karl Dietrich Erdmann, for the Federal Archive of Hans Booms, Marx cabinets I/II, vol. 1 and 2, (Die Kabinette Marx I und II, Band 1 und 2), Vol. I: 30 November 1923 till 3 June 1924, Boppard/Rhine: 1973. Vol. 2: 3 June 1924 till January 1925, Boppard/Rhine: 1977.

Files of Chancellery of the Reich, Weimar Republic, ed., for the Historical Commission at the Bavarian Academy of Science by Karl Dietrich Erdmann, for the Federal Archive of Hans Booms, Luther cabinets I/II, vol. 1 and 2 (Die Kabinette Luther I und II, Band 1 und 2), Vol. 1: 15 January 1925 till 20 January 1926. Vol. 2: 20 January 1926 till 17 May 1926, Boppard/Rhine: 1977.

Files of Chancellery of the Reich, Weimar Republic, ed. for the Historical Commission at the Bavarian Academy of Science by Karl Dietrich Erdmann, for the Federal Archive of Hans Booms, Stresemann cabinets I/II, vol. I (Die Kabinette Stresemann I und II, Band 1), 13 August bis 6 October 1923, Vol 2, 6 October to 30 November 1923, Boppard/Rhine: 1978.

Files of Foreign Policy of the Federal Republic of Germany, commissioned by the German Foreign Office, ed. the Institute of Contemporary History (IfZ), 1949/1950, publ. Hans-Peter Schwarz, Munich: 1997.

Files of Foreign Policy of the Federal Republic of Germany, commissioned by the German Foreign Office, ed. the Institute of Contemporary History (IfZ), publ. Hans-Peter Schwarz 1951, 1 January to 31 December 1951, Munich: 1999.

Files of Foreign Policy of the Federal Republic of Germany, commissioned by the German Foreign Office, ed. the Institute of Contemporary History (IfZ), Vol. 2: Adenauer and the High Commissioners 1952 (Adenauer und die Hohen Kommissare 1952), ed. Hans-Peter Schwarz with Reiner Pommerin, Munich: 1990.

Files of Foreign Policy of the Federal Republic of Germany 1951, publ. and commissioned by the German Foreign Office, ed. the Institute of Contemporary History (IfZ), Vol 2: Adenauer and the High Commissioners 1952, publ. Hans-Peter Schwarz with Reiner Pommerin, Munich: 1990.

America's Plans for War against the Soviet Union 1945–1950. A 15–volume set reproducing in facsimile 98 plans and studies created by the Joint Chiefs of Staff, Vol. 14: Long Range Planning: Dropshot. Publ. by Steven T. Ross und David Alan Rosenberg, New-York: 1989.

Remarks Chief of the Army Command, Colonel General von Seeckt during visits and manoeuvres between the years 1920 and 1926, publ. Reichswehr Ministry, German Army Training Department (Heeresausbildungsabteilung), Berlin: 1927.

Provisions on promotion and transfer of the volunteers of the Reichsheer (non-commissioned officers and privates) during peacetime with supplementary provisions for officers of November 1920, Berlin: 1920. Bestimmungen über die Beförderung und Versetzung der Freiwilligen des Reichsheeres (Unteroffiziere und Mannschaften) im Frieden mit Offiziersergänzungsbestimmungen vom November 1929, Berlin: 1920.

Documents on the history of the German constitution since 1789, Vol. V World War, revolution and reformation of the German Reich 1914 – 1919,

(Deutsche Verfassungsgeschichte seit 1789, Bd. V Weltkrieg, Revolution und Reichserneuerung 1914–1919), ed. Ernst R. Huber, Stuttgart: 1978.

Documents on the history of the German constitution, Vol. VI, The Weimar Republic (Deutsche Verfassungsgeschichte, Bd. VI, Die Weimarer Republik), ed. Ernst R. Huber, Stuttgart: 1981.

Documents on the history of the German constitution, German constitutional documents 1919 – 1933, Vol. 4 (Deutsche Verfassungsgeschichte, Deutsche Verfassungsdokumente 1919–1933 Band 4), ed. Ernst R. Huber, Stuttgart: 1992.

Documents on German policy III series / Vol. 3 (Deutschland Politik III Reihe / Band 3), 1st January till 31. December 1957, ed. Federal Ministry of All-German Affairs (Bundesministerium für Gesamtdeutsche Fragen) Bonn/ Berlin, Frankfurt/Main: 1967.

Descriptive lists of the historical stock of the Federal Archive, Vol. 19, stock no.247 (Findbücher zu den Beständen des Bundesarchivs, Band 19, Bestand N 247), literary remains of Colonel General Hans von Seeckt, Koblenz: 1981.

Drilling Regulation for the infantry (Exerzier-Reglement für die Infanterie D.V.E. No. 130, Berlin: 1909.

Rules of field-duty [Felddienst-Ordnung (F.O.) D.V.E. No. 267, Berlin: 1908.]

Command and combined arms combat, Army regulation 487 [Führung und Gefecht der verbundenen Waffen, Heeresdienstvorschrift H.Dv.487, (FuG)], Publisher 'Offene Worte': Berlin 1921, 1923, Part 1 (section I-XII): 1921, Part 2 (section XIII-XVIII): 1923.

Army Regulation (Heeres-Verordnungsblatt), publ. Ministry of the Reichswehr (Army Command/ Military Administration [Reichswehrministerium (Heer-esleitung/ Heeresverwaltung)] year 1920–1926, Berlin: 1921–1927.

Military Science Review (Militärwissenschaftliche Rundschau), publ. Reich War Ministry (Reichskriegsministerium), Berlin: 1936.

Reichswehr and Red Army, Documents of German and Russian Military Archives from 1925 – 1931, publ. Federal Archive, Official Russian Archives Services, Official Russian Military Archive: ed. for the Federal Archive 'Friedrich P. Kahlenberg', for the Official Russian Archive Service 'Rudilf G. Pichoja", for the Official Russian Military Archive 'Ljudmila V. Dvojnych', Koblenz 1995. [Reichswehr und Rote Armee, Dokumente aus den Militärarchiven Deutschlands und Russlands 1925 – 1931, Publ. Bundesarchiv, Russischer Staatlicher Archivdienst, Russisches Staatliches Militärarchiv: herausgegeben für das Bundesarchiv: Friedrich P. Kahlenberg, für den Russischen Archivdienst Rudilf G. Pichoja, für das Russische Staatliche Militärarchiv: Ljudmila V. Dvojnych, Koblenz: 1995.]

Reichswehr Ministry, Army Personnel Office, Ranking List of the German Imperial Army, (Reichswehrministerium, Heeres-Personalamt, Ranglisten des deutschen Reichsheeres), Berlin, 1923 to 1926.

Sources on the relations between Germany and its neighbours in the 19th and 20th century, Vol. 8, sources on the German-Soviet relations 1917 – 1945, publ. by Horst Günther Linke, Darmstadt: 1998.

Sources on the history of parliamentarism and the political parties, second series: Military and Policy. On behalf of the Commission for history of parliamentarism and the political parties and the Military History Research Institution. Publ. by Erich Matthias and Hans Meier-Welcker, Vol. 2. Between revolution and Kapp-Coup, Military and Domestic Policy 1918 – 1920, (Zwischen Revolution und Kapp-Putsch, Militär und Innenpolitik 1918–1920, ed. by Heinz Hürten, Düsseldorf: 1977.

Sources on the history of parliamentarism and the political parties, Second Series: Military and Policy. On behalf of the Commission for history of parliamentarism and the political parties and the Military History Research Institution. Publ. by Erich Matthias and Hans Meier-Welcker, Vol. 3. The beginnings of the era Seeckt, Military and Domestic Policy 1920 – 1922 (Die Anfänge der Ära Seeckt, Militär und Innenpolitik 1920–1922), ed. by Heinz Hürten, Düsseldorf: 1979.

Sources on the history of parliamentarism and the political parties, second series: Military and Policy. On behalf of the Commission for history of parliamentarism and the political parties and the Military History Research Institution. Publ. by Erich Matthias and Hans Meier-Welcker, Vol. 4. The crisis year 1923, Military and Domestic Policy (Das Krisenjahr 1923, Militär und Innenpolitik 1922–1924), ed. by Heinz Hürten, Düsseldorf: 1980.

Ceasefire 1918 – 1919, The documentary material of the ceasefire negotiations of Compiegne, Spa, Trier and Brussels, exchange of notes/ protocols of the negotiations / contracts / reports about total activities, on behalf of the German ceasefire commission, Vol. I, the ceasefire contract of Compiègne and its renewals in addition to the financial conditions, Berlin 1940. (Der Waffenstillstandsvertrag von *Compiègne* und seine Verlängerungen nebst den finanziellen Bestimmungen, Berlin: 1940).

3. References

Abenheim, Donald: Bundeswehr und Tradition. Die Suche nach einem gültigen Erbe des deutschen Soldaten, Munich: 1989.

Absolon, Rudolf: Die Wehrmacht im Dritten Reich, Vol. I to IV, Schriften des Bundesarchivs 16, Boppard: 1969. Vol. I, 30 January 1933 till 2 August 1934. Mit einem Blick auf das Militärwesen in Preussen, im Kaiserreich und in der Weimarer Republik.

Adamthwaite, Anthony P.: Britain and the world, 1945 – 1949: the view from the Foreign Office, in: Power in Europe? Great Britain, France, Italy and Germany in a postwar world, 1945 – 1950, ed. by Josef Becker, Franz Knipping. – Berlin: 1986, p. 9 to 26.

Adjutant im preussischen Kriegsministerium June 1918 till October 1919, Aufzeichnungen des Hauptmanns Gustav Böhm, Publ. for MGFA, Heinz Hürten and Georg Mayer, Stuttgart: 1977.

Airpower journal: (APJ) professional journal of the United States Air Force, Washington, DC, Publ. Air University Maxwell Air Force Base, Ala.

Albrecht, Clemens, Behrmann, Günter C., Bock, Michael: Die intellektuelle Gründung der Bundesrepublik, eine Wirkungsgeschichte der Frankfurter Schule, Frankfurt / Main: 1999.

Altrichter, Friedrich: Das Wesen der soldatischen Erziehung, Berlin: 1942.

Alvensleben, Udo von: Lauter Abschiede, Frankfurt / Main: 1971.

Andrew, Christopher und Gordiewsky, Oleg: KGB, die Geschichte seiner Auslandsoperationen von Lenin bis Gorbatschow, Munich: 1990.

Anfänge westdeutscher Sicherheitspolitik 1945 – 1956, Vol. 1, Von der Kapitulation bis zum Pleven-Plan, Publ. MGFA, Munich: 1982.

Anfänge westdeutscher Sicherheitspolitik 1945 – 1956, Vol. 3, Die NATO-Option, Publ. MGFA, Munich: 1993

Anfänge westdeutscher Sicherheitspolitik 1945 to 1956, Vol. 4, Wirtschaft und Rüstung Souveränität und Sicherheit, Publ. MGFA, Munich: 1997.

Armee für Frieden und Sozialismus, Geschichte der nationalen Volksarmee der DDR, Berlin: 1985.

Aufstand des Gewissens. Militärischer Widerstand gegen Hitler und das NS – Regime 1933 – 1945, Publ. MGFA, Hamburg: 2000.

Bald, Detlef und Uwe Hartmann (Publ.): Klassiker der Pädagogik im deutschen Militär, Baden-Baden: 1999.

Barker, Elisabeth: The British between the Superpowers 1945 – 1950, London: 1983.

Baudissin, Wolf Graf von: Soldat für den Frieden, Munich 1969.

Baudissin, Wolf Graf von: Nie wieder Sieg! Programmatische Schriften von 1951 – 1981, Munich: 1986.

Baudissin, Wolf Graf von, interview led by Charles Schüddekopf, p. 203 to 225 in: Die zornigen alten Männer, Gedanken über Deutschland seit 1945, Publ. by Axel Eggebrecht, Hamburg: 1979.

Baudissin, Wolf Graf von, interview on 6 December 1968 in his Hamburg appartment, led by Klaus von Schubert. The author owed its documents to Lieutenant Colonel (ret.) Professor Dr. Claus von Rosen, Baudissin Archive at the Command and Staff College, Lieutenant General Wolf-Graf-von-Baudissin barrack, Hamburg

Baudissin, Wolf Graf von, Dagmar Gräfin zu Dohna: als wären wir nie getrennt, Briefe 1941 – 1947, Bonn: 2001

Beck, Ludwig: Colonel General von Seeckton his 70th birthday, in: Militärgeschichtliche Rundschau, 1936, booklet 3, p. 285–291.

Becker, Josef, Franz Knipping (Publ.): Power in Europe? Great Britain, France, Italy and Germany in a postwar world, 1945 – 1950, Berlin: 1986.

Beförderungspraxis in der Reichswehr: Untersuchungen zur Geschichte des Offizierskorps Publ. by MGFA, Stuttgart: 1962.

Below, Günter von: Lebenserinnerungen, Part 1 and 2 without any information about the year and the location.

Provisions on promotion and transfer of the volunteers of the Reichsheer (non-commissioned officers and privates) during peacetime with supplementary provisions for officers of November 1920, Berlin.

Bonner Kommentar zum Grundgesetz, Heidelberg: 2005.

Borgert, Heinz-Ludger: Grundzüge der Landkriegführung von Schlieffen bis Guderian, in: Handbuch zur deutschen Militärgeschichte 1648 – 1939, by Hans Meier-Welcker, Publ. by MGFA, o. A. v. J. u. O. p.427 to 584.

Bracher, Karl Dietrich: Die Auflösung der Weimarer Republik, eine Studie zum Problem des Machtverfalls in der Demokratie, Villingen: 1964.

Bracher, Karl Dietrich: Auflösung der Weimarer Republik. Eine Studie zum Problem des Machtverfalls in der Demokratie, Villingen: 1964.

Breit, Gotthard: Das Staats- und Gesellschaftsbild deutscher Generale beider Weltkriege im Spiegel ihrer Memoiren, in: Wehrwissenschaftliche Forschungen, Band 17, Publ. by MGFA, Boppard: 1973.

Brugmann, Gerhard: Heeresmanöver der Bundeswehr, Buchholz in der Nordheide: 2004.

Brühl: Nationale Volksarmee – Armee für den Frieden, Baden-Baden: 1995, p. 157 to 165.

Buffet, Cyril: Rapallo: Sirens and Phantoms, in: Haunted by History: Myths in International Relations, Publ. by Cyril Buffet und Beatrice Heuser, Oxford: 1998, p. 235 to 258.

Bülow, Friedrich: Volkswirtschaftslehre, Leipzig 1931.

Busch, Eckard: Staatsverfassung und Wehrverfassung, p. 104 to123, in: De officio, zu den ethischen Herausforderungen des Offizierberufes, Hannover: 1985.

Busch, Eckhard: Der Oberbefehl; Seine rechtliche Struktur in Preussen und Deutschland seit 1848, Boppard / Rhine: 1967.

Carsten, Fancis L.: Reichswehr und Politik 1918–1933, Cologne: 1965.

Carsten, Fancis L.: The Reichswehr and Politics 1918–1933, Oxford: 1966.

Citino, Robert M.: The Path to Blitzkrieg. Doctrine and training in the German Army 1920–1939, Mechanicsburg: 2008[2].

Clausewitz, Carl von: Vom Kriege, Troisdorf: 1980, 19th edition.

Clifford, Garry J.: Bureaucratic Politics, p. 91 to 102, in: Michael J. Hogan and Thomas G. Paterson (Publ.): Explaining the History of American Foreign Relations, Cambridge: 2004.

Cochenhausen, Konrad von: Der Weg zum Offizier im Reichsheer (unter besonderer Berücksichtigung der Lehrgänge an den Waffenschulen) Berlin: 1923.

Cornish, Paul: British Military Planning for the Defence of Germany 1945 – 1950, London: 1996.

Corum, James, S.: The Roots of Blitzkrieg, Hans von Seeckt and the German Military Reform, Kansas: 1992.

Costigliola, Frank: Reading the Meaning: Theory, Language, and Metaphor, p. 279 to 303, in: Michael J. Hogan and Thomas G. Paterson (Publ.): Explaining the History of American Foreign Relations, Cambridge: 2004.

Craig, Gordon. A.: Die preussisch-deutsche Armee 1640 – 1945, Staat im Staate, Düsseldorf: 1960.

Creveld, Martin: Kampfkraft, Militärische Organisation und militärische Leistung 1939 to 1945, Freiburg: 1989.

Critchfield, James: Partners at the Creation, the men behind postwar Germany´s Defense and Intelligence establishments, Annapolis: 2003.

Deighton, Anne: The impossible Peace, Britain, the Division of Germany and the Origins of the Cold War, Oxford: 1990.

Deist, Wilhelm: Die Reichswehr und der Krieg der Zukunft, in: Militärgeschichtliche Mitteilungen, Publ. MGFA, Freiburg: 1989, year 45, booklet 1, p. 81 to 92.

Deist, Wilhelm: Strategy and Unlimited Warfare in Germany: Moltke, Falkenhayn, and Ludendorff, in: Great War, Total War. Combat and Mobiliziation on the Western Front, 1914 – 1918, Cambridge: 2000, p. 265 to 280.

Deist, Wilhelm: The road to ideological war: Germany, 1918 – 1945, in: The making of strategy. Rulers, states, and war, Publ. Williamson Murray, Macgregor Knox, Cambridge: 1996, p. 352 to 392.

Delmer, Sefton: Die Deutschen und ich, Hamburg: 1962.

Demeter, Karl: Das deutsche Offizierkorps in Gesellschaft und Staat 1650 – 1945, Frankfurt/Main: 1963.

Demeter, Karl: Das Reichsarchiv, Tatsachen und Personen, Frankfurt/Main: 1969.

Denkschrift des militärischen Expertenausschusses über die Aufstellung eines deutschen Kontingents im Rahmen einer übernationalen Streitmacht zur Verteidigung Westeuropas vom 9. October 1950, BA-MA BW 9/3119.

Deutscher Oktober 1923. Ein Revolutionsplan und sein Scheitern, Publ. Bernhard H. Bayerlein, Leonid G. Babicenko, Friedrich I Firsov und Aleksandr Ju. Vatlin, in Archive des Kommunismus, Pfade des XX. Jahrhunderts, Vol. 3, Berlin: 2003.

Die Deutsche Revolution 1848/49 in Augenzeugenberichten (Publ. by Hans Jessen), Munich: 1973.

Diedrich, Torsten und Rüdiger Wenzke: Die getarnte Armee, Geschichte der Kasernierten Volkspolizei der DDR 1952 – 1956, in: Militärgeschichte der DDR, Vol.1, Publ. MGFA, Berlin: 2001.

Diedrich, Torsten: Herrschaftssicherung, Aufrüstung und Militarisierung im SED-Staat, in: Militär, Staat und Gesellschaft in der DDR, Forschungsfelder, Ergebnisse, Perspektiven, Publ. by MGFA, Vol. 8, Berlin: 2004, p. 257 to 285.

Diedrich, Torsten: Vincenz Müller, Patriot im Zwiespalt, in: Genosse General, die militärische Elite der DDR in biographischen Skizzen, Vol. 7, Publ. by MGFA, Berlin: 2003, p. 125 to 159.

Dietz, Andreas: Das Primat der Politik in kaiserlicher Armee, Reichswehr, Wehrmacht und Bundeswehr: Rechtlicher Sicherungen der Entscheidungsgewalt über Krieg und Frieden zwischen Politik und Militär, Tübingen: 2003.

Ditté, Rainer: Zur Geschichte Führergehilfen- und Generalstabsausbildung des Heeres. Die Auswahl und Ausbildung im Reichsheer und im Heer der Wehrmacht von 1919 – 1945, Hamburg: 1975.

Djakow, J.L. und T.S. Buschujewa: Das faschistische Schwert wurde in der Sowjetunion geschmiedet. Die geheime Zusammenarbeit der Roten Armee mit der Reichswehr 1922 till 1933, Unbekannte Dokumente Russland in Personen, Dokumenten, Tagebuchaufzeichnungen, Moskau: 1992.

Dockrill, Saki: The evolution of Britain's policy towards a European army 1950 – 54, in: The journal of strategic studies. Year 12, 1989, Book 1, 38 to 62.

Dockrill, Saki: Britain's policy for West German rearmament 1950 to 1955, Cambridge Univ. Press: 1991 (Cambridge studies in international relations, 13).

Dockrill, Saki: Grossbritannien und die Wiederbewaffnung Deutschlands 1950 – 1955, in: Die doppelte Eindämmung: europäische Sicherheit und deutsche Frage in den Fünfzigern. (Tutzinger Schriften zur Politik, Vol. 2, Publ. Akademie für Politische Bildung, Tutzing). Publ. Rolf Steininger, mit Beitr. von Rolf Badstübner, Munich: 1993, 63 to 74.

Doepner, Friedrich: Die Bildung des Offiziers I und II, p. 135 to 143 und 204 to 208 in: Wehrkunde, 1972.

Doepner, Friedrich: Zur Auswahl der Offizieranwärter im 100 000-Mann-Heer I und II p. 200–203 and p. 259 to 263 in: Wehrkunde, 1973.

Doepner, Friedrich: Die Entscheidung für den Offizierberuf, in: Wehrkunde, 1974, Book 4 p. 421 to 428.

Dreetz, Dieter: Zur Entwicklung der Soldatenräte des Heimatheeres (November 1918 – March 1919), in: Zeitschrift für Militärgeschichte, Berlin: 1970, Year 9, Book 4, p. 429 to 438.

Driftmann, Hans: Grundzüge des militärischen Erziehungs- und Bildungswesen in der Zeit 1811 to 1938, Regensburg: 1980.

Dürrenmatt, Friedrich: Die Physiker, Zürich: 1962.

Eisele, Willi: Die Haltung von Spartacusbund und KPD (1918/19) zur parlamentarischen Demokratie, in: Schutz der Demokratie, Texte zur Inneren Sicherheit, Bonn: 1992, p. 17 to 51.

Entschieden für Frieden: 50 Jahre Bundeswehr 1955 bis 2005, Publ. by MGFA, Freiburg: 2005.

Enzyklopädie Erster Weltkrieg, Publ. Gerhard Hirschfeld, Gerd Krumreich and Irina Renz, Paderborn: 2003.

Epstein, Julius: Der Seeckt-Plan, from unpublished documents, in: Der Monat, eine internationale Zeitschrift, 1948, booklet 2, p. 42 to 50.

Epstein, Julius: Seeckt, Stalin und Europa, in: Der Monat, eine internationale Zeitschrift, 1948, Book 2, p. 55-58.

Epstein, Julius: Seeckt und Tschiang-Kai-Schek, in: Wehrwissenschaftliche Rundschau, Zeitschrift für Europäische Sicherheit, 1954, p. 534 to 543.

Erfurth, Waldemar: Die Geschichte des deutschen Generalstabes 1918–1945, Göttingen: 1957.

Faulenbach, Bernd: Deutsche Geschichtswissenschaft nach den beiden Weltkriegen, p. 214 to 240, in: Lernen aus dem Krieg? Deutsche Nachkriegszeiten 1918 und 1945, Beiträge zur historischen Friedensforschung, Publ. by Gottfried Niedhart and Dieter Riesenberger, Munich: 1992.

Fernsehgespräch Heusinger – Woller, 24 October 1982, Arbeitsmaterialien Dr. Georg Meyer.

Fingerle, Stephan: Waffen in Arbeiterhand? Die Rekrutierung des Offizierskorps der Nationalen Volksarmee und ihrer Vorläufer, in series: Militärgeschichte der DDR, Vol. 2, Publ. by MGFA, Berlin: 2001.

Fischer, Fritz: Griff nach der Weltmacht. Die Kriegszielpolitik des kaiserlichen Deutschland 1814/1918, Düsseldorf: 1967.

Fischer, Johannes: Militärpolitische Lage und militärische Planung bei Aufstellungsbeginn der Bundeswehr, in: Militärgeschichte Probleme – Thesen – Wege, Stuttgart: 1982.

Fischer, Peter: Atomenergie und staatliches Interesse: Die Anfänge der Atompolitik in der Bundesrepublik Deutschland 1949–1955, Nuclear History Program (NHP), Vol. 30/3 Baden-Baden: 1994.

Foerster, Roland: Das operative Denken des deutschen Generalstabs 1870–1945, in: Dietmar Schössler, (Publ.): Die Entwicklung des Strategie- und Operationsbegriffs seit Clausewitz, in: Beiträge zur Sicherheitspolitik und Strategieforschung, Militärwissenschaftliches Colloquium des Clausewitz-Gesellschaft e.V. April 1995, Dresden, Munich: 1997, p. 36 to 64.

Foley, Robert T.: From Volkskrieg to Vernichtungskrieg: German concepts of warfare, 1871 – 1935, in: War, peace and world orders in European history, Publ. by Anja V. Hartmann, London: 2001, p. 214 to 225.

Forster, Thomas M.: NVA, die Armee der Sowjetzone, Cologne: 1966/67.

Forster, Thomas M.: The East German Army, The second power in the Warsaw pact, London: 1980.

Förster, Stig: Der Deutsche Generalstab und die Illusion des kurzen Krieges, 1871–1914. Metakritik eines Mythos, in: Militärgeschichtliche Mitteilungen, Publ. MGFA, Freiburg: 1955, (54), p. 61 to 95.

Freedman, Lawrence David: Deterrence: a reply, in: The journal of strategic studies. 28 (2005), H. 5, p. 789 to 801.

Fritz, Ernst: Aus dem Nachlass des Generals Walther Reinhardt, Stuttgart: 1958.

Fuchs, Günter: 25 Jahre Verteidigungshaushalt, p. 235 to 238 in: Bundeswehrverwaltung, 1981, Books 10 to 12, p. 235 to 238.

Fuhrer, Hans Rudolf: Die Wehrmacht aus Schweizer Sicht, in: Die Wehrmacht. Mythos und Realität, Publ. by Rolf-Dieter Müller und Hans Erich Volkmann, im Auftrag des MGFA, Munich: 1999, p. 123 to 146.

Funke, Manfred: Die Republik der Friedlosigkeit. Äussere und innere Belastungsfaktoren der Epoche von Weimar 1918–1933, in: Aus Politik und Zeitgeschichte, Beilage zur Wochenzeitung Das Parlament, B 32–33/94, 12 August 1994, p. 11 to 19.

Funke, Manfred: Republikschutz in Weimar, in: Schutz der Demokratie, Texte zur Inneren Sicherheit, Bonn: 1992, p. 7 to 16.

Gablik, Axel: Walter Reinhardt in: Detlef Bald (Publ.): Klassiker der Pädagogik im deutschen Militär, Baden-Baden: 1999.

Gaertingen, Friedrich Freiherr Hiller von: Militärgeschichte in Deutschland von 1918 bis 1945, in: Militärgeschichte in Deutschland und Österreich vom 18. Jahrhundert bis in die Gegenwart, Bonn: 1985.

Generalstäbe in Deutschland 1871–1945, Aufgaben in der Armee und Stellung im Staat, Vol. 3, in: Beiträge zur Militär- und Kriegsgeschichte, Publ. by MGFA, Stuttgart: 1962.

Genschel, Dietrich: Wehrreform und Reaktion, die Vorbereitung der Inneren Führung 1951–1956, Hamburg: 1957.

Gessler, Otto: Reichswehrpolitik in der Weimarer Republik, Stuttgart: 1958.

Geyer, Michael: Die Wehrmacht der Deutschen Republik ist die Reichswehr: Bemerkungen zur neueren Literatur, in: Militärgeschichtliche Mitteilungen, Publ. MGFA, Vol. 16, Year, 2/1973, Freiburg: 1973, p. 152 to 199.

Geyer, Michael: Der zur Organisation erhobene Burgfrieden, in: Militär und Militarismus in der Weimarer Republik, Publ. by Klaus Jürgen Müller und Eckardt Opitz, Düsseldorf: 1978.

Geyer, Michael: Aufrüstung oder Sicherheit, die Reichswehr in der Krise der Machtpolitik 1924–1936, Wiesbaden: 1980.

Glatzke, Hans W: Von Rapallo nach Berlin Stresemann und die deutsche Russlandpolitik, in Vierteljahreshefte, 1956, Heft 1, p. 1 to 28.

Goethe, Johann Wolfgang: Faust, Frankfurt/Main: 1994.

Goodpaster, Andrew und Huntington, P. Samuel: Civil-Military Relations, Washington: 1977.

Gordon, Harold J.: The Reichswehr and the German Republic 1919–1926, Princeton: 1957.

Gordon, Harold J.: Reichswehr und die Weimarer Republik, Frankfurt / Main: 1959.

Gordon, Harold J.: Reichswehr und Politik in der Weimarer Republik, in: Politische Studien, 22 year, 1971, booklet: Jan/Feb., p.34 to 45.

Gordon, Harold J.: Hans von Seeckt als Mensch, in: Wehrwissenschaftliche Rundschau, Zeitschrift für die Europäische Sicherheit, Frankfurt/Main: 1957, p. 575 to 584.

Gordon Harold J. Jr.: Der Hitlerputsch 1923, Machtkampf in Bayern 1923–1924. Frankfurt/Main: 1971.

Görlitz, Walter: Kleine Geschichte des deutschen Generalsstabs, Berlin: 1977.

Grant, Ted: The unbroken Thread, the development of Trotskyism over 40 years, London: 1989.

Grau, Roland: Zur Rolle der Soldatenräte der Fronttruppen in der Novemberrevolution, in: Zeitschrift für Militärgeschichte, Berlin: 1968, year 7, booklet 5, p. 550 to 564.

Groehler, Olaf: Selbstmörderische Allianz, Deutsch-russische Militärbeziehungen 1920–1941, Berlin: 1992.

Groener, Wilhelm: Lebenserinnerungen – Jugend – Generalstab – Weltkrieg, Göttingen: 1957.

Groener-Geyer, Dorothea: General Groener, Soldat und Staatsmann, Frankfurt/Main: 1955.

Gross, Gerhard P.: Das Dogma der Beweglichkeit. Überlegungen zur Genese der deutschen Heerestaktik im Zeitalter der Weltkriege, in: Erster Weltkrieg – Zweiter Weltkrieg. Ein Vergleich Krieg, Kriegserlebnis, Kriegserfahrungen in Deutschland. Publ. MGFA, Paderborn: 2002, p. 143 to 166.

Gross, Gross, Gerhard P.: Mythos und Wirklichkeit. Geschichte des operativen Denkens im deutschen Heer von Moltke d.Ä. bis Heusinger, Paderborn: 2012.

Guderian, Heinz: Die Panzerwaffe. Ihre Entwicklung, ihre Kampftaktik und ihre operativen Möglichkeiten bis zum Beginn des grossdeutschen Freiheitskampfes, Stuttgart: 1943.

Guske, Claus: Das politische Denken des Generals von Seeckt, ein Beitrag zur Diskussion des Verhältnisses Seeckt – Reichswehr-Republik, in: Historische Studien, booklet 422, Lübeck: 1971.

Habeck, Mary: Storm of Steel, the Development of Armour Doctrine in Germany and the Sovietunion, 1919–1939, New-York: 2003.

Halperin, Morton H.: Bureaucratic Politics and Foreign policy, Washington: 1974.

HD.v. 487, Heeresdienstvorschrift, Führung und Gefecht (F.u.G) der verbundenen Waffen, Neudruck der Ausgabe 1921–1924 in 3 Teilen, Osnabrück: 1994.

Hallgarten, Georg W.F.: General Hans von Seeckt and Russia, 1920–1922, in: Journal of Military History, Chicago: 1949, March edition.

Hammerstein, Kunrath von: Spähtrupp, Stuttgart: 1963.

Hansen, Ernst Willi: Zum 'Militärisch-Industriellen Komplex' in der Weimarer Republik, in: Militär und Militarismus in der Weimarer Republik, Publ. by Klaus Jürgen Müller und Eckardt Opitz, Düsseldorf: 1978.

Harder, Hans Joachim: Politische und operative Begründung der Umfangszahlen der Bundeswehr und des Heeres, Bergisch Gladbach: 1993.

Howard Michael: The First World War, Oxford: 2002.

Hauck, Friedrich Wilhelm: Generaloberst Hans von Seeckt, in: Studien zur Militärgeschichte, Militärwissenschaft und Konfliktforschung, Band 15, Osnabrück: 1977.

Heiber, Helmut: Die Republik von Weimar, dtv – Weltgeschichte des 20. Jahrhunderts, Munich: 1966.

Heinemann, Winfried: Buchbesprechung von Rüdiger Schönrade: General Joachim von Stülpnagel und die Politik, eine biographische Skizze zum Verhältnis von militärischer und politischer Führung in der Weimarer Politik, Berlin: 2007, in: Militärgeschichtliche Zeitschrift: MGZ / Publ. by Militärgeschichtlichen Forschungsamt, Munich: 2008, Year 67, p. 531.

Hermann, Erich: Innere Führung in: Wehrwissenschaftliche Rundschau. Year 19, 1969, p. 492 to 507.

Herzfeld, Hans: Politik, Heer und Rüstung in der Zwischenkriegszeit, p. 255 to 277, in: Herzfeld, Hans: Ausgewählte Aufsätze, Berlin: 1962.

Hesse, Kurt: Der Reichswehrsoldat, Berlin: 1927.

Hesse, Kurt: Der Geist von Potsdam, Mainz: 1967.

Heuser, Beatrice und Robert O´Neill: Securing Peace in Europa, 1945–62. Thoughts for post-Cold War Era, London: 1992.

Heuser, Beatrice: Transatlantic Relations, Sharing the ideals and costs, London: 1996.

Heuser, Beatrice: NATO; Britain, France and the FRG, Nuclear Strategies and Forces for Europe, 1949–2000, London: 1997.

Heuser, Beatrice: Die Strategie der NATO während des Kalten Krieges, in: Entschieden für Frieden, 50 Jahre Bundeswehr 1955 till 2000, Publ. MGFA, Freiburg: 2005, p. 51 to 62.

Heuser, Beatrice: The Evolution of Strategy. Thinking War from Antiquity to the Present, Cambridge: 2010.

Heusinger, Adolf: Befehl im Widerstreit, Schicksalsstunden der deutschen Armee 1923–1945, Tübingen: 1950.

Heuss, Theodor: Die grossen Reden, der Staatsmann, Tübingen: 1965.

Hillard, Gustav: Herren und Narren der Welt, Munich: 1955.

Thomas Hobbes: Leviathan or the matter from power of a commonwealth, ecclesiastical and civil. London: 1894.

Hoffmann, Peter: Claus Schenk Graf von Stauffenberg und seine Brüder, Stuttgart: 1992.

Hogan, Michael J. und Thomas G. Paterson (Publ.): Explaining the History of American Foreign Relations, Cambridge: 2004.

Höhne, Heinz: Mordsache Röhm Hitlers Durchbruch zur Alleinherrschaft 1933 – 1934, Hamburg: 1984.

Höhne, Heinz: Der Krieg im Dunkeln, Macht und Einfluss der deutschen und russischen Gemeindienste, Munich: 1985.

Honig, Jan Willem: Clausewitz and the Politics of Early Modern Warfare, in: Clausewitz, the State and War, Stuttgart: 2011, p. 29 to 48.

Hoppe, Christoph: Zwischen Teilhabe und Mitsprache: Die Nuklearfrage in der Allianzpolitik Deutschland s 1970–1966, Nuclear History Program (NHP), Vol. 30/2, Baden – Baden: 1993.

Hornung, Klaus: Staat und Armee, Studien zur Befehls- und Kommandogewalt und zum politisch-militärischen Verhältnis in der Bundesrepublik Deutschland, Mainz: 1975.

Horst, Cornelis van der: Die Bendlerstrasse, Entscheidungen und Kämpfe 1918–1933, Stuttgart: o.J.

Hossbach, Friedrich: Zwischen Wehrmacht und Hitler 1934–1938, Hannover: 1949.

Huber, Ernst R., Doepner, Friedrich: 50 Jahre Soldat – Der Offizieran wärterjahrgang 1930, p. 191 to 213 in: Europäische Wehrkunde, 1980.

Huber, John, D. und Charles R. Shipan: Deliberate Discretion? The Institutional Foundations of Bureaucratic Autonomy, Cambridge: 2002.

Huber, Rudolf Günter: Gerd von Rundstedt, Sein Leben und Wirken im Spannungs feld gesellschaftlicher Einflüsse und persönlicher Standortbestimmungen, Frankfurt am Main: 2004.

Huntington, P. Samuel: The Soldier and the State. The Theory and Politics of Civil-Military Relations, Cambridge/Massachusetts: 1959.

Huntington, P. Samuel: Interservice Competition and the Political Roles of the Armed Services, p. 40 to 52, in: American Political Science Review, 55, (1961).

Huntington, P. Samuel und Andrew Goodpaster: Civil-Military Relations, Washington: 1977.

Hürten, Heinz: Das Offizierskorps des Reichsheeres p. 231 to 246 in: Deutsche Führungsgeschichte in der Neuzeit, Band 11, Das deutsche Offizierkorps 1860–1960, Büdinger Vorträge 1977, Publ. by Hanns Hubert Hofmann, Boppard: 1980.

Hürten, Heinz: Der Kapp-Putsch als Wende, über Rahmenbedingungen der Weimarer Republik seit dem Frühjahr 1920, Publ. by Rheinisch-Westfälische Akademie der Wissenschaften, Opladen: 1989.

Hürten, Heinz: Reichswehr und Ausnahmezustand, ein Beitrag zur Verfassungsproblematik der Weimarer Republik in ihrem ersten Jahrfünft, Opladen: 1977.

Information für die Truppe, Beiheft 3/87, Adolf Heusinger, ein deutscher Soldat im 20. Jahrhundert, Publ. by Bundesministerium der Verteidigung, Führungsstab der Streitkräfte, Bonn: 1987, erschienen in: Schriftenreihe der Innere Führung, Vol. 3/1987.

Iriye, Akira: Culture and International History, p. 241 to 256, in: Michael J. Hogan und Thomas G. Paterson (Publ.): Explaining the History of American Foreign Relations, Cambridge: 2004.

Janis, Irving L.: Victims of Groupthink. A spychological study of foreign-policy decisions and fiascoes, Boston: 1972.

Jasper, Gotthard: Der Schutz der Republik. Studien zur staatlichen Sicherung der Demokratie in der Weimarer Republik 1922–1930, (Tübinger Studien zur

Geschichte und Politik, Publ. Hans Rothfels, Josef Engel, Vol. 16) Tübingen: 1963.

Junker, Detlef: Über die Legitimität von Werturteilen in den Sozialwissenschaften und der Geschichtswissenschaft, p. 1 to 33 in: Historische Zeitschrift, Vol. 211, Oldenbourg: 1970.

Kant, Immanuel: Zum Ewigen Frieden, Bern: 1944.

Kapp-Lüttwitz-Ludendorff-Putsch, Der, Publ. Erwin Könnemann, Gerhard Schulze, Munich: 2002.

Kaulbach, Eberhardt: Generaloberst Hans von Seeckt – Zur Persönlichkeit und zur Leistung, in: Wehrwissenschaftliche Rundschau, Zeitschrift für Europäische Sicherheit, Frankfurt/Main: 1966, 666 to 681.

Keller, Peter: 'Die Wehrmacht der Deutschen Republik ist die Reichswehr'. Die deutsche Armee 1918–1921, Paderborn: 2014.

Kessel, Eberhard: Militärgeschichte und Kriegstheorie in neuerer Zeit, Ausgewählte Aufsätze, Historische Forschungen, Vol. 33, Berlin: 1987.

Kessel, Eberhard: Moltke, Stuttgart: 1957.

Kessel, Eberhard: Seeckts politisches Programm von 1923, in: Spiegel der Geschichte, Festgabe für Max Braubach, Münster: 1964, p.887 to 914.

Kesselring, Agilof: 60 Jahre NATO, wechselnde Bedrohungen – neue Strategien, in: Militärgeschichte, Zeitschrift für historische Bildung, Militärgeschichte, Zeitschrift für historische Bildung, Publ. MGFA, Year. 1/2009, p. 4 to 7.

Kessler, Mario: Die kommunistische Linke und die Weimarer Republik, in: Aus Politik und Zeitgeschichte, Beilage zur Wochenzeitung Das Parlament, Vol. 32–33/94, 12 August 1994, p. 20 to 30.

Keynes, John Maynard: Die wirtschaftlichen Folgen des Friedensvertrages, Munich: 1920.

Kiessling, Günter: Der versäumte Widerspruch, Mainz: 1993.

Kolb, Eberhard: Die Weimarer Republik, Munich: 2009.

Köllner, Lutz: Militärausgaben in der deutschen staatstheoretischen und ökonomie-theoretischen Literatur vom 17. Jahrhundert bis zur Gegenwart Publ. by Sozialwissenschaftlichen Institut der Bundeswehr, SOWI-Berichte, Heft 36, Munich: 1984.

Kozak, David C. und James M. Keagle (Publ.): Bureaucratic Politics and national Security. Theory and Practice, London: 1988.

Krakow, Jürgen: Die Genehmigung, Mainz: 1991.

Kroener, Bernhard R.: Auf dem Weg zu einer 'nationalsozialistischen Volksarmee', die soziale Öffnung des Heeresoffizierskorps im Zweiten Weltkrieg, in: Von Stalingrad zur Währungsreform, zur Sozialgeschichte des Umbruchs in Deutschland, Publ. by Martin Broszat, Klaus-Dietmar Henke u.a., Munich: 1990, p. 651 to 682.

Kroener, Bernhard R.: Das Heeresoffizierkorps im Zweiten Weltkrieg, in: Quellen und Darstellungen zur Zeitgeschichte, Vol. 26: Von Stalingrad zur Währungsreform, zur Sozialgeschichte des Umbruchs in Deutschland, Publ. by Martin Broszat u.a., Munich: 1990, p. 651 to 682.

Kroener, Bernhard R.: Strukturelle Veränderungen in der militärischen Gesellschaft des Dritten Reiches, in: Nationalsozialismus und Modernisierung, Darmstadt: 1991, p. 267 to 296.

Kroener, Bernhard R.: Mobilmachungen gegen Recht und Verfassung. Kriegsvorbereitungen in Reichsheer und Wehrmacht 1918 bis 1939, in: Erster Weltkrieg – Zweiter Weltkrieg. Ein Vergleich Krieg, Kriegserlebnis, Kriegserfahrungen in Deutschland. Im Auftrag MGFA, Publ. Bruno Thoss und Hans-Erich Volkmann, Paderborn: 2002, p. 57 to 78.

Kroener, Bernhard R.: Generaloberst Fromm, der starke Mann im Heimatkriegsgebiet, Paderborn: 2005.

Krosigk, Lutz Graf Schwerin von: Es geschah in Deutschland, Menschenbilder unseres Jahrhunderts, Tübingen: 1951.

Krug, Paul: Rückschau auf Potsdam und Friedensjahre im 9. (Preuss.) Infanterie-Regiment, in: Axel von dem Bussche, Publ. by Gevinon von Medem, Mainz: 1994.

Krüger, Dieter: Das Amt Blank. Die schwierige Gründung des Bundesministeriums der Verteidigung, Freiburg: 1993.

Krüger, Gabriele: Die Brigade Erhardt, Hamburg: 1971.

Krüger, Peter: Die Aussenpolitik der Republik von Weimar, Darmstadt: 1985.

Krumeich, Gerd: Der Ruhrkampf als Krieg, in: Düsseldorfer Schriften zur neuen Landesgeschichte und zur Geschichte Nordrhein-Westfalens, Vol. 69, Der Schatten des Weltkriegs: Die Ruhrbesetzung 1923, Publ. by Gerd Krumeich and Joachim Schröder, Essen: 2004.

Lahne, Walter: Unteroffiziere, Gestern – Heute – Morgen, Herford: 1974.

Lange, Sven: Der Fahneneid, die Geschichte der Schwurverpflichtung im deutschen Militär, Publ. by Eckhardt Opitz, Vol. 19, Bremen: 2002.

Lania, Leo: Der Hitler-Prozess, Berlin: 1925.

Lapp, Peter Joachim: General bei Hitler und Ulbricht, Vincenz Müller – Eine deutsche Karriere, Berlin: 2003.

Laughland, John: A history of political trials. From Charles I to Saddam Hussein. Witney, Oxfordshire: 2008.

Leeb, Generalfeldmarschall Wilhelm Ritter von: Tagebuchaufzeichnungen und Lagebeurteilungen aus zwei Weltkriegen, aus dem Nachlass herausgegeben und mit einem Lebensabriss versehen von Georg Meyer, Stuttgart: 1976.

Leistenschneider, Stefan: Normalangriff oder Freiheit der Form, die Entstehung der Auftragstaktik im preussisch-deutschen Heer 1871–1914, Munich: 1992.

Lernen aus dem Krieg, deutsche Nachkriegszeiten 1918/1945, Beiträge zur deutschen Friedensforschung, Munich: 1992.

Liddell Hart, Basil: The German Generals Talk, New York: 1948.

Liddell, Basil Hart: The German Generals Talk, New York: 1948

Linke, Horst Günther: Deutsch-sowjetische Beziehungen bis Rapallo, Cologne: 1970.

Loth, Wilfried: Stalins ungeliebtes Kind. Warum Moskau die DDR nicht wollte, Hamburg: 1994.

Luban, Ottokar: Karl Radek (1885–1939) in: Internationale wissenschaftliche Korrespondenz zur Geschichte der deutschen Arbeiterbewegung 41, 2005, booklet 4, p. 518 to 527.

Ludendorff, Erich: Kriegführung und Politik, Berlin: 1922.

Ludendorff, Erich: Der totale Krieg, Berlin: 1935.

Mann, Siegrid: Bundesministerium der Verteidigung, Bonn: 1971.

Manstein, Erich von: Aus einem Soldatenleben 1887–1939, Bonn: 1958.

Martini, Winfried: Der 'Ungehorsam' Seeckts oder die Kunst des Abschreibens, in: Europäische Wehrkunde: Organ für alle Wehrfragen; Organ der Gesellschaft für Wehrkunde, Munich: 1962, booklet 1, p. 128 to 134.

Meier-Welcker, Hans: Die Stellung der Chefs der Heeresleitung in den Anfängen der Republik, in: Vierteljahreshefte für Zeitgeschichte, Year 4, 1956, booklet 2, p. 145 to 160.

Meier-Welcker, Hans: Über den Unterricht in Kriegsgeschichte, in: Wehrwissenschaftliche Rundschau, Zeitschrift für die Europäische Sicherheit, 1956, booklet 10, p. 539 to 546.

Meier-Welcker, Hans: Seeckt über die Chefstellung im Generalstab, p. 15 to 21 in: Wehrwissenschaftliche Rundschau, Year. 17, 1967.

Meier-Welcker, Hans: Seeckt, Frankfurt / Main: 1967.

Meier-Welcker, Hans: Seeckt in der Kritik, in: Wehrwissenschaftliche Rundschau, Zeitschrift für die Europäische Sicherheit, 1969, Year 19, p. 265 to 284.

Meier-Welcker, Hans: Soldat und Geschichte, Freiburg i. Br.: 1979.

Meier-Welcker, Hans: Der Weg zum Offizier im Reichsheer der Weimarer Republik in: Militärgeschichtliche Mitteilungen, Publ. MGFA, Vol. 19, Year 1/1976, Freiburg: 1976, p. 147 to 180.

Meineke, Stefan: Parteien und Parlamentarismus im Urteil Friedrich Meineckes, p. 51 to 93 in: Friedrich Meinecke in seiner Zeit, Studien zu Leben und Werk, Publ. by Gisela Bock and Daniel Schönpflug, Beiträge zur Universitäts- und Wissenschaftsgeschichte, Vol. 19, Stuttgart: 2006.

Meyer, Georg: Menschenführung im Heer der Bundeswehr, in: Menschenführung im Heer, p. 204 to 251 in: Vorträge zur Militärgeschichte, Vol. 3, Publ. MGFA, Bonn: 1982.

Meyer, Georg: Soldaten ohne Armee in: Von Stalingrad zur Währungsreform – Zur Sozialgeschichte des Umbruchs in Deutschland, Publ. by Martin Broszat, Munich: 1988.

Meyer, Georg: Soldat im Ghetto, Eine Denkschrift der Gruppe Innere Führung im Bundesministerium für Verteidigung, in Militärgeschichte, 1991, booklet 4, p. 63 to 66.

Meyer, Georg: Innenpolitische Voraussetzungen der westdeutschen Wiederbewaffnung, in: Wiederbewaffnung in Deutschland nach 1945, Schriftenreihe der Gesellschaft für Deutschlandforschung, Vol. XI, Berlin: 1986.

Meyer, Georg: Auswirkungen des 20. Juli 1944 auf das innere Gefüge der Wehrmacht bis Kriegsende und auf das soldatische Selbstverständnis im Vorfeld des westdeutschen Verteidigungsbeitrages 1950/51, in: Vorträge zur Militärgeschichte, Vol. 5 Der militärische Widerstand gegen Hitler und das NS-Regime 1933–1945, Bonn: 1984.

Meyer, Georg: Drei deutsche Generale. Dienst in der Diktatur und im Spannungsfeld des Kalten Krieges, in: 'Vom Kalten Krieg zur deutschen Einheit' (Publ. MGFA) Munich: 1995.

Meyer, Georg: Personalfragen beim Aufbau der Bundeswehr, p. 99 to 120 in: Adenauer und die Wiederbewaffnung, Rhöndorfer Gespräche, Publ. by Wolfgang Krieger, Vol. 18, Bonn: 2000.

Meyer, Georg: Adolf Heusinger. Dienst eines deutschen Soldaten 1915 bis 1964, Hamburg: 2001.

Militär-Wochenblatt, Unabhängige Zeitschrift für die deutsche Wehrmacht, 1920–1926, Berlin: 1921–1927.

Millotat, Christian E.O.: Auftragstaktik, das oberste Führungsprinzip im Heer der Bundeswehr, ihre Entwicklung und Darstellung in deutschen militärischen Führungsgrundlagen, Österreichische Militärzeitung 2001, booklet 3, p. 299 to 310.

Mirwald, Siegried: Zur Entwicklung der Führungsgrundsätze im deutschen Heer, eine vergleichende Untersuchung der H.Dv. 487 (FuG) und 1921–23 und der H.Dv. 300 (T.F.) von 1933–34, unterbesonderer Betrachtung des hinhaltenden Gefechts und des hinhaltenden Widerstandes, Hamburg: 1968.

Mittwochs-Gesellschaft, Die, Protokolle aus dem geistigen Deutschland 1932 bis 1944, Berlin: 1982.

Model, Hansgeorg: Der deutsche Generalstabsoffizier, Seine Auswahl und Ausbildung in der Reichswehr, Wehrmacht und Bundeswehr, Frankfurt/Main: 1968.

Model, Hansgeorg, Prause, Jens: Generalstab im Wandel, neue Wege bei der Generalstabsausbildung in der Bundeswehr, Munich: 1982.

Mohr, Ernst Günther: Die unterschlagenen Jahre, China vor Mao Tse Tung, Munich: 1985.

Mommsen, Hans: Die politischen Folgen der Ruhrbesetzung, in: Düsseldorfer Schriften, Vol. 69, Essen: 2004.

Montecue, Lowry, J.: The forge of West German Rearmament, Theodor Blank and the Amt Blank, (American University Studies, Series 9, History, Vol. 83), New York: 1989.

Montgomery, Bernhard: Memoiren, Munich: 1958.

Mühlhausen, Walter: Friedrich Ebert, Reichspräsident der Weimarer Republik, Bonn: 2006.

Müller, Klaus-Jürgen: Armee, Politik und Gesellschaft in Deutschland 1933–1945, Studien zum Verhältnis von Armee und NS-System, Paderborn: 1979.

Müller, Klaus-Jürgen: Deutsche Militär-Elite in der Vorgeschichte des Zweiten Weltkrieges in: die deutschen Eliten und der Weg in den Zweiten Weltkrieg, Publ. by Martin Broszat and Klaus Schwabe, Munich: 1989, p. 226 to 290

Müller, Klaus-Jürgen: Das Heer und Hitler, Armee und nationalsozialistisches Regime, 1933–1940, Stuttgart: 1969.

Mulligan, William: The creation of the modern German Army, General Walther Reinhardt and the Weimar Republic, 1914–1930, New York: 2005.

Murray, Williamson: The collapse of empire: British strategy, 1919–1945, in: The Making of strategy. Rulers, states, and war, Publ. Williamson Murray, Macgregor Knox u.a., Cambridge: 1995, p. 393 to 427.

Nägler, Frank: 'Innere Führung': Zum Entstehungszusammenhang einer Führungsphilosophie, in: Entschieden für Frieden, 50 Jahre Bundeswehr, 1955–2005, Publ. MGFA, Freiburg: 2005, p. 321 to 334.

Nakata, Jun: Der Grenz- und Landesschutz in der Weimarer Republik 1918–1933, die geheime Aufrüstung und die deutsche Gesellschaft, Publ. by MGFA, Rombach: 2002.

Nayhauss-Cormons, Mainhardt Graf von: Zwischen Gehorsam und Gewissen, Richard von Weizsäcker und das Infanterie-Regiment 9, Bergisch Gladbach: 1994.

Neill, Robert J.: The German Army and the Nazi Party, 1933–1939, London: 1966.

Neue Dokumente zur Geschichte der Reichswehr 1930–1933 in: Vierteljahresschrift zur Zeitgeschichte, 1954, booklet 4 (October), p. 397 to 436.

Neugebauer, Karl-Volker: Operatives Denken zwischen dem Ersten und Zweiten Weltkrieg, in: Operatives Denken und Handeln in deutschen Streitkräfte im 19. und 20. Jahrhundert, Vorträge zur Militärgeschichte, Vol. 9, Herford: 1988.

Nicholls, A.J: Myth of the German Sonderweg, in: Haunted by History: Myths in International Relations, Publ. Cyril Buffet and Beatrice Heuser, Oxford: 1998, p. 209 to 222.

Niemetz, Daniel: Besiegt, gebraucht, gelobt, gemieden. Zum Umgang mit ehemaligen Wehrmachtoffizieren im DDR-Militär, in: Deutschland Archiv, 1999, Year 32, booklet 3, p. 378 to 392.

Nipperdey, Thomas: Deutsche Geschichte 1866–1918, Machtstaat vor der Demokratie, Vol. 2, Munich: 1993.

Noak, Peter: Reichswehr und Landesverteidigung, eine Untersuchung über die Möglichkeiten für das Zusammenwirken der obersten militärischen Führung 1921 – 1932, Hamburg: 1969.

Nolte, Ernst: Historische Existenz: zwischen Anfang und Ende der Geschichte? Munich [u.a.]: 1998.

Noske, Gustav: Von Kiel bis Kapp, zur Geschichte der deutschen Revolution, Berlin: 1920.

Oertzen, R. von: Gedanken über die Mannszucht in: Wissen und Wehr, 1925, 2nd booklet, p. 65 to 79 and 157 to 176.

Offiziere im Bild von Dokumenten aus drei Jahrhunderten, Beiträge zur Militär- und Kriegsgeschichte, Publ. MGFA, Vol. 6, Einführung von Manfred Messerschmidt, Dokumente Manfred Messerschmidt und Ursula von Gersdorff, Stuttgart: 1964.

Opitz, Eckardt: Exkurs: Sozialdemokratie und Militarismus in der Weimarer Republik, in: Militär und Militarismus in der Weimarer Republik, Publ. by Klaus Jürgen Müller and Eckardt Opitz, Düsseldorf: 1978.

Opposition gegen Hitler und der Staatsstreich vom 20. Juli 1944, Geheime Dokumente aus dem ehemaligen Reichsicherheitshauptamt, Publ. by Hans-Adolf Jacobsen, o.A.v.J.u.O.

Paul, Wolfgang: Das Potsdamer Infanterie-Regiment 9, 1918 – 1945, preussische Tradition in Krieg und Frieden, Textband, Osnabrück: 1983.

Paul, Wolfgang: Das Potsdamer Infanterie-Regiment 9, 1918 – 1945, preussische Tradition in Krieg und Frieden, Dokumentenband, Osnabrück: 1984.

Phelps, Reginald: Aus den Seeckt-Dokumenten, I. Die Verabschiedung Seeckts 1926, in: Deutsche Rundschau 1952, Year 58, booklet 9, p. 881 to 891, booklet 10, Aus den Seeckt-Dokumenten II: Seeckt und die Innenpolitik, p. 1013 to 1023.

Plehwe, Friedrich-Karl von: Reichskanzler Kurt von Schleicher Weimars letzte Chance gegen Hitler, Esslingen: 1983.

Pöhlmann, Markus: Von Versailler nach Armageddon: Totalisierungserfahrung und Kriegserwartungen in deutschen Militärzeitschriften, in: An der Schwelle zum Totalen Krieg. Die militärische Debatte über den Krieg der Zukunft 1919–1939, Publ. Stig Förster (= Krieg in der Geschichte, Vol. 13, Publ. Stig Förster), Paderborn: 2002, p. 323 to 393.

Pommerin, Rainer: Die Wehrpflicht, legitimes Kind der Demokratie oder überholter Ballast in der Einsatzarmee, in: Entschieden für Frieden, 50 Jahre Bundeswehr 1955–2005 Freiburg: 2005, p. 299 to 321.

Prerardovich, Nikolaus von: Die militärische und soziale Herkunft der hohen Generalität des deutschen Heeres am 1. Mai 1944 in: Wehrwissenschaftliche Rundschau, Zeitschrift für die Europäische Sicherheit, 1970, p. 44 to 55.

Rabenau, Friedrich von: Seeckt – Aus meinem Leben 1866–1918, Leipzig: 1938 und Aus seinem Leben 1918–1936, Leipzig: 1940.

Raesfeld, Werner von: Führung durch Auftrag oder durch bindenden Befehl? In: Wehrkunde, 1960, booklet 4, p. 165 to 169.

Rahn, Werner: Reichsmarine und Landesverteidigung 1919–1928, Konzeption und Führung der Marine in der Weimarer Republik, Munich: 1976.

Range, Clemens: Die geduldete Armee, Berlin: 2005.

Rehm, Walter: Reichswehr und politische Parteien der Weimarer Republik, in: Wehrwissenschaftliche Rundschau, Zeitschrift für Europäische Sicherheit, 1958, p. 692 to 708.

Rehm, Walter: Wiederbewaffnung und Wiedervereinigung, in: Wiederbewaffnung in Deutschland nach 1945, Berlin: 1986.

Reichherzer, Frank: Alles ist Front! Wehrwissenschaften in Deutschland und die Bellefizierung der Gesellscahft vom Ersten Weltkrieg bis in den Kalten Krieg, Paderborn: 2012.

Reichswehr und Rote Armee, Dokumente aus den Militärarchiven Deutschlands und Russlands 1925–1931, Publ. by Bundesarchiv, Russischer Archivdienst und Russisches Staatliches Militärarchiv, Koblenz: 1995.

Reinhardt, Walther: Wehrkraft und Wehrwille, aus seinem Nachlass mit einer Lebensbeschreibung, Berlin: 1932.

Reinicke, Adolf: Das Reichsheer 1921–1934, Ziele, Methoden der Ausbildung und Erziehung sowie der Dienstgestaltung, Osnabrück: 1986.

Richter, Ludwig: Die Weimarer Reichsverfassung, in: Aus Politik und Zeitgeschichte, Beilage zur Wochenzeitung Das Parlament, Vol. 32–33/94, 12 August 1994, p. 3 to 10.

Ringsdorf, Ulrich: Organisatorische Entwicklung und Aufgaben der Abteilung Fremde Heere Ost im Generalstab des Heeres, in: Aus der Arbeit der Archive: Beiträge zum Archivwesen, zur Quellenkunde und zur Geschichte, Festschrift für Hans Booms, Publ. Friedrich P. Kahlenberg, Boppard am Rhein: 1989, p. 800 to 810.

Ritter, Gerhard: Staatskunst und Kriegshandwerk. Das Problem des 'Militarismus' in Deutschland, Vol one: Die altpreussische Tradition (1740–1890), Munich: 1954.

Rosenberg, Arthur: Entstehung und Geschichte der Weimarer Republik, Frankfurt/Main: 1955.

Rosenfeld, Günter: Sowjetrussland und Deutschland 1917 – 1922, Berlin: 1960.

Rosenfeld, Günter: Sowjetunion und Deutschland: 1922 – 1933, Cologne: 1984.

Ruge, Wolfgang: Neue Dokumente über den Soldatenrat bei der Obersten Heeresleitung, in: Zeitschrift für Geschichtswissenschaften, 1968, booklet 11, p. 1402 to 1421.

Salewski, Michael: Entwaffnung und Militärkontrolle in Deutschland 1919 – 1927, Munich: 1966.

Schäfer, Kirstin A.: Werner von Bloomberg – Hitlers Generalfeldmarschall, eine Biographie, Paderborn: 2006.

Schlaffer, Rudolf J.: Schleifer a.D.? Zur Menschenführung im Heer in der Aufbauphase, in: Sicherheitspolitik und Streitkräfte der Bundesrepublik Deutschland, Vol. 3, Das Heer 1950 bis 1970. Konzeption, Organisation, Aufstellung, Hrg MGFA, Munich: 2006, p. 615 to 698.

Schmädecke, Jürgen: Militärische Kommandogewalt und parlamentarische Demokratie. Zum Problem der Verantwortlichkeit des Reichswehrminsiters in der Weimarer Republik, Lübeck: 1966.

Schmidt, Helmut: Was fehlt der Bundeswehr Mängel der Armee – Notwendigkeiten der Konsolidierung, p. 104 to 118 in: Armee gegen den Krieg, Publ. by Wolfram von Raven, Stuttgart: 1966.

Schmidt, Helmut: Militärische Befehlsgewalt und parlamentarische Kontrolle, in: Festschrift für Adolf Arndt, Frankfurt/Main: 1969.

Schmückle, Gerd: Ohne Pauken und Trompeten, Erinnerungen an Krieg und Frieden, Stuttgart: 1982.

Schönrade, Rüdiger: General Joachim von Stülpnagel und die Politik. Eine biographische Skizze zum Verhältnis von militärischer und politischer Führung in der Weimarer Republik, Berlin: 2007.

Schössler, Dietmar (Publ.): Die Entwicklung des Strategie- und Operationsbegriffs seit Clausewitz, in: Beiträge zur Sicherheitspolitik und Strategieforschung, Militärwissenschaftliches Colloquium des Clausewitz-Gesellschaft e.V. April 1995, Dresden, Munich: 1997.

Schüddekopf, Otto-Ernst: Karl Radek in Berlin. Ein Kapitel deutsch-russischer Beziehungen im Jahre 1919, in: Archiv für Sozialgeschichte, Publ. by der Friedrich-Ebert Stiftung, Vol. II, 1962, p. 87 to 166.

Schulze, Hagen: Freikorps und Republik 1918–1920, Wehrwissenschaftliche Forschungen, Band 8, Publ. MGFA, Boppard: 1969.

Schulze, Hagen: Weimar Deutschland 1917–1933 in: Die Deutschen und ihre Nation: Neuere Deutsche Geschichte, in 6 Bänden, Vol. 4, Berlin: 1982.

Schwadlo-Gesterding, Joachim: Das Reichsheer, Sonderdruck aus 'Soldat in der Reichswehr, das soldatische Erlebnis 1918–1933, Bonn: 1966.

Schwerin von Krosigk, Lutz Graf: Es geschah in Deutschland, Menschenbilder unseres Jahrhunderts, Tübingen: 1951.

Searle, Alaric: A very special relationship: Basil Liddell Hart, Wehrmacht Generals and the debate on West German rearmament, 1945–1953, in: War in History, Vol. 5, 1998.

Seeckt, Hans von: Die Reichswehr, Leipzig: 1933.

Seeckt, Hans von: Die Zukunft des Reiches, Urteile und Forderungen, Berlin: 1929.

Seeckt, Hans von: Gedanken eines Soldaten, Berlin: 1929.

Seeckt, Hans von: Gedanken eines Soldaten, Berlin: 1935.

Seeckt, Hans von: Landesverteidigung, Berlin: 1930.

Seeckt, Hans von: Moltke, ein Vorbild, Leipzig: 1931.

Seidt, Hans Ulrich: Berlin Kabul Moskau; Oskar Ritter von Niedermayer und Deutschlands Geopolitik, Munich: 2002.

Semler, Paul (Hrg): Wehrgesetz vom 23. März 1921, mit Einleitung und Erläuterungen des Wehrgesetzes vom 18. Juni 1921, Berlin: 1921.

Severing, Carl: Memoiren Volume I, Volume II, Cologne: 1950.

Shipan, Charles R, and Huber, John D.: Deliberate Discretion? The Institutional Foundations of Bureaucratic Autonomy, Cambridge: 2002.

Shearer, Donald: Truppenbewegungen, II. Notes on Early Mobilization Planning: 1921–1926, o.A. des Ortes: 1978 (= Bestand des BA-MA, Freiburg, unter der Signatur : Msg 2/2168).

Simon, Ulrich: Die Integration der Bundeswehr in die Gesellschaft. Das Ringen um die Innere Führung, Hamburg: 1980.

Snider, Don: The US Military in Transition to Jointness: Surmounting Old Nations of Interservice Rivalry, p. 16 to 33, in: Airpower Journal, 1966, booklet 3

Soldatengesetz, Publ. and Commentary by Martin Rittau, Munich: 1957.

Sontheimer, Kurt: Die Adenauer-Ära, Grundlegung der Bundesrepublik, Munich: 1991.

Speidel, Hans: Aus unserer Zeit. Erinnerungen, Berlin: 1977.

Speidel, Helm: Reichswehr und Rote Armee, in Vierteljahreshefte für Zeitgeschichte, 1953, booklet 1, p. 9 to 45.

Stellenbesetzung im Reichsheer from 16 May 1920, 1st October 1920 and 1st October 1921, in Bibliotheca Rerum Militarium, Quellen und Darstellungen zur Militärwissenschaft und Militärgeschichte, Neudruck der Originalausgaben 1920–1921, Publ. MGFA, Osnabrück: 1928.

Stolz, Gerd und Grieser, Eberhard: Geschichte de Kavallerie-Regiments 5 'Feldmarschall von Mackensen', Geschichte seiner Stamm-Regimenter in Abrissen und Erinnerungen (1741–1944), Munich: 1975.

Steininger, Rolf, Jürgen Weber (Hrg): Die doppelte Eindämmung. Europäische Sicherheit und Deutsche Frage in den fünfziger Jahren, Tutzinger Schriften zur Politik, Book 2, Munich: 1993.

Steininger, Rolf: Deutschland und die Sozialistische Internationale nach dem Zweiten Weltkrieg. Die deutsche Frage, die Internationale und das Problem der Wiederbewaffnung der SPD auf den internationalen sozialistischen Konferenzen bis 1951, unter besonderer Berücksichtigung der Labour Party, Darstellung und Dokumentation, in: Archiv für Sozialgeschichte, Publ. by der Friedrich-Ebert-Stiftung in Verbindung mit dem Institut für Sozialgeschichte Braunschweig/Bonn, Book 7, Bonn: 1979.

Steininger, Rolf: Zwischen Pariser Verträgen und Genfer Gipfelkonferenz: Grossbritannien und die deutsche Frage 1955, in: Die doppelte Eindämmung: europäische Sicherheit und deutsche Frage in den Fünfzigern. Publ. by Rolf Steininger, Munich: 1993, p. 177 to 211.

Steininger, Rolf: Westdeutschland ein 'Bollwerk gegen den Kommunismus'?, in: Militärgeschichtliche Mitteilungen, Publ. MGFA, Freiburg: 1985, Year 38, Book 2, p. 163 to 207.

Strachan, Hew: On total war and modern war, in: The International History Review, 22, 2, 2000, p. 341–370.

Strachan, Hew: Ausbildung, Kampfgeist und die zwei Weltkriege, in: Erster Weltkrieg – Zweiter Weltkrieg. Ein Vergleich Krieg, Kriegserlebnis,

Kriegserfahrungen in Deutschland. Publ. MGFA, Paderborn: 2002, p. 265 to 286.

Strachan, Hew: The Lost Meaning of Strategy, in: Survival: the IISS Quarterly, Vol. 47, 2005, Book 3, p. 33 to 54.

Strachan, Hew: Making Strategy: Civil-Military Relations after Iraq, in: Survival: the IISS Quarterly, Vol. 48, Book 3, autumn 2006, p. 59 to 82.

Strachan, Hew: Clausewitz and the Dialectics of War, in: Clausewitz in the Twenty-First Century, ed. by Hew Strachan and Andreas Herberg-Rothe, Oxford: 2007, p. 14 to 44.

Strachan, Hew: Strategy in the Twenty-First-Century, in: The Changing Character of War, Publ. Hew Strachan and Sybille Scheipers, Oxford: 2011, p. 50 to 523.

Strenge, Irene: Kurt von Schleicher, Politik im Reichswehrministerium am Ende der Weimarer Republik, Berlin: 2006.

Stresemann, Gustav: Vermächtnis, der Nachlass in drei Bänden, erster Band, Berlin: 1932.

Stuhlmann, Friedrich: Deutsche Wehrmacht, Berlin 1934.

Stülpnagel, Joachim von: 75 Jahre meines Lebens, Düsseldorf: Photo Copie GmbH, 1955.

Stumpf, Reinhard: Die Wehrmacht-Elite, Rang- und Herkunftsstruktur der deutschen Generale und Admirale 1933–1944, in Wehrwissenschaftliche Forschungen, Abteilung Militärgeschichtliche Studien, Publ. MGFA, Vol. 29, Boppard/Rhein: 1982.

Stürmer, Michael: Wanderer zwischen zwei Welten, Hans Meier Welcker: Seeckt: in Neue politische Literatur, Year 13, 1968, p. 91 to 396.

Teske, Hermann: Die silbernen Spiegel, Generalstabsdienst unter der Lupe, Heidelberg: 1952.

Teske, Hermann: Analyse eines Reichswehr-Regiments, p. 252 to 269 in: Wehrwissenschaftliche Rundschau, Zeitschrift für Europäische Sicherheit, Frankfurt/Main: 1962.

Thaer, Albrecht von: Generalstabsdienst an der Front und in der Obersten Heeresleitung, aus Briefen und Tagebuchaufzeichnungen 1915–1919, Göttingen: 1959.

Thoss, Bruno: Menschenführung im Ersten Weltkrieg und im Reichsheer, p. 113 to 138: Menschenführung im Heer, Vol. 3, in Vorträge zur Militärgeschichte, Publ. MGFA, Bonn: 1982.

Tracey, Donald: Reform in the Early Weimarer Republic: The Thuringian Example, in: Journal of Modern History, 1974, Year. 44, p. 195 to 212.

Tradition und Reformen im militärischen Bewusstsein. Von der preussischen Allgemeinen Kriegsschule zur Führungsakademie der Bundeswehr, eine Dokumentation 1810–1985; herausgegeben von Detlef Bald, Gerhild Bald-Gerlich, Eduard Ambros, Baden-Baden: 1985.

Trucotte, William: Service Rivalry Overshadowed, p. 28 to 33, in: Airpower Journal, 1966, booklet 3.

Untersuchungen zur Geschichte des Offizierskorps, Anciennität und Beförderung nach Leistung, in: Beiträge zur Militär- und Kriegsgeschichte, Vol. 4, Publ. MGFA, Stuttgart: 1962.

Ursachen und Voraussetzungen der deutschen Kriegspolitik, Publ. Wilhelm Deist, Manfred Messerschmidt, Hans-Erich Volkmann und Wolfram Wette, Stuttgart: 1979.

Vardi, Gil-li: The Enigma of German Operational Theory: The Evolution of Military Thought in Germany, 1919–1938. London: 2008.

Vardi, Gil-li: The Change from Within, in: The Changing Character of War, Ed. Hew Strachan and Sibylle Scheipers, Oxford: 2011, p. 79 to 90.

Vaupel, Rudolph: Die Reorganisation des preussischen Staates unter Stein und Hardenberg, Zweiter Teil; Das Preussische Heer vom Tilsiter Frieden bis zur Befreiung, 1807–1814, Leipzig: 1938.

Vierteljahreshefte für Zeitgeschichte, Second Year, 1954, booklet 3, Juli: Ausgewählte Briefe von Generalmajor Helmuth Stieff.

Vogelsang, Thilo: Reichswehr, Staat und NSDAP, Beiträge zur deutschen Geschichte 1930–1932, Stuttgart: 1962.

Waffenstillstand, Der 1918–1919, Das Dokumentenmaterial der Waffenstillstand-Verhandlungen von *Compiègne*, Spa, Trier und Brüssel, Notenwechsel / Verhandlungsprotokolle / Verträge Gesamttätigkeitsberichte, im Auftrag der Deutschen Waffenstillstandskommission, Vol. I., Der Waffenstillstandsvertrag von *Compiègne* und seine Verlängerungen nebst den finanziellen Bestimmungen, Berlin: 1940.

Wagner, Armin: Die Bildung des DDR-Verteidigungsministeriums. Politische und militärische Entscheidungen zur Spitzengliederung der NVA 1955/56, in: Militärgeschichte, Zeitschrift für historische Bildung, Publ. MGFA, Potsdam, Year 10/2000, Hamburg: 2000, p. 55 to 63.

Wagner, Armin: Geburtswehen einer jungen sozialistischen Armee, Die Bildung des DDR-Verteidigungsministerium und der NVA 1955/56, in: Deutschland Archiv, 2001, booklet 6, p. 967 to 980.

Wallach, Jehuda L.: Das Dogma der Vernichtungsschlacht. Die Lehren von Clausewitz und Schlieffen und ihre Wirkungen in zwei Weltkriegen, Frankfurt/Main: 1967.

Wallach, Jehuda L.: Kriegstheorien. Ihre Entwicklungen im 19. und 20. Jahrundert, Frankfurt/Main: 1972.

Weckmann, Kurt: Führergehilfenausbildung, in: Wehrwissenschaftliche Rundschau, Zeitschrift für die Europäische Sicherheit, Frankfurt/Main: 1954, p. 268 to 277.

Wege eines Soldaten, Heinz Gaedcke, Publ. by Gerhard Brugmann, Nordertstedt: 2005.

Wehler, Hans–Ulrich: Deutsche Gesellschaftsgeschichte, Vom Beginn des Ersten Weltkriegs bis zur Gründung der beiden deutschen Staaten, 1914 – 1949, Vol. 4, Munich: 2003[2].

Wehrgesetz vom 23. März 1921, Publ. by Martin Rittau, Berlin: 1924.

Wehrs, Nikolai: Demokratie durch Diktatur? Meinecke als Vernunftrepublikaner in der Weimarer Republik, in: Friedrich Meinecke in seiner Zeit, Studien zu Leben und Werk, Publ. by Gisela Bock und Daniel Schönpflug, Beiträge zur Universitäts- und Wissenschaftsgeschichte, Vol. 19, Stuttgart: 2006.

Wells, Samuel F.: The first cold war build-up: Europe in United States Strategy and Policy, 1950–1953, in: Western Security: The formative years, European and Atlantic Defence 1947–1953, Publ. by Olav Riste, New York: 1985, p. 181 to 197.

Weniger, Erich: Inhalt und Formen des politischen Unterrichts in der Truppe, p. 327–338, in: Der deutsche Soldat in der Armee von morgen, Wehrverfassung, Wehrsystem, Inneres Gefüge, erschienen in: Veröffentlichungen des Institutes für Staatslehre und Politik e.V. Mainz, Vol. 4, Frankfurt/Main: 1954.

Wenzke, Rüdiger: Militärjustiz und Disziplinarrecht in der NVA, in: Militärgeschichte, 6/1995, Hamburg: 1995, p. 45 to 51.

Wenzke, Rüdiger: Wehrmachtsoffiziere in den DDR- Streitkräften in: Nationale Volksarmee – Armee für den Frieden Publ. by Detlef Bald, Reinhard Brühl, Andreas Prüfert, Baden-Baden: 1995.

Wenzke, Rüdiger: Das unliebsame Erbe der Wehrmacht, S 1113–1138, in: Die Wehrmacht: Mythos und Realität, Publ. by Rolf-Dieter Müller und Hans-Erich Volkmann, Munich: 1999.

Westphal, Siegried: Erinnerungen, Mainz: 1975.

Wette, Wolfram: Die deutsche militärische Führungsschicht in den Nachkriegszeiten, in: Lernen aus dem Krieg, deutsche Nachkriegszeiten 1918 und 1945, Munich: 1992, p. 39–66.

Wettig, Gerhard: Entmilitarisierung und Wiederbewaffnung in Deutschland 1943–1955, internationale Auseinandersetzungen um die Rolle der Deutschen in Europa, Munich: 1967.

Wettig, Gerhard: Neue Erkenntnisse aus sowjetischen Geheimdokumenten über den militärischen Aufbau in der SBZ/DDR 1947–1952, in: Militärgeschichtliche Mitteilungen, Hamburg: 1994, Year 53, Publ. MFGA, Potsdam, p. 399 to 419.

Wheeler-Bennet: John. W.: The Nemesis of Power, The German Army in the Politcs 1918–1945, London: 1956.

Wiggershausen, Norbert: Bedrohungsvorstellungen des Bundeskanzlers Adenauers nach Ausbruch des Korea-Krieges, p. 79 to 122, booklet 1, in: Militärgeschichtliche Mitteilungen (MGM), Publ. MGFA, Freiburg: 1979.

Wiggershausen, Norbert: Zur Bedeutung und Nachwirkung des militärischen Widerstandes in der Bundesrepublik Deutschland und in der Bundeswehr, p. 207 to 233 in: Vorträge zur Militärgeschichte. Publ. Militärgeschichtlichen Forschungsamt, Bd. 5, Der militärische Widerstand gegen Hitler und das NS-Regime 1933–1945, Herford: 1984.

Wild, Klaus: Zur Führergehilfen- und Generalstabsausbildung in der Reichswehr und Wehrmacht. Die Entwicklung des Fortbildungskurses für Offiziere der Reichswehr bis 1933 und die Ausbildung an der Wehrmachtakademie von

1935 bis 1938, Lehrgangsarbeit an der Führungsakademie der Bundeswehr, Hamburg: 1976.

Wild, Klaus: der Fortbildungskurs für Offiziere der Reichswehr (Reinhardt-Kurs) von 1928 – 1933, in: Europäische Wehrkunde, 1978, booklet 10, column 519–523.

Wildenmann, Rudolf: Macht und Konsens als Problem der Innen- und Aussenpolitik, in: Kölner Schriften zur Politischen Wissenschaft, Vol. 2, Publ. by Ferdinand A. Hermens, Frankfurt/Main: 1963.

Wirsching, Andreas und Jürgen Eder, Publ.: Vernunftrepublikanismus in der Weimarer Republik. Politik, Literatur, Wissenschaft (= Stiftung Bundespräsident-Theodor-Heuss-Haus, Wissenschaftliche Reihe, Vol. 9), Stuttgart: 2008.

Wittekind, Kurt: Aus 20 Jahren deutscher Wehrwirtschaft 1925–1945, in: Wehrkunde, Zeitschrift für alle Wehrfragen, Vol. VI, Year 1957.

Woertz, Franz: Die Verschwörung der Offiziere, in: Die Tat, 1930, booklet 8, p. 610 to 619.

Wohlfeil, Rainer: Handbuch zur deutschen Militärgeschichte 1648 – 1939. – 3, Section V, VI. Von der Entlassung Bismarcks bis zum Ende des Ersten Weltkrieges 1890 – 1918, Vol. 3, Section VI, Reichswehr und Republik 1918–1933, Publ. by MGFA, Munich: 1970.

Wohlfeil, Rainer und Dollinger, Hans: Die Deutsche Reichswehr, Bilder, Dokumente, Texte, zur Geschichte des Hunderttausend-Mann-Heeres 1919–1933, Wiesbaden: 1977.

Zeidler, Manfred: Reichswehr und Rote Armee 1920–1933, Wege und Stationen einer ungewöhnlichen Zusammenarbeit, Munich: 1993.

Zeidler, Manfred: The strange allies – Red Army and Reichswehr in the Inter-war Period, p. 99 to 118 in: Russian-German special relations in the twentieth century: a closed chapter? Oxford: 2006.

12th Infanterie-Regiment der Deutschen Reichswehr, 1.1.1921 bis 1.10.1934, ein Beispiel für den Übergang von der alten Armee zum neuen deutschen Volksheer, Osterwieck/Harz und Berlin: 1939.

Notes

1. See Hans Meier-Welcker: *Seeckt*, Frankfurt/Main: 1967. For information concerning his biography and personal background Introduction

2. The End of World War I. Manfred Funke: *Die Republik der Friedlosigkeit. Äussere und innere Belastungsfaktoren der Epoche von Weimar 1918–1933*, in: *Aus Politik und Zeitgeschichte, Beilage zur Wochenzeitung: Das Parlament*, B 32–33/94, 12 August 1994, p. 11.

3. Thomas Nipperdey: *Deutsche Geschichte 1866–1918*, Vol. II, *Machtstaat vor der Demokratie*, Munich: 1993², p. 872, cf. also p. 863–867.

4. Nipperdey: *Deutsche Geschichte 1866–1918*, Vol. II, p. 874.

5. *Der Waffenstillstand 1918–1919*, Hrg. im Auftrag der Deutschen Waffenstillstands-Kommission. *Das Dokumenten-Material der Waffenstillstands-Verhandlungen von Compiègne, Spa, Trier und Brüssel, Notenwechsel / Verhandlungs protokolle / Verträge* Gesamttätigkeitsbericht. Vol. 1: *Der Waffenstillstandsvertrag von Compiègne und seine Verlängerungen nebst den finanziellen Bestimmungen*, Berlin 1940, p. 61.

6. *Der Waffenstillstand 1918 – 1919*, Vol. 1, p. 22–26.

7. *Der Waffenstillstandsvertrag von Compiègne und seine Verlängerungen nebst finanziellen Bestimmungen*, Berlin 1940, Vol. 1. p. 11.

8. John Laughland: *A history of political trials. From Charles I to Saddam Hussein*, Witney, Oxfordshire: Lang, 2008, p. 43, 1–43.

9. Michael Salewski: *Entwaffnung und Militärkontrolle in Deutschland 1919 – 1927*, Munich: 1966, p. 32. Cf. this for the troop strength of the peacetime forces prior to World War I. BA-MA Nachlass Seeckt N 247/67, Speech by Seeckt on 20 February 1920 in Hamburg, slide no. 31.

10. Rainer Wohlfeil: *Reichswehr und Republik (1918–1933)* in: *Handbuch zur deutschen Militärgeschichte*, Abschnitt VI, Munich 1979, p. 20. Ulrich Wehler: *Deutsche Gesellschaftsgeschichte, 1914 – 1949*, Vol. 4, Munich: 2003², p. 241. Concerning the Treaty of Versailles, Gerhard Ritter wrote that the peace treaty threatened to 'prolong into all eternity the most violent emotions and animosities' in the German people for as long as it remained in effect. In: Bernd Faulenbach: *Deutsche Geschichtswissenschaft nach den beiden Weltkriegen*, in: *Lernen aus dem Krieg? Deutsche Nachkriegszeiten 1918 und 1945*, Beiträge zur historischen Friedensforschung, Hrg. von Gottfried Niedhart und Dieter Riesenberger, Munich: 1992, p. 220.

11. For information on the origins of Part V of the peace treaty, see: Salewski: *Entwaffnung und Militärkontrolle in Deutschland*, p. 30–36.

12. The above-mentioned war-guilt paragraphs, arms limitations and military controls came to be described as the 'Dictate of Versailles'. Cf.: Salewski:

Entwaffnung und Militärkontrolle, p. 17. Rainer Wohlfeil: *Reichswehr und Republik*, p. 17–21.

13. Wehler: *Deutsche Geschichte*, Vol. 4, p. 243, 251–252. The Federal Republic of Germany only paid off the remainder of its debt in 1953.

14. Germany was still to comply with the economic terms specified in the Treaty of Versailles, but the socio-economic conditions in society, which had worsened in the Depression, were to be lightened to some extent by this.

15. *Treaty of Versailles Articles 159–180 Military Clauses*, Articles 181–197 Naval Clauses, 198–202 Air Clauses.

16. *Treaty of Versailles Article 160*, paragraphs 1 and 2.

17. *Treaty of Versailles Article 173*.

18. *Das Wehrgesetz vom 23. März 1921*, Hrg. Martin Rittau, Berlin: 1924, p. 29, 31: § 2: The number of the soldiers and military officials of the Reichsheer amounts to no more than 100,000. This number includes 4,000 officers and military officials of officer rank as a maximum. To these, 300 medical officers and 200 veterinary officers were added. §5: The maximum number of soldiers and military officials of the Reichsmarine amounted to 15,000. This number included 1,500 officers and deck officers.

19. *Treaty of Versailles Article 160*, § 1, paragraph 2: 'The Army shall be devoted exclusively to the maintenance of order within the territory and to the control of the frontiers.'

20. *Treaty of Versailles* Articles 203–210.

21. Ludwig Richter: *Die Weimarer Reichsverfassung*, in: *Aus Politik und Zeitgeschichte*, Beilage zur Wochenzeitung: *Das Parlament*, B 32–33/94, 12 August 1994, p. 3–4.

22. Richter: *Die Weimarer Reichsverfassung*, p. 6.

23. Richter: *Die Weimarer Reichsverfassung*, p. 10.

24. Richter: *Die Weimarer Reichsverfassung*, p. 7.

25. Huber: *Dokumente zur Deutschen Verfassungsgeschichte*, Vol. VI, Stuttgart: 1981, p. 612. Huber: *Dokumente zur Deutschen Verfassungsgeschichte* Vol. 4, Stuttgart: 1992, p. 86 and p. 196. Huber: *Dokumente zur Deutschen Verfassungsgeschichte*, Vol. VI, p. 583.

Chapter 1: Seeckt According to Existing Literature

1. Seeckt according to existing Literature. John W. Wheeler-Bennet: *Nemesis of Power, The German Army in Politics 1918–1945*, London: 1956. Samuel P. Huntington: *The Soldier and the State. The Theory and Politics of Civil-Military Relations*, Cambridge / Massachusetts: 1959. Gordon, Harold J.: *The Reichswehr and the German Republic 1919–1926*, Princeton: 1957. Francis L. Carsten: *The Reichswehr and Politics 1918–1933*, Oxford: 1966. Jehuda L. Wallach: *Das Dogma der Vernichtungsschlacht. Die Lehren von Clausewitz und Schlieffen und ihre Wirkungen in zwei Weltkriegen*, Frankfurt / Main: 1967.

2. Klaus-Jürgen Müller: *Das Heer und Hitler, Armee und nationalsozialistisches Regime 1933–1940*, Stuttgart: 1969. Michael Geyer: *Die Wehrmacht der Deutschen Republik ist die Reichswehr: Bemerkungen zur neueren Literatur*, in: *Militärgeschichtliche Mitteilungen*, Publ. MGFA, Vol. 16, Year, 2/1973,

Freiburg: 1973, p. 152 to 199. Geyer: *Der zur Organisation erhobene Burgfrieden*, in: *Militär und Militarismus in der Weimarer Republik*, Publ. by Klaus Jürgen Müller und Eckardt Opitz, Düsseldorf: 1978. Klaus Jürgen Müller: *Armee, Politik und Gesellschaft in Deutschland 1933–1945, Studien zum Verhältnis von Armee und NS-System*, Paderborn: 1979. Geyer: *Aufrüstung oder Sicherheit, die Reichswehr in der Krise der Machtpolitik 1924–1936*, Wiesbaden: 1980.

3. Karl-Volker Neugebauer: *Operatives Denken zwischen dem Ersten und Zweiten Weltkrieg*, in: *Operatives Denken und Handeln in deutschen Streitkräfte im 19. und 20. Jahrhundert, Vorträge zur Militärgeschichte*, Vol. 9, Herford: 1988. James, S. Corum: *The Roots of Blitzkrieg, Hans von Seeckt and the German Military Reform*, Kansas: 1992. Gerhard P. Gross: *Das Dogma der Beweglichkeit. Überlegungen zur Genese der deutschen Heerestaktik im Zeitalter der Weltkriege*, in: *Erster Weltkrieg – Zweiter Weltkrieg. Ein Vergleich, Krieg, Kriegserlebnis, Kriegserfahrung in Deutschland*, im Auftrag des MGFA, Hrg. Bruno Thoss und Hans-Erich Volkmann: Überlegungen zur Genese der deutschen Heerestaktik im Zeitalter der Weltkriege, in: *Erster Weltkrieg – Zweiter Weltkrieg*, Paderborn: 2002. Robert M Citino, *The Path to Blitzkrieg. Doctrine and training in the German Army 1920–1939*, Mechanicsburg: 2008². Gli-li Vardi: *The Enigma of German Operational Theory: The Evolution of Military Thought in Germany*, 1919–1938, London: 2008. Peter Keller: *'Die Wehrmacht der Deutschen Republik ist die Reichswehr'. Die deutsche Armee 1918–1921*, Paderborn: 2014. Gerhard P. Gross: *Mythos und Wirklichkeit. Geschichte des operativen Denkens im deutschen Heer von Moltke d.Ä. bis Heusinger*, Paderborn: 2012. Marco Sigg: *Der Unterführer als Feldherr im Taschenformat. Theorie und Praxis der Auftragstaktik im deutschen Heer 1869 bis 1945*, Paderborn: 2014.

4. Matthias Strohn: *Hans von Seeckt and his Vision of a 'Modern Army'*, in: *War in History*, Vol. 12, No. 3, July 2005. Matthias Strohn: *The German Army and the Defence of the Reich. Military Doctrine and the Conduct of the Defensive Battle 1918–1939*, Oxford: 2011.

5. James S. Corum: *Roots of Blitzkrieg, Hans von Seeckt and the German Military Reform*, Kansas: 1992. Mary Habeck: *Storm of Steel, the Development of Armour Doctrine in Germany and the Soviet Union, 1919–1939*, New Yoor: 2003. Robert M. Citino: *The Path to Blitzkrieg, Doctrine and Training in the German Army 1920–39*, Mechanicsburg: 2008².

6. Gerhard P. Gross: *Das Dogma der Beweglichkeit. Überlegungen zur Genese der deutschen Heerestaktik im Zeitalter der Weltkriege*, in: *Erster Weltkrieg – Zweiter Weltkrieg. Ein Vergleich, Krieg, Kriegserlebnis, Kriegserfahrung in Deutschland*, im Auftrag des MGFA, Hrg. Bruno Thoss und Hans-Erich Volkmann: Überlegungen zur Genese der deutschen Heerestaktik im Zeitalter der Weltkriege, in: *Erster Weltkrieg – Zweiter Weltkrieg*, Paderborn: 2002, p. 155. Gerhard P. Gross: *Mythos und Wirklichkeit. Geschichte des operativen Denkens im deutschen Heer von Moltke d.Ä. bis Heusinger*, Paderborn: 2012, p.149. Marco Sigg: *Der Unterführer als Feldherr im Taschenformat. Theorie und Praxis der Auftragstaktik im deutschen Heer 1869 bis 1945*, Paderborn: 2014, pp. 63–64,106, 118, 229 footnote 303.

7. Wilhelm Deist: *Strategy and Unlimited Warfare in Germany: Moltke, Falkenhayn, and Ludendorff*, in: *Great War, Total War. Combat and Mobilization on the Western Front, 1914–1918*, Cambridge: 2000, pp. 265–280. Cf. Rainer Wohlfeil: *Heer und Republik*.

8. Sigg: *Der Unterführer als Feldherr im Taschenformat*, p. 63. Kroener: *Mobilmachungsplanungen gegen Recht und Verfassung*, p.62ff.

9. Sigg: *Der Unterführer als Feldherr im Taschenformat*, pp. 63, 64, 77.

10. Wheeler-Bennet: *Nemesis of Power, the German Army in Politics 1918–1945*, London: 1956, p. 86–87, cf. p. 90–91. Cf. J. Neill: *The German Army and the Nazi party, 1933–1939*, p. 62. Peter Keller: '*Die Wehrmacht der Deutschen Republik ist die Reichswehr*'. *Die deutsche Armee 1918–1921*, Paderborn: 2014, pp. 2–10, 12, 163, 170.

11. Gil-li Vardi: *The Enigma of German Operational Theory: The Evolution of Military Thought in Germany*, 1919–1938, London: 2008, p. 167.

12. Vardi: *The Change from Within*, in: *The Changing Character of War*, Ed. Hew Strachan and Sybille Scheipers, Oxford: 2011, p. 81.

13. Müller: *Das Heer und Hitler, Armee und nationalsozialistisches Regime 1933–1940*, Stuttgart: 1969, p. 23.

14. Peter Keller: *Die Wehrmacht der Deutschen Republik ist die Reichswehr*, p. 272.

15. Citino: *Path to Blitzkrieg*, p. 16. Mary Habeck: *Storm of Steel, The Development of Armour Doctrine in Germany and the Soviet Union, 1919–1939*, New York: 2003, p. 19–20.

16. Neugebauer: *Operatives Denken zwischen dem Ersten und Zweiten Weltkrieg*, p. 102.

17. Neugebauer: *Operatives Denken zwischen dem Ersten und Zweiten Weltkrieg*, p. 102.

18. David Jablonsky: *Roots of Strategy*, Book 4, 3 *Military Classics, Mahan, Corbett, Douhet, Mitschell*, Mechanisburg: 1999, p. 3.

19. Cf. Honig: *Clausewitz and the Politics of Early Modern Warfare*, pp. 29–48. Cf. also Hew Strachan: *Clausewitz and the Dialectics of War*; both articels are to be found in: *Clausewitz in the Twenty-First Century*, ed. by Hew Strachan and Andreas Herberg-Rothe, Oxford: 2007, pp. 14–44.

20. Keller: '*Die Wehrmacht der Deutschen Republik ist die Reichswehr*', pp. 9, 274f.

21. The Politico-Military Situation in 1918. Michael Geyer: *Die Wehrmacht der Deutschen Republik ist die Reichswehr: Bemerkungen zur neueren Literatur* in: *Militärgeschichtliche Mitteilungen*, MGFA, Vol. 16, issue 2/1973, Freiburg: 1973, p. 156.

22. Geyer: *Die Wehrmacht der Deutschen Republik ist die Reichswehr*, p. 182.

23. Geyer: *Die Wehrmacht der Deutschen Republik ist die Reichswehr*, p. 182.

24. Geyer: *Aufrüstung oder Sicherheit, die Reichswehr in der Krise der Machtpolitik 1924–1936*, Wiesbaden: 1980, p. 32.

25. Keller: *Die Wehrmacht der deutschen Republik ist die Reichswehr*, p. 11; see also pp. 274–276.

26. Geyer: *Aufrüstung oder Sicherheit*, p. 32.

27. Geyer: *Aufrüstung oder Sicherheit*, p. 32. Cf. Rainer Wohlfeil: *Heer und Republik*, in: *Handbuch zur deutschen Militärgeschichte 1648–1939*, Vol. 3, section VI, *Reichswehr und Republik 1918–1933*, ed. MGFA, Munich: 1979, p. 207.

28. Geyer: *Aufrüstung oder Sicherheit*, p. 35.
29. Vardi: *The Enigma of German Operational Theory*, p. 165.
30. Vardi: *The Enigma of German Operational Theory*, p. 162.
31. The 'Problem of Professionalism' of the Military Elite and Total War. Müller: *Armee, Politik und Gesellschaft in Deutschland 1933–1945, Studien zum Verhältnis von Armee und NS-System*, Paderborn: 1979, p. 22.
32. Keller: *Die Wehrmacht der Deutschen Republik ist die Reichswehr*, p. 170.
33. Müller: *Das Heer und Hitler, Armee und nationalsozialistisches Regime*, p. 23.
34. Müller: *Armee, Politik und Gesellschaft in Deutschland 1933–1945*, p. 21.
35. Müller: *Armee, Politik und Gesellschaft in Deutschland 1933–1945*, p. 23. Cf. Wheeler-Bennet: *Nemesis of Power*, p. 87, 89, 95, 96, 143. Otto-Ernst Schüddekopf: *Das Heer und die Republik, Quellen zur Politik der Reichswehrführung, 1918 bis 1933*, Frankfurt/Main: 1955, p. 128.
36. Geyer: *Burgfrieden*, p. 17. Seeckt: *Schlagworte* (1928), in: *Gedanken eines Soldaten*, 1935, p.14. [Thoughts of A Soldier, Ernest Benn Limited, London, 1930, p. 34 (Translator's note: The English translation of Seeckt's: *Gedanken eines Soldaten* is based on the first publication in 1929, not on the enlarged edition of 1935].
37. Geyer: *Der zur Organisation erhobene Burgfrieden*, in: *Militär und Militarismus in der Weimarer Republik*. Eds. Klaus Jürgen Müller and Eckardt Opitz, Düsseldorf: 1978, pp. 18, 29.
38. Michael Geyer: *Aufrüstung oder Sicherheit*, p. 28f. Werner Rahn: *Reichsmarine und Landesverteidigung 1919–1928, Konzeption und Führung der Marine in der Weimarer Republik*, Munich: 1976, p. 210. Andreas Dietz: *Das Primat der Politik in kaiserlicher Armee, Reichswehr, Wehrmacht und Bundeswehr: Rechtliche Sicherungen der Entscheidungsgewalt*. über Krieg und Frieden zwischen Politik und Militär, Tübingen: 2003, p. 235.
39. Vardi: *The Enigma of German Operational Theory*, p. 165. Cf. Wheeler-Bennet: *Nemesis of Power*, p. 119–120. Cf. Carsten: *The Reichswehr and Politics*, pp. 142ff.
40. Vardi: *The Enigma of German Operational Theory*, p. 162.
41. Geyer: *Die Wehrmacht der Deutschen Republik ist die Reichswehr*, p. 198. Cf. Wheeler-Bennet: *Nemesis of Power*, p. 86–87, 90.
42. Robert J. Neill: *The German Army and the Nazi Party*, 1933–1939, London: 1966, p. 62.
43. Eberhard Birk, Gerhard P. Gross: *Von Versailles über Paris nach Moskau*, Teil 1, in: Österreichische militärische Zeitschrift: ÖMZ, 2013, Heft 2, p. 134.
44. Kroener: *Mobilmachungen gegen Recht und Verfassung*, p. 65.
45. Kroener: *Mobilmachungen gegen Recht und Verfassung*, p. 62.
46. BArch Nachlass Seeckt N 247/139, slide no. 4, dated 14 January 1921.
47. Kroener: *Mobilmachungen gegen Recht und Verfassung*, p. 63. In the original text, the expression used is not 'dilution' but rather: 'In connection with the abolition of the Treaty of Versailles, the introduction of compulsory military service, and a combination of the standing (professional) army and the militia for a transitional period' BArch Nachlass Seeckt N 247/139 dated 14 January 1921, slide no. 4. Cf. Meier-Welcker: *Seeckt*, p. 532.
48. Kroener: *Mobilmachungen gegen Recht und Verfassung*, p. 63.

49. Vardi: *The Change from Within*, p. 81.

50. Eberhard Birk, Gerhard P. Gross: *Von Versailles über Paris nach Moskau*, Teil 1, p. 137.

51. Vardi: *The Change from Within*, p. 80.

52. Vardi: *The Enigma of German Operational Theory*, p. 146. Cf. Mary Habeck: *Storm of Steel, the Development of Armour Doctrine in Germany and the Soviet Union, 1919–1939*, New York: 2003, p. 19f-20.

53. Wheeler-Bennet: *Nemesis of Power*, p. 86–87, 90, 96, 97.

54. Geyer: *Die Wehrmacht der Deutschen Republik ist die Reichswehr*, pp. 152–199, p. 162.

55. Geyer: *Die Wehrmacht der Deutschen Republik ist die Reichswehr*, p. 176.

56. Müller: *Das Heer und Hitler*, pp. 23, 24.

57. Ulrich Wehler: *Deutsche Gesellschaftsgeschichte*, Vol. no. 4: *Vom Beginn des Ersten Weltkrieges bis zur Gründung des beiden deutschen Staaten 1914–1949*, Munich: 2003, p. 417.

58. Geyer: *Die Wehrmacht der Deutschen Republik ist die Reichswehr*, p. 197. Cf. Keller: *Die Wehrmacht der Deutschen Republik ist die Reichswehr*, p. 12.

59. Citino: *Path to Blitzkrieg*, p. 9. Vardi: *The Enigma of German Operational Theory*, p. 151f. Reichherzer: *Alles ist Front*, p. 162.

60. Jehuda L. Wallach: *Das Dogma der Vernichtungsschlacht. Die Lehren von Clausewitz und Schlieffen und ihre Wirkungen in zwei Weltkriegen*, Frankfurt / Main: 1967, pp. 313–325, 342, 350; cf. p. 339f, where he writes: 'It is difficult to know whether this was truly Seeckt's intention or whether it was actually only a more recent consideration of Rabenau's...' Corum: *Roots of Blitzkrieg*, p. 32, 50. Vardi: *The Enigma of German Operational Theory*, p. 151f.

61. Birk/Gross: *Von Versailles über Paris nach Moskau*, Teil 1, p. 137.

62. Geyer: *Die Wehrmacht der Deutschen Republik ist die Reichswehr*, p. 155.

63. The Organization of the Army and Advance in Arms Technology. Among more recent researchers, Matthias Strohn is the only one to point out that quite the reverse is true and that Seeckt did learn something and put it to practical use. Matthias Strohn: *The German Army and the Defence of the Reich. Military Doctrine and the Conduct of the Defensive Battle 1918–1939*, Oxford: 2011, p. 94.

64. Vardi: *The Enigma of German Operational Theory*, p. 171.

65. Vardi: *The Enigma of German Operational Theory*, p. 168.

66. Vardi: *The Enigma of German Operational Theory*, p. 168.

67. Vardi: *The Enigma of German Operational Theory*, p. 169. Cf. Matthias Strohn: *Hans von Seeckt and his Vision of a 'Modern Army'*, in: *War in History*, Vol. 12, No. 3, July 2005, p. 324; in this, Strohn already called attention to Seeckt's intention in his letter to Groener. He stated that political and military changes determined the formation, organization and structure of any army. 'Seeckt wrote that he aimed at a professional army... he emphasized that no organization is made for eternity and that changing political and military situations might make a conscript army necessary.'

68. Vardi: *The Enigma of German Operational Theory*, pp. 168–169.

69. Vardi: *The Enigma of German Operational Theory*, p. 168.

70. Gross: *Das Dogma der Beweglichkeit*, p. 155.

71. Vardi: *The Enigma of German Operational Theory*, p. 154. Cf. Carsten: *Reichswehr und Politik*, p. 233f. Vardi: *The Change from Within*, pp. 81–83.

72. Vardi: *The Enigma of German Operational Theory*, pp. 145–146.

73. Vardi: *The Enigma of German Operational Theory*, p. 146.

74. Vardi: *The Enigma of German Operational Theory*, p. 168.

75. Vardi: *The Enigma of German Operational Theory*, p. 168.

76. Vardi: *The Enigma of German Operational Theory*, p. 146. Cf. Carsten: *The Reichswehr and Politics*, p. 213f. Cf. Habeck: Storm of Steel, p. 20.

77. *Führung und Gefecht der verbundenen Waffen*, FuG parts I and II = H.Dv. 487, Berlin: 1921 and 1923.

78. Wallach: *Das Dogma der Vernichtungsschlacht*, pp. 317f, 332f.

79. Vardi: *The Enigma of German Operational* Theory, p. 147.

80. Vardi: *The Change from Within*, pp. 83–85.

81. Vardi: *The Change from Within*, p. 80.

82. Carsten: *Reichswehr and Politik*, p. 213.

83. Sigg: *Der Unterführer als Feldherr im Taschenformat*, pp. 59, 61–64, 65, 229.

84. Sigg: *Der Unterführer als Feldherr im Taschenformat*, p. 40.

85. Sigg: *Der Unterführer als Feldherr im Taschenformat*, p. 77.

86. An Army of 200 000. Independent Social Democratic Party of Germany (USPD. = Unabhängige Sozialdemokratische Partei Deutschlands). Cf. Robert J. Neill: *German Army and the Nazi Party, 1933–1939*, London: 1966, p. 84. Corum: Roots of Blitzkrieg, p. 29.

87. Vardi: *The Enigma of German Operational Theory*, p. 159.

88. Vardi: *The Enigma of German Operational Theory*, p. 162.

89. Vardi: *The Enigma of German Operational Theory*, p. 162. Cf. Carsten: The Reichswehr and Politics, p. 113.

90. Civil-Military Relations. Müller: *Das Heer und Hitler*, p. 22. Cf. Keller: *Die Wehrmacht der Deutschen Republik ist die Reichswehr*, p. 230.

91. Geyer: *Die Wehrmacht der Deutschen Republik ist die Reichswehr*, p. 198. Rainer Wohlfeil: *Handbuch zur deutschen Militärgeschichte 1648–1939. – 3.* Abschnitt V, VI. *Von der Entlassung Bismarcks bis zum Ende des Ersten Weltkrieges 1890 – 1918*, Abschnitt VI: *Reichswehr und Republik 1918–1933*, Hrg. vom MGFA, Munich: 1970. Carsten: *The Reichswehr and Politics*, p. 173. Cf. Strohn: *Hans von Seeckt and his vision of a 'Modern Army'*, p. 321.

92. *Offiziere im Bild von Dokumenten aus drei Jahrhunderten*, Beiträge zur Militär- und Kriegsgeschichte, ed. MGFA, vol.6, Einführung von Manfred Messerschmidt, Dokumente Manfred Messerschmidt und Ursula von Gersdorff, Stuttgart: 1964, p. 92.

93. Keller: *Die Wehrmacht der Deutschen Republik ist die Reichswehr*, p. 230.

94. Keller: *Die Wehrmacht der Deutschen Republik ist die Reichswehr*, p. 12.

95. Otto-Ernst Schüddekopf: *Das Heer und die Republik, Quellen zur Politik der Reichswehrführung, 1918 bis 1933*, Frankfurt/ Main: 1955, S. 116. Gessler: *Reichswehrpolitik in der Weimarer Republik*, Stuttgart: 1958, p. 69. Concerning Nazi censoring of the work of Rabenau and other editions published by Rabenau on Seeckt see: BArch Nachlass Rabenau N 62/5, slides nos. 5–18. In Strohn: *Hans von Seeckt and his vision of a "Modern Army"*, p. 322, Strohn also took this into account in his analysis. Cf. also Strohn: *The German Army and the*

Defence of the Reich, p. 103f. In Meier-Welcker: *Seeckt*, p. 350, Fn. 4, the author also refers to the interpretations made bei Rabenau. By contrast, in Otto-Ernst Schüddekopf: *Herr und Republik*, S. 116, in Keller: *Die Wehrmacht der deutschen Republik ist die Reichswehr*, p. 10, Fn. 4, Keller referred to Rabenau. An incorrect approach is also to be found in the biography by Franz Uhle-Wettler: *Erich Ludendorff Soldat – Feldherr – Revolutionär*, Graz: 2013, in which the author draws on Rabenau: *Seeckt I* and *Seeckt* II, for his description of the relationship between Ludendorff and Seeckt. Kroener: *Mobilmachungen gegen Recht und Verfassung*, p. 63, quotes Rabenau and yet gives erroneous information concerning the source in Meier-Welcker: *Seeckt*, p. 532. The source in Seeckt is not mentioned at all: see BArch Nachlass Seeckt N 247/139 slide no. 4ff.

96. Gessler: *Reichswehrpolitik*, pp. 287–288.
97. Vardi: *The Enigma of German Operational Theory*, pp. 143, 154.
98. Keller: *Die Wehrmacht der Deutschen Republik ist die Reichswehr*, p. 221.
99. Vardi: *The Enigma of German Operational Theory*, p. 162.
100. Carsten: *Reichswehr and Politics*, pp. 92–93. Wheeler-Bennet: *Nemesis of Power*, p. 96. Gross: *Mythos und Wirklichkeit*, pp. 149, 150. Robert J. Neill: *The German Army and the Nazi Party*, 1933–1939, London: 1966, p. 62.
101. Robert J. Neill: *The German Army and the Nazi Party*, 1933–1939, London: 1966, p. 62. Wheeler-Bennet: *Nemesis of Power*, p. 96.
102. Birk/Gross: *Von Versailles über Paris nach Moskau*, Teil 1, p. 137. Geyer: *Die Wehrmacht der Deutschen Republik ist die Reichswehr: Bemerkungen zur neueren Literatur*, in: *Militärgeschichtliche Mitteilungen*, MGFA, vol. 16, issue 2/1973, Freiburg: 1973, p. 176.
103. Vardi: *The Enigma of German Operational Theory*, p. 161.
104. Vardi: *The Change from Within*, p. 81.
105. Geyer: *Aufrüstung oder Sicherheit*, p. 35.
106. Geyer: *Aufrüstung oder Sicherheit*, p. 45.
107. Carsten: *The Reichswehr and Politics*, p. 162.
108. Keller: *Die Wehrmacht der Deutschen Republik ist die Reichswehr*, pp. 221, 230f, 272, 275.
109. Keller: *Die Wehrmacht der Deutschen Republik ist die Reichswehr*, p. 241.
110. Garry J. Clifford: *Bureaucratic Politics*, pp. 91–102, in: Michael J. Hogan and Thomas G. Paterson (eds.): *Explaining the History of American Foreign Relations*, Cambridge: 2004. John D. Huber and Charles R. Shipan: *Deliberate Discretion? The Institutional Foundations of Bureaucratic Autonomy*, Cambridge: 2002. John C. Reis: *The Management of Defense. Organization and Control of the U.S. Armed Services*, Baltimore: 1964. Morton H. Halperin: *Bureaucratic Politics and Foreign Policy*, Washington: 1974. Samuel P. Huntington: *Interservice Competition and the Political Roles of the Armed Services*, pp. 40–52, in: *American Political Science Review*, 55 (1961). Samuel P. Huntington and Andrew Goodpaster: *Civil-Military Relations*, Washington: 1977. David C. Kozak and James M. Keagle (eds.): *Bureaucratic Politics and National Security. Theory and Practice*, London: 1988. Irving L. Janis: *Victims of Groupthink. A psychological study of foreign-policy decisions and fiascoes*, Boston: 1972.
111. Irving L. Janis: *Victims of Groupthink*.

112. Samuel P. Huntington: *The Soldier and the State. The Theory and Politics of Civil-Military Relations*, Cambridge/Massachusetts: 1959, p 111. Cf. Wheeler-Bennet: *Nemesis of Power*, p. 87, 91, 110. Corum: *Roots of Blitzkrieg*, p. 173.

113. Samuel P. Huntington: *The soldier and the state in the 1970s*, in: Andrew Goodpaster and Samuel P. Huntington: *Civil-Military Relations*, Washington: 1977, p. 6.

114. Huntington: *The Soldier and the State*, pp. 59–79.

115. Huntington: *The Soldier and the State*, p. 15.

116. Huntington: *The Soldier and the State*, p. 14.

117. Huntington: *The Soldier and the State in the 1970s*, p. 6.

118. Huntington: *Civil-Military Relations*, p. 6.

119. Huntington: *Interservice Competition and the Political Roles of the Armed Services*, p. 40, in: *American Political Science Review*, 1961, 55.

120. Huntington: *Interservice Competition and the Political Roles of the Armed Services*, p. 40 in: *American Political Science Review*, 1961, 55.

121. Strachan: *Making Strategy: Civil-Military Relations after Iraq*, in: *Survival*, Vol. 48, No. 3, autumn 2006, p. 62.

122. Strachan: *Making Strategy: Civil-Military Relations after Iraq*, p. 67.

123. Strachan: *Making Strategy: Civil-Military Relations after Iraq*, p. 76.

124. Carl von Clausewitz: *Vom Kriege*, 6. Kapitel B: *Der Krieg ist ein Instrument der Politik*, Troisdorf: 1980, pp. 991–998, particularly p. 995.

125. Outlook. Michael Geyer: *Der zur Organisation erhobene Burgfrieden*, in: *Militär und Militarismus in der Weimarer Republik*. Eds. Klaus Jürgen Müller and Eckardt Opitz, Düsseldorf: 1978, p. 17.

126. Geyer: *Die Wehrmacht der Deutschen Republik ist die Reichswehr*, pp. 153, 198. Müller: *Armee, Politik und Gesellschaft*, p. 22.

127. Geyer: *Aufrüstung oder Sicherheit*, p. 45. *Offiziere im Bild von Dokumenten aus drei Jahrhunderten*, p. 92.

128. Müller: *Das Heer und Hitler*, p. 22.

129. Müller: *Armee, Politik und Gesellschaft*, p. 28.

130. Liddell Hart: *The German Generals Talk*, New York: 1948, p. 14. Citino: *Path to Blitzkrieg*, p. 9. In this regard, James Corum also argued against Liddell Hart and added some important key training aspects to Seeckt's concept. Cf: *Corum: Roots of Blitzkrieg*, p. 54, 97, 101, 103–121.

131. Wilhelm Deist: *Die Reichswehr und der Krieg der Zukunft*, in: *Militärgeschichtliche Mitteilungen* 1989, Jahrgang 45, Heft 1, p. 86.

132. Geyer: *Aufrüstung oder Sicherheit*, p. 45.

133. Neugebauer: *Operatives Denken zwischen dem Ersten und Zweiten Weltkrieg*, p. 103. Vardi: *The Enigma of German Operational Theory*, p. 151. Gross: *Mythos und Wirklichkeit*, pp.154f, 158. Corum: *Roots of Blitzkrieg*, p. 1f. Citino: *Path to Blitzkrieg*, p. 10–11, 16.

134. Corum: *Roots of Blitzkrieg*, p. 54, 97, 101, 103–121.

135. Harold J. Gordon: *The Reichswehr and the German Republic 1919–1926*, Princeton: 1957, p. 201. Müller: *Armee, Politik und Gesellschaft in Deutschland 1933–1945*, p. 23. Carsten: *Reichswehr and Politics*, pp.198–220, 212–215.

136. Cf. Huntington: *The Soldier and the State in the 1970s*.

Chapter 2: Military-Strategic Considerations in the Weimar Republic

1. Paul Hindenburg (2 October 1847 – 2 August 1934).
2. Marianne Weber: *Max Weber, ein Lebensbild*, Tübingen: 1984, p. 664f.
3. Ludendorff's Total War Theory. Erich Ludendorff: *Der totale Krieg*, Munich: 1935, p. 8f. Cf. Leon Daudet: *La Guerre totale*, Paris: 1928, quoted from: Heuser: *The Evolution of Strategy. Thinking War from Antiquity to the Present*, Cambridge: 2010, p. 137.
4. Cf. Heuser: *The Evolution of Strategy*, pp. 113–123, 157.
5. Ludendorff: *Der totale Krieg*, p. 5.
6. Ludendorff: *Der totale Krieg*, p. 3.
7. Ludendorff: *Kriegführung und Politik*, p. 10.
8. Ludendorff: *Der totale Krieg*, p. 6.
9. Ludendorff: *Der totale Krieg*, p. 6.
10. Ludendorff: Kriegführung und Politik, p. 11. Concerning the history of the concept of a people's war since 1870, see also: Robert T. Foley: *From Volkskrieg to Vernichtungskrieg: German concepts of warfare, 1871 – 1935*, in: *War, Peace and World Orders in European History*, edited by Beatrice Heuser and Anja V. Hartmann, London: 2001, pp. 214–225.
11. Ludendorff: *Der totale Krieg*, p. 4f.
12. Erich Ludendorff: *Kriegführung und Politik*, Berlin: 1922, pp. 11–12. See also Robert T. Foley: *From Volkskrieg to Vernichtungskrieg: German concepts of warfare, 1871 – 1935*, pp. 214–225.
13. Ludendorff: *Der totale Krieg*, p. 7.
14. Ludendorff: *Der totale Krieg*, p. 21.
15. Ludendorff: *Der totale Krieg*, p. 12.
16. Ludendorff: *Der totale Krieg*, pp. 11, 12, 16, 20, 21, 26, 27, 57.
17. Ludendorff: *Der totale Krieg*, p. 6.
18. Ludendorff: *Der totale Krieg*, p. 13.
19. Ludendorff: *Der totale Krieg*, pp. 19, 33.
20. Ludendorff: *Der totale Krieg*, p. 19.
21. Ludendorff: *Der totale Krieg*, p. 17.
22. Ludendorff: *Der totale Krieg*, p. 17.
23. Ludendorff: *Der totale Krieg*, p. 17.
24. Ludendorff: *Der totale Krieg*, p. 6.
25. Ludendorff: *Der totale Krieg*, p. 17.
26. Ludendorff: *Der totale Krieg*, p. 17. Cf. Heuser: *The Evolution of Strategy*, pp. 192–193.
27. Ludendorff: *Der totale Krieg*, p. 28.
28. Ludendorff: *Der totale Krieg*, p. 19.
29. Ludendorff: *Der totale Krieg*, p. 24.
30. Ludendorff: *Der totale Krieg*, pp. 11, 13, 15, 16.
31. Ludendorff: *Der totale Krieg*, p. 25.
32. Ludendorff: *Der totale Krieg*, p. 61.
33. Ludendorff: *Der totale Krieg*, p. 61.
34. Cf. Robert T. Foley: *From Volkskrieg to Vernichtungskrieg*, p. 214f.
35. Ludendorff: *Der totale Krieg*, p. 9.

36. Ludendorff: *Der totale Krieg*, p. 9.
37. Ludendorff: *Der totale Krieg*, p.10.
38. Ludendorff: *Kriegführung und Politik*, p. 23.
39. Cf. Robert T. Foley: *From Volkskrieg to Vernichtungskrieg: German concepts of warfare, 1871–1935*, p. 214, in: *War, Peace and World Orders in European History*, London: 2001.
40. Ludendorff: *Kriegführung und Politik*, p. 12. Ludendorff: *Der totale Krieg*, p. 3.
41. Ludendorff: *Der totale Krieg*, p.3.
42. Ludendorff: *Der totale Krieg*, pp.3, 10. Erich Ludendorff: *Kriegführung und Politik*, Berlin: 1922, p. 12.
43. Ludendorff: *Der totale Krieg*, p. 10.
44. Immanuel Kant: *Zum Ewigen Frieden*, Bern: 1944, p. 11.
45. Hew Strachan: *The Lost Meaning of Strategy*, in: Survival: *IISS Quarterly*, Vol. 47, 2005, No. 3, p. 42.
46. Wilhelm Deist: *The road to ideological war: Germany, 1918–1945*, in: *The making of strategy*. Rulers, states, and war, eds. Williamson Murray, Macgregor Knox, Cambridge: 1996, p. 360f.
47. Strachan: *The Lost Meaning of Strategy*, p. 45. Cf. Hew Strachan: *On total war and modern war*, in: *The International History Review*, 22, 2, 2000, p. 31–370.
48. Ludendorff: *Der totale Krieg*, pp. 79, -84.
49. Gordon: *Der Hitlerputsch 1923, Machtkampf in Bayern 1923–1924*. Frankfurt/Main: 1971, p. 270.
50. Meier-Welcker: *Seeckt*, p. 410. Cf. Rabenau: *Seeckt II*, p. 146.
51. Seeckt: *Clausewitz* (1930), in: *Gedanken eines Soldaten*, 1935, p. 26.
52. Harold J. Gordon: *The Reichswehr and the German Republic 1919–1926*, Princeton: 1957, p. 440. See also: *Der Kapp-Lüttwitz-Ludendorff-Putsch*, ed. by Erwin Könnemann and Gerhard Schulze, Munich: 2002, p. 197.
53. Claus Guske: *Das politische Denken Seeckts*, p. 67.
54. Marianne Weber: *Max Weber*, p. 665.

Chapter 3: Seeckt's Military Strategy

1. Heuser: *The Evolution of Strategy*, p. 3.
2. Heuser: *The Evolution of Strategy*, pp. 4–28, 39–110. Karl-Volker Neugebauer: *Operatives Denken zwischen dem Ersten und Zweiten Weltkrieg*, in: *Operatives Denken und Handeln in deutschen Streitkräften im 19. und 20. Jahrhundert*, Vorträge zur Militärgeschichte, Vol. 9, Herford: 1988, pp. 97–121.
3. Heuser: *The Evolution of Strategy*, p. 13.
4. Heuser: *The Evolution of Strategy*, p. 13–17.
5. Heuser: *The Evolution of Strategy*, p. 13–17.
6. Seeckt: *Staatsmann und Feldherr* (1928), in: *Gedanken eines Soldaten*, 1935, p. 39.
7. Another reason for utilizing the term 'military strategy' is the excessive use of the word 'strategy'. This is the case, for instance, in information technology, where people talk of the "strategic leading role" of the IT sector or in financial affairs, where officials drew up "strategic reflections" concerning the "cum and ex deals" of the banks in order to counteract the years of tax evasion of

the banks. In order to specifically limit the term to one area, the adjective "military" is added; this can be done in the German language by constructing a compound noun.

8. Seeckt: *Moderne Heere* (1928), in: *Gedanken eines Soldaten*, Berlin: 1935, p. 53. For more information on strategic doctrine and political education, see: Offiziere im Bild von Dokumenten aus drei Jahrhunderten, in: *Beiträge zur Militär- und Kriegsgeschichte*, vol. 6, ed. MGFA, Stuttgart: 1964, p. 228f. Cf. Matthias Strohn: *The German Army and the Defence of the Reich. Military Doctrine and the Conduct of the Defensive Battle 1918–1939*, Oxford: 2011, p. 96.

9. Seeckt: *Schlagworte* (1928), in: *Gedanken eines Soldaten*, 1935, p.15.

10. Seeckt: *Landesverteidigung*, 1930, p. 68f. Seeckt: *Grundsätze moderner Landesverteidigung*, (1930), in: *Gedanken eines Soldaten*, 1935, p. 77.

11. Seeckt: *Clausewitz* (1930), in: *Gedanken eines Soldaten*, 1935, pp. 23–29.

12. Seeckt: *Clausewitz* (1930), in: *Gedanken eines Soldaten*, 1935, p. 24f.

13. Seeckt: *Clausewitz* (1930), in: *Gedanken eines Soldaten*, 1935, pp. 25, 26.

14. Seeckt: *Clausewitz* (1930), in: *Gedanken eines Soldaten*, 1935, p. 25. Clausewitz: *Vom Kriege*, pp. 990–991.

15. Cf. Clausewitz: *Vom Kriege*, p. 995.

16. Seeckt: *Staatsmann und Feldherr* (1928), in: *Gedanken eines Soldaten*, 1935, p. 40.

17. Seeckt: *Clausewitz* (1930), in: *Gedanken eines Soldaten*, 1935, p. 26.

18. Seeckt: *Reichswehr*, p. 41.

19. Clausewitz: *Vom Kriege*, p. 991.

20. Seeckt: *Staatsmann und Feldherr* (1928), in: *Gedanken eines Soldaten*, 1935, p. 45.

21. Seeckt: *Staatsmann und Feldherr* (1928), in: *Gedanken eines Soldaten*, 1935, p. 40.

22. Seeckt: *Clausewitz* (1930), in: *Gedanken eines Soldaten*, 1935, p. 26.

23. Seeckt: *Staatsmann und Feldherr* (1928), in: *Gedanken eines Soldaten*, 1935, p. 39.

24. Seeckt: *Staatsmann und Feldherr* (1928), in: *Gedanken eines Soldaten*, 1935, p. 39. Clausewitz: *Vom Kriege*, pp. 991, 993, 994.

25. Seeckt: *Moderne Heere* (1928), in: *Gedanken eines Soldaten*, p. 51. BArch Nachlass Seeckt N 247/89 Reichswehrministerium Chef des Truppenamtes, Berlin 26 February 1920, slides nos. 14–19. BArch Nachlass Seeckt N 247/89 Reichswehrministerium Chef des Truppenamtes, Berlin 31 July 1920, slide nos. 22–27. BArch Nachlass Seeckt N 247/104 Reichswehrministerium Chef der Heeresleitung, 11 March 1922, slides nos. 3–12. Cf. Meier-Welcker: *Seeckt*, p. 538, footnote 48.

26. Thomas Hobbes: Leviathan or the matter from power of a commonwealth, ecclesiastical and civil. London: 1894, see Chapter XIII.

27. Seeckt: *Staatsmann und Feldherr* (1928), in: *Gedanken eines Soldaten*, 1935, p. 40.

28. Seeckt: *Schlagworte* (1928), in: *Gedanken eines Soldaten*, 1935, p. 15.

29. Seeckt: *Clausewitz* (1930), in: Seeckt: *Gedanken eines Soldaten*, 1935, p. 26.

30. Seeckt: *Staatsmann und Feldherr* (1928), in: *Gedanken eines Soldaten*, 1935, p. 40.

31. Seeckt: *Das erreichbare Ziel* (1927), in: *Gedanken eines Soldaten*, 1935, p. 48.

32. Seeckt: *Staatsmann und Feldherr* (1928), in: *Gedanken eines Soldaten*, 1935, p. 41.

33. Seeckt: *Moderne Heere* (1928), in: *Gedanken eines Soldaten*, 1935, p. 51.

34. Meier-Welcker: *Seeckt*, pp. 40, 39–40. General Staff officer Tappen had been in Berlin since 1895. Together with Seeckt, he attended the War Academy in Berlin and, like him, was trained as a General Staff officer. In 1895, Seeckt, Tappen and General Groener all attended the War Academy. Cf. Rabenau: *Seeckt II*, p. 35.

35. Cf. Strohn: *The German Army and the Defence of the Reich*, pp. 118, 124f.

36. Seeckt: *Landesverteidigung*, 1930, p. 42f.

37. Seeckt: *Staatsmann und Feldherr* (1928), in: *Gedanken eines Soldaten*, 1935, p.44.

38. Cf. Wheeler-Bennet: *Nemesis of Power*, p. 86, 100. Cf. Citino: *Path to Blitzkrieg*, p. 13, 120–122.

39. Clausewitz – Bismarck – Moltke – Seeckt: *Staatsmann und Feldherr* (1928), in: *Gedanken eines Soldaten*, 1935, p. 39f. Cf. Seeckt: *Clausewitz* (1930), in: *Gedanken eines Soldaten*, 1935, p. 26.

40. Seeckt: *Clausewitz* (1930), in: *Gedanken eines Soldaten*, 1935, p.23f. Clausewitz: *Vom Kriege*, pp. 990–998.

41. Seeckt: *Moderne Heere* (1928), in: *Gedanken eines Soldaten*, Berlin: 1935, p. 56. Cf. Seeckt: *Moltke, ein Vorbild*, 1931, pp. 127f, 140f.

42. FuG, 1923, p. 352, paragraph 5. See also: Seeckt: *Schlagworte* (1928), in: *Gedanken eines Soldaten*, 1935, p. 18.

43. Seeckt: *Clausewitz* (1930), in: *Gedanken eines Soldaten*, 1935, p. 28. Cf. Clausewitz: *Vom Kriege*, p. 994.

44. Clausewitz: *Vom Kriege*, pp.990–994.

45. Seeckt: *Schlagworte* (1928), in: *Gedanken eines Soldaten*, 1935, p. 15.

46. BArch Nachlass Seeckt N 247/77, *Entwurf Heeresorganisation* of [*Army Organisation draft* of] 17 February 1919, slide no. 8. Clausewitz: *Vom Kriege*, p. 995.

47. Seeckt: *Moltke*, p. 127.

48. Seeckt: *Moltke*, p. 128.

49. Seeckt: *Moltke*, pp. 128–129.

50. Seeckt: *Moltke*, p.70.

51. Seeckt: *Staatsmann und Feldherr* (1928), in: *Gedanken eines Soldaten*, 1935, p. 39f.

52. BArch Nachlass Seeckt N 247/141, slide no. 82.

53. BArch Nachlass Seeckt N 247/141, slide no. 58.

54. Seeckt: *Moltke*, p.39. Seeckt: *Staatsmann und Feldherr* (1928), in: *Gedanken eines Soldaten*, 1935, p. 43f.

55. Seeckt: *Staatsmann und Feldherr* (1928), in: *Gedanken eines Soldaten*, 1935, p. 43f.

56. Cf. Gessler: *Reichswehrpolitik*, pp.343, 347.

57. Civil-Military Cooperation. Seeckt: *Staatsmann und Feldherr* (1928), in: *Gedanken eines Soldaten*, 1935, p. 43.

58. Seeckt: *Staatsmann und Feldherr* (1928), in: *Gedanken eines Soldaten*, 1935, p. 43.

59. Seeckt: *Staatsmann und Feldherr* (1928), in: *Gedanken eines Soldaten*, 1935, p. 39.

60. Seeckt: *Staatsmann und Feldherr* (1928), in: *Gedanken eines Soldaten*, 1935, pp.40–41.

61. Strachan: *Making Strategy*, p. 66.

62. Strachan: *Making Strategy*, p. 71.

63. Seeckt: *Staatsmann und Feldherr* (1928), in: *Gedanken eines Soldaten*, 1935, p. 41.

64. Seeckt: *Staatsmann und Feldherr* (1928), in: *Gedanken eines Soldaten*, 1935, p. 43.

65. Seeckt: *Staatsmann und Feldherr* (1928), in: *Gedanken eines Soldaten*, 1935, pp. 40, 41.

66. Seeckt: *Clausewitz* (1930), in: *Gedanken eines Soldaten*, 1935, p. 28.

67. Strachan: *Making Strategy*, p. 68.

68. Seeckt: *Staatsmann und Feldherr* (1928), in: *Gedanken eines Soldaten*, 1935, p. 40f.

69. Seeckt: *Staatsmann und Feldherr* (1928), in: *Gedanken eines Soldaten*, 1935, p. 41. Cf. Strachan: *Making Strategy*, p. 78.

70. Seeckt: *Staatsmann und Feldherr* (1928), in: *Gedanken eines Soldaten*, 1935, p. 41.

71. Seeckt: *Staatsmann und Feldherr* (1928), in: *Gedanken eines Soldaten*, 1935, p. 45.

72. Seeckt: *Clausewitz* (1930), in: *Gedanken eines Soldaten*, 1935, p. 26.

73. Strachan: *Making Strategy*, p. 67.

74. Seeckt: *Clausewitz* (1930), in: *Gedanken eines Soldaten*, 1935, p. 28. Cf. Clausewitz: *Vom Kriege*, pp. 994, 995.

75. Seeckt: *Staatsmann und Feldherr* (1928), in: *Gedanken eines Soldaten*, 1935, p. 44.

76. Seeckt: *Staatsmann und Feldherr* (1928), in: *Gedanken eines Soldaten*, 1935, p. 43.

77. Seeckt: *Staatsmann und Feldherr* (1928), in: *Gedanken eines Soldaten*, 1935, p. 45. Cf. Clausewitz: *Vom Kriege*, pp. 991, 994.

78. Strachan: *Making Strategy*, p. 68.

79. Clausewitz: *Vom Kriege*, p. 991.

80. Strachan: *Making Strategy*, pp. 67, 76.

81. Seeckt: *Staatsmann und* Feldherr (1928), in: *Gedanken eines Soldaten*, 1935, p. 44.

82. Strachan: *Making Strategy*, p. 76.

83. Strachan: *Making Strategy*, p. 77.

84. Seeckt: *Clausewitz* (1930), in: *Gedanken eines Soldaten*, 1935, p. 27.

85. Seeckt: *Clausewitz* (1930), in: *Gedanken eines Soldaten*, 1935, pp. 26–28. Clausewitz: *Vom Kriege*, pp. 991. 993.

86. Seeckt: *Moltke*, p. 108.

87. BArch, Nachlass Seeckt N 247/89 Aus der Akte „Chef der Heeresleitung, Führerreise 1923, *Geheim*, *Schlussbesprechung*, f. 56. *Offiziere im Bild von*

Dokumenten aus drei Jahrhunderten, in: *Beiträge zur Militär- und Kriegsgeschichte*, pp. 222, 228f. BA-MA, RH 37/783 Reichswehrministerium, Heeresleitung No. 550.7.23. T 1 III dated 24/7/23. 12–2/94 Reichswehrministerium Heer Heeresleitung No. 382. 22. T 4 pers. 31 July 1922, pp. 3f, 6. Seeckt: *Moltke*, p. 54. BA-MA RH 12–2/93, Reichswehrministerium Chef der Heeresleitung No. 200. 22. Adj. No. 273.4.22. T4 II. dated 1 April 1922. Rabenau: *Seeckt II*, p. 507. Ludwig Beck: *Studien*, Stuttgart: 1955, pp. 41–45; From 1 October 1923 until 30 September 1925, Beck was the director of the principal staff assistant training of the Military District Command VI in Münster/Westphalia.

88. Clausewitz: *Vom Kriege*, p. 995.

89. BArch Nachlass Seeckt N 247/9, slide no. 22.

90. Joachim von Stülpnagel: *75 Jahre meines Lebens*, Düsseldorf: Photo Copie GmbH, 1955, p.194.

91. Seeckt: *Reichswehr*, p. 79.

92. *Offiziere im Bild von Dokumenten aus drei Jahrhunderten*, in: *Beiträge zur Militär- und Kriegsgeschichte*, p. 228f. Clausewitz: *Vom Kriege*, p. 995.

93. Seeckt: *Clausewitz* (1930), in: *Gedanken eines Soldaten*, 1935, pp. 27–28.

94. Seeckt: *Clausewitz* (1930), in: *Gedanken eines Soldaten*, 1935, p. 28.

95. Hew Strachan: *Strategy in the Twenty-First Century*, in: *The Changing Character of War*, Eds. Hew Strachan and Sibylle Scheipers, Oxford: 2011, p.506.

96. Hew Strachan: *Making Strategy*, p. 68.

97. Clausewitz: *Vom Kriege*, pp. 991–995.

98. Hew Strachan: *Making Strategy*, p. 62.

99. Huntington: *The Soldier and the State*, p. 68.

100. Groener: *Lebenserinnerungen*, Göttingen: 1957, p. 520.

101. Seeckt: *Gedanken eines Soldaten*, p. 9.

102. Seeckt: *Reichswehr*, p. 32.

103. Vardi: *The Enigma of German Operational Theory*, p.154.

104. Vardi: *The Enigma of German Operational Theory*, p. 159.

105. Vardi: *The Enigma of German Operational Theory*, p. 162.

106. BArch Nachlass Seeckt N 247/75 *Chef der Heeresleitung*, dated 10 July 1920, slides nos. 21–22.

107. *The Enigma of the German Operational Theory*, p. 162, further on see: p. 159, footnote 225. The text refers Chapter I, to page 15 of the book.

108. Vardi has pretended that, see: *The Enigma of the German Operational Theory*, p. 162, further on see also: p. 159, footnote 225.

109. BArch Nachlass Seeckt N 247/75, 10 July 1920, slide no. 23. Cf. Meier-Welcker: *Seeckt*, pp. 282–291. Corum: *Roots of Blitzkrieg*, p. 14, 18.

110. Deist: *Die Reichswehr und der Krieg der Zukunft*, p.88.

111. Geyer: *Die Wehrmacht der Deutschen Republik ist die Reichswehr*, p. 166.

112. Gordon: *Reichswehr*, p. 421.

113. Carsten: *Reichswehr and Politics*, p. 154. (German edition p. 175). Cf. Wheeler-Bennet: *Nemesis of Power*, p. 108.

114. BArch Nachlass Rabenau N 62/7 slide no. 23.

115. Realpolitik and Crisis Prevention. Seeckt: *Staatsmann und Feldherr* (1928), in: *Gedanken eines Soldaten*, 1935, p. 53.

116. Seeckt: *Clausewitz* (1930), in: *Gedanken eines Soldaten*, 1935, p. 26f.
117. Seeckt: *Reichswehr*, p. 41.
118. Seeckt: *Schlagworte* (1928), in: *Gedanken eines Soldaten*, 1935, p. 15.
119. Seeckt: *Schlagworte* (1928), in: *Gedanken eines Soldaten*, 1935, p. 15.
120. Seeckt: *Schlagworte* (1928), in: *Gedanken eines Soldaten*, 1935, p. 16.
121. Seeckt: *Schlagworte* (1928), in: Seeckt: *Gedanken eines Soldaten*, 1935, p. 16.
122. BA-MA, Nachlass Seeckt N 247/77 *Heeresorganisation* dated 17 February 1919, slide no. 8.
123. Seeckt: *Schlagworte* (1928), in: *Gedanken eines Soldaten*, 1935, p.13. Cf. Clausewitz: *Vom Kriege*, p. 992.
124. Seeckt: *Staatsmann und Feldherr* (1928), in: *Gedanken eines Soldaten*, 1935, p. 43. Cf. Strohn: *Hans von Seeckt and his vision of a "Modern Army"*, p.327.
125. Seeckt: *Staatsmann und Feldherr* (1928), in: *Gedanken eines Soldaten*, 1935, p. 41.
126. Seeckt: *Staatsmann und Feldherr* (1928), in: *Gedanken eines Soldaten*, 1935, p. 41.
127. Seeckt: *Staatsmann und Feldherr* (1928), in: *Gedanken eines Soldaten*, 1935, p. 42.
128. Seeckt: *Staatsmann und Feldherr* (1928), in: *Gedanken eines Soldaten*, 1935, p. 44.
129. Seeckt: *Staatsmann und Feldherr* (1928), in: *Gedanken eines Soldaten*, 1935, p. 44f.
130. Seeckt: *Staatsmann und Feldherr* (1928), in: *Gedanken eines Soldaten*, 1935, p. 47.
131. Seeckt: *Staatsmann und Feldherr* (1928), in: *Gedanken eines Soldaten*, 1935, p. 41.
132. Seeckt: *Staatsmann und Feldherr* (1928), in: *Gedanken eines Soldaten*, 1935, p. 45.
133. Seeckt: *Clausewitz* (1930), in: *Gedanken eines Soldaten*, 1935, p. 27. Cf. Clausewitz: *Vom Kriege*, pp. 991, 993, 994.
134. Seeckt: *Staatsmann und Feldherr* (1928), in: *Gedanken eines Soldaten*, 1935, p. 46.
135. Seeckt: *Clausewitz* (1930), in: *Gedanken eines Soldaten*, 1935, p. 27.
136. Seeckt: *Staatsmann und Feldherr* (1928), in: *Gedanken eines Soldaten*, 1935, p. 46.
137. Seeckt: *Staatsmann und Feldherr* (1928), in: *Gedanken eines Soldaten*, 1935, p. 46.
138. Seeckt: *Staatsmann und Feldherr* (1928), in: *Gedanken eines Soldaten*, 1935, p. 46.
139. Seeckt: *Staatsmann und Feldherr* (1928), in: *Gedanken eines Soldaten*, 1935, p. 46.
140. Seeckt: *Staatsmann und Feldherr* (1928), in: *Gedanken eines Soldaten*, 1935, p. 46.
141. Seeckt: *Clausewitz* (1930), in: *Gedanken eines Soldaten*, 1935, p. 27.
142. Seeckt: *Staatsmann und Feldherr* (1928), in: *Gedanken eines Soldaten*, 1935, pp. 43–44.

143. Seeckt: *Clausewitz* (1930), in: *Gedanken eines Soldaten*, 1935, p. 26. Clausewitz: *Vom Kriege*, pp. 994–995.

144. Claus Guske: *Das politische Denken Seeckts*, p. 67. See also Groener: *Lebenserinnerungen*, p. 421; he shared Seeckt's view: 'he [Ludendorff] encroached increasingly on the political sphere as well, impetuously seizing overall control of German affairs'. Heuser: *The Evolution of Strategy*, p. 120.

145. Claus Guske: *Das politische Denken Seeckts*, p. 67. Meier-Welcker: *Seeckt*, p. 410. Cf. Rabenau: *Seeckt* II, p. 146. In his '*Lebenserinnerungen*' (memoirs), p. 421, Groener wrote that Ludendorff had wanted to control "political affairs". See also Groener's lecture to the Wednesday Society on 3 June 1936, in: *Die Mittwochs-Gesellschaft, Protokolle aus dem geistigen Deutschland 1932 bis 1944*, ed. Klaus Scholder, Berlin: 1982, pp. 142–146.

146. See Wallach: *Das Dogma der Vernichtungsschlacht*, pp. 292–294f concerning the differences between Seeckt and Hindenburg, Ludendorff and Groener.

147. Deist: *Die Reichswehr und der Krieg der Zukunft*, p. 83.

148. *Offiziere im Bild von Dokumenten aus drei Jahrhunderten*, in: *Beiträge zur Militär- und Kriegsgeschichte*, vol. 6, ed. MGFA, Stuttgart: 1964, p. 228f. Cf. Habeck: *Storm of Steel*, p. 20, 24f.

149. Seeckt: *Staatsmann und Feldherr* (1928), in: *Gedanken eines Soldaten*, 1935, p. 44.

150. BArch Nachlass Seeckt N 247/104, Reichswehrministerium Chef der Heeresleitung, 11. März 1922.

151. Heuser: *The Evolution of Strategy*, pp. 176–178, 183–185.

152. BArch Nachlass Seeckt N 247/104 Reichswehrministerium Chef der Heeresleitung, 11. März 1922, slide no. 6.

153. BArch Nachlass Seeckt N 247/104 Reichswehrministerium Chef der Heeresleitung, 11. März 1922, slide no. 6.

154. Keller: *Die Wehrmacht der Deutschen Republik ist die Reichswehr*, p. 11.

155. Seeckt: *Heer im Staat* (1928), in: *Gedanken eines Soldaten*, 1935, p. 92f.

156. Mass and Technology. Seeckt: *Moderne Heere* (1928), in: *Gedanken eines Soldaten*, 1935, p. 56. Seeckt: *Landesverteidigung*, 1930, p. 42.

157. Seeckt: *Moderne Heere* (1928), in: *Gedanken eines Soldaten*, 1935, p. 56.

158. Seeckt: *Moderne Heere* (1928), in: *Gedanken eines Soldaten*, 1935, p. 56.

159. Heuser: *The Evolution of Strategy*, p. 168.

160. Seeckt: *Moderne Heere* (1928), in: *Gedanken eines Soldaten*, 1935, p. 58.

161. Seeckt: *Landesverteidigung*, 1930 p. 42. cf. p. 37f, 47, 65; Seeckt: *Grundsätze der modernen Landesverteidigung* (1930), in: *Gedanken eines Soldaten*, 1935, p. 84 f.

162. Seeckt: *Landesverteidigung*, 1930, p. 64–65, cf. p. 37

163. Seeckt: *Landesverteidigung*, 1930, p. 64. Seeckt: *Landesverteidigung*, 1930, p. 64–65, cf. p. 37. Stig Förster: *Der Deutsche Generalstab und die Illusion des kurzen Krieges, 1871–1914. Metakritik eines Mythos*, in: *Militärgeschichtliche Mitteilungen*, 1955, (54), p. 61–95.

164. Seeckt: *Moderne Heere* (1928), in: *Gedanken eines Soldaten*, 1935, p. 53.

165. Seeckt: *Moderne Heere* (1928), in: *Gedanken eines Soldaten*, 1935, p. 60 f. Seeckt: *Landesverteidigung*, 1930, p. 65, 87.

166. Seeckt: Moderne Heere (1928), in: Gedanken eines Soldaten, 1935, p. 55.

167. Seeckt: *Moderne Heere* (1928), in: *Gedanken eines Soldaten*, 1935, p. 60.

168. Seeckt: *Moderne Heere* (1928), in: *Gedanken eines Soldaten*, 1935, p. 53.

169. Seeckt: *Landesverteidigung*, 1930, p. 29 and 68–70.

170. Corum: *Roots of Blitzkrieg*, p. 31, 33, 50, 68, 169, 183. Citino: *Path to Blitzkrieg*, p. 9, 35

171. Seeckt: *Moderne Heere* (1928), in: *Gedanken eines Soldaten*, 1935, p. 60.

172. Seeckt: *Reichswehr*, p. 42 f. Seeckt: *Grundsätze moderner Landesverteidigung* (1930), in: *Gedanken eines Soldaten*, 1935, p. 81.

173. BArch Nachlass Seeckt N 247/77, *Entwurf Heeresorganisation* of [*Army Organisation draft* of] of 17 February 1919, slide no. 9.

174. Seeckt used the terms levy in mass and battle of despair for the first time in the event of an external attack in his '*Grundlegende Gedanken für den Wiederaufbau unserer Wehrmacht*' *(Fundamental Thoughts for the Reconstruction of our Wehrmacht)*. N 247/130 No. 220, 14 January 1921, slide no. 4.

175. Seeckt: *Landesverteidigung*, 1930, p. 70. Seeckt: *Grundsätze moderner Landesverteidigung* (1930), in: *Gedanken eines Soldaten*, 1935, p. 78.

176. For information on the term people's army in contrast to the professional army or operating army, see Seeckt: *Landesverteidigung*, p. 68, 70, 76 f, 78, 88f. Seeckt: *Die Reichswehr*, p. 100.

177. Seeckt: *Landesverteidigung*, p. 70. Cf.: Seeckt: *Landesverteidigung*, p. 29 f, 81; Seeckt: *Grundsätze moderner Landesverteidigung* (1930), in: *Gedanken eines Soldaten*, 1935, p. 79.

178. Seeckt: *Moderne Heere* (1928), in: *Gedanken eines Soldaten*, 1935, p. 59. Cf. Seeckt: *Grundsätze moderner Landesverteidigung* (1930), in: *Gedanken eines Soldaten*, 1935, p. 79.

179. Seeckt: *Grundsätze der Landesverteidigung* (1930), in: *Gedanken eines Soldaten*, 1935, p. 82. Cf. Seeckt: *Landesverteidigung*, p. 77.

180. Seeckt: *Landesverteidigung*, p. 78.

181. Seeckt: *Grundsätze moderner Landesverteidigung*, (1930), in: *Gedanken eines Soldaten*, 1935, p. 78, 80–82.

182. Seeckt: *Landesverteidigung*, p. 78–79.

183. Seeckt: *Grundätze moderner Landesverteidigung* (1930), in: *Gedanken eines Soldaten*, 1935, p. 84.

184. Meier-Welcker: *Seeckt*, p. 532.

185. Seeckt: *Grundsätze moderner Landesverteidigung* (1930), in: *Gedanken eines Soldaten*, 1935, p. 80, 81.

186. Seeckt: *Moderne Heere* (1928), in: *Gedanken eines Soldaten*, 1935, p. 59. Seeckt: *Grundsätze moderner Landesverteidigung* (1930), in: *Gedanken eines Soldaten*, 1935, p. 80, 81. Cf. Nachlass Seeckt N 247/77 *Army Organisation*, 17 February 1919, slide no. 9.

187. Seeckt: *Landesverteidigung*, p. 85.

188. Seeckt: *Landesverteidigung*, p. 70. Seeckt: *Grundsätze moderner Landesverteidigung* (1930), in: *Gedanken eines Soldaten*, 1935, p. 78.

189. Seeckt: *Landesverteidigung*, 1933, p. 82.

190. Seeckt: *Grundsätze moderner Landesverteidigung* (1930), in: *Gedanken eines Soldaten*, 1935, p. 78.

191. Seeckt: *Landesverteidigung*, p. 74–77. Meier-Welcker: *Seeckt*, p. 532.

192. Seeckt: *Grundsätze moderner Landesverteidigung*, (1930), in: *Gedanken eines Soldaten*, 1935, p. 81. Seeckt: *Landesverteidigung*, p. 78. Cf. Seeckt: *Landesverteidigung*, p. 70, 74 f.

193. Seeckt: *Grundsätze moderner Landesverteidigung* (1930), in: *Gedanken eines Soldaten*, 1935, p. 81.

194. Seeckt: *Landesverteidigung*, p. 78–81.

195. Seeckt: *Reichswehr*, p. 42 f. Seeckt: *Grundsätze moderner Landesverteidigung* (1930), in: *Gedanken eines Soldaten*, 1935, p. 78.

196. Seeckt: *Landesverteidigung*, p. 78.

197. Seeckt: *Landesverteidigung*, p. 68 f.

198. Deist: *Die Reichswehr und der Krieg der Zukunft*, p. 84.

199. Seeckt: *Grundsätze moderner Landesverteidigung*, (1930), in: *Gedanken eines Soldaten*, 1935, p. 81.

200. Cf. Citino: *Path to Blitzkrieg*, p. 9.

201. BArch Nachlass Seeckt 247/77 *Army Organisation*, 17 February 1919, slide no. 9.

202. Seeckt: *Landesverteidigung*, p. 54.

203. Seeckt: *Grundsätze moderner Landesverteidigung* (1930), in: *Gedanken eines Soldaten*, 1935, p. 77.

204. Seeckt: *Landesverteidigung*, p. 67. Seeckt: *Landesverteidigung*, 1930, p. 54.

205. Meier-Welcker: *Seeckt*, p. 11.

206. Heuser: *The Evolution of Strategy*, p.113 ff, 163, 167.

207. Seeckt: *Landesverteidigung*, p. 90.

208. Seeckt: *Heer im Staat* (1928) in: *Gedanken eines Soldaten*, 1935, p. 89.

209. BArch Nachlass Seeckt N 247/77 *Army Organisation* of 17 February 1919, slide no. 8.

210. Seeckt: *Landesverteidigung*, 1930, p. 37; cf. Seeckt: *Moderne Heere*, (1928), in: *Gedanken eines Soldaten*, 1935, p. 58, 89.

211. Seeckt: *Landesverteidigung*, 1930, p. 64–65 and cf. p. 37.

212. Seeckt: *Grundsätze der Landesverteidigung* (1930), in: *Gedanken eines Soldaten*, 1935, p.83. Seeckt: *Landesverteidigung*, 1930, p. 88.

213. Seeckt: *Moderne Heer* (1928), in: *Gedanken eines Soldaten*, 1935, p. 53. cf. BArch N 247/158 Die internationale Bedeutung der Abrüstungsfrage (1930), p. 16.

214. Seeckt: *Grundsätze moderner Landesverteidigung* (1930), in: *Gedanken eines Soldaten*, 1935, p. 83.

215. Seeckt: *Moderne Heere* (1928), in: *Gedanken eines Soldaten*, 1935, p. 53.

216. Seeckt: *Moderne Heere* (1928), in: *Gedanken eines Soldaten*, 1935, p. 60.

217. Heuser: *The Evolution of Strategy*, p. 175, 186, 329.

218. Seeckt: *Moderne Heere* (1928), in: *Gedanken eines Soldaten*, 1935, p. 54.

219. Cf. Heuser: *The Evolution of Strategy*, p. 180.

220. Corum: *Roots of Blitzkrieg*, p. 144–148. Habeck: *Storm of Steel*, p. 21, 24, 49, 51.

221. Kroener: *Generaloberst Fromm, der starke Mann im Heimatkriegsgebiet*, Paderborn: 2005, p. 174.

222. Liddell Hart: *The German Generals Talk*, New York: 1948, p. 14: 'He gave the Reichswehr a gospel of mobility'. Gross: *Das Dogma der Beweglichkeit*, p. 154. Heinz-Ludger Borgert referred in his article to Liddell Hart, see: *Grundzüge der Landkriegführung von Schlieffen bis Guderian*, in: *Handbuch zur deutschen Militärgeschichte 1648–1939*, begründet von Hans Meier-Welcker, Hrg. vom MGFA, o.A.v.J.u.O., p. 551.

223. The Professional Army. Cf. Heuser: *The Evolution of Strategy*, p. 154.

224. Seeckt: *Landesverteidigung*, p. 27, 29, 73, 92. Seeckt: *Die Zukunft des Reiches*, p. 157. Seeckt: *Grundsätze moderner Landesverteidigung* (1920), in: *Gedanken eines Soldaten*, 1935, p. 84. BArch Nachlass Seeckt N 247/77, *Entwurf Heeresorganisation* of [*Army Organisation draft* of], 17 February 1919, p. 1.

225. BArch Nachlass Seeckt N 247/77, *Entwurf Heeresorganisation* of [*Army Organisation draft*] of 17 Febrary 1919, slide no. 8.

226. BArch Nachlass Seeckt N 247/77, *Entwurf Heeresorganisation* of [*Army Organisation draft*], of 17 February 1919, slide no. 8. Cf. Meier-Welcker: *Seeckt*, p. 200.

227. Seeckt: *Reichswehr*, p. 100.

228. Seeckt: *Reichswehr*, p. 44.

229. BArch Nachlass Seeckt N 247/77, *Entwurf Heeresorganisation* of [*Army Organisation draft* of], 17 February 1919, slide no. 9a. In her text, Vardi translated the German term 'Stosstrupp' as elite force. This is not the same thing. Vardi: The Enigma of German Operational Theory, p. 168.

230. Seeckt: *Grundsätze der Landesverteidigung* (1930), in: *Gedanken eines Soldaten*, 1935, p. 78.

231. BArch Nachlass Seeckt N 247/77 *Entwurf Heeresorganisation* of [*Army Organisation draft* of], 17 February 1919, slide no. 9.

232. BArch Nachlass Seeckt N 247/77, *Entwurf Heeresorganisation* of [*Army Organisation draft* of], 17 February 1919, slide no. 9.

233. Seeckt: *Grundsätze der Landesverteidigung* (1930), in: *Gedanken eines Soldaten*, 1935, p. 78. Cf. Part II, Seeckt's military considerations.

234. Seeckt: *Moderne Heere* (1928), in: *Gedanken eines Soldaten*, 1935, p. 58.

235. Seeckt: *Moderne Heere* (1928), in: *Gedanken eines Soldaten*, 1935, p. 59.

236. Seeckt: *Grundsätze moderner Landesverteidigung* (1930), in: *Gedanken eines Soldaten*, 1935, p. 65.

237. Seeckt: *Moderne Heere* (1928), in: *Gedanken eines Soldaten*, 1935, p. 59.

238. Seeckt: *Moderne Heere* (1928), in: *Gedanken eines Soldaten*, 1935, p. 83–84.

239. Seeckt: *Grundsätze moderner Landesverteidigung* (1930), in: *Gedanken eines Soldaten*, 1935, p. 76.

240. Seeckt: *Moderne Heere* (1928), in: *Gedanken eines Soldaten*, 1935, p. 58.

241. FuG, 1924, p. 18.

242. BArch Bw 2/1800 presentation to officers on a course in Adenau on 14 January 1957, slide no. 3. Cf. Seeckt: *Reichswehr*, p. 42. Corum: *Roots of Blitzkrieg*, p. 31.

243. Stig Förster: *Der Deutsche Generalstab und die Illusion des kurzen Krieges, 1871–1914. Metakritik eines Mythos*, in: *Militärgeschichtliche Mitteilungen*, 1955, (54), p. 61–95.

244. Seeckt: *Moderne Heere* (1928), in: *Gedanken eines Soldaten*, 1935, p. 58.

245. Seeckt: *Das erreichbare Ziel* (1927), in: *Gedanken eines Soldaten*, 1935, p.48.

246. Seeckt: *Moderne Heere* (1928), in: *Gedanken eines Soldaten*, 1935, p. 57.

247. FuG, 1923, p. 352. Cf. Wheeler-Bennet: *Nemesis of Power*, p. 86.

248. FuG, 1923, p. 350. Geneva Convention: FuG, 1921, p. 243.

249. FuG, 1923, p. 350, 352.

250. Deist: *Die Reichswehr und der Krieg der Zukunft*, p. 83.

251. *Bemerkungen des Chefs der Heeresleitung* [*Observations of the Chief of the Army Command*], Colonel General von Seeckt, during visits and manoeuvres in the years 1920 to1926, ed. Ministry of the Reichswehr, Army Training Division, Berlin: 1927, p 48 f.

252. Seeckt: *Moderne Heere* (1928), in: *Gedanken eines Soldaten*, 1935, p. 57.

253. Seeckt: *Moderne Heere* (1928), in: *Gedanken eines Soldaten*, 1935, p. 57.

254. Seeckt: *Moderne Heere* (1928), in: *Gedanken eines Soldaten*, 1935, p. 57.

255. *Bemerkungen des Chefs der Heeresleitung* [*Observations of the Chief of the Army Command*], 1927, p. 38 f.

256. Deist: *Die Reichswehr und der Krieg der Zukunft*, p. 84.

257. Corum: *Roots of Blithkrieg*, p. 33, 54, 68, 169, 183. Citino: *Path to Blithkrieg*, p. 9.

258. Tactical and Operational Training Army Regulation. 487, H.D. v. 487 *Führung und Gefecht der verbundenen Waffen* (FuG,), re-print of the 1921–1294 edition, Osnabrück: 1994.

259. FuG, Introduction and index 1924, p. 3.

260. *Bemerkungen des Chefs der Heeresleitung* [*Observations of the Chief of the Army Command*], Colonel General von Seeckt, during visits and manoeuvres in the years 1920 to 1926, Berlin: 1927 is a consolidation of the years 1922–1926.

261. FuG, 1921, p. 3.

262. Deist: *Die Reichswehr und der Krieg der Zukunft*, p. 85. Cf. Dietz: *Primat der Politik*, p. 228.

263. FuG, 1921: p. 56, 61, 74, 1923, p 9 f. Seeckt: *Staatsmann und Feldherr* (1928), in: *Gedanken eines Soldaten*, 1935, p. 57 f.

264. Rabenau: *Seeckt II*, p. 529. Paul: *Das Potsdamer Infanterie-Regiment 9*, p. 34 f.

265. Seeckt: *Neuzeitliche Kavallerie* (1927), in: *Gedanken eines Soldaten*, 1935, p. 109.

266. Wallach: *Dogma der Vernichtungsschlacht*, p. 343.

267. FuG, 1921, item 4, p. 6, item 54, p. 29. *Bemerkungen des Chefs der Heeresleitung* [*Observations of the Chief of the Army Command*], 1927, p. 40, 41. Seeckt: *Staatsmann und Feldherr* (1928), in: *Gedanken eines Soldaten*, 1935, p. 40 f.

268. FuG, 1921, item 57, p. 31.

269. FuG, 1921, item 58, p. 31 f.

270. FuG, 1921, item 54, p. 29. Cf. Seeckt: *Die neuzeitliche Kavallerie* (1927), in: *Gedanken eines Soldaten*, 1935, p. 109.

271. FuG, 1921, item 54, p. 29f, cf. p. 56–63, 64–65. *Bemerkungen des Chefs der Heeresleitung* [*Observations of the Chief of the Army Command*],, p. 28, 98 f.

272. FuG, 1921, item 18, p. 15 f.

273. FuG, 1921, item 54, p. 25.

274. FuG, 1921, item 43 p. 24 f.
275. FuG, 1921, item 43, p. 24 f.
276. *Bemerkungen des Chefs der Heeresleitung* [*Observations of the Chief of the Army Command*], 1927, p. 41.
277. BArch Nachlass Seeckt N 247/110 Observations of the Chief of the Army Command based on his visits in 1923, slide no. 4.
278. Seeckt: *Staatsmann und Feldherr* (1928), in: *Gedanken eines Soldaten*, 1935 p. 43 f. Cf. Neugebauer: *Operatives Denken zwischen dem Ersten und Zweiten Weltkrieg*, p. 106.
279. FuG, 1921, item 55, p. 30.
280. Observations of the Chief of the Army Command, 1927, p. 18. In F.u.G item 9 there is a reference to the fact that adhering rigidly to the decision and the order leads to mistakes in the conduct of war.
281. FuG, 1921, item 35, p. 21.
282. FuG, 1921, item 9, p. 8.
283. Meier-Welcker: *Seeckt*, p. 40–43.
284. Rabenau: *Seeckt II*, p. 511.
285. FuG, 1921, item 5, p. 7, item 9, p. 8.
286. Seeckt: *Die Reichswehr*, p. 100. Cf. Seeckt: *Die Reichswehr*, p. 98.
287. Gross: *Das Dogma der Beweglichkeit*, p. 155.
288. Gross: *Das Dogma der Beweglichkeit*, p. 155.
289. FuG, 1921, item 332, p. 176.
290. *Bemerkungen des Chefs der Heeresleitung* [*Observations of the Chief of the Army Command*], 1927, p. 41.
291. FuG, 1921, item 15, p. 12.
292. Gross: *Das Dogma der Beweglichkeit*, p. 155.
293. FuG, 1921, item 413, p. 225f.
294. Meier-Welcker: *Seeckt*, p. 40–43.
295. FuG, 1921, item 12, p. 11.
296. Gross: *Das Dogma der Beweglichkeit*, p. 155. For information on the concept and meaning of the main battle line, see Robert M. Citino: *The Path to Blitzkrieg. Doctrine and Training in the German Army 1920–39*, p. 21. Cf. FuG, 1921, items. 387 and 389.
297. FuG, 1921, item 344, p. 183.
298. FuG, 1921, item 393, p. 215.
299. *Bemerkungen des Chefs der Heeresleitung* [*Observations of the Chief of the Army Command*], 1927, p. 43.
300. FuG, 1923, item 534, p. 47.
301. FuG, 1923, item 534, p. 47.
302. FuG, 1923, item 535, p. 47.
303. FuG, 1923, item 537, p. 49.
304. FuG, 1923, item 572, p. 60.
305. FuG, 1923, item 533, p. 46.
306. FuG, 1923, item 581, p. 65.
307. FuG, 1923, item 581, p. 65.
308. FuG, 1923, item 534, p. 46 f. Cf. BArch N 247/ *Bemerkungen des Chefs der Heeresleitung* [*Observations of the Chief of the Army Command*], p. 4.

309. FuG, 1923, item 548, p. 52, item 551, p. 53. Cf. Meier-Welcker: Seeckt, p. 55.
310. BArch RH12–2/84 Ministry of the Reichswehr Army Command No. 503/12.23. vol. 2. Wooden model of an infantry gun Berlin, 17.1.1924. BA-MA, RH 37/427 Bavarian Army District Command VII (Bavarian 7th Div.) No. 1155 geh. Art. 189 geh. 8.10.1923. RH 37/427 II. Batl. 19 (Bavarian) Inf. Reg. No 589/88 – Cdr – 30.9.1924. RH 37/778 Ministry of the Reichswehr Army Command IV No. 601, 26 geh. vol. (6) Description of modern combat vehicle 10 November 1926. RH 37/454 Ministry of the Reichswehr Army Command NO: 9. 24 1.22. Vol: 2.2. IV Berlin, 5.5.22 practice M.G. made of wood. Cf. Paul: *Das Potsdamer Infanterie-Regiment 9*, p. 34.
311. *Bemerkungen des Chefs der Heeresleitung* [*Observations of the Chief of the Army Command*], 1927, p. 41.
312. Rabenau: *Seeckt II*, p. 510. Seeckt: *Reichswehr*, p. 111f.
313. FuG, 1923, p. 229, for the term war of movement cf. also item 905, p. 217.
314. Wallach: *Dogma der Vernichtungsschlacht*, p. 344.
315. Citino in his work: Robert M. Citino: *The Path to Blitzkrieg*, analysed these armoured units more closely and proved that training using cardboard tanks formed an important part of military education.
316. Citino: *The Path to Blitzkrieg*, p. 11–145.
317. *Bemerkungen des Chefs der Heeresleitung* [*Observations of the Chief of the Army Command*], 1927, p. 26.
318. FuG, 1921, p. 46 f, item 102, p. 52.
319. FuG, 1921, item 16, p. 13 and item 358, 194f. Cf. FuG, 1921, item 13, p. 11, item 16, p. 13. FuG, 1924, p. 20, on breakthrough, envelopment in the method of attack.
320. FuG, 1921, item 355, p. 192. For information on the various types and methods of combat FuG, Berlin 1921, items 327–332, 414, p. 174–176, 191, 198, 226 and 1924: 20 f and *Bemerkungen des Chefs der Heeresleitung* [*Observations of the Chief of the Army Command*], 1927, p. 36.
321. FuG, 1921, item 327, p. 174.
322. FuG, 1924, p. 27.
323. FuG, 1924, p. 27. *Bemerkungen des Chefs der Heeresleitung* [*Observations of the Chief of the Army Command*], 1927, p. 36.
324. FuG, 1921, item 327, p. 174.
325. FuG, 1921, p. 174, 191, 220. FuG, 1923, p. 27–29, p. 174.
326. *Bemerkungen des Chefs der Heeresleitung*, [*Observations of the Chief of the Army Command*], 1927, p. 26.
327. FuG, 1921, item 318, p. 168 f. FuG, 1924, p. 20, 27. Cf. Meier-Welker: *Seeckt*, p. 40.
328. FuG, 1921, item 327, item 328, p. 174.
329. Seeckt: *Schlagworte* (1928), in: *Gedanken eines Soldaten*, 1935, p. 13–15.
330. *Bemerkungen des Chefs der Heeresleitung* [*Observations of the Chief of the Army Command*], 1927, p. 36.
331. James S. Corum: *The Roots of Blitzkrieg, Hans von Seeckt and the German Military Reform*, Kansas: 1992, p. 26. Wheeler-Bennet: *The Nemesis of Power*, p. 101. Gil-li Vardi's assumption that Seeckt was adhering to outdated rules

of the operational level of command without having considered the mistakes of the military leadership in the battle of envelopment is not entirely correct. 'If we give the conception "Cannae" its right meaning, we find that it implies insistence on that method of warfare which leads to the destruction of the enemy. This is to be the most surely attained by a vigorous envelopment of his two flanks – see 'Cannae'. Seekt held to pre-existing operational truths, even when aware of drawbacks that might prevent the fulfillment of the Germany army's prescribed formula. Seeckt concluded that 'it must at all costs be kept in mind that any form of envelopment, if only on one flank, is the surest road to annihilating success'. Vardi: *The Enigma of German Operational Theory*, p. 151.

332. Seeckt: *Schlagworte* (1928), in: *Gedanken eines Soldaten*, 1935, p. 15.

333. BArch Nachlass Seeckt N 247/110 *Bemerkungen des Chefs der Heeresleitung* [*Observations of the Chief of the Army Command*], p. 4.

334. BArch RH 12–2/93 *Ministry of the Reichswehr Chief of the Army Command* No. 200.22. Adj. No. 273 .4.22. T 4 II Berlin, 1 April 1922: Military district exercise trip 1921, slide no. 6 (2). Cf. BArch Nachlass N 247/110, 1 December 1923, p. 16.

335. BArch Nachlass Rabenau N 62/39 slide no. 173.

336. 'Gorlice became the textbook example of the breakthrough' in: Wilhelm Groener: Lebenserinnerungen. Jugend, Generalstab, Weltkrieg, Göttingen: 1957, p. 232. Cf. Wheeler-Bennet: *Nemesis of Power*, p. 101.

337. Seeckt: *Schlieffentag* (1928), in: *Gedanken eines Soldaten*, 1935, p. 23.

338. Seeckt: *Schlagworte* (1928), in: *Gedanken eines Soldaten*, 1935, p. 14. Cf. Seeckt: *Staaatsmann und Feldherr* (1928), in: *Gedanken eines Soldaten*, 1935, p. 42.

339. FuG, 1923, item 318, p. 168 and items 328, 329, p. 174 f.

340. FuG, 1923, item 535, p. 47 and item 549, p. 53.

341. Seeckt: *Schlagworte* (1928), in: *Gedanken eines Soldaten*, 1935, p. 13 f.

342. Meier-Welker: *Seeckt*, p. 41.

343. Observations of the Chief of the Army Command 1927, p. 37, 56.

344. FuG, 1921, p. 11.

345. Seeckt: *Clausewitz* (1930), in: *Gedanken eines Soldaten*, 1935, p. 29.

346. FuG, 1921, item 51, 52, 54, 56–59, p. 29–32, item 123–131, p. 58–63. FuG, 1923, item 467 – 517, p. 9–40. FuG, 1923, item 631–634, p. 86–92. Bemerkungen des Chefs der Heeresleitung, p. 29, 38–41, 44–47, 50 f, 57, 64, 70, 90, 98, 112. Seeckt: *Moderne Heere* (1928), in: *Gedanken eines Soldaten*, 1935: p. 57 f.

347. Seeckt: *Neuzeitliche Kavallerie* (1927), in: *Gedanken eines Soldaten*, 1935, p. 101.

348. Heinz Guderian: *Die Panzerwaffe. Ihre Entwicklung, ihre Kampftaktik und ihre operativen Möglichkeiten bis zum Beginn des grossdeutschen Freiheitskampfes*, Stuttgart: 1943. Cf. Neugebauer, in: *Operatives Denken zwischen dem Ersten und Zweiten Weltkrieg*, p. 119, 120.

349. Rabenau: *Seeckt II*, p. 511–512.

350. Walach: *Dogma der Vernichtungsschlacht*, p. 342.

351. FuG, 1921, p. 7, item 5.

352. Gross: *Das Dogma der Beweglichkeit*, p. 154.

353. Seeckt: *Reichswehr*, p. 96.

354. Gross: *Das Dogma der Beweglichkeit*, p. 154. Gross: *Mythos und Wirklichkeit*, p. 154. Cf. Schüddekopf: *Heer und Republik*, p. 119.

355. *Bemerkungen des Chefs der Heeresleitung, [Observations of the Chief of the Army Command]* 1927, p. 12.

356. Observations of the Chief of the Army Command, 1927, p. 18.

357. BArch Nachlass Seeckt N 247/110 Observations of the Chief of the Army Command during his visits in 1923, p. 3. The 'Observations' published by General Heye in 1927 should not be confused with the individual ones published annually. The 'Observations' published in 1927 are a consolidation of the years 1922 to 1925, they are incomplete and make generalisations about the educational idea on which training is based.

358. Seeckt: *Reichswehr*, p. 44.

359. Heinz-Ludger Borgert: *Grundzüge der Landkriegführung von Schlieffen bis Guderian*, in: *Handbuch zur deutschen Militärgeschichte 1648–1939*, Eds. Hans Meier-Welcker, ed. MGFA, o.A.v.J.u.O., p. 542. Cf. Wallach: *Das Dogma der Vernichtungsschlacht*, pp. 317f, 332f.

360. The Passive Electoral Rights and Political Activities of Soldiers. Heuser: *The Evolution of Strategy*, p. 153.

361. BArch Nachlass Rabenau N62/40. slide no. 87.

362. BArch Nachlass Rabenau N62/39, slide no. 59.

363. BArch Nachlass Rabenau N62/39, slides nos. 59, 76. Carsten: *The Reichswehr and Politics*, p. 110.

364. BArch Nachlass Rabenau N62/39, slide no. 60. Carsten: *The Reichswehr and Politics*, p. 192.

365. BArch Nachlass Seeckt N 247/89 T 1 III No. 56.8.22 of 2 August 1922, slide no. 46.

366. BArch Nachlass Rabenau N62/39, slide no. 75a.

367. BArch Nachlass Rabenau N62/39, slide no. 77.

368. BArch Nachlass Rabenau N62/40, slide no. 6, N 62/11, slide no. 11.

369. BArch RH 37–783, Reichswehr Ministry Army Command No. 550.7.23 T 1 III of 24 July 1923. Printed in: *Quellen zur Geschichte des Parlamentarismus und der politischen Parteien*, Zweite Reihe: *Militär und Politik*. Im Auftrag der Kommission für Geschichte des Parlamentarismus und der politischen Parteien und des Militärgeschichtlichen Forschungsamtes, Ed. Erich Matthias and Hans Meier-Welcker, Vol. 4. *Das Krisenjahr 1923. Militär und Innenpolitik 1922–1924*, edited by Heinz Hürten, Düsseldorf: 1980, p. 59. (Hürten: *Das Krisenjahr 1923*)

370. Seeckt: *Landesverteidigung*, 1930, p. 54.

371. BArch Nachlass Rabenau N 62/39, slide no. 167. Cf. Wheeler-Bennet: *Nemesis of Power*, p. 109–110, 112.

372. Schüddekopf: *Heer und Republik*, p. 186. BArch, Nachlass Seeckt N 247/89 Reichswehr Ministry Director of the Truppenamt, Berlin 26 February 1920, slides nos. 14–19. N 247/89 Reichswehr Ministry Director of the Truppenamt, Berlin 31 July 1920, slides nos. 22–27. N 247/104, Reichswehr Ministry Chief of the Army Command, 11 March 1922, slides nos. 3–12. N 247/ 89 T 1 III No. 56.8.22 Berlin, August 1922, slide no. 46.

373. BArch RH 37/783 *Chief of the Army Command No.* 167/24 T. 1 III per., 27 February 1924.

374. *Quellen zur Geschichte des Parlamentarismus und der politischen Parteien*, Zweite Reihe: *Militär und Politik*. Im Auftrag der Kommission für Geschichte des Parlamentarismus und der politischen Parteien und des Militärgeschichtlichen Forschungsamtes. Ed. Erich Matthias and Hans Meier-Welcker, Vol. 2. *Zwischen Revolution und Kapp-Putsch, Militär und Innenpolitik 1918–1920*, edited by Heinz Hürten, Düsseldorf: 1977. (Hürten: *Zwischen Revolution und Kapp-Putsch*, p. 146.

375. *Quellen zur Geschichte des Parlamentarismus und der politischen Parteien*, Zweite Reihe: *Militär und Politik*. Im Auftrag der Kommission für Geschichte des Parlamentarismus und der politischen Parteien und des Militärgeschichtlichen Forschungsamtes, Ed. Erich Matthias and Hans Meier-Welcker, Vol. 3. *Die Anfänge der Ära Seeckt, Militär und Innenpolitik 1920–1922*, edited by Heinz Hürten, Düsseldorf: 1979, p. 283. (Hürten: *Die Ära Seeckt*)

376. Schüddekopf: *Heer und Republik*, p. 185. Cf. Wheeler-Bennet: *Power of Nemesis*, p. 112.

377. BArch RH 37/783 *Chief of the Army Command*, No. 580. 9. 24. T. 1 III, Berlin 22 September 1924.

378. Wehler: *Deutsche Gesellschaftsgeschichte*, vol. 4, p. 417.

379. Further Focal Points of the Military Strategy. Seeckt: *Staatsmann und Feldheer* (1928), in: *Gedanken eines Soldaten*, 1935 (p. 40ff, 45). Seeckt: *Grundsätze moderner Landesverteidigung* (1930), in: *Gedanken eines Soldaten*, 1935 (p. 64). Seeckt: *Die Reichswehr* (p. 41). BArch Nachlass Seeckt N 247/158, Die Internationale Bedeutung der Abrüstungsfrage, 1930, slides nos. 18, 16–19.

380. BArch Nachlass Seeckt N 247 /158, slides nos. 16, 17, 19.

381. Seeckt: *Zukunft des Reiches*, p. 5.

382. Seeckt: *Staatsmann und Feldherr* (1928) [*Statesman and Soldier* (1930]*, in: Seeckt: *Gedanken eines Soldaten*, 1935, p. 39. Seeckt: Clausewitz (1930), in: *Gedanken eines Soldaten*, 1935, p. 26.

383. The People BArch Nachlass Seeckt N247/158, slides nos. 15, 16.

384. Cf. Seeckt: *Grundsätze moderner Landesverteidigung*, (1930), in: *Gedanken eines Soldaten*, 1935, p. 63.

385. Seeckt: *Das erreichbare Ziel* (1927) [The Attainable Object], in: *Gedanken eines Soldaten*, 1935, p. 50. [Thoughts of A Soldier, 1930, p. 50].

386. Seeckt: *Grundsätze moderner Landesverteidigung* (1930), in: *Gedanken eines Soldaten*, 1935, p. 63, 64.

387. BArch Nachlass Seeckt N 247/158, slide no.15.

388. Seeckt: *Clausewitz* (1930), in: *Gedanken eines Soldaten*, 1935, p. 26.

389. Seeckt: *Grundsätze der Landesverteidigung* (1930), in: *Gedanken eines Soldaten*, 1935, p. 80 ff, cf. also p. 79.

390. Seeckt: *Grundsätze moderner Landesverteidigung* (1930) in: *Gedanken eines Soldaten*, 1935, p. 81. cf. BArch Nachlass Seeckt N247/158, slide no. 13.

391. Competition in Armament – Disarmament – Balance of Armament BArch Nachlass Seeckt N 247/158, slide no. 20.

392. Seeckt: *Das erreichbare Ziel* (1927) [*The Attainable Object* (1930)], in: *Gedanken eines Soldaten*, 1935, p. 48 [*Thoughts of A Soldier* (1930)].

393. BArch Nachlass Seeckt N 247/158, slide no. 15.

394. Seeck: *Grundsätzer moderner Landesverteidigung* (1930), in: *Gedanken eines Soldaten*, 1935 (p. 64). *Moderne Heere*, (1928), in: *Gedanken eines Soldaten*, 1935, p. 55.

395. BArch Nachlass Seeckt N 247/58, slide no. 14.

396. Seeckt: *Moderne Heere* (1928), in: *Gedanken eines Soldaten*, 1935, p. 55.

397. Seeckt: *Das erreichbare Ziel* (1927), in: *Gedanken eines Soldaten*, 1935, p. 48.

398. BArch Nachlass Seeck N 247/158, slide no. 20.

399. Seeckt: *Grundsätze moderner Landesverteidigung* (1930) in: *Gedanken eines Soldaten*, 1935, p. 63.

400. BArch Nachlass Seeck N 247/158, slide no. 15.

401. BArch Nachlass Seeckt N 247/158, slide no. 14.

402. BArch Nachlass Seeckt N 247/158, slide no. 15. Seeck: *Grundsätze moderner Landesverteidigung* (1930) in: *Gedanken eines Soldaten*, 1935., p. 84.

403. BArch Nachlass Seeckt N 247/158, slide no. 15. Seeckt: *Moderne Heere*, (1928), in: *Gedanken eines Soldaten*, 1935, p. 55. Seeckt: *Grundsätze moderner Landesverteidigung* (1930) in: *Gedanken eines Soldaten*, 1935, p. 64.

404. Seeckt: *Das erreichbare Ziel* (1927) [*The Attainable Object* (1930), in: *Gedanken eines Soldaten*, 1935, p. 50 [*Thoughts of A Soldier* (1930].

405. Seeck: *Grundsätze moderner Landesverteidigung*, (1930), in: *Gedanken eines Soldaten*, 1935, p. 63. Cf. Heuser: *The Evolution of Strategy*, p.124, 129. Seeckt's reference to Moltke.

406. BArch Nachlass Seeckt N 247/158, slides nos. 12, 14.

407. Seeckt: *Grundsätze moderner Landesverteidigung*, (1930), in: *Gedanken eines Soldaten*, 1935, p. 66.

408. Seeckt: *Grundsätze moderner Landesverteidigung*, (1930), in: *Gedanken eines Soldaten*, 1935 p. 63.

409. Seeckt: *Moltke*, p. 108.

410. BArch Nachlass Seeckt N 247/158, slide no. 18.

411. BArch Nachlass Seeckt N 247/158, slide no. 16.

412. Seeckt: *Grundsätze moderner Landesverteidigung*, (1930), in: *Gedanken eines Soldaten*, 1935, p. 63.

413. *Akten der Reichskanzlei*, *das Kabinett Cuno* p. 395ff. BArch Nachlass Seeckt N 247/158, slide no. 13.

414. Seeckt: *Grundsätze moderner Landesverteidigung*, (1930), in: *Gedanken eines Soldaten*, 1935, p. 63.

415. Seeckt: *Grundsätze moderner Landesverteidigung*, (1930), in: *Gedanken eines Soldaten*, 1935, p. 64.

416. Seeckt: *Moderne Heere*, (1928) [Modern Armies (1930)], in: *Gedanken eines Soldaten*, 1935, p. 55. [*Thoughts of A Soldier* (1930), (p. 58)] Cf. Seeckt: *Grundsätze moderner Landesverteidigung* (1930), in: *Gedanken eines Soldaten*, 1935, p. 64.

417. Seeck: *Clausewitz* (1930), in: *Gedanken eines Soldaten*, 1935, p. 26.

418. Seeckt: *Staatsmann und Feldherr* (1928) [*Statesman and Soldier* (1930)], in: *Gedanken eines Soldaten*, 1935, p. 40 [*Thoughts of A Soldier* (1930), p. 34, 35].

419. BArch Nachlass Seeck N 247/158, slide no. 19.

420. Seeckt: *Grundsätze moderner Landesverteidigung* (1930), in: *Gedanken eines Soldaten*, 1935, p. 78.

421. Seeckt: *Grundsätze moderner Landesverteidigung* (1930), in: *Gedanken eines Soldaten*, 1935, p. 63.

422. Seeckt: *Moderne Heere* (1928) [*Modern Armies* (1930)], in: *Gedanken eines Soldaten*, 1935 (p. 55) [*Thoughts of A Soldier* (1930), p. 57, 58]. Cf. loc. cit.: *Grundsätze moderner Landesverteidigung* (1930), p. 64.

423. Seeckt: *Reichswehr*, p. 44.

424. Seeckt: *Grundsätze moderner Landesverteidigung* (1930), in: *Gedanken eines Soldaten*, 1935, p. 79.

425. Seeck: *Landesverteidigung*, 1930, p. 87.

426. Seeckt: *Moderne Heere*, (1928) [*Modern Armies* (1930), in: *Gedanken eines Soldaten*, 1935, p. 55 [*Thoughts of A Soldier*] (1930), p. 67].

427. Seeckt: *Landesverteidigung*, 1930, p. 22.

428. BArch Nachlass Seeckt N 247/158, slide no. 13.

429. Seeckt: *Moderne Heere* (1928), in: *Gedanken eines Soldaten*, 1935, p. 61.

430. Seeckt: *Moderne Heere* (1928) [*Modern Armies* (1930)], in: *Gedanken eines Soldaten*, 1935, p. 61 [*Thoughts of A Soldier* (1930), p. 66].

431. Seeckt: *Landesverteidigung* p. 29 ff.

432. Seeckt: *Landesverteidigung*, 1930, p. 29.

433. Seeck: *Grundsätze moderner Landesverteidigung* (1930) in: *Gedanken eines Soldaten*, 1935, p. 63.

434. Seeckt: *Das erreichbare Ziel* (1927) [*The Attainable Object* (1930)], in: *Gedanken eines Soldaten*, 1935, p. 50. [*Thoughts of A Soldier* (1930), p. 49].

435. Seeckt: *Moderne Heere*, (1928), in: *Gedanken eines Soldaten*, 1935, p. 55.

436. A Balance of Armament through International Negotiations and Alliance Policy Seeckt: *Grundsätze moderner Landesverteidigung* (1930) in: *Gedanken eines Soldaten*, 1935, p. 78.

437. Seeckt: *Landesverteidigung*, 1930, p. 22ff and Seeckt: *Grundsätze moderner Landesverteidigung* (1930), in: *Gedanken eines Soldaten*, 1935, p. 63ff.

438. Seeck: *Grundsätze moderner Landesverteidigung*, (1930), in: *Gedanken eines Soldaten*, 1935, p. 63. Seeckt: *Landesverteidigung*, 1930, p. 22.

439. Seeck: *Grundsätze moderner Landesverteidigung*, (1930), in: *Gedanken eines Soldaten*, 1935, p. 63.

440. Seeckt: *Zukunft des Reiches*, p. 155.

441. Seeckt: *Das erreichbare Ziel* (1927) [*The Attainable Object* (1930)], in: *Gedanken eines Soldaten*, 1935, p. 50 [*Thoughts of A Soldier* (1930), p. 49].

442. Seeckt: *Clausewitz* (1930), in: *Gedanken eines Soldaten*, 1935, p. 27.

443. Seeckt: *Staatsmann und Feldherr* (1928), in: *Gedanken eines Soldaten*, 1935, p. 45. [*Statesman and Soldier* (1930), *Thoughts of A Soldier*, (1930), p. 42, 43].

444. Seeckt: *Staatsmann und Feldherr* (1929), in: *Gedanken eines Soldaten*, 1935, p. 41. BArch Nachlass Seeckt N 247/158, slides nos. 20, 21.

445. Seeckt: *Zukunft des Reiches*, Berlin: 1929, p. 157). Seeckt: *Grundsätze moderner Landesverteidigung* (1930), in: *Gedanken eines Soldaten*, 1935, p. 65.

446. BArch Nachlass Seeckt N 247/77, slide no. 8.

447. BArch Nachlass Seeckt N 247/158, slide no. 18)

448. Akira Iriye: *Culture and International History*, in: Michael J. Hogan und Thomas G. Paterson (Publ.): Explaining the History of American Foreign Relations, Cambridge: 2004, p. 245.

449. The Geographic and Geopolitical Positions. Seeckt: *Reichswehr*, p. 41.

450. Seeck: *Grundsätze moderner Landesverteidigung* (1930) in: *Gedanken eines Soldaten*, 1935, p. 64, 65.

451. BArch Nachlass Seeckt N 247/158, slide no. 16.

452. Seeckt: *Zukunft des Reiches*, p. 156.

453. Seeckt: *Grundsätze moderner Landesverteidigung* (1930) in: *Gedanken eines Soldaten*, 1935, p. 64, p. 79 ff.

454. Commerce. BArch Nachlass Seeckt N 247/160: *Deutschland und Europa*.

455. BArch Nachlass Seeckt N 247/160 *Deutschland und Europa*, slide no. 3.

456. BArch Nachlass Seeckt N 247/160 *Deutschland und Europa*, slide no. 4.

457. For an overarching analysis of the situation regarding Germany after 1918, see the publication by British economist John Maynard Keynes: *Die wirtschaftlichen Folgen des Friedensvertrages* (Economic Consequences of the Peace), Munich, 1920.

458. BArch Nachlass Seeckt N 247/160 *Deutschland und Europa*, slide no. 7.

459. BArch Nachlass Seeckt N 247/160 *Deutschland und Europa*, slide no. 4.

460. BArch Nachlass Seeckt N 247/160 *Deutschland und Europa*, slide no. 2.

461. BArch Nachlass Seeckt N 247/160 *Deutschland und Europa*, slide no. 5.

462. BArch Nachlass Seeckt N 247/160 *Deutschland und Europa*, slide no. 8.

463. Post-War Economic Systems and Ideology BArch Nachlass Seeckt N 247/160 *Deutschland und Europa*, slide no. 2.

464. BArch Nachlass Seeckt N 247/158, slide no. 16.

465. BArch Nachlass Seeckt N 247/141, slide no. 80.

466. Schüddekopf: *Heer und Republik*, p. 186. BArch, Nachlass Seeck N 247/89 *Reichswehrministerium Chef des Truppenamtes*, Berlin 26 February 1920, slides nos. 14–19. N 247/89 *Reichswehrministerium Chef des Truppenamtes*, Berlin 31 July 1920, slides nos. 22–27. N 247/104, *Reichswehrministerium Chef der Heeresleitung*, 11 March 1922, slides nos. 3–12). N 247/ 89 T 1 III Nr. 56.8.22 Berlin, August 1922, slide no. 46.

467. BArch Nachlass Seeckt N 247/160 *Deutschland und Europa*, slide no. 4.

468. BArch Nachlass Seeckt N 247/160 *Deutschland und Europa*, slide no. 8.

469. Meier-Welcker: *Seeckt*, p. 200.

470. The Right of Self-Defence. BArch Nachlass Seeckt N247/77. Seiner Excellenz dem Ersten Generalquartiermeister Herrn Generalleutnant Gröner – Heeresorganisation – *Entwurf Heeresorganisation* of [*Army Organisation draft of*], 17 February 1919, slides nos. 8–11.

471. BArch Nachlass Rabenau N 62/39, slide no. 155.

472. BArch Nachlass Seeckt N 247/104 *Reichswehrministerium Chef der Heeresleitung*, Berlin 11 March 1922, slide no. 11.

473. BArch Nachlass Seeckt N 247/104, slide no. 11.

474. Akten der Reichskanzlei, *Das Kabinett Cuno*, p. 394. Cf. BArch N247/104 slides nos. 3–10.

475. BArch Nachlass Seeckt N 247/104, slide no. 12.

476. In April 1919, he wrote to his wife: 'This war was once – for many years – a fixed necessity for me and still is my prospect for a distant future. But now, nobody can believe that our armies, which have been defeated and artifically deprived of discipline and their leaders' respect, would achieve, together with the disorderly Russian hordes, what the splendid imperial army did not achieve', BArch Nachlass Rabenau N 62/48, slide no. 30.

477. Germany's Foreign Policy during the 1923 Ruhr Crisis. Beatrice Heuser and Anja V. Hartmann (Eds.): *War, Peace and World Orders in European History*, London: 2001, p. 9ff.

478. BArch Nachlass Seeckt N 247/58, slide no. 17.

479. BArch Nachlass Seeckt N 247/58, slide no. 16.

480. *Akten der Reichskanzlei, Weimarer Republik*, Publ. by Karl Dietrich Erdmann und Wolfgang Mommsen, Boppard am Rhein: 1968, *Das Kabinett Cuno 22. November 1922 bis 12. August 1923*, Nr. 42, p. 138, footnote 6.

481. *Akten der Reichskanzlei, Das Kabinett Cuno*, Nr. 42, p. 138, footnote 7. The French government's reparations policy and strategic interests vis-à-vis the German government since 1920: Eberhard Kolb: *Die Weimarer Republik*, Munich: 2009, p. 45 ff, 51 ff.

482. Cf. Funke: *Die Republik der Friedlosigkeit*, p. 12–14.

483. *Akten der Reichskanzlei, Das Kabinett Cuno*, Nr. 42, p. 138.

484. *Akten der Reichskanzlei, Das Kabinett Cuno*, Nr. 42, p. 141.

485. *Akten der Reichskanzlei, Das Kabinett Cuno*, Nr. 37, p. 124.

486. *Akten der Reichskanzlei, Das Kabinett Cuno*, Nr. 42, p. 137, footnote 3.

487. BArch Nachlass Rabenau N 62/11, slide no. 11. Cf. Carsten: *The Reichswehr and Politics*, p. 154.

488. Akten der Reichskanzlei, *Das Kabinett Cuno*, Nr. 37, p. 123, footnote 3.

489. Gerd Krumeich: *Der Ruhrkampf als Krieg*, in: *Düsseldorfer Schriften zur neuen Landesgeschichte und zur Geschichte Nordrhein-Westfalens*, Band 69, Der Schatten des Weltkriegs: *Die Ruhrbesetzung 1923*, Publ. by Gerd Krumeich und Joachim Schröder, Essen: 2004, p. 16–18. Akten der Reichskanzlei, Weimarer Republik, Publ. by Karl Dietrich Erdmann und Wolfgang Mommsen, Boppard am Rhein: *Akten der Reichskanzlei, Das Kabinett Cuno*, Nr. 37, p. 124.

490. *Akten der Reichskanzlei, Das Kabinett Cuno*, Nr. 37, p.123, footnote 3, no. 37, p. 127. Cf. Carsten: *The Reichswehr and Politics*, p. 154.

491. Hans Mommsen: *Die politischen Folgen der Ruhrbesetzung*, in: Düsseldorfer Schriften, Vol. 69, p. 305–311 and Gerd Krumeich: *Der Ruhrkampf als Krieg*, in: Düsseldorfer Schriften Vol. 69, p. 20. *Das Kabinett Cuno*, Nr. 37 (p. 122–123, footnote 3). Meier-Welcker: *Seeckt*, p. 363. Seeckt wrote a similar position paper in 1922, cf. Meier-Welcker: *Seeckt*, p. 322.

492. Gerd Krumeich: *Der Ruhrkampf als Krieg*, p. 11.

493. Akten der Reichskanzlei, *Das Kabinett Cuno*, Nr. 37 p. 128, footnote 17.

494. *Akten der Reichskanzlei, Das Kabinett Cuno*, p. 392–395, dated 16 April 1924. BArch Nachlass Rabenau N 62/8.

495. *Akten der Reichskanzlei, Das Kabinett Cuno* 22., Nr. 124, p. 392–395 dated 16 April 1924. Meier-Welcker: *Seeckt*, p. 348–350, 357ff, p. 363.

496. *Akten der Reichskanzlei, Das Kabinett Cuno*, p. 393–394. Cf. also BArch Nachlass Seeckt N 247/104, slide '11. März 1922', slide no. 8. Seeckt on the French Chamber negotiations: 'Declarations that Germany had to have the means to protect its borders and that other powers were not inclined to guarantee Germany's security were also made on behalf of the government in the French chamber negotiations on the peace treaty and the disarmament of Germany.'

497. *Akten der Reichskanzlei, Das Kabinett Cuno* p. 394.

498. *Akten der Reichskanzlei, Das Kabinett Cuno* p. 395. BArch Nachlass Rabenau 62/8 slide no. 12.

499. BArch Nachlass Rabenau N 62/39, slides no. 147, 148. Nachlass Rabenau N 62/7, slide no. 37ff.

500. *Akten der Reichskanzlei, Das Kabinett Cuno*, p. 395.

501. *Akten der Reichskanzlei, Das Kabinett Cuno*, p. 395.

502. Seeckt: *Das erreichbare Ziel* (1927) [The Attainable Object (1930)], in: *Gedanken eines Soldaten*, 1935, p. 50 [*Thoughts of a Soldier*, p. 50]

503. Akten der Reichskanzlei, *Das Kabinett Cuno*, p. 395.

504. BArch Nachlass Rabenau N 62/11, slide no. 11. Cf. Wheeler-Bennet: *Nemesis of Power*, p. 108f.

505. Seeckt: *Clausewitz* (1930), in: Seeckt: *Gedanken eines Soldaten*, 1935, p. 26.

506. BArch Nachlass Seeckt N 247/89 Reichswehrministerium Chef der Heeresleitung, 31 July 1920, slide no. 25.

507. BArch Nachlass Rabenau N 62/39, slide no. 149.

508. Cf. BArch Nachlass Seeckt: N 247/141, slides nos. 47–51.

509. Seeckt's Orientation towards the East and His Policy of Alliance with the USSR. BArch Nachlass Seeckt N 247/158, slide no. 18. Cf. Rabenau: Seeckt II, p. 118. Meier-Welcker: Seeckt p. 200.

510. BArch Nachlass Seeckt N 247/77, slide no. 8. Cf. BArch Nachlass Seeckt N 247/104, slide no. 5.

511. BArch Nachlass Rabenau N 62/48, slide no. 31.

512. Meier-Welcker: *Seeckt* p. 200.

513. BArch Nachlass Seeckt N 247/77, slide no. 8.

514. BArch Nachlass Seeckt N 247/77, slide no. 8.

515. Seeckt: *Grundsätze moderner Landesverteidigung* (1930) in: *Gedanken eines Soldaten*, 1935 p. 78.

516. Seeckt: *Grundsätze moderner Landesverteidigung* (1930) in: *Gedanken eines Soldaten*, 1935 p. 78.

517. BArch Nachlass Seeckt N 247/140 (slide no. 20). Article 198 of the Treaty of Versailles.

518. BArch Nachlass Seeckt N247/67 (slide no. 29).

519. Wheeler-Bennet: *Nemesis of Power*, p. 120, 124, 127, 131f.

520. BArch Nachlass Seeckt N 247/141 (slides nos. 79–81).

521. BAarch Nachlass Seeckt N 247/141 slide 81.

522. Wheeler-Bennet: *Nemesis of Power*, p. 119f.

523. Schüddekopf: *Heer und Republik,* p. 148. Manfred Zeidler: *Reichswehr und Rote Armee 1920–1933. Wege und Stationen einer ungewöhnlichen Zusammenarbeit,* Munich: 1993 (p. 47, 295).

524. BArch Nachlass Seeckt N 247/141 (slide no. 80). Cf. Wheeler-Bennet: *Nemesis of Power,* p. 119–120

525. BArch Nachlass Seeckt N 247/141 (slides nos. 94, 84). BA-MA, Nachlass N 247/89 T 1 III Nr. 56.8.22 dated 2 August 1922 (slide no. 146).

526. BArch Nachlass Seeckt N 247/141, slide no. 93.

527. Hürten: *Die Anfänge der Ära Seeckt,* p. 213,

528. BArch Nachlass Seeckt N 247/158, slide no. 13.

529. BArch Nachlass Seeckt N 247/89, slides nos. 14–19. BArch Nachlass Seeckt N 247/141, slide no. 93 ff.

530. BArch Nachlass Seeckt N 247/141, slides nos. 74, 83.

531. BArch Nachlass Seeckt N 247/141, slide no. 86.

532. BArch Nachlass Seeckt N 247/141, slide no. 92.

533. Military Co-operation with the Red Army. Lenin supported this opinion at the 9th CPSU party congress in March 1920, in: Horst Günther Linke: *Deutsch-sowjetische Beziehungen bis Rapallo,* Cologne: 1970, p. 97. Cf. Ruth Fischer: *Stalin und der deutsche Kommunismus, der Übergang zur Konterrevolution,* Frankfurt / Main: 1948, p. 642. Bei Carsten: *Reichswehr und Politik,* p. 80. Meier-Welker: *Seeckt,* p. 324. In Manfred Zeidler: *Reichswehr und Rote Armee 1920–1933.* Page 47, it is assumed that the initial contacts between the military leaders date back to mid-1920. Meier-Welker believes that Radek and Seeckt established contact on 10 February 1922, Meier-Welcker: *Seeckt* p. 322. For more details, see BArch Nachlass Stülpnagel N 62/39, slides nos. 111, 116, 112.

534. J.L. Djakow, T.S. Buschujewa: *Das faschistische Schwert wurde in der Sowjetunio geschmiedet, Die geheime Zusammenarbeit der Roten Armee mit der Reichswehr 1922–1933,* Unbekannte Dokumente. Russland in Personen, Dokumenten, Tagebuchaufzeichnungen, Moscow: 1992, p. 11–13. Ruth Fischer: *Stalin* p. 36. For more information on the personality of Karl Radek and his importance for the workers' and soldiers' councils in the first post-war years, see: Linke: *Deutsch-sowjetische Beziehungen bis Rapallo,* p. 28–38. Otto-Ernst Schüddekopf: *Karl Radek in Berlin. Ein Kapitel deutsch-russischer Beziehungen im Jahre 1919,* in: *Archiv für Sozialgeschichte,* Publ. by Friedrich-Ebert-Stiftung, II. Vol., 1962, p. 87–166.

535. Otto-Ernst Schüddekopf: *Karl Radek in Berlin,* p. 109, 152. Carsten: *Reichswehr und Politik* p. 80. Zeidler: *Reichswehr und Rote Armee,* p. 59. Groehler: *Selbstmörderische Allianz, deutsch-russische Militärbeziehungen 1920–1941,* p. 261. He was detained because he had entered Germany illegally in order to attend the first German workers' and soldiers' councils congress. See also: Linke: *Deutsch-sowjetische Beziehungen,* p. 34, 36–37. Carsten: *Reichswehr und Politik,* p. 80, it is assumed that Seeckt and Rade first established contact in Berlin as early as in the summer / autumn of 1919. BArch Nachlass Rabenau N 62/39, slides nos. 111, 116, 112. Cf. Wheeler-Bennet: *Nemesis of Power,* p. 124, 127.

536. Wohlfeil: *Reichswehr und Republik*, p. 236. Hans Ulrich Seidt: *Berlin Kabul Moskau. Oskar Ritter von Niedermayer und Deutschlands Geopolitik*, Munich 2002, p. 128ff, 133. Cf. Zeidler: *Rote Armee*, p. 59. Meier-Welker, *Seeckt*, p. 326.

537. Hürten: *Die Anfänge der Ära Seeckt*, p. 212.

538. Carsten: *The Reichswehr and Politics*, p. 135–147.

539. Hürten: *Die Anfänge der Ära Seeckt*, p. 213.

540. Cf. Wheeler-Bennet: *Nemesis of Power*, p. 124, 127.

541. Rudolf Absolon: *Die Wehrmacht im Dritten Reich*, vol. I to IV, Schriften des Bundesarchivs 16, Boppard: 1969. Vol. I, 30 January 1933 to 2 August 1934. With an eye to military affairs in Prussia, during the German Empire and the Weimar Republic, vol. 1, p. 33, 'Special Group R' at the Troop Office of the Army High Command = Russia. Cf. BArch Nachlass Rabenau N 62/7 (slide no. 26ff). Wohlfeil: *Reichswehr und Republik* p. 236ff and Seidt: *Berlin Kabul Moskau*, p. 146.

542. Zeidler: *Reichswehr und Rote Armee*, p. 52, 55, 330. R. Absolon: *Die Wehrmacht im Dritten Reich*, vol. I to IV, Schriften des Bundesarchivs 16, I, 30 January1933 to 2 August 1934, Boppard: 1969, p. 33. Helm Speidel: *Reichswehr und Rote Armee*, in: *Vierteljahrshefte für Zeitgeschichte*, 1953, Book 1, p. 19.

543. Seidt: *Berlin Kabul Moskau*, p. 146, 150.

544. BArch Nachlass Rabenau N 62/7 slide no. 27.

545. Speidel: *Reichswehr und Rote Armee*, p. 26.

546. (Gesellschaft für landwirtschaftliche Artikel GmbH; Gela); *Reichswehr und Rote* Armee, documents from the German and Russian military archives 1925–1931, p. 43, footnote 3, p. 43–50. Gessler: *Reichswehrpolitik*, p. 199ff.

547. Zeidler: *Reichswehr und Rote Armee*, p. 222. Cf. Rudolf Absolon: *Die Wehrmacht im Dritten Reich.* Vol. I, p. 33.

548. BArch Nachlass Rabenau N 62/39, slide no.132. Cf. Carsten: *The Reichswehr and Politics*, p. 142.

549. Peter Krüger: *Die Aussenpolitik der Republik von Weimar,* Darmstadt: 1985, p. 148. For information on Seeck and Ebert see Wohlfeil: *Reichswehr und Republik*, p. 235. Cf. Mühlhausen: *Friedrich Eber* p. 486 and p. 492 on his latent anti-Bolshevism.

550. Schüddekopf: *Heer und Republik*, p. 161–165. Carsten: *Reichswehr und Politik*, p. 143. Meier-Welker: *Seeckt*, pages 341–343 go into the details of the dispute between Rantzau and Seeckt and Wirth. Wirth had not informed the Reich President about his politico-military negotiations in advance and justified his going it alone, Seeckt justified his unauthorised actions in his memorandum dated 15 July 1922 published in Schüddekopf: *Heer und Republik* p. 165f. Cf. BArch Nachlass Seeckt, N 247/92 dated 4 February 1920.

551. Julius Epstein: *Der Seeckt-Plan*, from unpublished documents, in: *Der Monat*, 1948, Book 2, p. 47. Cf. Gessler: *Reichswehrpolitik*, p. 200.

552. Zeidler: *Reichswehr und Rote Armee*, p. 69. Viktor Kopp, the Soviet representative, issued a similar assurance to Maltzan as early as June 1920 Horst Günter Linke: *Deutsch-sowjetische Beziehungen bis Rapallo*, p. 104.

553. Seeckt: *Schlagworte* (1928), in: Seeckt: *Gedanken eines Soldaten*, 1935, p. 18.

554. Zeidler: *Reichswehr und Rote Armee*, p. 68–70. For information on the budgetary situation concerning the Reichswehr, see: Helm Speidel: *Reichswehr und Rote Armee*, p. 22ff, Meier-Welcker: *Seeckt*, p. 351ff.

555. (Gesellschaft zur Förderung gewerblicher Unternehmen; GEFU). Epstein: *Der Seeckt-Plan* (from unpublished documents), Book 2, p. 49.

556. Zeidler: *Reichswehr und Rote Armee* p. 79–82.

557. Zeidler: *Reichswehr und Rote Armee* p. 85.

558. *Reichswehr und Rote Armee, Dokumente aus den Militärarchiven Deutschlands und Russlands 1925–1931*, p. 38. Zeidler: *Reichswehr und Rote Armee* p. 96.

559. Zeidler: *Reichswehr und Rote Armee* p. 93–97.

560. Zeidler: *Reichswehr und Rote Armee* p. 334. Speidel: *Reichswehr und Rote Armee* p. 26, 29–30.

561. Schüddekopf: *Heer und Republik*, p. 216.

562. Zeidler: *Reichswehr und Rote Armee 1920–1933* p. 72.

563. Zeidler: *Reichswehr und Rote Armee 1920–1933* p. 104ff.

564. Zeidler: *Reichswehr und Rote Armee 1920–1933* p. 105.

565. (Deutsche Volkspartei), Krüger: *Die Aussenpolitik der Republik von Weimar* p. 296. Cf. Carsten: *The Reichswehr and Politics*, p. 206 f). Seeckt and Locarno: Cf. Wheeler-Bennet: *Nemesis of Power*, p. 131f, 141f.

566. Epstein: *Der Seeckt-Plan* (from unpublished documents) in: *Der Monat*, 1948, Book 2, p. 49. Glatzke: *Von Rapallo nach Berlin Stresemann* p. 28.

567. Zeidler: *Reichswehr und Rote Armee 1920–1933* p. 138.

568. *Reichswehr und Rote Armee, Dokumente aus den Militärarchiven Deutschlands und Russlands 1925–1931* (p. 57, p. 53–60). (BArch RH 2/2293). General Fiebig was assigned as a teacher to the War Academy of the USSR, later he commanded an air force unit und served at Stalingrad.

569. Speidel: *Reichswehr und Rote Armee* p. 34.

570. Djakow/Buschujewa: *Das faschistische Schwert* p. 77.

571. *Reichswehr und Rote Armee, Dokumente aus den Militärarchiven Deutschlands und Russlands 1925–1931*, p. 121.

572. *Reichswehr und Rote Armee, Dokumente aus den Militärarchiven Deutschlands und Russlands 1925–1931*, p. 116 ff.

573. BArch Nachlass Rabenau N 62/7, slide no. 29.

574. Heusinger's testimonies as a prisoner of war: QR documents from G. Meyer. His assertion that the beginning of rearmament in 1935 was accompanied by a decline in quality is confirmed by Hew Strachan in his study: *Ausbildung, Kampfgeist und die zwei Weltkrieg*, in: *Erster Weltkrieg – Zweiter Weltkrieg. Ein Vergleich Krieg, Kriegserlebnis, Kriegserfahrungen in Deutschland*. Publ. MGFA, Paderborn: 2002 p. 280.

575. BArch Nachlass Seeckt N 247/141, slides nos. 48, 81.

576. Schüddekopf: *Heer und Republik*, p. 164. Citino: *Path to Blitzkrieg*, p. 145.

577. Seeckt: *Zukunft des Reiches*, p. 157.

578. Geyer: *Aufrüstung oder Sicherheit*, p. 45.

Chapter 4: Factional Dispute over Military Strategy at the Reichswehr Ministry

1. Neugebauer: *Operatives Denken zwischen dem Ersten und Zweiten Weltkrieg*, p. 103. Cf. Geyer: *Aufrüstung oder Sicherheit*, p. 100, he wrote about a 'functioning guerrilla organization,' which, however, did not yet exist in 1924/1925. Stülpnagel however, suggested 'sabotage and assassinations of individuals' (p. 99). Cf. Geyer on similar suggestions by Bussche-Ippenburg: *Burgfrieden*, p. 106 f. On page 205 of his work *75 Jahre meines Lebens*, Stülpnagel wrote about his activities in 1923: 'As mentioned earlier, I had dealt with the question of a people's war – what is today called a partisan war – and began to set up a Feldjäger service as a practical preparation for it.'
2. Gordon: *Reichswehr*, p. 263. Lt Col Bussche-Ippenburg, who was one of his supporters, had already been posted to Hanover before Stülpnagel. Waldemar Erfurth: *Die Geschichte des deutschen Generalstabs 1918–1945*, Göttingen: 1957, p. 107.
3. BArch Nachlass Rabenau N 62/11, slide no. 18. N 62/7 slides nos. 8–9, N 62/40, slide 93. Corum: *Roots of Blitzkrieg*, p. 51–67.
4. Geyer: *Aufrüstung oder Sicherheit*, p. 101 f.
5. Joachim von Stülpnagel and the Ruhr Crisis in 1923. Schönrade: *Stülpnagel* pp. 23, 29.
6. BArch Nachlass Rabenau N 62/139, slide no. 146 f.
7. *Rangliste des Deutschen Reichsheeres*, Berlin: 1921, 1922, 1923, 1924, 1925, 1926, 1927.
8. Carsten: *The Reichswehr and Politics*, p. 199 ff.
9. Carsten: *The Reichswehr and Politics*, p. 212.
10. Carsten: *Reichswehr und Politik*, p. 175. Cf. Deist: *Die Reichswehr und der Krieg der Zukunft*, p. 85 f. Schönrade: *Stülpnagel*, p.57. P. 270. Hürten: *Das Krisenjahr 1923*, p. 270.
11. BArch Nachlass Stülpnagel N 5/20, slide no. 26 f.
12. Carsten: *Reichswehr und Politik*, p. 175. For information on the conflict at the Reichswehr Ministry, see also Meier-Welcker: *Seeckt*, pp. 517–519.
13. Carsten: *Reichswehr und Politik*, p. 176. (English edition, p. 154)
14. BArch Nachlass Stülpnagel N 5/10, slides nos. 10–48. BArch RH 2/417 of 31 March 1923.
15. BArch RH 8I/1385, slides nos. 15–16 '*Denkschrift über die Ziele und Wege der nächsten Jahre für unsere Kriegsvorbereitungen.*' Cf. Nachlass Stülpnagel N5/20, slide no. 2.
16. Cf. Nachlass Stülpnagel N5/10, slide 2–48, BArch RH 8/1385, slides nos. 15–20, '*Denkschrift über die Ziele und Wege der nächsten Jahre für unsere Kriegsvorbereitungen,*' slides 85–99, „*Die zahlenmässig beschränkte Qualitätsarmee und das Massenheer in ihrer wechselseitigen Bewertung in künftigen Kriegen vom Standpunkt moderner Waffentechnik. Wo liegen für beide die oberen und unteren Grenzen ihres Umfanges?*"
17. BArch Nachlass Stülpnagel N 5/20, slides nos. 25 and 112.
18. BArch Nachlass Stülpnagel N 5/20, slide no. 27.
19. BArch Nachlass Stülpnagel N 5/20, slide no. 30.

20. BArch RH 8 I/1385, slides nos. 15–20, 85–99. Cf. Heinz Hürten: *Reichswehr und Ausnahmezustand, ein Beitrag zur Verfassungsproblematik der Weimarer Republik in ihrem ersten Jahrfünft*, Opladen: 1977, footnote no. 87, p. 36. This anonymous memorandum about the state of emergency has its roots in the Truppenamt Division T.1.III, which was headed by Stülpnagel.

21. Stülpnagel: *75 Jahre meines Lebens*, pp. 194, 200. Cf. Meier-Welcker: *Seeckt*, p. 518. In 1919, Major Alexander von Falkenhausen made a remark to Major von Schleicher on his disdain of Prussian bureaucracy, stating 'that only a dictatorship can save us'. Sources on the history of parliamentarism and the political parties, second series, Militär und Politik, vol. 2. *Zwischen Revolution und Kapp-Putsch*, p. 138. Cf. BArch Nachlass Stülpnagel N2/21, slides nos. 4–15. Cf. BArch Nachlass Rabenau N 62/40, slide no. 93.

22. BArch Nachlass Stülpnagel N 5/20, slide no. 22.

23. Stülpnagel's Concept of a People's War. BArch Nachlass Stülpnagel N 5/10, slide no. 24.

24. BArch Nachlass Stülpnagel N 5/20, slides nos. 29–36, 72, 105–109.

25. Stülpnagel: *75 Jahre meines Lebens*, p. 218.

26. Hürten: *Das Krisenjahr 1923*, p. 267.

27. BArch Nachlass Stülpnagel N 5/10, slide no. 24. Cf. also RH 8/896, slides nos. 213, 214, 217–223.

28. BArch Nachlass Stülpnagel N 5/20, slides nos. 34–35.

29. Carsten: *The Reichswehr and Politics*, p. 155.

30. BArch Nachlass Stülpnagel N 5/20, slide no. 29. Nachlass Rabenau N 62/39 slide no. 149.

31. BArch Nachlass Stülpnagel N 5/20, slide no. 34 f.

32. BArch Nachlass Stülpnagel N 5/10.

33. Hürten: *Das Krisenjahr*, pp. 266–272. Cf. for the year of 1927: BArch RH 8 I /1385 '*Denkschrift über die Ziele und Wege der nächsten Jahre für unsere Kriegsvorbereitungen*', slides nos. 15–20. Presentation on 28 January 1927: '*Die zahlenmässig beschränkte Qualitätsarmee und das Massenheer in ihrer wechselseitigen Bewertung in künftigen Kriegen vom Standpunkt moderner Waffentechnik. Wo liegen für beide die oberen und unteren Grenzen ihres Umfanges?*' Slide nos. 86–99.

34. BArch Nachlass Stülpnagel N 5/20, f. 27.

35. BArch RH 8 I /1385, *Die zahlenmässig beschränkte Qualitätsarmee und das Massenheer*, slides nos 90, 92.

36. Hürten: *Das Krisenjahr 1923*, p. 271. Cf. also pp. 268, 269, 270.

37. Hürten: *Das Krisenjahr 1923*, p. 243.

38. Hürten: *Das Krisenjahr 1923*, p. 271. Cf. Carsten: *The Reichswehr and Politics*, p. 206. While Winfried Heinemann's review of Rüdiger Schönrade's biography of Joachim von Stülpnagel does not deal with the causes and motives in detail, it makes clear that there were considerable differences between Seeckt and Stülpnagel regarding 'the issue of the relationship between armed force and politics.' Heinemann is also of the opinion that this led to 'Seeckt finally (1924) having Stülpnagel posted away to Brunswick as a regimental commander'. In: *Militärgeschichtliche Zeitschrift*: MGZ / Published by Militärgeschichtliches Forschungsamt, Munich: 2008, year 67, p. 531: Winfried Heinemanns

Buchbesprechung von Rüdiger Schönrade: *General Joachim von Stülpnagel und die Politik, eine biographische Skizze zum Verhältnis von militärischer und politischer Führung in der Weimarer Politik*, Berlin: 2007.

39. BArch Nachlass Stülpnagel N 5/20, slide no. 20.
40. Hürten: *Das Krisenjahr 1923*, p. 270.
41. BArch Nachlass Stülpnagel N5/29, slide no. 32.
42. BArch Nachlass Stülpnagel N 5/10 *Gedanken über den Krieg der Zukunft*, February 1924, slides nos. 21–23.
43. BArch Nachlass Sülpnagel N 5/ 20, slide no. 72.
44. BArch Nachlass Stülpnagel N 5/ 20, slides nos. 30, 31.
45. Cf. Geyer: *Aufrüstung oder Sicherheit*, pp. 98 ff. deal with the war games of the years of 1924 and 1925. Their object was the people's war, which was favoured by the Truppenamt Director, General Wetzell, and the officers Stülpnagel, Bussche-Ippenburg, Bonin and Hasse.
46. BArch RH 8 I /1385 *Denkschrift über die Ziele und Wege der nächsten Jahre für unsere Kriegsvorbereitungen*, slide no. 16.
47. BArch RH 2/2200, no. 42/25 T 2 III 1 pers. 22 January 1925 as well as RH 2/2200 of 15 May 1926 and RH 8 I/911.
48. Ludendorff knew Major Freiherr von dem Bussche since the autumn of 1918. He informed the Reichstag on Ludendorff's behalf about the imminent military defeat and that the war was as good as lost. Cf. Ludendorff: *Meine Kriegserinnerungen*, Berlin: 1936², p. 201. Hürten: *Das Krisenjahr 1923*, pp. 23–25. Stülpnagel's concept was supported by Hindenburg, Heye, Schleicher and Gessler; cf. Stülpangel: *75 Jahre meines Lebens*, pp. 230, 234.
49. Kroener: *Mobilmachungen gegen Recht und Verfassung. Kriegsvorbereitungen in Reichsheer und Wehrmacht 1918 bis 1939, in: Erster Weltkrieg – Zweiter Weltkrieg. Ein Vergleich Krieg, Kriegserlebnis, Kriegserfahrungen in Deutschland*. On behalf of the Military History Research Institute; publishers: Bruno Thoss and Hans-Erich Volkmann, Paderborn: 2002, p 66. Michael Geyer: *Aufrüstung oder Sicherheit*, p 99. Schönrade: *Stülpnagel*, pp. 76, 83, 85, 117, 119.
50. Hürten: *Das Krisenjahr* 1923, p. 267.
51. Hürten: *Das Krisenjahr* 1923, p. 267.
52. Ludendorff: *Der totale Krieg*, p 6. BArch Nachlass Stülpnagel N 5/ 20, slides nos. 26 f.
53. Stülpnagel: *75 Jahre meines Lebens*, p. 207.
54. BArch Nachlass Rabenau N62/40 slide no. 6. Carsten: *The Reichswehr and Politics*, pp. 173, 182.
55. BArch Nachlass Rabenau N62/11 slide no. 13, 2, N 62/7 slide no. 23, N 62/40, slide no. 29. Documents of the Chancellery of the Reich, Stresemann Cabinets I and II, vol. 2, p. 1177.
56. Stülpnagel: *75 Jahre meines Lebens*, p. 212.
57. Stülpnagel: *75 Jahre meines Lebens*, p. 212.
58. Stülpnagel: *75 Jahre meines Lebens*, p. 223. Cf. also Schönrade: *Stülpnagel*, p. 118.
59. I was unable to verify whether Seeckt, as stated on page 210 of Rahn's work *Reichsmarine und Landesverteidigung 1919–1928*, really gave a speech in

favour of war during a cabinet meeting on 09 February 1923; neither the diary entries of Paul Behnckes, whom he cites here as a contemporary witness, nor his private official correspondence corroborate this claim. BArch Nachlass Paul Behncke N 173/8, 9. (Film signatures: GC 3052 and GC 3053).

60. Gordon: *Reichswehr*, p. 338, p. 251. Cf. Meier-Welcker's report: *Seeckt*, p. 353.

61. Meier-Welcker: Seeckt, p. 417.

62. Stülpnagel: *75 Jahre meines Lebens*, p. 214. Cf. Carsten: *The Reichswehr and Politics*, p. 154 f. Wilhelm Marx, Member of the Centrum Party, took up the cancellorship at 30.11.1923.

63. Stülpnagel: *75 Jahre meines Lebens*, p. 223.

64. Carsten: *Reichswehr und Politik*, p. 233 f. (Engl. edition, p. 212). Cf. Meier-Welcker: *Seeckt*, p. 518. Cf. Schüddekopf: *Das Heer und die Republik*, p. 128.

65. BArch Nachlass Stülpnagel N 5/20, slide no. 112 of 12 July 1925. Cf. Carsten: *The Reichswehr and Politics*, p. 212 f. Cf. Gordon: *Reichswehr*, p. 581.

66. BArch Nachlass Stülpnagel N 5/20, slide no. 111.

67. Meier-Welker: *Seeckt*, p. 537. Schönrade: *Stülpnagel, p.* 58.

68. Carsten: *Reichswehr und Politik*, p. 233 f. (Engl. edition, p. 213). Underlining by author. Cf. Meier-Welcker: *Seeckt*, p. 518.

69. Stülpnagel: *75 Jahre meines Lebens*, pp. 214, 215. Meier-Welcker: *Seeckt*, pp. 387, 390, 393, 397. BArch, Nachlass Rabenau N 62/11, slide no. 27. Documents of the Chancellery of the Reich, Cabinets I/II of Stresemann, p. 1190. Carsten: *The Reichswehr and Politics*, p. 189.

70. Stülpnagel: *75 Jahre meines Lebens*, p. 223 f.

71. Stülpnagel: *75 Jahre meines Lebens*, pp. 192, 196, 197.

72. Stülpnagel: *75 Jahre meines Lebens*, pp. 212, 230, 229, 234. Cf. Carsten: *The Reichswehr and Politics*, p. 212.

73. Cf. e.g. Gordon: *Reichswehr*, p. 338, p. 251. Cf. Meier-Welcker: *Seeckt*, p. 353.

74. Stülpnagel: *75 Jahre meines Lebens*, pp. 209, 223–224, 227. BArch Nachlass Rabenau N 62/39, slide no. 159. Cf. Meier-Welcker: Seeckt, p. 410.

75. Stülpnagel: *75 Jahre meines Lebens*, p. 189. Gessler: *Reichswehrpolitik in der Weimarer Zeit*, p. 286.

76. Meier-Welker: *Seeckt*, p. 537.

77. For example: Geyer: *Aufrüstung oder Sicherheit*, p. 101. Cf. Wheeler-Bennet: *Nemesis of Power*, p. 143.

78. Stülpnagel: *75 Jahre meines Lebens*, p. 234, cf. also p. 230.

79. BArch Nachlass Rabenau N 62/39 slide no. 154.

80. BArch RH 8/1385 slide no. 16.

81. Hürten: *Das Krisenjahr 1923*, p. 271.

82. BArch RH 8 I /1385 Die zahlenmässig beschränkte Qualitätsarmee, presentation on 28 January 1927, Major Joachim von Stülpnagel.

83. Corum: *Roots of Blitzkrieg*, p. 62.

84. Dietz: *Primat der Politik*, p. 235. Cf. Wheeler-Bennet: *Nemesis of Power*, p. 13ff.

85. Stülpnagel: *75 Jahre meines Lebens*, p. 234. Cf. Carsten: *The Reichswehr and Politics*, p. 206 f. BArch Nachlass Seeckt N 247/112, Weltpressedienst, 31 December 1924, slide no. 3. Dorothea Groener-Geyer: *General Groener, Soldat und Staatsmann*, Frankfurt/Main: 1955, p. 279. The affiliation regarding the

regiments of the Old Army was also a factor in the Reichswehr. Soldiers of the 3rd Garde Regiment of the Old Army were not always friends with those of the 1st Garde Regiment zu Fuss. Cf. Gessler: Reichswehrpolitik, p. 556.

86. BArch RH 8 I /1385 *Denkschrift über die Ziele und Wege der nächsten Jahre für unsere Kriegsvorbereitungen*, slide no. 18.

87. BArch RH 8 I /1385 *Die zahlenmässig beschränkte Qualitätsarmee und das Massenheer in ihrer wechselseitigen Bewertung in künftigen Kriegen vom Standpunkt moderner Waffentechnik. Wo liegt für beide die oberen und unteren Grenzen ihres Umfanges?* Presentation of 28 January 1927 by Major Joachim von Stülpnagel, slide no. 86.

88. Nachlass Stülpnagel N 5/20 slide no. 38.

89. Geyer: *Aufrüstung oder Sicherheit*, p. 100.

90. Hürten: *Zwischen Revolution und Kapp-Putsch*, p. 288.

91. Hürten: *Das Krisenjahr 1923*, p. 243.

92. Hürten: *Das Krisenjahr 1923*, p. 270.

93. Hürten: *Das Krisenjahr 1923*, p. 268.

94. Hürten: *Das Krisenjahr 1923*, p. 269.

95. Geyer: *Aufrüstung oder Sicherheit*, p. 99.

Chapter 5: Seeckt's Political Programme in 1923/24

1. Meier-Welcker: Seeckt, p. 410.

2. Cf. Wheeler-Bennet: *Nemesis of Power*, p. 110.

3. Hürten: *Reichswehr und Ausnahmezustand*, p. 45. Cf. Carsten: *The Reichswehr and Politics*, p. 153 f.

4. Hürten: *Reichswehr und Ausnahmezustand*, p. 47. Carsten: *The Reichswehr and Politics*, pp. 187, 189.

5. Mühlhausen: *Friedrich Ebert*, p. 667.

6. Hürten: *Ausnahmezustand und Reichswehr*, p. 47.

7. Hürten: *Reichswehr und Ausnahmezustand*, p. 47.

8. Hürten: *Das Krisenjahr 1923*, p. XVI.

9. Hürten: *Reichswehr und Ausnahmezustand*, p. 41.

10. Mühlhausen: *Friedrich Ebert*, p. 691. Carsten: *The Reichswehr and Politics*, pp. 180, 187, 189, 195.

11. Mühlhausen: *Friedrich Ebert*, p. 667. Cf. Carsten: *The Reichswehr and Politics*, p. 207 f.

12. Hürten: *Das Krisenjahr 1923*, p. XXIX. Hürten: *Ausnahmezustand und Reichswehr*, p. 47.

13. Huber: *Dokumente zur Deutschen Verfassungsgeschichte*, vol VII, p. 413.

14. Hürten: *Das Krisenjahr 1923*, p. XXIV.

15. Hürten: *Das Krisenjahr 1923*, p. 89, no. 43. Cf. Mühlhausen: *Friedrich Ebert*, p. 653 f. and footnote 272. For information on the division of the states into military district commands and the nomination of civilian government commissioners, cf.: Files of the Chancellery of the Reich, Stresemann cabinets I/II, vol. 1, pp. 384 f., 390, 396 f. For information on the government commissioners' function, cf. p. 406.

16. Hürten: *Das Krisenjahr 1923*, p. 93, no. 46. Cf. Wheeler-Bennet: *Nemesis of Power*, p. 112–113.

17. Cf. Carsten: *The Reichswehr and Politics*, p. 188.

18. Files of the Chancellery of the Reich, Weimar Republic, *Marx cabinets* I/II, vol. 1: 30 November 1923 until 3 June 1924, Boppard am Rhein: 1973. Vol. 2: 3 June 1924 until January 1925, Boppard am Rhein: 1977, vol. 1, p. 176.

19. Files of the Chancellery of the Reich, *Marx cabinets* I/II, vol. 1, p. 176.

20. Files of the Chancellery of the Reich, *Marx cabinets* I/II, vol. 1, p. 176. Cf. the files of the Chancellery of the Reich, *Marx cabinets*, vol. 1, p. 228–231 of 11 January 1924. For information on the maintenance of the state of emergency until 6 February 1924, cf. pp. 322–324.

21. Files of the Chancellery of the Reich, *Marx cabinets* I/II, vol. 1, p. 244, annotation 2.

22. Hürten: *Das Krisenjahr 1923*, p. 273, annotation no. 2.

23. Files of the Chancellery of the Reich, Stresemann cabinets I/II, pp. 944 f., 967 f., 974 f, 1011 f.

24. Dietz: *Das Primat der Politik*, p. 263, cf. 289. Cf. Wheeler-Bennet: *Nemesis of Power*, p. 87–95.

25. BArch Nachlass Rabenau N 62/40 slides nos. 43, 46–57. Files of the Chancellery of the Reich, Stresemann cabinets I/II, p. 1193 f. Mühlhausen: Friedrich Ebert, p. 687 f. Carsten: *The Reichswehr and Politics*, pp. 170, 181, 115, 203 Carsten mentioned that the relationship between Ebert and Seeckt had never been good.

26. Cf. Wheeler-Bennet: *Nemesis of Power*, p. 115–116.

27. BArch Nachlass Rabenau N 62/40, slides nos. 46–47.

28. BArch Nachlass Rabenau N 62/40, slide no. 6. Seeckt had tried to influence Lossow through Gessler and Schleicher since March 1923. Files of the Chancellery of the Reich, *Stresemann cabinets* I/II, pp. 1177, 1197, annotation 101.

29. Carsten: *The Reichswehr and Politics*, p. 186.

30. Files of the Chancellery of the Reich, *Stresemann cabinets* I/II, vol. 2, p. 1197. Carsten: *The Reichswehr and Politics*, p. 182.

31. BArch Nachlass Rabenau N 62/48, slide no. 14.

32. Mühlhausen: *Friedrich Ebert*, pp. 682–691. BArch Nachlass Rabenau N 62/11 slides nos. 9, 13, 27. N 62/7 slide no. 22, N 62/40, slides nos. 46–47. Files of the Chancellery of the Reich, *Stresemann cabinets* I/II, pp. 1178 f., 1182, 1190, 1191, 1203 and footnote 127. BArch Nachlass Seeckt N 247/113, slide no. 30.

33. BArch Nachlass Seeckt N 247/139, *Ein Regierungsprogramm*, slides nos. 2–15.

34. BArch Nachlass Seeckt N 247/139, *Ein Regierungsprogramm*, slide no. 12.

35. BArch Nachlass Seeckt N 247/139, *Ein Regierungsprogramm*, slide no. 6.

36. BArch Nachlass Seeckt N 247/139, *Ein Regierungsprogramm*, slide no. 9.

37. BArch Nachlass Seeckt N 247/139 *Ein Regierungsprogramm*, slides nos. 6 and 11.

38. BArch Nachlass Rabenau N 62/39, slide no. 155.

39. BArch Nachlass Seeckt N 247/139, *Ein Regierungsprogramm*, slide no. 10.

40. BArch Nachlass Seeckt N 247/139, *Ein Regierungsprogramm*, slide no. 10.
41. BArch Nachlass Seeckt N 247/139, *Ein Regierungsprogramm*, slides nos. 6 and 10.
42. BArch Nachlass Seeckt N 247/139, *Ein Regierungsprogramm*, slides nos. 7 and 12. Cf. Wheeler-Bennet: Nemesis of Power, p. 120.
43. BArch Nachlass Seeckt N 247/139, *Ein Regierungsprogramm*, slides nos. 7, 12.
44. T = Truppenamt 1= Heeresabteilung.
45. Hürten: *Das Krisenjahr 1923*, pp. 273–283 and 334–362.
46. Hürten: *Das Krisenjahr 1923*, pp. 353 – 354.
47. Hürten: *Das Krisenjahr 1923*, p. 273, footnote no. 2.
48. BArch Nachlass Seeckt N 247/113, slide no. 28.
49. BArch Nachlass Seeckt N 247/113, slide no. 30.
50. BArch Nachlass Seeckt N 247/113, slide no. 27.
51. BArch Nachlass Seeckt N 247/113, slide no. 27.
52. BArch Nachlass Seeckt N 247/113, slide no. 26.
53. BArch Nachlass Seeckt N 247/113, slide no. 26.
54. BArch Nachlass Seeckt N 247/113, slide no. 32.
55. BArch Nachlass Seeckt N 247/113, slide no. 25.
56. Stresemann: *Das Vermächtnis*, vol. 1, p. 210.
57. For example: Karl Heinz Bracher, Francis Carsten, Gordon Craig, Wilhelm Deist, Klaus Jürgen Müller, Stig Förster, Michael Geyer, Gerhard Gross, Bernhard Kroener, Manfred Messerschmidt, Gli-li Vardi, Bennet-Wheeler, Ulrich Wehler, Thilo Vogelsang.
58. Mrs. von Seeckt was of Jewish origin. In a letter to her, he wrote about Jewish talent, saying that it "rests with criticism, i.e. on the negative side, and that it can never have a state-building effect". BArch Nachlass Rabenau N 62/48, slide no. 24.
59. BArch Nachlass Rabenau N 62/11, slide no. 27.
60. Files of the Chancellery of the Reich, *Stresemann cabinets I/II* vol. 2, p. 1181.
61. Kessel: *Seeckt's political programme of 1923*, p. 895.
62. BArch Nachlass Rabenau N 62/39, slide no. 110. Cf. Francis Carsten, Otto-Ernst Schüddekopf about his ambitious.

Index